School–University–Community Research in a (Post) COVID-19 World

A volume in
Current Perspectives on School/University/Community Research
R. Martin Reardon and Jack Leonard, *Series Editors*

Current Perspectives on School/University/ Community Research

R. Martin Reardon and Jack Leonard, *Series Editors*

School–University–Community Collaboration for Civic Education and Engagement in the Democratic Project (2022)
  R. Martin Reardon and Jack Leonard

Learning to Read the World and the Word: School-University-Community Collaboration to Enrich Immigrant Literacy and Teacher Education (2021)
  R. Martin Reardon and Jack Leonard

A Place Called Home: School-University-Community Collaboration and the Immigrant Educational Experience (2021)
  Jack Leonard and R. Martin Reardon

Alleviating the Educational Impact of Adverse Childhood Experiences: School–University–Community Collaboration (2020)
  R. Martin Reardon and Jack Leonard

Integrating Digital Technology in Education: School–University–Community Collaboration (2019)
  R. Martin Reardon and Jack Leonard

Innovation and Implementation in Rural Places: School–University–Community Collaboration in Education (2018)
  R. Martin Reardon and Jack Leonard

Making a Positive Impact in Rural Places: Change Agency in the Context of School-University-Community Collaboration in Education (2018)
  R. Martin Reardon and Jack Leonard

Exploring the Community Impact of Research–Practice Partnerships in Education (2017)
  R. Martin Reardon and Jack Leonard

School–University–Community Research in a (Post) COVID-19 World

edited by

R. Martin Reardon
East Carolina University

Jack Leonard
University of Massachusetts Boston (retired)

INFORMATION AGE PUBLISHING, INC.
Charlotte, NC • www.infoagepub.com

Library of Congress Cataloging-in-Publication Data

A CIP record for this book is available from the Library of Congress
http://www.loc.gov

ISBN: 979-8-88730-349-9 (Paperback)
979-8-88730-350-5 (Hardcover)
979-8-88730-351-2 (E-Book)

Copyright © 2023 Information Age Publishing Inc.

All rights reserved. No part of this publication may be reproduced, stored in a
retrieval system, or transmitted, in any form or by any means, electronic, mechanical,
photocopying, microfilming, recording or otherwise, without written permission
from the publisher.

Printed in the United States of America

CONTENTS

Introduction..ix

SECTION I

ONLINE LEARNING FOR SPECIFIC GROUPS OF STUDENTS

1 COVID-19 and the Retrenchment of the IDEA...................................3
   Christina Payne-Tsoupros

2 Surviving the Pandemic: Empowering Immigrant Families
   to Advocate and Support Their Children/Youth With
   Disabilities at Home..19
   Lusa Lo and Kimberly Lee

3 Suggestions for Promising Practices for Black Autistic Children
   and Their Families Post-Pandemic..43
   *Elizabeth Holliday Morgan, Margaret L. Sebastian,
   and Kanwardeep Kaur Singh*

4 The Disruption of Mentoring for Black Youth During COVID-19:
   No One to Turn to...63
   Jay Matthew and Detra D. Johnson

v

vi ▪ Contents

5 Educational and Mental Health Challenges of Grandchildren
Raised by Grandparents During the COVID-19 Pandemic
in South Carolina: Qualitative Results From a
Community-Based Study..83
*Theresa M. Harrison, Yanfeng Xu, Patrice Forrester, Sue Levkoff,
Ashlee A. Lewis, Gina M. Kunz, and Karen Utter*

SECTION II
PERSPECTIVES ON LEARNING

6 Study Buddy: An Online Individualized Tutoring Program
for Racialized, Indigenous, and Immigrant Students 111
*Wendy Cukier, Bincy Wilson, Donna Fradley, Aaron Smajda,
and Stefan Karajovic*

7 "If You Ever Did Need the Help, It Would Be There in a
Second. No Questions Asked": A Study of Perceived Impact
of Out-of-School STEM Programs During COVID-19 135
*Christopher J. Fornaro, Kimberly Sterin, Katrina Struloeff,
and Alonzo M. Flowers III*

8 Remote Instructional Coaching During the COVID-19
Pandemic: An Exploration of Coaching Moves and
Teacher Reflection 155
Jeanna R. Wieselmann and Marc T. Sager

SECTION III
TWIN EPIDEMICS

9 Youth Curation as Collective Disruption: Making in Museums
During the COVID-19 Pandemic 181
*Kristina M. Stamatis, Joseph L. Polman,
and José Rogelio Manriquez-Hernandez*

10 Leveraging University Partners as Brokers to Navigate
Research Practice Partnerships During Intertwined
Global Pandemics.. 207
Holly Plank, Eleanor R. Anderson, and Cassie Quigley

Contents • **vii**

SECTION IV

REFLECTIONS AND ROADMAPS

11 Video Documentation of the International Rural School Leadership Project: A Retrospective Case Study of University–School–Community Collaboration 235
Jerry D. Johnson and Hobart L. Harmon

12 Building Reciprocal University–School–Community Relationships to Explore the Impact of COVID-19 on Rural Schools in Aotearoa New Zealand 259
Jennifer Tatebe and Carol Mutch

13 Emergent Program Evaluation (Post) COVID-19 287
Nicole Weinberg, Elissa Bryant, Kayla Bullard, and Gabriel Huddleston

About the Editors 309

About the Contributors...311

INTRODUCTION

*Historically, pandemics have forced humans to break with the past
and imagine their world anew. This one is no different. It is a portal,
a gateway between one world and the next.*

—Roy, 2020, para. 48

A news item as I finalize the components of this volume focused on a warning from the White House chief medical advisor (Dr. Anthony Fauci) that the United States is at a crossroads as new COVID-19 omicron "lineage variants" (Kimball, 2022, para. 3) begin to challenge BA.5 as the predominant strain of the virus. Fauci went on to recommend vaccination to avoid a healthcare "negative trifecta" (Kimball, 2022, para. 8) among COVID-19, seasonal influenza, and respiratory syncytial virus, and deplored the approximately 400 deaths per day currently due to COVID-19.

Nevertheless, there are indications that people are ready to focus on a pandemic-free future. As an initial step in this direction, Oster (2022) recently advocated for a pandemic amnesty. Oster pointed out that decisions had to be made by health care officials "under conditions of tremendous uncertainty" (para. 3) and implied that it should come as no surprise that some of the choices they made arguably proved more harmful than helpful. As an example of a choice that had harmful effects, Oster instanced the protracted closing of schools in the United States—given the relatively low risk of in-school transmission of infection. Oster's dispassionate assessment was that, with the benefit of hindsight, some decisions that turned out to be right "were right for the wrong reasons. In other instances,

---

School–University–Community Research in a (Post) COVID-19 World, pages ix–xvi
Copyright © 2023 by Information Age Publishing
www.infoagepub.com
All rights of reproduction in any form reserved.

ix

[decision makers] had a prescient understanding of the available information" (para. 7). Oster's amnesty proposal received a mixed reception on social media with one poignant thread of lament demanding a reckoning for those who made decisions that resulted in many loved ones dying alone (e.g., D'Couto, 2022) and being hastily and unceremoniously buried (e.g., O'Donnell, 2020).

To recap, the news of the COVID-19 pandemic began to startle and dismay the world in late 2019 when a cluster of patients in Hubei Province in China suffered from an "atypical pneumonia-like illness" (Centers for Disease Control and Prevention, n.d.-a, label 1) that could not be treated effectively with standard approaches. By late December, the World Health Organization had been notified of a similar situation centered on the Wuhan Seafood Wholesale Market and on January 5, 2020 the genetic sequence of Wuhan-Hu-1 was published through an online database. Against a backdrop of earnest denial, unfounded hubris, and political posturing, on March 12, 2020 Ohio was the first U.S. state to close all K–12 school buildings (Grossman et al., 2021).

An impartial observer might have anticipated that, faced with a pandemic caused by the first novel, highly contagious, deadly virus to emerge since 1918 when the H1N1 virus killed an estimated one-third of the world's population (Centers for Disease Control and Prevention, n.d.-b, para. 2), political differences would be set aside. Indeed, as Education Week (2021) documented, every state in the United States (except Montana and Wyoming) either ordered or recommended that schools close for the remainder of the 2019–2020 school year upheaving the education of upward of 55 million students and the lives of their parents as well as the lives of the administrators, teachers, and staff members of their schools.

The consequences soon became manifest. The American Psychological Association (2020) reported that some 81% of teenage children (13–17 years of age) were negatively impacted in a range of ways due to school closures, including 47% who indicated that they "didn't learn as much as they did in previous years" (para. 21). That perhaps many more than 47% of teenage children in the United States did not learn as much as they did in previous years was documented in a subsequent National Assessment of Educational Progress (NAEP) report which found that "the national average score declines in mathematics for fourth and eighth graders were the largest ever recorded in that subject" (Wilburn & Elias, 2022, para. 1). The National Center for Educational Statistics commissioner commented somewhat hyperbolically that the results showed that "every student was vulnerable to the pandemic's disruptions" (Wilburn & Elias, 2022, para. 5) and called for a single-minded emphasis on ways to assist students to recover from their trauma and accelerate their learning. Wilburn and Elias

(2022) joined those who have pointed out that the learning declines associated with COVID-19 did not occur equitably. For example, they noted that the eighth grade reading scores declined only for White students (by four points), eighth grade mathematics scores declined for most racial and ethnic groups and across the performance distribution, fourth grade reading scores declined for American Indian/Alaska Native, Black, Hispanic, and White students, and fourth grade mathematics scores declined for all racial and ethnic groups except native Hawaiian-Pacific Islander students.

The likelihood of a single-minded policy response to change the system and address the achievement gaps exposed by the range of responses to COVID-19 seems small. On the one hand, doubting the sustainability of innovative responses, education historian Larry Cuban referenced the dominant stability of schooling which, if anything, "produces this huge public and professional need to resume schooling as it was" (Young, 2022, para. 18). On the other hand, diverse political agendas will diffuse concerted efforts. Grossman et al. (2021) discussed a pertinent example from Michigan where "public health data, partisanship, and collective bargaining" (p. 637) each played a role in determining school reopening decisions. On this same issue of school reopening, there is credible evidence from Massachusetts that the much maligned and politically explosive masking policies implemented in some schools may have saved lives (Cowger et al., 2022).

I opened my introduction with an epigraph consisting of the second-to-last paragraph of Roy's (2020) essay. Roy's concluding paragraph proposed a stark dichotomy: We can choose to walk through the portal to the (post)-COVID-19 world "dragging the carcasses of our prejudice and hatred, our avarice, our data banks and dead idea, our dead rivers and smoky skies . . . or we can walk lightly, with little luggage, ready to imagine another world. And ready to fight for it" (para. 49). The contributors to this volume offer suggestions regarding the remnants of carcasses that (still) should be buried as well as what is worth fighting for in this other (post)-COVID-19 world.

My colleague Jack Leonard pointed out to me how easily the chapters fell into various dichotomies: narrow focus versus broad focus, students-at-risk versus those not at-risk, challenges and unexpected benefits versus undesirable outcomes of the pandemic. We decided to group the chapters into four groups: Section I: Online Learning for Specific Groups of Students, Section II: Perspectives on Learning, Section III: Twin Epidemics, and Section IV: Reflections and Roadmaps. The backdrop to all sections and chapters is the understanding, as Oster (2022) acknowledged, that decisions had to be made with unaccustomed haste by educational leaders amid great uncertainty as the pandemic unfolded.

xii • Introduction

SECTION I: ONLINE LEARNING FOR SPECIFIC GROUPS OF STUDENTS

Section I opens with a sobering assessment from Payne-Tsoupros of the state of the legislative guard-rails that the members of that broader community in the United States have long understood to guarantee that students with disabilities will receive a free and appropriate education in the least restrictive educational environment. Payne-Tsoupros contended that the overall impact of some decisions made by educational leaders amounted to a retrenchment of the protections guaranteed by the landmark Individuals With Disabilities Education Improvement Act of 2004. As the pandemic subsides into endemic status, the guard rails need to be refurbished.

In Chapter 2, Lo and Lee focused on the burden on families of students with disabilities brought about by the pivot from the established in-person, school-based learning environment to socially distanced online learning. They highlighted the additional disruption of such a change for families from culturally and linguistically diverse backgrounds. Extraordinary times demanded extraordinary measures and they chronicled the emergence of a support group that effected an educationally oriented partnership among Chinese immigrant families of children with disabilities. What emerged in response to a crisis has implications for the future.

Picking-up on the implications for the future theme, in Chapter 3, Morgan, Sebastian, and Singh focused on promising practices for Black autistic children and their families. Drawing on the data from a national qualitative study that involved interviews with Black mothers of children on the autism spectrum, they highlighted the dawning realization among the "mother/educators" of what their children needed and how they could address those needs. Far from distancing the families from the school, their realization strengthened the school–community partnership and revealed the shortcomings of the customary once-a-year Individualized Education Plan meeting and the benefits of closer collaboration.

In Chapter 4, Matthew and Johnson focused on the disorientation of Black male youth who found that they had no one to turn to for advice and support during the pandemic. In a provocative analogy, they likened the onset of the pandemic to a rain deluge and the incremental return to normal as a drizzle. As they intended, the analogy raises the question of what it would take to bring fine weather for Black male youth. They advocated for providing mentoring oriented to equipping Black male youth with the support to weather the inconsistencies of their circumstances.

Surely grandparents provide mentoring and much more in supporting their grandchildren, and, in Chapter 5, Harrison and colleagues featured a statewide qualitative study of this situation. Specifically, the study was focused on surfacing both educational and mental health challenges that grandchildren faced during the pandemic. Establishing the contours of the issue gave rise to advocacy for the empowerment of school personnel to support "grandfamilies" and for the creation and nurturance of reciprocal school–university–community relationships to sustain such support.

SECTION II: PERSPECTIVES ON LEARNING

In the first of the three chapters that highlight an international perspective, Cukier and colleagues open Chapter 6 with an illustration of the universality of the COVID-19 experience in developed counties. They drew attention to the convergence of multiple stresses—particularly for "equity-deserving groups." In response, the Diversity Institute convened a wide range of educational and community stakeholders to discern a way to address the issue: the Study Buddy program (684 students, 451 families, & 331 tutors). The outcome has been increased well-being of the participants.

Along similar lines in the United States, in Chapter 7, Fornaro and colleagues reported on their study of the perceived impact of an out-of-school science, technology, engineering, and mathematics program during COVID-19 but, in their instance, from the perspective of four administrators and four instructors. The students in the program (one branch of an organization aptly named Pathways) were in Grades 5 through 9. Semi-structured interviews bolstered by document analysis and observation verified the value of teaching and operational supports—both separately and in conjunction.

In Chapter 8, Wieselmann and Sager provide closure to this section by reporting that they took advantage of COVID-19 to conduct a single case study (with three participants). They applied an interaction analysis approach to dissect the coaching moves their participants implemented in an online coaching context. Their major finding related to the extent to which the context prompted teacher reflection in addition to affirming teacher practice, directing attention to how students learn, and the pertinent pedagogical approach.

SECTION III: TWIN EPIDEMICS

Both the chapters in Section 3 evoked the "twin epidemics of racism," and both emanated from a collaboration in the context of museums. In Chapter 9, Stamatis, Polman, and Manriquez-Hernandez explored the role of youth in the curation historical narratives as critically literate participants. In their case, the historical narrative was that of Latino youth in a small city in the mountain west of the United States. They highlighted the potential

xiv ▪ Introduction

for youth curation to deeply engage participants in reflective deconstruction of their lived experience in school and community.

Collectively, the focus of Stamatis and colleagues and Plank, Anderson, and Quigley in Chapter 10 effectively bracket the museum experience from grass roots to institutional. Plank and colleagues provide a reflection on their experience as invited external brokers in a three-way research–practitioner partnership between a school and a museum. This singular partnership arose pre-pandemic—born out of the necessity to share building resources. The leaders of the school and museum were astute enough to realize that their quite disparate cultures did not bode well for an unbrokered collaboration. Plank and colleagues reflect on their role as brokers as they worked toward eliminating their role from the partnership.

SECTION IV: REFLECTIONS AND ROADMAPS

Two of the chapters in this final section, complete the trio of contributions focused on the international impact of COVID-19. In the first of these two, in Chapter 11, Johnson and Harmon were spurred by their shared interest in education in rural contexts in the United States to make contact with educational leaders in similarly rural contexts in the state of Queensland, Australia. In their chapter they distill a wealth of data into 21 key collaborative activities; nine essential elements of public-sector collaboration involving schools, universities, and communities; and seven critical incidents related to success.

Maintaining the rural education orientation, the second of the two contributions in this section focused on the international context of Aotearoa New Zealand. Readers in the United States will be well aware of how the measures implemented by Prime Minister Jacinda Ardern to restrict the spread of COVID-19 were viewed as either draconian or admirable depending on the political persuasion of the viewer. In Chapter 12, Tatebe and Mutch discuss how those measures impacted the students, teachers, and community members in a set of rural schools. In the process, they provide some insight into the respect for the indigenous language and culture that permeates the educational landscape in the land of the long white cloud.

Returning to the United States, Weinberg and colleagues brought this volume to a fitting conclusion in Chapter 13 with a future-focused consideration of the adaptations to institutional norms that were implemented in response to COVID-19. They pondered their role as community-based researchers amid what they characterized as the aftershocks of COVID-19 and proposed a framework grounded in core principles and practices to facilitate future collaborative responses.

Introduction • **xv**

* * *

Front Cover: Jack Leonard, my esteemed colleague and co-editor since the inception of this series, retired from UMass Boston to an idyllic location overlooking a large bay in Nova Scotia that opens to the Atlantic Ocean a few years before COVID-19. A few weeks prior to the onslaught of Hurricane Ian, his canoe was set adrift from its moorings in a heavy windstorm. He presumed it was lost forever but notified the community members through his Facebook page "just in case." A few weeks after Hurricane Ian, he was pleasantly surprised when one of his neighbors retrieved it from a tree and brought it back. To his further surprise, it still floated although the gunwale was badly damaged. Another of his admirable neighbors informed him that the makers of that brand of canoe provide replacement gunwales, so he can repair it. To me, Jack's canoe is a metaphor for the educational endeavor as we emerge from COVID-19—damaged but still floating and repairable.

Back Cover: Carol Mutch (co-author of Chapter 12) provided a photo of a mural painted by four girls (Abigail, Hadie, Mikelya, & Charlotte; names included with permission) who attend Greendale School *Kānuka Ruru-hau*—one of the rural schools featured in Chapter 12. A *kānuka* is a tree that provides protection for new growth and reflects the school's Māori name, gifted by the local *iwi* (tribe). The birds (clockwise from the top) are ruru (Morepork owl), *kererū* (wood pigeon), *piwakawaka* (fantail), *kākāpō* (ground parrot), *tūī* (no translation) and they match each of the school's values. The mural symbolizes the Māori whakatauikī (proverb): *Kia maru, kia poipoi, kia puāwai* (by providing shelter and nourishment, the new growth will flourish).

REFERENCES

American Psychological Association. (2020). *Stress in America, 2020: A national mental health crisis.* https://www.apa.org/news/press/releases/stress/2020/report-october

Centers for Disease Control and Prevention. (n.d.-a). *CDC museum COVID-19 timeline.* https://www.cdc.gov/museum/timeline/covid19.html

Centers for Disease Control and Prevention. (n.d.-b). *History of the 1918 flu pandemic.* https://www.cdc.gov/flu/pandemic-resources/1918-commemoration/1918-pandemic-history.htm

Cowger, T. L., Murray, E. J., Clarke, J., Bassett, M. T., Ojikutu, B. O., Sánchez, S. M., Linos, N., & Hall, K. T. (2022, November 24). Lifting universal masking in schools—Covid-19 incidence among students and staff. *The New England Journal of Medicine*, 1–12. https://doi.org/10.1056/NEJMoa2211029

xvi ▪ Introduction

D'Couto, H. T. (2022, March 7). *Forcing my COVID patients to die alone is inhumane—and unnecessary.* WBUR. https://www.wbur.org/cognoscenti/2022/03/07/covid-patients-icu-dying-alone-helen-t-dcouto

Education Week. (2021, October 13). *Map: Coronavirus and school closures in 2019–2020.* https://www.edweek.org/leadership/map-coronavirus-and-school-closures-in-2019-2020/2020/03

Grossman, M., Reckhow, S., Strunk, K. O., & Turner, M. (2021). All states close but red districts reopen: The politics of in-person schooling during the COVID-19 pandemic. *Educational Researcher, 50*(9), 637–648. https://doi.org/10.3102/0013189X211048840

Kimball, S. (2022, November 3). *U.S. faces pandemic crossroads with Covid deaths still too high and new omicron variants emerging, Fauci says.* CNBC. https://www.cnbc.com/2022/11/03/fauci-us-at-crossroads-with-covid-deaths-too-high-and-omicron-variants-emerging.html

O'Donnell, M. (2020, April 24). Coronavirus pandemic leads to drive-through wakes: "You have to have an opportunity to say goodbye." *Chicago Sun Times.* https://chicago.suntimes.com/2020/4/24/21232114/coronavirus-drive-through-wakes-funerals-rosemarie-santilli-kolssak-funeral-home-wheeling

Oster, E. (2022, October 31). Let's declare a pandemic amnesty: Let's focus on the future and fix the problems we still need to solve. *The Atlantic.* https://www.theatlantic.com/ideas/archive/2022/10/covid-response-forgiveness/671879/

Roy, A. (2020, April 3). The pandemic is a portal. *Financial Times.* https://www.ft.com/content/10d8f5e8-74eb-11ea-95fe-fcd274e920ca

Wilburn, G., & Elias, J. (2022, October 22). *Mathematics and reading scores of fourth- and eighth-graders declined in most states during pandemic, nation's report card shows.* https://www.nationsreportcard.gov/mathematics/supportive_files/2022_rm_press_release.docx

Young, J. R. (2022, January 18). *How will COVID-19 impact school reform movements.* https://www.edsurge.com/news/2022-01-18-how-will-covid-19-impact-school-reform-movements

SECTION I

ONLINE LEARNING FOR SPECIFIC GROUPS OF STUDENTS

CHAPTER 1

COVID-19 AND THE RETRENCHMENT OF THE IDEA

Christina Payne-Tsoupros
Gallaudet University

ABSTRACT

This chapter explores the effects of the COVID-19 pandemic in U.S. K–12 public schools focusing on children receiving special education services. Using disability critical race theory and critical race policy analysis, I argue that school leaders' responses to the pandemic have contributed to a retrenchment of the protections guaranteed to students with disabilities under the Individuals With Disabilities Education Improvement Act of 2004.

The COVID-19 pandemic has affected many aspects of K–12 public education, including special education. In this chapter, I argue that the pandemic and school leaders' responses to it have contributed to a retrenchment of the Individuals With Disabilities Education Improvement Act of 2004 (IDEA)—focusing specifically on the impact of deaf and hard-of-hearing students as well as students with other disabilities. Using a critical race policy analysis (Valles & Villalpando, 2022), I analyze families' rights in the individualized education program (IEP) process and teachers' and students'

School–University–Community Research in a (Post) COVID-19 World, pages 3–17
Copyright © 2023 by Information Age Publishing
www.infoagepub.com
All rights of reproduction in any form reserved.

4 • C. PAYNE-TSOUPROS

experiences amid the COVID-19 pandemic. While the long-term effects of the COVID-19 pandemic are still unfolding, I posit that school leaders' responses to the COVID-19 pandemic constitute a retrenchment of the protections guaranteed under the IDEA.

This chapter will proceed in four parts. In the first part, I provide a brief overview of the IDEA (2004), focusing on the procedural safeguards afforded to students and families. The IDEA requires that the child's IEP set forth the programs and services the student will receive to achieve a "free appropriate public education" (FAPE; IDEA, 2004, Part A (c)(3)), which is the core substantive right guaranteed to eligible children under the IDEA. I then address specific considerations in the IDEA for deaf and hard-of-hearing students.

In the second part of the chapter, I discuss school leaders' responses to the COVID-19 pandemic. Then, in the third part of the chapter, I discuss disability critical race theory (DisCrit, Annamma et al., 2013) and critical race policy analysis (Valles & Villalpando, 2022). Introduced by Annamma et al. (2013), DisCrit is a theoretical framework to analyze race and disability. I use Valles and Villalpando's (2022) work on critical race policy analysis to operationalize the tenets of DisCrit in the context of school leaders' responses to the COVID-19 pandemic, specifically with respect to the procedural safeguards in the IDEA (2004). I examine dynamics favoring school organizational structures over families in the context of the IDEA, which I argue, have become exacerbated during the COVID-19 pandemic. I use this (disability) critical race policy framework to contextualize teachers' and students' experiences in deaf education and then in special education more broadly.

I argue that using DisCrit (Annamma et al., 2013) in this critical race policy framework (Valles & Villalpando, 2022) demonstrates that school leaders' responses to the COVID-19 pandemic have in some ways rolled back protections in the IDEA (2004), exacerbating inequities, particularly for students from marginalized groups, using deaf and hard-of-hearing[1] children as an example. Deaf and hard-of-hearing children may have specific language and communication needs not shared by the larger population of students receiving specific education services. Constricting the power of the families in this way is contrary to Congress's intent in passing the IDEA. I specifically address families' rights and students' rights under the IDEA.

I conclude the chapter with a preliminary exploration of ways to disrupt this retrenchment of the IDEA (2004), including considerations at the individual level, local school district level, and federal level.

IDEA

In this section, I provide an overview of the IDEA (2004). I then discuss provisions in the IDEA that have specific applications to deaf and hard-of-hearing students; namely, the requirement that an eligible child with a disability receive special education services in the "least restrictive environment" (LRE, 20 U.S.C. § 1406(b)(2)) and the related "special factors" provision (20 U.S.C. § 1414(d)(3)(B)).

Overview of the IDEA and FAPE

Originally passed in 1975 as the Education for All Handicapped Children Act, the IDEA (2004) is the federal special education law that guarantees children with disabilities the right to an education from birth through the earlier of attaining age 26 or graduating from high school. A cornerstone of the IDEA is its guarantee of FAPE to eligible children with disabilities through the program of services set forth in the child's "individualized education program" (IEP, 20 U.S.C. §§ 1400(d)(1)(A); 1414(d)). The IDEA itself does not define FAPE, so its interpretation has been left to the courts.

According to the U.S. Supreme Court, to satisfy FAPE, "a school must offer an IEP reasonably calculated to enable a child to make progress appropriate in light of the child's circumstances" (*Endrew F. v. Douglas County School District Re-1.*, 2017, p. 11).

The IEP includes a statement of the student's present level of development and a statement of the measurable results or expected outcomes (20 U.S.C. § 1414(d)(1)-(d)(5)). The IEP states the anticipated length, duration, and frequency of services. The IEP is reviewed annually with mandatory re-evaluation at least every 3 years. Under the IDEA (2004), families are necessary parties in the development of the student's IEP. The IEP team considers the child's strengths, the families' concerns for enhancing the child's education, and the academic, developmental, and functional needs of the child.

The IDEA (2004) is federally funded, with receipt of fund contingent upon an agreement by state officials to provide FAPE for eligible children ages 3 through 26 years of age. Federal legislators developed a funding formula, recognizing the increased costs of educating a child with a disability, estimated at 2:1 (Dragoo, 2019). Under the funding formula, the federal government would pay a certain amount of the excess costs of educating a child with a disability, with states and localities to pay the rest. Since its inception, Congress has never funded the IDEA to the promised levels.

The IDEA (2004) sets forth a specific procedural process for resolving special education disputes before a complaint may be heard in court. The administrative procedure before a case is heard in court is referred to as due process and consists of the following sequential steps: (a) a family/student files a complaint, (b) the school district responds to the complaint, (c) a resolution session between family and school district is held, (d) there

6 ▪ C. PAYNE-TSOUPROS

are prehearing disclosures exchanged between the parties, and (e) a mediation session is conducted (20 U.S.C. § 1415(b)-(f)). The resolution session and mediation session are two of the three formal dispute resolution processes set forth in the IDEA. If mediation is unsuccessful, the parties may move to a due process hearing.

A qualified impartial hearing officer presides over the due process hearing. If a party is unsatisfied after the due process hearing, then it may file an appeal. In some states, the appeal is directly to court. Other states have a second tier of administrative review, in which a party first appeals to a second administrative body, before the party may bring the case to court. In addition, states may supplement the protections and processes set forth in the IDEA (2004).

LRE and Special Factors

The IDEA (2004) requires that "to the maximum extent appropriate," a child with a disability must be educated with nondisabled children, with removal "from the regular educational environment occur[ing] only when the nature or severity of the disability of a child is such that education in regular classes with the use of supplementary aids and services cannot be achieved satisfactorily" (20 U.S.C. § 1412(a)(5)(A)).

Following similarly worded 1992 policy guidance from the U.S. Department of Education, the 1997 reauthorization of the IDEA included a specific provision related to language and communication of deaf and hard-of-hearing children (as well as several other populations). The IDEA (2004) and the regulations thereunder stipulate special factors that must be considered in developing an IEP for deaf and hard-of-hearing children. For a child who is deaf or hard-of-hearing, the IEP must

> consider the communication needs of the child, and . . . the child's language and communication needs, opportunities for direct communication with peers and professional personnel in the child's language and communication mode, academic level, and full range of needs, including opportunities for direct instruction in the child's language and communication mode. (20 U.S.C. § 1414(d)(3)(B)(iv))

The special factors provision was incorporated into the IDEA in its 1997 reauthorization, after recognition that LRE was often inappropriately applied to deaf and hard-of-hearing children (Deaf Students Education Services, 1992; National Association of the Deaf, n.d.).

SCHOOL LEADERS' RESPONSES TO THE COVID-19 PANDEMIC

In this section, I summarize the legal guidance regarding IDEA (2004) compliance promulgated in Spring 2020 and discuss research addressing effects of the pandemic on teachers and students in special education.

Legal Backdrop

The Spring 2020 shift to remote learning occurred amid a moving backdrop of legal obligations, as school districts navigated the evolving landscape from the U.S. Department of Education. On March 12, 2020, the U.S. Department of Education (2020a) issued guidance reaffirming the importance of meeting IDEA (2004) mandates declaring that "if a [local education authority] LEA continues to provide educational opportunities to the general student population during a school closure, the school must ensure that students with disabilities also have equal access to the same opportunities, including the provision of FAPE" (U.S. Department of Education, 2020b, p. 2). This guidance led to some confusion as some states and local education agencies interpreted this guidance to mean they should not offer remote learning opportunities for anyone if they could not meet the requirements of the IDEA for some of their students (Jameson et al., 2020). On March 21, 2020, U.S. Department of Education clarified this "serious misunderstanding that has recently circulated within the educational community" (p. 1). On April 27, 2020, the U.S. Department of Education advised that it was not asking Congress to waive the right to FAPE during the pandemic.

Following this initial period, administrators in K–12 schools engaged in a variety of strategies to deliver the educational experience to students amid the COVID-19 pandemic. These strategies included a nationwide shift to remote learning, variations on hybrid learning, masking, vaccination and testing policies, limitations on number of people at in-person events (if any) such as extracurricular events, as well as other changes (Toste et al., 2021).

Special Education

Among early childhood special educators, Steed and Leech (2021) found inclusion and communication with general education teachers a challenge in the first spring of the pandemic. Glessner and Johnson (2020) conducted a qualitive study of five special education teachers as they transitioned to remote learning during Spring 2020. They found that teachers identified themes of needing supports, routines, as well as special education specific constraints of keeping up with paperwork and monitoring student progress. Their findings also indicated that inequities and imbalances with respect to families' rights have become exacerbated over the course of the pandemic while at the same time families were taking on more tasks that were typically assigned to teachers or staff due to the school buildings being closed. Specifically in the context of the referrals and evaluations for special education services, they found that teachers felt that more responsibility was shifted to the parents in the special education process, because the children were not in class in front of the teachers.

Within special education itself, different populations have different needs, and it is important that researchers and policy makers consider how policies may affect specific populations. I use deaf and hard-of-hearing children as an example of one group that may have specific needs in this context.

Deaf and Hard-of-Hearing Children

There is limited research on the effects of the COVID-19 pandemic on deaf education. In Fall 2020, Schafer et al. (2021) conducted a qualitative survey of 416 educational personnel who work with students with hearing loss across a range of educational settings. Noting that at the time of the study there were no published studies on the impact of COVID-19 on deaf and hard-of-hearing students, they highlighted the following commonly reported educational challenges for students with hearing loss given the educational changes during the pandemic: (a) the use of face masks contributed to auditory signal attenuation and loss of visual cues, (b) reduced access to sign language interpreters, (c) issues with technology reliability, (d) lack of captioning or transcripts for online lectures or meetings, and (e) social distancing added to the attenuation of auditory signaling.

For in-person learning, Schafer et al. (2021) found that face masks and social distancing requirements posed substantial listening challenges. For remote learning, they found that technology issues interfered with remote learning; in addition, many caregivers were uncomfortable with the technology skills required for remote learning. Of note, they found that, with the exception of American Sign Language (ASL) interpreters, common accommodations were not consistently provided to students with hearing loss.

In the early childhood context, Steed and Leech (2021) found that teachers used indirect instructional approaches during the pandemic with more emphasis on meeting with families and providing activities to families compared to instructing children. It is worth considering the extent to which this also applied in the deaf education context, particularly given issues of language deprivation that may appear with deaf and hard-of-hearing children.

DISABILITY CRITICAL RACE THEORY AND CRITICAL RACE POLICY ANALYSIS

Formally introduced in 2013 by Annamma et al., disability critical race theory (DisCrit) is an intersectional (Crenshaw, 1989) theoretical framework to analyze how the dual systems of racism and ableism reinforce each other and offer insight into "why the location of being both a person of color *and* a person labeled with a dis/ability is qualitatively different for students of color than White students with a dis/ability" (Annamma et al., 2013, p. 5). Annamma et al. developed seven tenets of DisCrit "to operationalize what kinds of specific questions can be illuminated from a DisCrit approach" (p. 11).

Valles and Villalpando (2022) set forth an approach to using a critical race policy analysis. They noted that a critical race policy analysis "is helpful in centering race and thereby unmasking the process and ways in which policies marginalize and oppress communities of color" (p. 397). Writing in the context of school discipline policies, they set out the following four steps in their critical race policy analysis. First, research how the policies arose nationally and statewide "and the process used to approve these policies" (p. 397). Second, identify the key stakeholders and their motivations for supporting or not supporting the policy. Third, apply "a discourse analysis using [critical race theory] CRT and LatCrit to guide the analysis used to unpack drafted legislation and policies" (p. 397). Fourth, analyze "the impact on the implementation of the policy" (p. 397).

DISCRIT AND CRITICAL RACE POLICY ANALYSIS OF EDUCATIONAL POLICIES IN RESPONSE TO THE COVID-19 PANDEMIC

In this section, I analyze one of these responses—specifically, the return to in-person learning—under a critical race policy analysis, using the approach outlined by Valles and Villalpando (2022). While they used critical race policy analysis to operationalize CRT and LatCrit theories in the context of school discipline policies, I seek to operationalize DisCrit theory in context of school policies amid the COVID-19 pandemic. Specifically, I propose this approach to analyze school administrators' responses to the COVID-19 pandemic with respect to deaf and hard-of-hearing students.

School Administrators' Responses to the COVID-19 Pandemic

I propose using the critical race policy analysis set forth by Valles and Villalpando (2022) to analyze the IDEA protections and how those protections have been affected by school administrators' responses to the COVID-19 pandemic. Adapting the critical race policy analysis approach of Valles and Villalpando to this context raises several important issues. I use the example of school administrators' policies around the return to in-person learning during the pandemic as an example to illustrate the kinds of questions this analysis can raise. This approach calls attention to the under-examined issue of how school administrators' responses to the COVID-19 pandemic may affect deaf and hard-of-hearing students.

Under the approach set forth by Valles and Villalpando (2022), the researcher considers how the policy under study arose. In the context of in-person learning, what prompted the pushes for the return to in-person learning? The researcher identifies stakeholders and their motivations. In this context, which parents and families pushed for the return to in-person learning? Which families were most vulnerable to negative consequences from COVID-19 upon a return to in-person learning?

Adapting Valles and Villalpando's (2022) approach to this context, the researcher applies a discourse analysis using DisCrit. Of particular relevance for this analysis are the following two tenets of DisCrit: (a) tenet2 4, which states: "DisCrit privileges voices of marginalized populations traditionally not acknowledged within research" (Annamma et al., 2013, p. 11), and (b) tenet 5, which states: "DisCrit considers legal and historical aspects of dis/ability and race and how both have been used separately and together to deny the rights of some citizens" (Annamma et al., 2013, p. 11).

DisCrit Tenet 4: Privileging Perspectives of Marginalized Populations

DisCrit tenet 4 emphasizes prioritizing the perspectives of those most affected by the return to in-person learning. Who has the authority to challenge decisions around COVID-19 and the return to in-person learning? In a longitudinal ethnographic study of rules around homework policy enforcement, Calarco (2020) reported that administrators in schools, as leaders of privilege-dependent organizations, strategically decided which students and families to exempt from homework rules. Poorer families were not "contentious enough, important enough, or compliant enough to warrant exemptions from rules" (p. 233). While the school in Calarco's study was comprised primarily (82%) of White families, Calarco's findings are comparable with Baldwin Clark's (2018), who described how privileged families used their positions to obtain preferred disability labels. Instead of catering to these families, DisCrit tenet 4 focuses on the perspectives of those traditionally excluded from these processes.

Consistent with DisCrit principles of recognizing power and perspectives, it is important to consider the researcher's position with respect to the population under study. I am a White, hearing, nondisabled researcher in the field of deaf education, which is overwhelmingly comprised of White hearing individuals like myself (Cawthon et al., 2017; Lawyer, 2018). It is important that I recognize my position as a member of privileged and dominant groups and prioritize the perspectives and work of people from within the community itself.

DisCrit Tenet 5: Interrogating Legal and Historical Power

Bryan and Emery (2014) stated that law is "the ultimate formal expression of cultural order" (p. 59). DisCrit tenet 5 requires the researcher to interrogate who historically has wielded power in schools. In this context, with respect to COVID-19 policies, the Center for Disease Control and Prevention reported that more parents who were of racial and ethnic minoritized groups expressed concerns about the reopening of school buildings than did White parents (Gilbert et al., 2020). During the same time frame, Parolin and Lee (2021) found that school building closures were more common in schools with higher proportions of students from racial and ethnic minoritized groups.

With respect to the IDEA, features of the law and how it has been implemented have raised concerns of racial disproportionalities through the IDEA as well as issues related to access to justice and power dynamics between schools and families. Specifically, with respect to deaf and hard-of-hearing children, the LRE provision of the IDEA contributed to disconcerting changes for some researchers and advocates of deaf and hard-of-hearing children and their families.

Racial disproportionalities. Researchers and advocates have raised concerns about disproportionality in special education since the inception of IDEA (Voulgarides et al., 2017). The 1997 reauthorization of IDEA first addressed disproportionality in the statute itself, reflecting federal legislators' concern that children of color were disproportionately placed into the most subjective disability categories of intellectual disability and emotional disturbance (Dragoo, 2019). In particular, researchers have analyzed how African American boys are over-represented in the highly stigmatized categories of emotionally disturbed (Broderick & Leonardo, 2016). Baldwin Clark (2018) analyzed how White children are over-represented in high resource special education categories, specifically autism. Clark tracked the consequence of a classification under emotional disturbance and of autism, finding that the underlying behaviors that lead to these labels may be almost the same. They found that White middle class parents manipulated

12 ▪ C. PAYNE-TSOUPROS

the system to their advantage to procure the more advantageous classification of autism for their children.

The change in the funding scheme in the 1997 reauthorization of the IDEA reflected federal legislators' "growing concern [that] a disproportionate number of minority children [were] being identified, particularly in the more subjective disability categories" (Dragoo, 2019, p. 10). In response, rather than use the number of children with disabilities living in the state to determine IDEA funding levels, federal legislators changed the formula to use the population of children living in the state. Payne-Tsoupros (2022) argued that the ongoing under-funding of the IDEA at the federal level disproportionately affects children of color with disabilities, as illustrated by the disparities in special education category placement mentioned above.

Access to IDEA enforcement. While families have the legal right under the IDEA to be part of the IEP process, there are power imbalances in the structure and enforcement of rights under the IDEA. Heldman et al. (2020) positioned special education along with child welfare and juvenile justice as three groups of children to whom the state owes legal obligations, stating: "The collaboration between parents of children with disabilities and schools that IDEA drafters originally sought has been illusory, even in the best of times" (p. 894). The IDEA's dispute resolution mechanism is an individual student-by-student process. By its nature as an individual rights mechanism, the structure of the IDEA may create barriers for poor families.

Pasachoff (2011) critiqued the private enforcement regime of the IDEA as insufficiently enforcing the law for the poor. Pasachoff analyzed how certain statutory features of private enforcement scheme incorporated in the IDEA—specifically, information asymmetries, the threat of litigation, and high transaction costs—led to wealthier families bringing private enforcement actions under the IDEA at higher rates than poor families.

In a qualitative study of the barriers that six parents of deaf children have experienced in the IEP process and the strategies these parents used to overcome those barriers, Trahan (2016) found that parents did not understand the IEP process sufficiently well enough to have a true voice in the process. Focusing on parents with culturally and linguistically diverse backgrounds, Trahan found the following as barriers experienced by the parents in the study: complex procedural safeguards, insufficient knowledge of IEP procedures, and lack of access to school personnel who were fluent in ASL.

Power dynamics: Schools and families. School districts often will prevail over parent plaintiffs in litigation. Zirkel (2012) analyzed the 65 hearing officers' decisions in Illinois between 1982 and 2010 that were subject to court appeal (and available in Westlaw or the Individuals With Disabilities Education Law Report database). Zirkel found the following: Outcomes were skewed in favor of school districts at both the administrative and court levels, the outcome upon judicial appeal was largely unchanged for most rulings, and the standard of judicial review did not appear relevant to the final court outcome.

Zirkel's (2012) findings are consistent with findings of other researchers. Schanding et al. (2017) analyzed 139 Texas due process hearings from 2011 to 2015 and found that the school district prevailed in 72% of the cases. In an analysis of Massachusetts due process hearings from 2005 to 2013, Blackwell and Blackwell (2015) found that the school district was the prevailing party in 62.5% of cases. The frequency with which school districts prevail over families in due process hearings and in court has been attributed to several factors, including the resources—namely, financial resources and attorneys—available to school districts (Schanding et al., 2017). Schanding et al. (2017) posited that, given the costs and relationship damage in continuing litigation, schools may be more likely to settle cases where they do not anticipate a favorable outcome.

LRE and deaf and hard-of-hearing children. Prior to the IDEA implementation, many deaf and hard-of-hearing children were educated in special residential and day schools with specialized curricula and various environmental modifications (Rose, 2002). As the overwhelming majority of deaf and hard-of-hearing children are born to hearing parents, schools for the deaf historically played a significant role in cultural transmission. Scully (2012) referred to this phenomenon as a "sociological novelty that the chief conduits for Deaf identity were institutional, . . . rather than familial" (p. 112). While based on disability inclusion principles, the LRE provision resulted in disruptions in this cultural transmission, as more and more deaf and hard-of-hearing children were mainstreamed in public schools.

As enrollment in schools for the deaf decreased, they lost some of their role as transmitters of culture (Jackson, 2010). Moores (2005) stated, "Education of deaf and hard-of-hearing students first began to lose its independence . . . with the passage of the Education of All Handicapped Children Act of 1975" (p. 80). DisCrit tenet 5 thus illuminates structural inequities within the IDEA when incorporated into a critical race theory policy analysis.

Finally, the researcher analyzes the implementation of these policies in schools today, considering questions such as: Which communities have more frequent and more severe outbreaks of COVID-19? Which communities incorporated mitigation techniques such as outdoor lunch, updated HVAC systems, high-quality masks, and physical distancing? Critical race policy analysis also sheds light on how specific populations of deaf and hard-of-hearing students may be affected differently by COVID-19 policies. Further, a critical race policy analysis framework is an approach to analyze how school-related COVID-19 polices may affect educational opportunities for deaf and hard-of-hearing students.

CONCLUSION

In this chapter, I proposed a preliminary analysis of school policies around in-person learning amid the COVID-19 pandemic. I used critical race policy analysis (Valles & Villalpando, 2022) to argue that school administrators' responses to the COVID-19 pandemic represent a retrenchment of the protections afforded to children and families under the IDEA. Disrupting this trajectory requires affirmative steps consistent with DisCrit (Annamma et al., 2013) and critical race policy analysis.

As preliminary considerations, at the individual level, students and families may consider bringing a lawsuit under the IDEA for failure to provide FAPE, however litigation is risky and burdensome on families. Teachers can find ways to capitalize on student strengths. For example, in a qualitative study conducted in summer 2020 of secondary students with disabilities in the United States, Toste et al. (2021) explored factors associated with students' resilience and self-determination during the pandemic. Toste et al. recommended the importance of personalized supports, maintaining high expectations of students with disabilities, and leveraging student strengths. At the school district level, school district administrators can prioritize students with highest needs to counter the power imbalances embedded in the IDEA. Reformers may look to lessons from other fields, such as Chang-Bacon's (2021) article that proposed that administrators of general education programs consider strategies used and advocated by professionals in the field of "students with interrupted formal education" (SIFE; p. 187).

However, as Grant (2020) cautioned: "Simply reminding school districts of their legal mandate to provide equitable and accessible educational opportunities is ineffective without the resources and financial support to implement the legal requirements safely" (p. 140). Thus, additional actions include Congress's immediate and full funding of the IDEA.

The unavoidable limits inherent in seeking individual solutions to systemic issues suggest that individual family and teacher responses alone will not be sufficient. Using DisCrit (Annamma et al., 2013) in a critical race policy analysis (Valles & Villalpando, 2022) can illuminate the power structures embedded in a proposed policy and help center the perspectives of those most affected.

NOTES

1. I use "deaf and hard-of-hearing" broadly to refer to the audiological condition of hearing loss.
2. Annamma et al. (2013) preferred to use "tenet" (with a lower case "t") in this context and maintained that practice subsequently. I maintain their preference.

REFERENCES

Annamma, S. A., Connor, D., & Ferri, B. (2013). Dis/ability critical race studies (DisCrit): Theorizing at the intersections of race and dis/ability. *Race Ethnicity and Education, 16*(1), 1–31. https://doi.org/10.1080/13613324.2012.730511

Baldwin Clark, L. (2018). Beyond bias: Cultural capital in anti-discrimination law. *Harvard Civil Rights-Civil Liberties Law Review, 53*, 381–443. https://ssrn.com/abstract=3282048

Blackwell, W. H., & Blackwell. V. B. (2015). A longitudinal study of special education due process hearings in Massachusetts: Issues, representation, and student characteristics. *SAGE Open, 5*(1), 1–11. https://doi.org/10.1177/2158244015577669

Broderick, A. A., & Leonardo, Z. (2016). What a good boy: The deployment and distribution of "goodness" as ideological property in schools. In S. A. Annamma, D. Connor, & B. Ferri (Eds.), *DisCrit: Disability studies and critical race theory in education* (pp. 55–67). Teachers College Press.

Bryan, A., & Emery, S. (2014). The case for deaf legal theory through the lens of deaf gain. In H. D. Bauman & J. J. Murray (Eds.), *Deaf gain: Raising the stakes for human diversity* (pp. 37–62). University of Minnesota Press.

Calarco, J. M. (2020). Avoiding us versus them: How schools' dependence on privileged "helicopter" parents influences enforcement of rules. *American Sociological Review, 85*(2), 223–246. https://doi.org/10.1177%2F0003122420905793

Cawthon, S. W., Garberoglio, C. L., & Hauser, P. C. (2017). Conclusion: Looking to the past and embracing the future. In S. W. Cawthon & C. L. Garberoglio (Eds.), *Research in deaf education: Contexts, challenges, and considerations* (pp. 361–377). Oxford University Press.

Chang-Bacon, C. K. (2021). Generation interrupted: Rethinking "students with interrupted formal education" (SIFE) in the wake of a pandemic. *Educational Researcher, 50*(3), 187–196. https://doi.org/10.3102/0013189X21992368

Crenshaw, K. (1989). Demarginalizing the intersection of race and sex: A Black feminist critique of antidiscrimination doctrine, feminist theory and antiracist policies. *The University of Chicago Legal Forum, 1989*(1), Article 8. https://chicagounbound.uchicago.edu/uclf/vol1989/iss1/8

Deaf Students Education Services; Policy Guidance, 57 F. R. 49274 (proposed Oct. 30, 1992). https://www.govinfo.gov/content/pkg/FR-1992-10-30/pdf/FR-1992-10-30.pdf

Dragoo, H. E. (2019). *The Individuals With Disabilities Education Act (IDEA) funding: A primer.* Congressional Research Service. https://crsreports.congress.gov/product/pdf/R/R44624

Education for all Handicapped Children Act, Pub. L. No. 94-142 (1975), codified as amended at 20 U.S.C. § 1400, et seq.

Endrew F. ex. rel. Joseph F. v. Douglas County School District, 580 U.S. ___ (2017). https://www.supremecourt.gov/opinions/16pdf/15-827_0pm1.pdf

Gilbert, L. K., Strine, T. W., Szucs, L. E., Crawford, T. N., Parks, S. E., Barradas, D. T., Njai, R., & Ko, J. Y. (2020, December 11). Racial and ethnic differences in parental attitudes and concerns about school reopening during the COVID-19 pandemic—United States, July 2020. *Morbidity and Mortality Weekly Report, 69,* 1848–1852. https://doi.org/10.15585/mmwr.mm6949a2

Glessner, M. M., & Johnson, S. A. (2020). The experiences and perceptions of practicing special education teachers during the COVID-19 pandemic. *The Interactive Journal of Global Leadership and Learning, 1*(2), Article 4. https://doi .org/10.55354/2692-3394.1013

Grant, C. (2020). COVID-19's impact on students with disabilities in under-resourced school districts. *Fordham Urban Law Journal, 48,* 127–141.

Heldman, J. K., Dalton, M. A., & Fellmeth, R. C. (2020). COVID-19 and preventing harm to vulnerable children. *San Diego Law Review, 57,* 865-918. https://digital .sandiego.edu/sdlr/vol57/iss4/2

Individuals With Disabilities Education Improvement Act of 2004, 20 U.S.C. § 1400 *et seq.* (2004). https://www.govinfo.gov/content/pkg/PLAW-108publ446/pdf/ PLAW-108publ446.pdf

Jackson, C. (2010). The Individuals With Disabilities Education Act and its impact on the deaf community. *Stanford Journal of Civil Rights & Civil Liberties, 6,* 355–390.

Jameson, J. M., Stegenga, S. M., Ryan, J., & Green, A. (2020). Free appropriate public education in the time of COVID-19. *Rural Special Education Quarterly, 39*(4), 181–192. https://doi.org/10.1177/8756870520959659

Lawyer, G. K. (2018). *Removing the colonizer's coat in deaf education: Exploring the curriculum of colonization and the field of deaf education* [Unpublished doctoral dissertation]. University of Tennessee. https://trace.tennessee.edu/utk_ graddiss/5036

Moores, D. F. (2005). The No Child Left Behind and the Individuals With Disabilities Education Acts: The uneven impact of partially funded federal mandates on education of deaf and hard of hearing children. *American Annals of the Deaf, 150*(2), 75–79. https://doi.org/10.1353/aad.2005.0028

National Association of the Deaf. (n.d.). *Position statement on inclusion.* https://www .nad.org/about-us/position-statements/position-statement-on-inclusion/

Parolin, Z., & Lee, E. K. (2021). Large socio-economic, geographic, and demographic disparities exist in exposure to school closures. *Nature Human Behavior, 5,* 522–528. https://www.nature.com/articles/s41562-021-01087-8.pdf

Pasachoff, E. (2011). Special education, poverty, and the limits of private enforcement. *Notre Dame Law Review, 86*(4), 1413–1493. https://scholarship.law .nd.edu/ndlr/vol86/iss4/2

Payne-Tsoupros, C. (2022). Using human resources planning to disrupt racism and ableism in the IDEA. *Journal of Education Human Resources.* Advance online publication. https://doi.org/10.3138/jehr-2021-0064

Rose, S. (2002). Inclusion of students with hearing loss in general education: Fact or fiction? *The Teacher Educator, 37*(3), 216–229. https://doi.org/10 .1080/08878730209555295

Schafer, E. C., Dunn, A., & Lavi, A. (2021). Educational challenges during the pandemic for students who have hearing loss. *Language, Speech, and Hearing Services in Schools, 52*(3), 889–898. https://doi.org/doi:10.1044/2021_LSHSS-21-00027

Schanding, G. T., Cheramie, G. M., Hyatt, H., Praytor, S. E., & Yellen, J. R. (2017). Analysis of special education due process hearings in Texas. *SAGE Open, 7*(2), 1–6. https://doi.org/10.1177/2158244017715057

Scully, J. L. (2012). Deaf identities in disability studies: With us or without us? In N. Watson, A. Roulstone, & C. Thomas (Eds.), *Routledge handbook of disability studies* (pp. 109–121). Routledge.

Steed, E. A., & Leech, N. (2021). Shifting to remote learning during COVID-19: Differences for early childhood and early childhood special education teachers. *Early Childhood Education Journal, 49*(5), 789–798. https://doi.org/10.1007/s10643-021-01218-w

Toste, J. R., Raley, S. K., Gross Toews, S., Shogren, K. A., & Coelho, G. (2021). "Eye opening and chaotic": Resilience and self-determination of secondary students with disabilities amidst the COVID-19 pandemic. *Journal of Education for Students Placed at Risk (JESPAR), 26*(2), 157–183. https://doi.org/10.1080/10824669.2021.1906248

Trahan, A. K. (2016). *An examination of parental experiences in the individualized education plans of their deaf children: A qualitative study* (Publication No. 10192616) [Doctoral dissertation, Lamar University]. ProQuest Dissertations and Theses Global.

U.S. Department of Education. (1992, October 26). *Deaf students education services; policy guidance.* https://www2.ed.gov/about/offices/list/ocr/docs/hq9806.html

U.S. Department of Education. (2020a). *Questions and answers on providing services to children with disabilities during the coronavirus disease 2019 outbreak.* https://www2.ed.gov/policy/speced/guid/idea/memosdcltrs/qa-covid-19-03-12-2020.pdf

U.S. Department of Education. (2020b, April 28). *Secretary DeVos reiterates learning must continue for all students, declines to seek congressional waivers to FAPE, LRE requirements of IDEA.* https://sites.ed.gov/idea/secretary-devos-declines-to-seek-congressional-fape-lre-waivers-to-idea-requirements

Valles, B. G., & Villalpando, O. (2022). A critical race policy analysis of the school-to-prison pipeline for Chicanos. In M. Lynn & A. D. Dixon (Eds.), *Handbook of critical race theory in education* (pp. 392–403). Routledge.

Voulgarides, C. K., Fergus, E., & King Thorius, K. A. (2017). Pursuing equity: Disproportionality in special education and the reframing of technical solutions to address systemic inequities. *Review of Research in Education, 41*(1), 61–87. https://doi.org/10.3102/0091732X16686947

Zirkel, P. A. (2012). Judicial appeals for hearing/review officer decisions under IDEA: An empirical analysis. *Exceptional Children, 78*(3), 375–384. https://doi.org/10.1177%2F001440291207800307

CHAPTER 2

SURVIVING THE PANDEMIC

Empowering Immigrant Families to Advocate and Support Their Children/ Youth With Disabilities at Home

Lusa Lo
University of Massachusetts Boston

Kimberly Lee
Parent Advocacy

ABSTRACT

The COVID-19 pandemic forced schools to make a last-minute decision to change the modality of student learning from in-person to distance learning. Although this sudden change had created difficulties for students and their families, it had been even more challenging for students with disabilities and their families, especially those who were culturally and linguistically diverse. While schools were overwhelmed with distributing materials and digital tools to students who were in need and implementing distance learning, less attention was placed on families' readiness to support their children's learning at home. The purpose of this chapter is to share the positive impact a family

School–University–Community Research in a (Post) COVID-19 World, pages 19–42
Copyright © 2023 by Information Age Publishing
www.infoagepub.com
All rights of reproduction in any form reserved.

support group had on the partnership between Chinese immigrant families of children with disabilities and schools. The participants encountered many challenges during the pandemic, including fiscal and racism issues and difficulties supporting children's distance learning. The family support group was not only able to provide a platform for the families to connect, support each other, and seek resources but also offer them opportunities to learn the skills they needed to support their children's distance learning and collaborate with schools to ensure that their children with disabilities received the needed services. Recommendations for practice and future research on how schools can further enhance their partnerships with families and community are discussed.

No matter where you were in 2020, everyone experienced the negative impact of the COVID-19 pandemic. The outbreak of COVID-19 shut down many parts of the world and led to a high mortality rate. In that year, there were approximately 375,000 deaths due to COVID-19 in the United States (Centers for Disease Control and Prevention, 2021). To protect everyone's health and safety, numerous measures were put in place across the entire United States including stay-at-home orders. Non-essential businesses, including schools, had to be closed (California Department of Education, 2020; Office of the Governor, 2020a; EducationWeek, 2020).

With the sudden mandate of school closure, without any contingent plans, many schools did not know how learning could continue taking place, especially when the closing period was extended (Office of the Governor, 2020b). Some schools scrambled to distribute hard copy learning materials for students to bring home, while others did not. Since student learning needed to continue, schools decided to implement distance learning. After one month of closing, some schools began shipping or asking families to pick up additional learning materials. A few schools also began loaning digital tools, such as Chromebooks, to students who did not own one (Klein, 2021). However, the actual implementation of online teaching and learning turned out to be more challenging than schools had ever anticipated. Most teachers did not have experience in providing online educational instruction. Their technological skills and pedagogical knowledge of teaching online were limited (Adams, 2020; Newton, 2020). Even when teachers were prepared, distance education could not be successfully implemented without the assistance of their students' families. However, many families were ill-equipped to take on these additional roles and responsibilities—especially for those who had children with disabilities and who were from culturally and linguistically diverse (CLD) backgrounds (Alexander & Ross, 2020; Nierman, 2020).

A REVIEW OF THE LITERATURE

Experiences of CLD Families

The United States has an estimated 45 million immigrants, with most coming from Mexico, China, India, the Philippines, and El Salvador (Esterline & Batalova, 2022). Approximately 67 million American residents speak a language other than English at home (Zeigler & Camarota, 2019). These demographics are reflected in the U.S. student population: CLD students comprise more than half of the general education (52%) and special education (53%) student population (National Center for Education Statistics, 2021). By 2028, the number of students who are White is projected to continue declining, while CLD students will continue to increase with Asian/Pacific Islander students being the largest growing group (National Center for Education Statistics, 2019).

Technological Needs

With the growing number of CLD students in today's classrooms, school professionals not only need to ensure that their curricula and instructional practices are culturally responsive but also determine ways to engage and effectively collaborate with their students' families. However, families from low socioeconomic status and CLD backgrounds are less likely to be actively involved in their children's school (Greene, 2011; Hirano et al., 2018; Kim et al., 2007; Lo & Bui, 2020). Reasons for their low involvement may include but are not limited to cultural and linguistic barriers, limited knowledge about the school system and expectations of involvement, lack of understanding of the special education process, and financial burdens (Lamorey, 2002; Lynch & Hanson, 2004; National Center on Safe Supportive Learning Environment, 2022). These barriers were amplified even more during the COVID-19 pandemic.

During the COVID-19 pandemic lockdown period, in order to interact and work/learn remotely, reliable Internet, computer, and mobile devices became basic necessities. However, such necessities were not always available to families. According to the National Telecommunications and Information Administration (2022), more than half of the U.S. families did not own a desktop computer (72%) or a laptop (53%), and many of them also did not have reliable Internet services. This digital divide hit U.S. immigrants the hardest (Cherewka, 2020). To close this gap, U.S. schools spent millions of dollars on refurbished or new devices and loaned them to students who needed one (Klein, 2021). With a low supply and huge demand for these devices, almost 1 year after the initial surge of COVID-19 cases, students in 44% of the largest districts were still waiting for devices to arrive

(Richards et al., 2021). Besides devices, prior to the implementation of the Affordable Connectivity Program, many low-income CLD families were unable to afford Internet connections with higher speed. Those who lived in rural areas were also unable to access reliable Internet services (Dao, 2020; Maher, 2020).

During in-person learning, school professionals are the sole individuals who provide instruction to students, manage classrooms, and offer interventions during school hours. Since the beginning of distance learning, more than half of these responsibilities have shifted to parents (Garbe et al., 2020; Power, 2020). More burdens were placed on parents' shoulders, especially those who had more than one child at home. Parents needed to keep track of their children's class schedules so they could prepare an uninterrupted space for their children at home and get them ready for remote classes—such as turning on computers, accessing Internet services, and logging into the online class platform. Following online classes, parents had to offer support to their children when completing online assignments and ensure that completed assignments were submitted to the correct online platform. However, results of the Program for the International Assessment of Adult Competencies survey indicated that only 12% of U.S. immigrants had high levels of proficiency using digital tools (Education GPS, 2019). With limited technological skills, immigrant parents faced difficulties supporting their children's distance learning.

Additional Struggles Faced by Families of Students With Disabilities

When parents are highly engaged in their child's education, many variables such as school behavior, attendance, homework completion, and academic performance are more likely to improve (Castro et al., 2015; Eagle, 1989; Henderson & Mapp, 2002). Parent engagement is especially needed in special education and is emphasized in U.S. legislation. For example, parents are the only ones who can advocate for their children with disabilities and make decisions about their special education services and placement, so they must be included in their child's individualized education program (IEP) team (Individuals With Disabilities Education Act [IDEA], 2004, §300.321, §300.322). Schools must receive parental consent prior to any type of formal testing taking place (§300.300). Additionally, school professionals cannot be absent from students' annual IEP meetings without the agreement of parents (§300.321). In order to take on these active roles, parents need to be knowledgeable about federal and state legislation, their parental rights, school curriculum, and interventions and strategies that are suitable for the specific needs of their children with disabilities. CLD parents, however, are rarely equipped with the expected knowledge and skills to effectively take on these roles.

Even though students with disabilities receive classroom instructions like all other students, they also require additional support and special education services. For instance, students with emotional and behavioral disorders frequently need teachers and/or paraprofessionals to redirect them or implement behavioral interventions to keep them calm and/or focused on class. Students with a reading disability or speech impairment may require one-on-one and/or small group instructions by related service providers, such as reading specialists and speech and language pathologists. Students with severe disabilities may also need a lot of hand-over-hand assistance during class. In online settings, a majority of these support and special education services are reduced or suspended (Adely, 2020). In May 2020, ParentsTogether Action (2020)—a national parent-led organization—surveyed more than 1,500 families of students with disabilities in the United States about the impact of COVID-19. Forty percent of the families reported that distance learning went poorly, and 39% reported that their children with disabilities did not receive any special education services and support.

For those who were fortunate to receive special education services, its quality remained questionable. Teachers and related service providers (e.g., speech and language pathologists) indicated that they were not confident that they had met the social, behavioral, and emotional needs of their students (Bruhn et al., 2022; Hebert et al., 2021). Surveys of service providers indicated that 90% did not have any experiences providing services remotely during the COVID-19 pandemic (American Speech-Language-Hearing Association, 2020a, 2020b). Among the respondents, only 5% reported having received training on how to provide services online (Sylvan et al., 2020).

When teaching or re-teaching certain skills to students with disabilities, teachers and related service providers employ a gradual release of a responsibility model (Pearson & Gallagher, 1983), which requires them to (a) mention what the expected tasks are and demonstrate how to perform them, (b) guide students to complete the tasks with supports, and (c) allow the students to perform the tasks together with peers and/or independently and then offer feedback. Specific strategies are also implemented to enhance the learning process. During online teaching, teachers and related service providers could only offer the first step of the model, while the remaining responsibilities rested on parents. Even when some teachers and related service providers attempted to create instructional videos or utilize some interactive apps for parents to use with their children with disabilities at home, it is important to note that parents had never been trained to provide this level of support. Parents not only had to manage their children's day-to-day lives, health, and emotional well-being, they suddenly had to also take on additional roles as hands-on instructors and service providers which they were unprepared to do (Fontanesi et al., 2020; Wintersmith, 2020).

Benefits of Community Engagement

When schools were overwhelmed with what they had to do to meet the needs of all students during the pandemic, limited attention was given to parents of students with disabilities about how they could support their children's distance learning at home. When help was not available at school, many families had to look elsewhere. As Epstein et al. (2018) stated, it was important to engage and integrate community resources and services that could help strengthen the partnerships between families and schools. For CLD parents, having someone in the community who understood their cultural and linguistic backgrounds was crucial. Community-based personnel or volunteers could often serve as cultural brokers between families and schools (Torres et al., 2015).

There are various types of support available in the community. For families of children with disabilities, each state has at least one federally funded Parent Training and Information Center which is expected to provide support for free or at a very low cost (U.S. Department of Education, 2020). For states that are larger and have many immigrants, such as California, they also have at least one federally funded Community Parent Resource Center that is specifically designed to serve low-income parents, parents of children who are English learners, and parents who have disabilities (U.S. Department of Education, 2020). Since not all states have Community Parent Resource Centers and not all Parent Training and Information Centers have bilingual staff, immigrant families often choose to connect with local parent groups due to language compatibility, close proximity, and scheduling flexibility. Furthermore, bonding with families who have the same cultural and linguistic backgrounds and have children with disabilities with similar needs is essential to these families (Lo et al., 2014). Previous studies also have shown that parents who participated in support groups not only gained knowledge and skills that prepared them for coping with their children's disabilities but also resulted in feeling a sense of belonging (Drake et al., 2008; Lo, 2008).

Chapter Focus

The purpose of this chapter is to share a study that focused on how one family support group offered emotional support, training, and resources to Chinese immigrant families of children with disabilities during the pandemic. Each family in the group had at least one school-age child with a disability. As the families in the group gained additional knowledge and skills from their participation in the group, many of them became community or school personnel who continued to support and advocate for other Chinese immigrant families of students with disabilities in their community.

METHOD

A total of 53 Chinese immigrant families participated in the study. Each family had at least one child with a disability. Only 28% of the families had an educational background beyond high school. A majority of them (85%) were non- or limited English speakers. Their children's or grandchildren's disability ranged from moderate to severe. Details of the characteristics of the participants and their children can be found in Table 2.1.

TABLE 2.1 Characteristics of the Parent Participants	
	Number of Participants
Roles	
Mother	42
Father	8
Grandparents	3
Education in Home Country or United States	
Not high school graduates	15
High school graduates	23
Associate degree or diploma	8
Bachelor's degree	5
Master's degree	2
Level of English Language Proficiency	
Illiterate	1
Non-English speaking	15
Limited English speaking	29
Fluent English speaking	8
Types of Their Children/Youth's Disabilities	
Specific learning disability	8
Speech and language impairment	3
Emotional and behavioral disorder	8
Autism	13
Developmental delay	5
Intellectual disability	6
Multiple disabilities	8
Hearing impairment	2
Grade Levels of Their Children/Youth's Disabilities	
Elementary school	15
Middle school	28
High school	18

We collected various types of data online in the study. First, we used pre- and post-test data from 18 multiple choice questions to determine participants' knowledge of special education legislation and their children/parental rights. Second, we used a survey with 12 Likert scale questions (scale of 1 through 4, where 4 as the highest) and three open-ended questions to evaluate families' satisfaction with the support and resources provided during the pandemic. We gave clear instructions to families to complete the pre- and post-test and survey and offered support to any families encountering difficulty. Finally, we conducted unstructured interviews in Cantonese, the participants' primary language, with 20 randomly selected participants online so they could further elaborate on their experiences during this period and their perceptions of the support offered by the group. We used data from the interviews to triangulate the participants' responses in the survey. Each interview lasted between one to two hours.

We calculated means and standard deviations from the data collected in the pre- and post-tests and Likert scale questions and transcribed the interviews verbatim, which were then translated into English by a professional translator. The research team, whose members were fluent in both English and Chinese, reviewed all transcriptions and translations for accuracy. Using the constant comparative method (Lincoln & Guba, 1985), we then categorized all interview data into pre-established themes that were relevant to the purpose of the study, and we identified sub-categories within each theme. After the process was completed, the research team met and reviewed the analysis. The interrater reliability was 96%. We discussed the differences until consensus was established.

RESULTS

Issues Faced During the Pandemic

When asked about their experiences during the pandemic, all participants shared numerous challenges, including financial and racism. Furthermore, many participants also faced barriers when trying to support their children/grandchildren with disabilities during distance learning.

Financial Challenges
Many families in the study, 65%, indicated that they were unable to work. One mother who was cleaning staff at a hotel commented that, due to the stay-at-home order and travel restrictions, hotels were closed. The restaurant where her husband was employed was also closed. She stated, "When we were working, we could barely cover our monthly expenses. When we stopped working, we had no income. We also had limited savings." Many

participants echoed the financial challenges they faced but appreciated the fiscal support the government offered later in the pandemic.

Some participants who worked in essential businesses, such as grocery stores and auto repair facilities, were able to work but were very anxious about the possibilities of getting infected by COVID-19. One father of a 9-year-old with multiple disabilities and fragile health commented,

> We couldn't find surgical masks anywhere. All we could do was to make our own. How could those be as effective as the hospital masks or the K-95N [*sic*]? I was worried. If I were the only one, being sick was fine. I have a family to take care of. I could infect them. You know [child's name] is very fragile.

Racism Issues

While maintaining good health was the biggest concern among all individuals, the participants of the study also had to worry about racial discrimination. Over half the families who were able to continue working mentioned that their co-workers blamed them for spreading the virus. More than three quarters of the parent participants mentioned that they were afraid to be the targets of hate crimes. A grandmother of two grandchildren with autism said,

> We started wearing masks before the state mandate. There were so many times that when we were walking outside, people drove by or people on public buses yelled some bad words at us.... I was at a grocery store once and a White lady told me to go shop somewhere else.... My grandson refused to wear a mask because other kids at the school laughed at him. The school didn't do anything about it.

Another mother also commented,

> [Son's name]'s classmate said my son should return to China, so he could take the virus back home to China. My son was born in the U.S. I know the students might be just ignorant, but this kind of message is hurtful. My son asked me why his classmates said those mean things.... I wish the teacher had done something about it.

Multiple Challenges During Distance Learning

Besides facing financial and racism issues, participants struggled during their children's distance learning. At the beginning of the pandemic, depending on the school districts, some students did not have books and digital tools for students to use for a long period of time. A few students who were fortunate to have received Chromebooks from their schools reported that the devices were unreliable. One mother mentioned that her daughter received a Chromebook from school, but it stopped working after 2 weeks.

28 ▪ L. LO and K. LEE

In addition to digital tools, the participants were in need of technological support, since many of them had never or rarely used computers. They were also unfamiliar with the technological applications teachers used. For instance, some students were required to have a Gmail account so they could be enrolled in Google classroom. One mother of a second grader with autism didn't know how to create a Gmail account for her daughter. The teacher also did not offer her help. Another parent of two children (each with an intellectual disability) reported that,

> My son had to use Zoom, but my daughter had to use Google [Google Meet]. I never heard of them. I didn't know how to get them in their online classes. I used my bad English to ask the teacher for help. She said she would but then I didn't hear from her. We missed a lot of classes at the beginning.

A mother of a son with a specific learning disability and speech impairment said,

> I got a text message from the teacher saying that my son hasn't turned in any homework. He told me that he didn't know how to submit homework to Google [Google Classroom]. He didn't ask me because he knew I wouldn't know how. His younger brother also didn't know how to get the assignments from Google [Google Classroom].

In addition to the technological needs, participants faced challenges when managing their children's online class schedule, especially for those who had more than one child. A mother of two children with disabilities and one child without disabilities mentioned,

> Juggling three of their class schedules was impossible. As you know, [oldest son] needs my help at all times. [Second son with Asperger's syndrome] has ADHD, so I also have to keep reminding him to join his classes on time and check on him. [Youngest daughter without a disability] can do most of the things by herself, but she is very young and still needs my help. All of their class schedules were different. I had to remember who had which class at what time. [Oldest son] and [second son] also had to attend ABA [applied behavioral analysis], speech, and PT [physical therapy].

Parents who had to return to work often left their children with their grandparents. A few also left their children with relatives who lived nearby. One father had to leave his son (who had an intellectual disability) with his parents. Since they couldn't help the child set up the computer or they forgot to remind him to join remote classes, he frequently missed classes. The father said,

Surviving the Pandemic ▪ **29**

I received a call from the teacher saying that my son missed a lot of classes. It would affect his grade. There's nothing I could do. I tried setting up alarms in the house to remind them. Maybe my mother, who is hard of hearing, didn't hear the alarm, or the alarm didn't work. I did what I could.

Perceptions of the Offered Support

We asked participants in this study to rate the usefulness of the support and training offered by the group during the pandemic. Survey results indicated that they were highly satisfied with the provided support and training.

- Monthly online group meetings ($M = 3.89$; $SD = 0.32$)
- Support from fellow parent members ($M = 3.79$; $SD = 0.41$)
- Technological training ($M = 3.92$; $SD = 0.27$)
- Advocacy training ($M = 3.91$; $SD = 0.30$)
- Guest speakers based on parents' interested topics ($M = 3.51$; $SD = 0.50$)

When asked to rank the top three supports they found most helpful in enhancing their partnerships with schools, participants chose technology and advocacy training ($n = 48$), monthly online group meetings ($n = 45$), and support from fellow group members ($n = 32$). One parent of a 9-year-old child with an emotional and behavioral disorder reported that one of the helpful technological skills she learned from the group was that she could ensure that her child did not go to other websites during his online classes.

After I made sure that he was in the Zoom class, I went to do some house chores or help his little sister. Several times I heard him laughing out loud. I thought he was having fun in class, but then I also heard him screaming. When I went to check on him, I found him watching a movie online instead of listening to his teachers. [The coordinator] taught us how to control the computer, so he would not be able to open some websites. The teacher didn't even know he was not paying attention in classes. I told her what happened, so she could pay attention to him in class.

Besides technological support, the parents also appreciated the advocacy training, since many encountered difficulties ensuring that their children with disabilities received the special education services they were supposed to receive. Pre- and post-test results of their knowledge of the special education legislation and the rights of children and parents showed a significant improvement from an average of 33% in pre-test to 90% in post-test. One parent of a 20-year-old daughter with an intellectual disability reported,

My daughter will need to be transitioning to state agencies soon. The school didn't give me any information about it and just told me to attend the meeting. I tried searching for information online, but everything was in English. Fortunately, our group talked about which adult agencies provided what and how to be prepared for the meeting. It was very helpful. When I went to the meeting, I already knew what needed to be done, so it went smoothly.

Another parent of a 13-year-old child with autism said,

[Child's name] used to get As in most of his classes and a few B+s. Now he failed a couple of his classes. I was shocked. I asked him. He said he didn't know. I also didn't get any text messages or emails from teachers about the problems. I emailed the teacher several times, but she didn't reply. The group suggested me to request for a virtual team meeting to find out why he failed those classes and ask for daily communication. During the meeting, I found out that my son forgot to submit many homework and did poorly in tests. [The coordinator] taught us to link our son's Google calendar with mine, so I could see his assignment deadlines and when he would have a test. I could then remind him.

Ongoing Issues Required Immediate Attention

Although the family group was able to provide a lot of needed support to increase parents' knowledge and skills so they could fully collaborate with schools, their partnerships with schools could not be successful without the schools' assistance. Several ongoing issues the participants faced required the schools' immediate attention.

During the pandemic, all school meetings took place online. Usually, oral messages were shared in English first and then interpreted into the target language. However, many schools chose to have interpreters provide simultaneous interpretations instead. Participants reported that the hired interpreters were not skilled to provide simultaneous interpretations. One parent said,

The interpreters often pause for a while and then gave only a very short interpretation. You know that's not everything the teachers said. One time, an interpreter even said that he wasn't sure what the speaker said, but he thought the overall message was about this, this, this.

Furthermore, the participants understood that schools were juggling a lot during the pandemic. However, they hoped schools understood that families also had many responsibilities. One parent, who had a child with cerebral palsy who was unable to move by himself, felt that she was always being notified, but schools never asked her whether or not she agreed or if she had any suggestions. The parent said,

> I had to attend all his classes with him. I adjusted my other schedules based on his class and therapy schedules. The teacher and the specialists frequently changed or canceled the schedules at the last minute. Sometimes he had doctor's appointments that I could not change. One time he was sick, and I thought he had COVID. His health is more important, so we missed some classes. The teacher blamed me for his absences.

This parent also mentioned that when she attended the online classes and service sessions with her child, an interpreter was not always present, which prevented her from fully understanding what teachers and related service providers said and hindered keeping her child engaged.

Many parents struggled to receive the special education services their children were entitled to during distance learning as well as compensatory services after school reopening. Three quarters of the participants indicated that their children either did not receive special education services or received a reduced number of services. More than 85% of the parents felt that distance learning went poorly. One parent of a non-verbal child with autism reported that,

> Based on his IEP, he was supposed to receive speech services three times a week and 30 minutes each time. When we went online, we only saw the speech teacher twice. When I complained about it, the school said that they would make up the services after we returned. Now that we are back, he is getting the same amount of speech services as before, but the school didn't make up the missed services. When I asked, they just didn't respond.

One grandparent also commented that, after school reopening, the school simply notified her about what they had already decided regarding services for her granddaughter with an intellectual disability. How the decisions were made were unknown to her.

DISCUSSION

The outbreak of COVID-19 began at the end of 2019 and rapidly turned into a global pandemic. Within a few months, the health of everyone in the world was jeopardized. The mortality rate also rapidly increased. The World Health Organization estimated an excess mortality rate of at least three million in 2020 (World Health Organization, 2022). This number continues to increase, as different parts of the world continue facing various waves of COVID-19 infections (Choy et al., 2022; Kingsley, 2022; Weise, 2022).

If distance learning must take place again, many lessons could be learned from this study. The family support group aspect of this study provided families with a better understanding of the types and levels of support that schools were unable to provide during the pandemic but also enhanced their skills to work collaboratively with schools and support their children during distance learning.

Powerfulness of the Community

With the sudden closure of schools, administrations were required to ensure that learning continued, and they provided digital tools to students who were in need. However, schools quickly learned that these were insufficient since teachers were not equipped with the skills to teach remotely. While schools were overwhelmed addressing these issues, they also did not have sufficient manpower and resources to address the needs of all families. Distance education required teachers to provide instruction on one side of the screen, while parents assisted their children with disabilities on the other side. Parents were also expected to continue supporting their children's learning offline. Beyond normal parental responsibilities, parents also had to become their children's technology support providers, teachers, reading and/or math specialists, behavior interventionists, and special education providers (Alexander & Ross, 2020). The schools' expectations on parents' ability to take on these additional roles and responsibilities were unrealistic as no training was provided to parents. Kurtz and colleagues (2021) surveyed more than 2,000 parents whose children attended public and private K–12 schools nationwide about their views on the schools' response to the pandemic. Only two-third of the parents found help from schools on using technology. In their study, 92% of the Chinese participants had limited to no technological skills, 85% of them spoke limited to no English, and 72% of them had an educational background of high school level or below. A majority of them received limited to no help from schools so expecting these parents to fulfill expected roles proved to be difficult.

The results of our study clearly suggested that the community, such as the family support group in the study, was able to train and prepare the Chinese immigrant families to fulfill, if not all, most of the school expectations. The participants were able to receive support and resources from their fellow group members. The group also provided various types of training to address the technological needs of the participants. Furthermore, the participants learned advocacy skills, so they could be prepared to communicate and collaborate with schools and ensure that their children with disabilities received the services they needed. The results of this study were consistent with the existing research about the positive impact of parent groups in the community. Allen et al. (1992) reviewed 20 parent support groups and found that these groups provided parents with opportunities to enhance their knowledge and skills about how to handle their children's disabilities. The parents' attitudes and skills about parenting were also increased. Furthermore, the parents were able to develop positive relationships with schools. While knowledge and skills were important, Twoy et al. (2007) found that parents who participated in support groups in the community felt that the opportunities to connect with other families of children with disabilities were extremely helpful. They felt that parents in the group understood what they went through and were able to offer assistance. This type of emotional support is especially needed for families of children with disabilities, since some families might not understand the causes of their child's disabilities and might blame themselves for causing their child to have a disability (National Information Center for Children and Youth With Disabilities, 2003).

Recommendation for Practice

There is no question that the family support group aspect of this study was able to provide the parent participants the levels of support that schools struggled to offer. Since not all families are aware of what services are available in their community, schools have a responsibility to assist them. Lo (2012) suggested that schools should provide families with a family resource directory that includes organizations in the community, the types of services they offer, fees for their services, languages they support, and contact information. This family resource directory should also be updated periodically, so that it is most useful to families. For instance, parents may need to convert their family vehicle if they have a child with disabilities requiring a wheelchair, so they can easily transport their children in and out of the vehicle. Many may not know that the expense of this type of conversion can be covered by some state agencies. Another example is that families of children with disabilities and fragile health have many unique needs. They could easily refer to the family resource directory and identify the organizations that can assist them.

Schools' Actions Are Urgently Needed

Although the family group was able to close the support gaps during the pandemic, there were still various challenges that the participants faced when collaborating with schools that could not be addressed by the community. These challenges included racism issues students faced in classes, a lack of or poor quality of interpretation services, and missing compensatory services.

Racism Issues

While everyone in the world was concerned about the spread of COVID-19, Asian Americans faced double threats. When COVID-19 began to affect the United States in March 2020, a photographer captured one of the speech notes of former U.S. President Donald Trump, where he crossed out the term "Corona Virus" and replaced it with "Chinese virus" (Chiu, 2020; Moynihan & Porumbescu, 2020). Such racialized language used publicly by a country's leader prompted and encouraged many Americans to blame the Chinese for the virus. Since the pandemic, hate crimes against Asian-Americans in the United States have risen dramatically. Between the middle of March and end of December 2020, Stop AAPI Hate, a coalition that tracked and responded to incidents against Asian Americans and Pacific Islanders in the United States, received almost 3,000 reports of anti-Asian hate incidents (Stop AAPI Hate, 2021). In some states, anti-Asian hate incidents increased by over 800% between 2019 and 2020 (Center for the Study of Hate and Extremism, 2021). School is supposed to be a safe place for children. However, children of the parent participants in the current study experienced firsthand anti-Asian racism sentiment in their online classes. Disappointedly, when teachers witnessed these incidents, no actions were taken.

Recommendation for practice. Children learn about race at an early age through watching or hearing what parents and teachers say/do and don't say/do, through watching television, playing with toys around them, and observing how they and others are being treated. Although children learn about race at home when they are young, teaching race and discrimination in school settings is critical. What teachers don't say and do is as important as what they say and do. Brey and Pauker (2019) observed 96 five to eight-year-old children and learned that they treated their peers much more favorably when these peers received positive non-verbal feedback, such as smiles, from teachers. When teachers ignored racist behaviors in their in-person or online classes, they were encouraging these behaviors to continue to take place. Culturally responsive teaching must be in place where students can connect what they learn in schools with their own and their classmates' cultures, languages, and life experiences (Burnham, 2020). Racist behaviors in schools must be addressed immediately and appropriately. Schools have a responsibility to train their teachers, so they are prepared to handle racism and discrimination issues in their classrooms and at their schools.

Quality of Interpreters

The race and ethnicity of U.S. teachers has not changed much for decades. A majority of the U.S. teachers remain White, 79%, while over half the student population is from CLD backgrounds (National Center for Education Statistics, 2021). Many of these students' parents may struggle communicating fluently in English (U.S. Census Bureau, 2020). Parents whose

English proficiency level is low rely on interpreters to help bridge the communication gap between them and schools. However, in this study, when teachers and related service providers expected the Chinese parents to assist them in providing services to their children with moderate to severe disabilities at home, interpreters were not always present to help facilitate the communication. The purpose of moving from in-person learning to distance learning was to prevent learning loss as much as possible. However, when parents were unable to support their children with disabilities during online classes, the impact of these sessions became limited.

The availability and quality of interpreters has remained a concern for over a decade. Lo (2010) observed 15 IEP meetings among five Chinese speaking parents of children with disabilities. Results indicated that jargon was used throughout the meetings. The interpreters were unfamiliar with these terms and frequently provided incorrect interpretations. For example, the "Wilson" reading program was interpreted as a person whose name was Wilson. One of the parents who understood some of the spoken English reported that the interpreter only provided 60% of the information. These experiences were consistent with what the parents of this study faced. During the pandemic, when all meetings took place online, schools attempted to use the meeting time efficiently and had interpreters provide simultaneous interpretations without confirming whether or not these interpreters had received the appropriate training to perform such services. The interpreters did not always interpret all the information school professionals communicated. Without knowing the content of all the oral messages, parents struggled to make the right decisions about their children's services.

Recommendation for practice. Due to budgeting issues, U.S. schools rarely have interpreters available on a daily basis. When interpreters are needed for meetings, schools often subcontract a third party and are unaware of the qualifications and quality of these interpreters. Some state legislators, such as in Massachusetts, have attempted to strengthen the qualifying requirements for interpreters in specialized school meetings, such as IEP and disciplinary meetings. They proposed a bill that requires these interpreters to have advanced training in interpretation, be assessed to demonstrate their competency, know the specialized terminology used in school settings, complete supervised field experiences, and participate in ongoing professional development in interpreting (The 192nd General Court, 2022). Meanwhile, in Massachusetts and elsewhere, the responsibility for ensuring that high quality, trained interpreters are used in meetings resides with schools. Even when the interpretation companies claim that their interpreters are highly qualified, schools still have the responsibility to verify and provide relevant training to the interpreters they hire. Being fluent in English and the target languages should not be the only criteria for these interpreters. They must also be trained and familiar with the terms that are used in specialized meetings (Lo, 2012). At the end of each meeting, professionals and parents should also have opportunities to evaluate their service, so schools can determine if the same interpreters should be used again for future meetings (Lo, 2022).

Collaboration vs. Cooperation

Collaboration is critical in effective teamwork. In school, this term is frequently being used, especially in regards to engaging students' families. In special education, collaboration is even more important, since without collaborating with families, schools would not be able to formally test students, make changes on students' placement, and implement students' IEPs. However, collaboration should be distinguished from cooperation. Cooperation requires all parties to follow and act on what has already been decided. These parties are mostly being informed when and how certain actions should be taken. However, collaboration requires more than just being informed. Collaboration requires all parties to maintain two-way communication, be involved in the development of any programs or projects, and provide feedback throughout the process (Kampwirth & Powers, 2015). When the participants of the current study attempted to collaborate with schools, they felt that their feedback was often not sought. Instead, they were only being informed of schools' decisions. For instance, 75% of the parent participants reported that their children with disabilities either did not receive special education services or received only a minimal amount of services. After reopening, schools were supposed to identify students who needed compensatory services. However, such processes were confusing to the parent participants. Many of them were also not invited to be involved in the process. When requesting compensatory services, schools often told parents that "based on our professional opinion" their children did not need them. When parents asked for explanations on how such decisions were made, they were often ignored. Furthermore, the participants expressed that it was very difficult for them to manage their children's distance learning schedules, especially when they had more than one child and/or a child that had multiple special education sessions. When issues arose and participants contacted the teachers, they often did not receive a response.

Recommendation for practice.   Students with disabilities are expected to have regressed the most during distance learning. During the pandemic, students with disabilities did not receive appropriate evaluations or special education services that they were entitled to receive. According to the U.S. Department of Education (2022), a group of individuals who were knowledgeable about the needs of the students, including their family, were required to be involved in the process to make such determinations. Instead of simply being informed, families must be part of the discussions and be involved in the decision-making process.

True partnership between home and school requires a lot more than just one-way communication. Informing families about changes and updates is only one step of the process. Families' feedback must be sought; otherwise, schools will have difficulty determining monitoring their own effectiveness. Although many schools did attempt to solicit some feedback from families during the pandemic, whether or not they have addressed those families' concerns is unknown. It would be helpful for schools to provide families with updates on what they have learned from gathering feedback, how they plan to address feedback, and why they may not be able to address some of the feedback. This process would enable families to see that their feedback is being taken seriously. Additionally, schools have the obligation to respond to families' phone/email/text communications in a timely manner, providing responses within no more than 48 hours and communicating with families if more time is needed to investigate reported issues.

CONCLUSION

Family engagement is a shared responsibility between schools and communities. This can clearly be seen in this study. The family support group was able to provide resources and training to enhance parents' knowledge and skills so they could properly support their children's learning at home. Parents were also able to utilize what they had learned to advocate for their children with disabilities. To make this partnership even more effective, all parties must be involved and work collaboratively to understand the students' and their families' cultures, languages, and beliefs, be aware of the interests and challenges of CLD families, and solicit feedback along the way. When this is done consistently and continuously, the ones who benefit are our children.

REFERENCES

Adams, C. (2020, April 17). Coronavirus 'confusion': Teachers had little training for how to do online classes. *USA Today*. https://www.usatoday.com/story/news/education/2020/04/17/coronavirus-teachers-online-class-school-closures/2972529001/

Adely, H. (2020, April 23). *'No one to help me': Special education families struggle with coronavirus school closures.* northjersey.com. https://www.northjersey.com/story/news/education/2020/04/23/coronavirus-special-education-students-disability-school-closures/3008234001/

Alexander, C., & Ross, N. (2020, May 22). 'It's been hell': Parents struggle with distance learning for their kids with disabilities. *USA Today*. https://www.

usatoday.com/story/news/education/2020/05/22/coronavirus-parents
-distance-learning-woes-kids-disabilities/5227887002/

Allen, M., Brown, P., & Finlay, B. (1992). *Helping children by strengthening families: A look at family support programs.* Children's Defense Fund.

American Speech-Langauge-Hearing Association. (2020a, March). *ASHA COVID-19 survey results–March 2020.* https://www.asha.org/siteassets/uploadedFiles/COVID-19-Tracker-Survey-March-2020.pdf

American Speech-Language-Hearing Association. (2020b, May). *ASHA COVID-19 survey results–May 2020.* https://www.asha.org/siteassets/uploadedFiles/COVID-19-Tracker-Survey-May-2020.pdf

Brey, E., & Pauker, K. (2019). Teachers' nonverbal behaviors influence children's stereotypic beliefs. *Journal of Experimental Child Psychology, 188*, 1–13. https://doi.org/10.1016/j.jecp.2019.104671

Bruhn, A., Choi, Y., McDaniel, S., Mathews, H., & Hirsch, S. (2022). Meeting the needs of students with emotional and behavioral disorders during the COVID-19 school closures. *Behavioral Disorders, 47*(4), 270–281. https://doi.org/10.1177/01987429211067472

Burnham, K. (2020, July 31). *5 culturally responsive teaching strategies.* Northeastern University. https://www.northeastern.edu/graduate/blog/culturally-responsive-teaching-strategies/

California Department of Education. (2020, March 18). *Guidance on COVID-19 school closures.* https://www.cde.ca.gov/ls/he/hn/covid19schoolclosures.asp

Castro, M., Expósito-Casas, E., López-Martín, E., Lizasoain, L., Navarro-Asencio, E., & Gaviria, J. (2015). Parental involvement on student academic achievement: A meta-analysis. *Educational Research Review, 14*, 33–46. https://doi.org/10.1016/j.edurev.2015.01.002

Center for the Study of Hate and Extremism. (2021). *Report to the nation: Anti-Asian prejudice and hate crime.* California State University San Bernardino. https://dataspace.princeton.edu/handle/88435/dsp01sq87bx76c

Centers for Disease Control and Prevention. (2021, April 9). *Provisional mortality data–United States, 2020.* https://www.cdc.gov/mmwr/volumes/70/wr/mm7014e1.htm

Cherewka, A. (2020, September 3). *The digital divide hits U.S. immigrant households disproportionately during the COVID-19 pandemic.* Migration Policy Institute. https://www.migrationpolicy.org/article/digital-divide-hits-us-immigrant-households-during-covid-19

Chiu, A. (2020, March 20). *Trump has no qualms about calling coronavirus the 'Chinese Virus.' That's a dangerous attitude, experts say.* https://www.washingtonpost.com/nation/2020/03/20/coronavirus-trump-chinese-virus/

Choy, G., Lam, N., & Magramo, K. (2022, Feb 10). *Coronavirus: Experts predict Hong Kong's fifth wave could peak at 28,000 cases a day, with 1,000 deaths by June, say 'Shanghai-style lockdown' should be considered.* https://www.scmp.com/news/hong-kong/health-environment/article/3166501/coronavirus-hong-kong-fifth-wave-could-peak-28000

Dao, E. (2020, August 5). *Remote learning creates issues for families without internet.* KXLY.com. https://www.kxly.com/remote-learning-creates-issues-for-families-without-internet/

Drake, J., Couse, L., DiNapoli, P., & Banach, M. (2008). Interdisciplinary best practice: A case study of family and school support for a young child with ASD. *International Journal of Nursing in Intellectual and Development Disabilities, 4*(1), article 3. https://findscholars.unh.edu/display/publication437090

Eagle, E. (1989, March 27–31). *Socioeconomic status, family structure, and parental involvement: The correlates of achievement* [Paper presentation]. Annual Meeting of the American Educational Research Association, San Francisco, CA. https://files.eric.ed.gov/fulltext/ED307332.pdf

Education GPS. (2019). *Survey of adult skills (PIAAC): Full selection of indicators.* OECD. https://gpseducation.oecd.org/IndicatorExplorer?query=0&indicators=P001

EducationWeek. (2020, July 1). *The coronavirus spring: The historic closing of U.S. schools (a timeline).* https://www.edweek.org/leadership/the-coronavirus-spring-the-historic-closing-of-u-s-schools-a-timeline/2020/07

Epstein, J., Sanders, M. G., Sheldon, S., Simon, B., Salinas, K., Jansorn, N., VanVoorhis, F., Martin, C., Thomas, B., Greenfield, M., Hutchins, D., & Williams, K. (2018). *School, family, and community partnerships: Your handbook for action* (4th ed.). Corwin.

Esterline, C., & Batalova, J. (2022, March 17). *Frequently requested statistics on immigrants and immigration in the United States.* Migration Policy Institute. https://www.migrationpolicy.org/article/frequently-requested-statistics-immigrants-and-immigration-united-states

Fontanesi, L., Marchetti, D., Mazza, C., Di Giandomenico, S., Roma, P., & Verrocchio, M. (2020). The effect of the COVID-19 lockdown on parents: A call to adopt urgent measures. *Psychological Trauma: Theory, Research, Practice, & Policy, 12*(31), S79–S81. http://dx.doi.org/10.1037/tra0000672

Garbe, A., Ogurlu, U., Logan, N., & Cook, P. (2020). COVID-19 and remote learning: Experiences of parents with children during the pandemic. *American Journal of Qualitative Research, 4*(3), 45–65. https://doi.org/10.29333/ajqr/8471

Greene, G. (2011). *Transition planning for culturally and linguistically diverse youth.* Brookes Publishing.

Hebert, M., Goodrich, J., & Namkung, J. (2021, April 10). *Characterizing remote instruction provided by elementary school teachers during COVID-19.* EurekAlert. https://www.eurekalert.org/news-releases/702013

Henderson, A., & Mapp, K. (2002). *A new wave of evidence: The impact of school, family, and community connections on student achievement.* Southwest Educational Development Laboratory.

Hirano, K., Rowe, D., Lindstrom, L., & Chan, P. (2018). Systemic barriers to family involvement in transition planning for youth with disabilities: A qualitative metasynthesis. *Journal of Child and Family Studies, 27*, 3440–3456. https://doi.org/10.1007/s10826-018-1189-y

Individuals With Disabilities Education Act, 20 U.S.C. 1400, *et seq.* (2004).

Kampwirth, T., & Powers, K. (2015). *Collaborative consultation in the schools: Effective practices for students with learning and behavior problems* (5th ed.). Pearson.

Kim, K., Lee, Y., & Morningstar, M. (2007). An unheard voice: Korean American parents' expectations, hopes, and experiences concerning their adolescent child's future. *Research and Practice for Persons With Severe Disabilities, 32*(4), 253–264. https://doi.org/10.2511/rpsd.32.4.253

Kingsley, T. (2022, June 27). *Covid: UK in 'fifth wave already' as experts warn summer events will see infections surge even higher.* https://www.independent.co.uk/news/health/covid-infections-glastonbury-spread-latest-b2108716.html

Klein, A. (2021, April 20). *During COVID-19, schools have made a mad dash to 1-to-1 computing. What happens next?* EducationWeek. https://www.edweek.org/technology/during-covid-19-schools-have-made-a-mad-dash-to-1-to-1-computing-what-happens-next/2021/04

Kurtz, H., Lloyd, S., Harwin, A., Chen, V., & Furuya, Y. (2021). *Parents and schools during a pandemic: Results of a national survey.* Editorial Projects in Education. https://epe.brightspotcdn.com/4a/ac/9a2d34e946618911c1931844d873/parents-and-schools-during-a-pandemic-final-4.26.21.pdf

Lamorey, S. (2002). The effects of culture on special education services: Evil eyes, prayer meetings, and IEPs. *Teaching Exceptional Children, 34*(5), 67–71. https://doi.org/10.1177/004005990203400511

Lincoln, Y. S., & Guba, E. G. (1985). *Naturalistic inquiry.* SAGE Publications.

Lo, L. (2008). Perceived benefits experienced in support groups for Chinese families of children with disabilities. *Early Child Development and Care, 180*(3), 405–415. https://doi.org/10.1080/03004430802002625

Lo, L. (2010). Chinese families' level of participation and experiences in IEP meetings. *Preventing School Failure: Alternative Education for Children and Youth, 53*(1), 21–27. https://doi.org/10.3200/PSFL.53.1.21-27

Lo, L. (2012). Demystifying the IEP process for diverse parents of children with disabilities. *Teaching Exceptional Children, 44*(3), 14–20. https://doi.org/10.1177/004005991204400302

Lo, L. (2022, April 15). *How to work effectively with interpreters.* Edutopia. https://www.edutopia.org/article/how-work-effectively-interpreters

Lo, L., & Bui, O. (2020). Transition planning: Voices of Chinese and Vietnamese parents of youth with autism and intellectual disabilities. *Career Development and Transition for Exceptional Individuals, 43*(2), 89–100. https://doi.org/10.1177/2165143419899938

Lo, L., Cheng, T., & Chan, K. (2014). A school-based parent support group: Empowering Hong Kong parents of children with disabilities to be advocates. In L. Lo & D. Hiatt-Michael (Eds.), *Promising practices to empower culturally and linguistically diverse families of children with disabilities* (pp. 113–124). Information Age Publishing.

Lynch, E., & Hanson, M. (2004). *Developing cross-cultural competence: A guide for working with children and their families* (3rd ed.). Brookes Publishing.

Maher, K. (2020, September 13). *Remote schooling out of reach for many students in West Virginia without internet.* The Wall Street Journal. https://www.wsj.com/articles/remote-schooling-out-of-reach-for-many-students-in-west-virginia-without-internet-11599989401

Moynihan, D., & Porumbescu, G. (2020, September 16). Trump's 'Chinese virus' slur makes some people blame Chinese Americans. But others blame Trump. *The Washington Post.* https://www.washingtonpost.com/politics/2020/09/16/

trumps-chinese-virus-slur-makes-some-people-blame-chinese-americans-others-blame-trump/

National Center for Education Statistics. (2019, April). *Projections of education statistics to 2028.* https://nces.ed.gov/pubs2020/2020024.pdf

National Center for Education Statistics. (2021, May). *Report on the condition of education 2021.* https://nces.ed.gov/pubs2021/2021144.pdf

National Center on Safe Supportive Learning Environment. (2022). *Family–school–community partnerships.* American Institutes for Research. https://safesupportivelearning.ed.gov/training-technical-assistance/education-level/early-learning/family-school-community-partnerships

National Information Center for Children and Youth with Disabilities. (2003). *Parenting a child with special needs* (News Digest 20, 3rd edition). https://www.autismtruths.org/pdf/3.%20Parenting%20a%20Child%20with%20Special%20Needs_National%20Information%20Center%20for%20Children%20and%20Youth%20with%20Disabilities.pdf

National Telecommunications and Information Administration. (2022, May 11). *NTIA data explorer.* Retrieved June 10, 2020 from https://www.ntia.doc.gov/data/digital-nation-data-explorer#sel=desktopUser&disp=map

Newton, D. (2020, March 26). *Most teachers say they are 'not prepared' to teach online.* Forbes. https://www.forbes.com/sites/dereknewton/2020/03/26/most-teachers-say-they-are-not-prepared-to-teach-online/?sh=2a4470877f2c

Nierman, M. (2020, September 30). *Families of students with special needs walk a tightrope between safety, falling behind in remote learning.* GBH News. https://www.wgbh.org/news/education/2020/09/30/families-of-students-with-special-needs-walk-a-tightrope-between-safety-falling-behind-in-remote-learning

Office of the Governor. (2020a, March 15). *Order temporarily closing all public and private elementary and secondary schools.* Commonwealth of Massachusetts. https://www.mass.gov/doc/march-15-2020-school-closure-order/download

Office of the Governor. (2020b, April 21). *Order extending the temporary closure of all public and private elementary and secondary schools.* Commonwealth of Massachusetts. https://www.mass.gov/doc/april-21-2020-school-closure-extension-order/download

ParentsTogether Action. (2020, May 27). *ParentsTogether survey reveals distance learning is failing our most vulnerable students.* https://parentstogetheraction.org/2020/05/27/parentstogether-survey-reveals-remote-learning-is-failing-our-most-vulnerable-students-2/

Pearson, P., & Gallagher, M. (1983). *The instruction of reading comprehension. Technical report No. 297.* Bolt, Berankek and Newman, Inc., & University of Illinois at Urbana-Champaign. https://files.eric.ed.gov/fulltext/ED236565.pdf

Power, K. (2020). The COVID-19 pandemic has increased the care burden of women and families. *Sustainability: Science, Practice & Policy, 16*(1), 67–73. https://doi.org/10.1080/15487733.2020.1776561

Richards, E., Aspegren, E., & Mansfield, E. (2021, February 4). A year into the pandemic, thousands of students still can't get reliable WiFi for school: The digital divide remains worse than ever. *USA Today.* https://www.usatoday.com/story/news/education/2021/02/04/covid-online-school-broadband-internet-laptops/3930744001/

Stop AAPI Hate. (2021, February 9). *New data on anti-Asian hate incidents against elderly and total national incidents in 2020.* https://stopaapihate.org/2021/03/16/2020-2021-national-report

Sylvan, L., Goldstein, E., & Crandall, M. (2020). Capturing a moment in time: A survey of school-based speech-language pathologists' experiences in the immediate aftermath of the COVID-19 public health emergency. *Perspectives of the ASHA Special Interest Groups, 5*(6), 1735–1749. https://doi.org/10.1044/2020_PERSP-20-00182

The 192nd General Court. (2022). *An act relative to the training, assessment, and assignment of qualified school interpreters in educational settings.* Commonwealth of Massachusetts. https://malegislature.gov/Bills/192/H3979

Torres, K., Lee, N., & Tran, C. (2015). *Building relationships bridging cultures: Cultural brokering in family engagement.* University of Washington College of Education. https://education.uw.edu/sites/default/files/programs/epsc/Cultural%20Brokers%20Brief_Web.pdf

Twoy, R., Connolly, P., & Novak, J. (2007). Coping strategies used by parents of children with autism. *Journal of the American Academy of Nurse Practitioners, 19*(5), 251–260. https://doi.org/10.1111/j.1745-7599.2007.00222.x

U.S. Census Bureau. (2020, April 8). *People that speak English less than "very well" in the United States.* https://www.census.gov/library/visualizations/interactive/people-that-speak-english-less-than-very-well.html

U.S. Department of Education. (2020, February 10). *Special education–Parent training and information centers.* https://www2.ed.gov/programs/oseppic/index.html

U.S. Department of Education. (2022, February). *Providing students with disabilities free appropriate public education during the COVID-19 pandemic and addressing the need for compensatory services under Section 504.* https://www2.ed.gov/about/offices/list/ocr/docs/fape-in-covid-19.pdf

Weise, E. (2022, May 18). It's happening again: COVID-19 cases are back on the rise. There are 3 main reasons why. *USA Today.* https://www.usatoday.com/story/news/health/2022/05/18/omicron-waning-immunity-rising-covid-cases/9823740002/

Wintersmith, A. (2020, May 19). *Specialists struggle to deliver special education services.* GBH News. https://www.wgbh.org/news/education/2020/05/19/specialists-struggle-to-deliver-special-education-services

World Health Organization. (2022). *The true death toll of COVID-19: Estimating global excess mortality.* https://www.who.int/data/stories/the-true-death-toll-of-covid-19-estimating-global-excess-mortality

Zeigler, K., & Camarota, S. (2019, October 29). *67.3 million in the United States spoke a foreign language at home in 2018.* Center for Immigration Studies. https://cis.org/Report/673-Million-United-States-Spoke-Foreign-Language-Home-2018

CHAPTER 3

SUGGESTIONS FOR PROMISING PRACTICES FOR BLACK AUTISTIC CHILDREN AND THEIR FAMILIES POST-PANDEMIC

Elizabeth Holliday Morgan
California State University Sacramento

Margaret L. Sebastian
Salisbury University

Kanwardeep Kaur Singh
California State University Sacramento

ABSTRACT

The global pandemic brought on by the SARS-COVID-19 outbreak literally dismantled and reconstructed U.S. K–12 and post-secondary schools (Darling-Hammond et al., 2020; Office for Civil Rights, 2021) allowing for existing

School–University–Community Research in a (Post) COVID-19 World, pages 43–62
Copyright © 2023 by Information Age Publishing
www.infoagepub.com
All rights of reproduction in any form reserved.

issues in school systems that create and perpetuate inequitable access to educational services and supports to be exposed and worsened (Kuhfeld, Soland, & Lewis, 2022; Kuhfeld, Soland, Lewis, & Mortan, 2022). Even prior to the pandemic, the groups of students that had the greatest disparities in academic achievement and outcomes struggled (Bailey et al., 2021). These students included those from historically marginalized populations such as students of color and students with disabilities (Averett, 2021; DePaoli et al., 2021; Wright et al., 2022). During the pandemic, students who were poor, rural, and/or required an individualized educational plan (IEP) often found themselves with little to no support and limited access to distance learning (Herold, 2020; Hill, 2020). These students required levels of individual support and resources that many school districts could not handle (Slavin & Storey, 2020). In this chapter, we will discuss evidence of promising practices to support student outcomes and academic achievement for Black students on the autism spectrum. Data from a national qualitative study involving interviews with Black mothers of children on the autism spectrum collected during the beginning of the pandemic suggest that the time and physical proximity that these mothers had with their children during the height of the pandemic allowed for opportunities and insight into their children's individual academic needs. Once these "mother/advocates" became "mother/educators," they recognized what their children needed and what they as mothers must do to support them as they engaged in distance learning through their high schools and colleges. Pulling upon resources and connections made prior to the pandemic, many of these mothers figured out ways to support their children. Our interviews suggested that traditional once-a-year meetings with teachers and intervention teams limit parental influence, which is key to their input in the child's learning outcomes. As mothers became more familiar with the academic needs and strengths of their child, they were more equipped to strengthen school–community partnerships to support the implementation of the IEP for their children. As parents became educational facilitators, they better understood the curriculum and had a voice in the learning process. In conclusion, the global pandemic school shutdown revealed cracks in special education, but for marginalized populations such as Black families of children with disabilities, these cracks became chasms. Findings from this analysis give evidence on how schools can (a) re-think their approaches to partnering with Black families and (b) transform previously superficial partnerships with families to authentic collaborations that support student outcomes.

Within the first 2 years of the SARS-COVID-19 global pandemic the lives of over one million people were shortened and many more millions worldwide were drastically changed. Those who were impacted the most were overwhelmingly from low-income and historically marginalized populations (Bailey & Moon, 2020). In the United States, these groups include but were not limited to people within the Black, Indigenous, and people of color (BIPOC) communities. U.S. schools were particularly vulnerable during the pandemic and were forced to close their doors and switch to distance learning (Darling-Hammond et al., 2020; Office for Civil Rights, 2021). During this time, children with intersectional marginalized identities, such as Black children with individualized educational plans (IEPs) due to a documented disability, struggled the most (Bailey et al., 2021; Kuhfeld, Soland, & Lewis, 2022). In this chapter we will give a brief historical overview of the offenses that Black Americans have faced and discuss how these historical injustices are connected to present-day disparities in care and barriers for school–home communication and partnership. This chapter will also present interviews with Black mothers in three states (California, Pennsylvania, and New York) gathered during the height of the pandemic (2020–2021); these mothers were helping their autistic children access virtual schooling and they found strategies for stronger school–home communication and partnership. Lastly, this chapter will offer suggestions to school practitioners on better approaches to partnering with Black families, which might transform previously superficial partnerships with families to authentic collaborations that support student outcomes.

HISTORICAL INJUSTICES

The practice of chattel slavery is the foundation of the American economy and a stain on American culture (Morris, 1996). The social constructs that were created to justify and rationalize the practice of enslaving captured Africans are the same found in racism, sexism, classism, and ableism today and continue to impact the descendants of enslaved Africans presently. For instance, before the 1863 Emancipation Proclamation not only was it a crime to teach any Black person to read, but any enslaved Black person also who attempted to read and write would be severely punished (Cornelius, 1983). This blatant denial of educational rights is at the root of generations of illiteracy in the Black community to this day. This is even more salient an issue when individuals hold two or more marginalized identities, such as being Black and disabled; they have experiences of double oppression, which often manifest in disparate supports and inadequate educational interventions (Proffitt, 2022).

After slavery became illegal in the United States in 1865, the country went through decades of reconstruction and Jim Crow laws that continued to disenfranchise Black Americans. The 1954 *Brown v. Board of Education of Topeka* outlawed racial segregation of schools and ruled that racial discrimination in schools was a violation of the 14th Amendment's Equal Protection Clause (Tushnet & Lezin, 1991). Three years later, in 1957, nine students affectionately called "The Little Rock Nine" entered Central High School in Little Rock, Arkansas guarded by the 101st Airborne Division of the U.S. Army to protect them from the over 1,100 White domestic terrorists threatening to murder them (Beals, 1995). These demonstrations of anti-Black progress continued as legislation and societal norms were created to maintain and perpetuate discrimination of Black children in schools. For example, 49 years after the Little Rock Nine, a 2007 federal study reported that Chicago's public school system had significant overrepresentation of suspensions and expulsions of Black students in their schools. Black students represented 23% of their student population but accounted for 44% of their yearly suspensions and 61% of expulsions (Bell, 2015). Most of the Black students who were suspended and expelled were Black boys and were considered disciplinary problems. "In the United States, schools, tasked with providing safe and generative learning environments for Black boys, often treat Black boys as problems" (Proffitt, 2022, p. 267). Using zero-tolerance policies to suspend and expel students leads to a higher chance of dropping out and incarceration (Belfield, 2014; Teasley & Miller, 2011). It is important to understand the severity of our nation's history of dehumanizing Black bodies in order to truly understand the desperate need to address the injustices of our schooling institutions. These deep roots of oppression now have grown in different directions making it difficult for Black students to learn and acquire appropriate supports when they have special learning accommodations needed.

The suffering of Black people is stitched into the fabric of our nation's history and the United States continues to present disparities in access to resources and outright oppression to this day. Along with racist epistemology, oppression is also embedded in the ableist logic of school structures that harm disabled students. In the 19th century, America constructed a standard of "normal," which centered on White able-bodied men (Jenkins, 2021). Although physical handicaps have always been recognized as disabilities, invisible intellectual, developmental, and mental disabilities have only been recognized in school systems within the last 50 years (Jenkins, 2021). Historically, people with physical impairments were ostracized, considered a nuisance to society, and often met with violence when interacting with the wider society (Braddock & Parish, 2001). Segregation expanded with the placement of students with disabilities in residential institutions rather than public schools (Braddock & Parish, 2001). In fact, during the first part of the 20th century, the United States supported the eugenics movement, which targeted, among others, people with disabilities (Braddock & Parish, 2001). The 1927 Supreme Court case *Buck v. Bell* affirmed that states had the right to sterilize anyone with a disability against their will (Braddock & Parish, 2001). It was not until 1975 that the United States passed the Education for All Handicapped Children Act, which secured the right to free and appropriate education for all students; this legislation was updated in 2004 as the Individuals With Disabilities Education Act (Braddock & Parish, 2001; IDEA, 2004). This act ensures free and appropriate public education to students in a least restrictive environment and serviced 7.5 million students in 2018–2019 of which 64% were taught in a general education classroom (IDEA, 2004; Montiel, 2014).

Exclusionary disciplinary practices, including suspensions and expulsions, are disproportionately applied to students with disabilities (Sullivan et al., 2014). Nationally, White students without disabilities are suspended less than students of color with a disability (Losen & Gillespie, 2012; Achilles et al., 2007). Despite IDEA protections and supports, students with disabilities are overexposed to discipline (Sullivan et al., 2014). Furthermore, Black students and students with poor social skills are more likely to be suspended over time (Sullivan et al., 2014). School suspensions subsequently result in students struggling both academically and socially (Krezmien et al., 2006).

In response to the SARS-COVID-19 pandemic in the United States, an estimated 55 million K–12 students experienced disruptions at their school sites (Bacher-Hicks et al., 2021). During the pandemic, the existing inequities in American schools became even more apparent. The most vulnerable students were less likely to have access to educational socialization through Internet access that would allow for online instruction and growth of the virtual community (Gauthier et al., 2021). As well, the pervasive lack of physical contact and socialization only exacerbated the particular needs of students, leading to inequities in access to resources and instructional quality (Fields et al., 2020). During the school closures, student homes became the only place where they could continue their academics. Educators began to realize how important families were in ensuring student learning (Munir, 2021). Given the history of oppression for Black and disabled people, we desired to investigate the experiences of Black families interacting with schools during the COVID-19 pandemic. In the next section, we will describe the theoretical framework, methodologies, and study design.

METHODS

Theoretical Framework

The theoretical framework for this study is based on the tenets of critical race theory (CRT). Critical race theory is a transdisciplinary theoretical framework that recognizes and considers the social-political construct of race, racism, and racist behaviors. It examines the relationship between race, racism, and oppression; as well as challenges dominant ideologies about power. There are six tenets that help form the theory (Bell, 1995; Crenshaw, 1995; Delgado & Stefancic, 2000, 2001): first, the permanence and pervasiveness of racism; second, Whiteness as property and privilege; third, race as a social construction; fourth, interest-convergence; fifth, intersectionality; and sixth, storytelling, counter-storytelling narratives (Bell, 1995; Crenshaw, 1995; Delgado & Stefancic, 2000, 2001). These are explained in the following paragraphs.

The permanence and pervasiveness of racism conveys that race and racism are central and fundamental in defining how the American society functions (Dixson & Anderson, 2018). Second, Whiteness as property and privilege define the dominant culture's perceptions of race and property and how it plays a critical role in establishing and maintaining racial and economic subordination (Bell, 1995; Crenshaw, 1995; Delgado & Stefancic, 2000, 2001). This is also rooted in the origins of property rights in the United States, the right to an education, and the right to a good reputation and high status (Delgado & Stefancic, 2000, 2001).

When we say that race is a social construction (Bell, 1995; Crenshaw, 1995; Delgado & Stefancic, 2000, 2001) we mean that it is not a natural, fixed, or biological concept. Furthermore, race has not been constructed neutrally but instead coercively as an ideological tool. Next, interest-convergence is grounded on the premise that the interest of people of color in achieving racial equality (and social, political and, economic progress) advances only when their interests align with those in power and those interests serve to benefit both groups—but inequitably (Delgado & Stefancic, 2000, 2001). The last two tenets are intersectionality and counter-storytelling. Intersectionality is the study of intersections between oppression, domination, and discrimination as coined by Kimberle Crenshaw (1995). Counter-stories can engage conscience and stir imagination in ways that more conventional discourse cannot. They are stories, parables, chronicles, and narratives that are powerful means for destroying White supremacist ideals.

In this study, CRT is paired with a phenomenological qualitative method of portraiture (following the methodology of Solórzano & Yosso, 2001) to investigate the experiences of Black mothers of children on the autism spectrum during the beginning of school closures during the U.S. SARS COVID-19 pandemic. We sought to understand strategies that parents with intersectional identities activate to overcome stressors associated with school–home communication during the pandemic across three states: California, Pennsylvania, and New York. To better appreciate these stressors, we developed this critical investigation to explore the experiences of intersectionally oppressed populations (impacted by racism, sexism, classism, ableism, etc.) or what Annamma and Hardy (2020) call, "multiply marginalized" populations, such as Black mothers (p. 41). We selected qualitative methods, specifically interviews, to provide more depth to the data obtained and to unearth the thoughts, feelings, and opinions of study collaborators that give insight to the barriers and strategies to school and home partnerships (Morgan, 2021). Using semi-structured open-ended interviews to learn about key relationships and interactions between each

Promising Practices for Black Autistic Children and Their Families Post-Pandemic • **49**

family and school professionals (Esterberg, 2001), the first author of this chapter (Morgan) was able to gather in-depth data about their experiences. Participants were called *collaborators* to counter the hierarchical and dominant positions associated with research and adhere to the CRT tenets that challenge dominant ideology and emphasize the centrality of experiential knowledge. We did this to confront the hierarchical power dynamics involved in social science research and to reimagine and redesign empirical investigations that recognize the value of partnership and collaboration in conducting high-quality qualitative inquiries (Ladson-Billings, 2000; Ladson-Billings, 2015; Lawrence-Lightfoot, 1994; Lawrence-Lightfoot & Hoffman Davis, 2002).

Portraiture is a methodology that is a mixture of art through creative writing using imagery, metaphors, data collection, and analysis (Lawrence-Lightfoot & Hoffman Davis, 2002). We believe that a strong emphasis on storytelling allows the data to speak for itself, helping readers come to their own conclusions as they take in the findings of the study. Lawrence-Lightfoot focused on three tenets to implement this methodology; first, how the researcher prepares for data collection; second, collecting the data with a holistic perspective; and third, understanding the themes to highlight in the data collection (Lawrence-Lightfoot & Hoffman Davis, 2002). After preparing for collecting the data, we began the data collection process with a holistic perspective, focusing on the context of the data, voice of the researched, and themes of the data while creating an aesthetic whole. The last step is the data analysis where we looked for themes from the data using five criteria: repetitive refrains, resonant metaphors, institutional rituals, cultural rituals, and revealing patterns; together these create a positive picture of a participant's experiences (Lawrence-Lightfoot & Hoffman Davis, 2002). Once themes were discovered, we made drafts of portraits and then gave these to the collaborators for input and member-checking to establish trustworthiness, authenticity, and to facilitate the co-creation of each portrait (Lawrence-Lightfoot & Hoffman Davis, 2002; Schwandt et al., 2007). This helped to create a clear focus of the data analysis, findings, and conclusions (Sebastian, 2021). The researcher portraits introduced the collaborator's background and setting. In this study, the participants' names and exact geographic location were all given pseudonyms to protect their privacy. Secondly, we maintained a focus on the voice of the researched; as researchers we listened *for* a story of the participant rather than *to* a story of the participant (Lawrence-Lightfoot & Hoffman Davis, 2002). Thus the creation of the story was being sought out in contrast to collecting data based on our own assumptions. For this study, we shared the stories of the participants as they were connected to the themes of the findings. Lastly, we used themes to create an aesthetic whole. As researchers, we highlighted experiences and themes that emerged over several different collaborator experiences. In the findings, we prefaced the stories with short summaries of the reason each story was connected to those themes. Due to the intersectionality of race, gender, and class in our study collaborators, we believe that this approach of collecting and analyzing the interviews were necessary to obtain a detailed snapshot of their lives and understand the role that race may have had in the development of school and home partnership and communication before, during, and after the pandemic (Crenshaw, 1989).

Interview Collection

The data used for analysis for this chapter came from a dissertation study involving interviews of seven Black mothers of children on the autism spectrum across three U.S. states (CA, PA, NY; Morgan, 2021). The goal of the dissertation study was to investigate advocacy development for these mothers; I (Morgan) asked questions about their experiences navigating service delivery systems (school, medical, etc.) to gain access to services and supports for their children. My interviews used semi-structured interview guides that allowed the mothers to include topics that were important to them that were not connected to any objectives of the study. Data collection for this study took place from November 2020–April 2021 during the height of the U.S. SARS COVID-19 at-home quarantine restrictions. Consequently, the seven mothers all discussed the pandemic and how it was impacting their families. I gathered four interviews per collaborator for a total of 28 interviews over the 5-month timespan. In addition to interviews, a family demographic questionnaire added to the analysis of interviews by providing an understanding of the family structure and educational and economic resources. Our research team extracted the names of school and community members.

Researcher Positionality

My positionality (Morgan) as a Black mother of a child on the autism spectrum allowed for in-group status with collaborators (Hsiung, 2008; Milner, 2007). In addition, our research team comprised two graduate level women of color. Sebastian identifies as a Black woman from a low-income background who is also a first-generation college student with expertise in qualitative research, applied statistical methods, and portraiture as a methodology. Singh identifies as a woman of Indian descent who is a second-year EdD student and current teacher in a public high school in Northern California. Our team's positionality informed our reflexivity and connection to the interviews (Holmes, 2020), giving us insight based on our insider

Promising Practices for Black Autistic Children and Their Families Post-Pandemic • **51**

privileges while keeping us curious to understand aspects of the mother's experiences that were outside our contextual understanding.

Collaborators

Seven collaborators met the following criteria for inclusion: (a) mother of a child who has a medical diagnosis or school classification of autism or autism spectrum disorder, (b) proficient English speaker, (c) has been a peer mentor or coach for at least one other family in their community over the last 3 years, and (d) identifies as Black or African American (Table 3.1).

Recruitment

We distributed research fliers and permission-to-contact forms to research coordinators at three university partners in California, Pennsylvania, and New York; these partners were associated with a randomized control trial research study to implement a parent coaching intervention for underserved communities. These research coordinators reached out to their Black parent coaches in the project to ask if they would be interested in participating in our proposed study and to give them the flier and permission-to-contact form. Once these were returned, the lead author conducted a phone screen for eligibility and collected consent documentation before setting up the interviews.

Procedures

We utilized the methodology of portraiture to collect and analyze four in-depth semi-structured interviews (60–90 minutes each) with seven Black mother peer coaches for a total of 28 in-depth, ethnographic, semi-structured interviews (Lawrence-Lightfoot & Hoffman Davis, 2002). We chose this methodology because it allows for a *thick description* of the data (Geertz, 1989). Interviews were audio-recorded, transcribed, and de-identified. Although I (the principal investigator, Morgan) had previously met with and conducted home visits with collaborators based in California, the COVID-19 pandemic required all interviews to be done virtually. I was the sole interviewer for all seven collaborators, taking jottings and notes during each virtual interview to observe the home environments and nonverbal communication (Pugh, 2013; Sacha, 2017).

We implemented a precoding process to identify deductive and inductive codes from each transcribed interview. We identified deductive concepts

TABLE 3.1 Collaborator Demographics

Name	Age	Education	Employment	Child Age	Income	Age of Child Diagnosis	Time From Diagnosis to Treatment
Ola	54	Bachelor's degree	Employed part-time	18	$40–49k	2 years	Less than 3 months
Hope	48	Bachelor's degree	Employed full-time	20	$100k or more	7 years	2+ years
Elizabeth	76	Bachelor's degree	Retired	9	$50–59k	2.5 years	Less than 3 months
Trust	49	Bachelor's degree	Employed full-time	19	$20–29k	3 years	3–6 months
Nandi	47	Some college	Unemployed	17	$10–19k	1.8 years	Less than 3 months
Sarge	61	Vocational certificate	Employed part-time	14	$50–59k	3 years	3–6 months
Faith	46	Associates degree	Employed part-time	19	$20–29k	3 years	3–6 months

Note: Mothers self-assigned pseudonyms for themselves, children, and significant people in their portrait.

Promising Practices for Black Autistic Children and Their Families Post-Pandemic • **53**

from the protocol and inductive concepts from the transcripts and these were summarized into a database format. Data analysis included a summary memo of each emerging theme concept, and each concept was then written into a portrait and then member-checked with the collaborators to produce the final portrait.

FINDINGS

In this section we will introduce portraits of two Black mothers demonstrating their experiences of navigating schooling systems during distance learning.

Connected Mothers Have Agency

In this portrait, readers will meet Faith and understand more about how she was able to pull upon established networks and partners within and outside the school to support her son during the pandemic.

Faith

Faith had one child, an 18-year-old son, Grey, who was tall, handsome, on the autism spectrum, and had minimal verbal communication skills. She was a petite woman with glowing caramel skin and auburn, cinnamon hair that was straightened, cut, and framed her oval face. Faith's advocacy for her son started when he was a baby because he had frequent ear infections and eventually had to have an operation to place tubes in his ears. Faith's marriage ended when Grey was a toddler; her 2.5-year-old son started to regress and lose words and her then husband could not cope with the idea that his son was not following the normal developmental trajectory. Faith described how she knew that she was going to be a good mother because she learned early when interacting with doctors that she would not take "no" for an answer. She was a single parent but knew how to partner with her son's teachers and medical providers to seek resources for her son's disability. As he progressed through elementary school, she had partnerships with teachers who were extremely helpful as she needed support for understanding how to best educate her son. She told a story of convincing her son's kindergarten teachers and intervention team that he needed a way to communicate; she advocated his use of American Sign Language, picture exchange communication boards (PECs), and an alternative augmentative communication device (e.g., Dynavox):

54 • E. H. MORGAN, M. L. SEBASTIAN, and K. K. SINGH

I was explaining it to them, you know, he has PECs. I made his PECs boards myself. I used to take pictures of things. I put them in a photo album, you know. And I was asking them [teachers], can they do it in the school? Because I taught him some sign language also. The school district said that it doesn't acknowledge sign language. So I said, he can't talk, he's in school, how will he communicate with you all and his peers? They really didn't have an answer for me. So I made up a picture book. I brought it to the school asked them could they use it? And then I was researching how I can give him a communication device. So I called agencies on my own to try to get a Dynavox for him. And they kept on turning me down. They would say I need to go through a speech teacher [SLP] or he wasn't ready. And I said well how is he supposed to communicate? He is ready. So I kept on pushing for it. And then I actually went out on my own and raised money and I bought one [Dynavox] myself (laughs). Right, so he had something to communicate with. And then maybe 6 months down the line, after I was teaching him how to use it to communicate, I showed the teachers and they all rallied around me. We met [IEP], I think twice, and the teachers actually helped me. They wrote letters and then he got a Dynavox for school. So I had to keep on fighting and he finally got one.

During the pandemic, both Faith and Grey worked virtually, as she worked as a school aid for elementary school students, and he was engaging in virtual learning. They worked side-by-side as they both learned how to navigate virtual environments. Since they were at home together, she realized that the individual attention she gave him allowed him to pick up skills that he had been challenged with while in physical school for a long time. These skills included adaptive skills like tying his shoes, using the restroom, and brushing his teeth. His teachers were impressed with his progress while he was engaged in virtual learning because they had been working with him for a while to develop those skills and he picked them up at home so much quicker. This is her account of their transition to distance learning and her ability to once again partner with teachers to produce positive outcomes for her son:

It was hard at first. You know, my son is used to his routines. He's all about routine. So, you know, school, horseback riding, swimming. We go skating, we are always on the go. So I'll always have him out in the community. Of course, that all came to a halt. And he had some behavior issues with dealing with it. I would try to explain to him we can't go out, we can't do this. We would do other things, play games—I ordered a lot of games off of Amazon. We used to play puzzles together, play memory, all types of games. We watch TV together. We read together. We spent more time with each

> other, which was good. With school, he's actually, like I tell the teachers all the time, he does better one-on-one than in a school setting because he can focus. So the teachers actually are so amazed how well he is doing. So school aspect is actually better than it was when he was actually in person, because I'm sitting there with him and it was one-on-one. He doesn't have any other distractions.

The pandemic forced schools and special education service providers to utilize a mixed-delivery model of intervention that parents like Faith had been using for years. Special education classrooms are often siloed and cut off from direct interaction with parents, but the virtual learning environment made that impossible to maintain. Parents like Faith who were once shut out of the classroom were now intimately connected to the curriculum and what was being taught which gave them a connection and role in the learning process for their children. In some instances, as with Faith and Gray, these connections and partnerships between school and home proved fruitful.

More Agency Produces Stronger Partnerships

In this portrait, readers will meet Nandi and understand more about how she was able to pull upon and reinforce the partnerships she had with her son's school intervention team to create stronger school-and-home communication during the pandemic.

Nandi

Nandi had a flawless gingerbread mocha complexion. Her shiny lip gloss popped on her perfectly full lips. Her hair was shaved on the sides with a thick, natural style on the top. She had shades of blond highlights on the top of her combed out natural hair puff, but the roots were a deep brunette. On her face sat a stylish pair of purple plastic framed glasses. She wore big tear drop silver hoops for earrings and had showed off her manicure that she did herself, but it appeared to be professionally done. One look and you could tell she took a lot of pride in her appearance and presentation. She also sat in a room that resembled a classroom. Nandi stated that she was in her basement, which she was turning it into a space where her 17-year-old non-speaking, autistic, son, Hayden, could do his distance learning due to COVID-19 restrictions. She hoped this would help with the distractedness he naturally has. Her name, Nandi, came from a movie about an African warrior, Shaka Zulu, and later found that it meant "sweet" in the language of the Zulu tribe in South Africa. In the neighboring country of Zambia, it is also known to be a Zulu word meaning "Queen." Nandi was born and raised in the Caribbean and she stated that her thick, rich accent was initially a hindrance in her being able to advocate for her two teenaged sons on the autism spectrum because she felt that no one could understand her when she talked. For Nandi, the process of becoming an advocate was not easy; she had the additional intersectional identity of being an immigrant. She found that in addition to the obstacles that other Black women faced, she also had the microaggressions of anti-immigrant and xenophobic attitudes, which were common for the times and which caused additional stress.

Prior to the pandemic and transition to distance learning, Nandi had made a point to have a strong relationship with all her children's teachers, but especially with Hayden's because he was the only child that could not communicate for himself. She described an interaction with one of Hayden's high school teachers:

> Well, in talking with his teachers, we both realized, OK, well, maybe he [Hayden] needs some more individual time. Maybe he needs more individual time in this area or more group time in other areas. They would help me understand what it is I need to understand and they would help to get me a clearer picture of what it means in the classroom . . . they would help break it down for me as to what all these terminologies and these classifications meant for Hayden and what it would look like in the classroom.

This type of two-way, collaborative communication between home and school proved to be helpful once the pandemic came because Nandi knew that she would have the support she needed to conduct distance learning. Nandi's intervention team had proven themselves reliable and trustworthy before the pandemic came, which is demonstrated in this story of an interaction she had with her son's speech language pathologist (SLP) when he was much younger. The SLP was a young, White, blond, petite woman who was assigned to her sons during the time they were in early intervention. Initially, this same therapist refused to come to Nandi's home without another person to support her because she judged the part of town that Nandi's family home was located to be unsafe. This SLP had a straight-forward "tell it like it is" approach to communicating with families. Nandi enjoyed this type of communication and ended up creating a strong relationship with the therapist so much so that the SLP advocated for her and her sons in venues where her family was being discriminated against. Here is one example during an IEP meeting.

There was a time when the boys were really young and we had to go to the city, to the city for, you know, because, of course, they were the purse strings [the location where the decision-makers that allocated funds were housed]. So we went in for a meeting. But for some reason, their dad and I were late getting to that meeting and all the therapists were there, along with the representative from the school [special education administrator]. And the chair of the meeting, she said, oh, where are these people coming from? So the therapist told them they're coming from the city and city of Rochester, she said. Oh, they're not going to come. So now we didn't know all of this happened. She said they're not gonna come. They're coming from the city and they're not going to show up. Let's just continue with the meeting. But the therapist said she had to tell them no. These parents will be here. And she said, like just after she said that, we showed up when she told us after the meeting that that's what the lady said. And she told me that those people from the city didn't care about their kids. So she had to advocate on our behalf saying, no, they will be showing up. It's not because they're from the city. They will be here. And we just need to wait for them. But that was kind of some example of like some prejudice that we weren't privy to at the time, but she later told us what happened.

This type of interaction with providers and teachers gave Nandi the confidence to partner with them and appreciate the contributions they brought to her son's intervention team. She had many great experiences with teachers and service professionals and found great allies in people that she did not think she would be able to partner with, which got stronger during the pandemic. She and the teachers would frequently communicate via email, text message, and Zoom to make sure that Hayden was making progress through the curriculum. It was a difficult transition; nonetheless, Nandi had a partnership between home and school that made the process much easier.

DISCUSSION

The silos and lack of effective communication between school and home have created a breakdown of partnerships between educators and families. For Black families, this disconnection can perpetuate stereotyping and lack of trust between schools and families. The pandemic accelerated universal communication between home and school which opened up opportunities for partnership. Nandi and Faith's examples give evidence of how powerful these partnerships can be, especially when in crisis.

Themes in the interviews suggest that traditional methods of communication that schools have used are (and have been) insufficient to create partnerships with Black families of children with disabilities. The annual, one-sided, non-collaborative IEP meetings with teachers and intervention teams limit the parental influence needed to give Black families input in their child's learning outcomes. As the Black mothers in our study became more familiar with the academic needs and strengths of their child, they became more equipped to partner with teachers and interventionists to support the implementation of IEP goals. And as these Black mothers became educational facilitators, their families had more understanding of the curriculum and a voice in the learning process. Findings from this analysis give evidence that partnership requires schools to rethink school–home communication practices; some of the types of communication strategies used during the pandemic should be maintained. Specifically, the option for virtual meetings and electronic signatures should be kept. More intentionality around empowering families with the information and knowledge of curriculum will support the implementation and evaluation of IEP goals. Lastly, we need to use these innovations to transform previously superficial partnerships with families to authentic collaborations that support student outcomes. This will require doing more and not less when it comes to engaging and involving historically marginalized families in the details of their child's educational career. The evidence from this study suggests and supports that when families are more informed, they have more agency in the intervention process which is advantageous for the student and school.

In conclusion, the global pandemic shutdown revealed cracks in special education systems; for marginalized populations such as Black families of children with disabilities, these cracks became chasms. Prior to the pandemic, the common practice of schools was to use reams of paper annually on printed out IEP meeting documents. However, during COVID-19 and school closures, school special education professionals met with families online in synchronous or asynchronous forums with many completing the IEP documents in a completely electronic format (Silva, 2020). This was a best practice for families in our study. During the pandemic, parents inevitably took on new responsibilities during online learning, which resulted in engaging in the learning experience and making them an intricate part of the daily learning practice. The promising practices of schools engaging in frequent, meaningful communication with families and utilizing alternative forms of communication (i.e., virtual options) seemed to give agency to groups of families that have been disenfranchised and marginalized. The school–community partnerships demonstrated in this study can inspire educators to take the experiences of the pandemic to build permanent bridges from school to home, especially for marginalized families. In the words of scholar and poet, Arundhati Roy, it is helpful for us think of the worldwide pandemic as an opportunity for change and to see "the pandemic as a portal," giving us the opportunity to leave thoughts and practices that no longer benefit us while bringing through thoughts and practices that do (Perry & Roy, 2020, para. 1). Our hope is that this chapter will inspire educators and investigators to think about leaving behind harmful, inequitable, and antiquated practices and research methodologies and embrace practices that build home–school–community partnerships to support our most vulnerable students and families.

REFERENCES

Achilles, G. M., McLaughlin, M. J., & Croninger, R. (2007). Sociocultural correlates of disciplinary exclusion among students with emotional, behavioral, and learning disabilities in the SEELS national dataset. *Journal of Emotional and Behavioral Disorders, 15*(1), 33–45. https://doi.org/10.1177/1063426607015 0010401

Annamma, S. A., & Handy, T. (2020). Sharpening justice through DisCrit: A contrapuntal analysis of education. *Educational Researcher, 50*(1), 41–50. https://doi.org/10.3102/0013189X20953838

Averett, K. H. (2021). Remote learning, COVID-19, and children with disabilities. *AERA Open, 7*. https://doi.org/10.1177/23328584211058471

Bacher-Hicks, A., Goodman, J., & Mulhern, C. (2021). Inequality in household adaptation to schooling shocks: Covid-induced online learning engagement in real time. *Journal of Public Economics, 193*, 104345. https://doi.org/10.1016/j.jpubeco.2020.104345

Bailey, D. H., Duncan, G. J., Murnane, R. J., & Au Yeung, N. (2021). Achievement gaps in the wake of COVID-19. *Educational Researcher, 50*(5), 266–275. https://doi.org/10.3102/0013189X211011237

Bailey, Z. D., & Moon, J. R. (2020). Racism and the political economy of COVID-19: Will we continue to resurrect the past? *Journal of Health Politics, Policy and Law, 45*(6), 937–950. https://doi.org/10.1215/03616878-8641481

Beals, M. (1995). *Warriors don't cry: Searing memoir of battle to integrate Little Rock's Central High.* Washington Square Press

Belfield, C. R. (2014). *The costs of high school failure and school suspensions for the state of California.* UCLA: The Civil Rights Project / Proyecto Derechos Civiles. https://escholarship.org/uc/item/8fb9x11w

Bell, C. (2015). The hidden side of zero tolerance policy: The African American perspective. *Sociology Compass, 9*(1), 14–22. https://doi.org/10.1111/soc4.12230

Bell, D. A. (1995). Who's afraid of critical race theory. *University of Illinois Law Review, 1995*(4), 893–910. ISSN: 0276-9948

Braddock, D., & Parish, S. (2001). An institutional history of disability. In G. L. Albrecht, K. Seelman, & M. Bury (Eds.), *Handbook of disability studies* (pp. 11–68). SAGE. https://dx.doi.org/10.4135/9781412976251.n2

Cornelius, J. (1983). "We slipped and learned to read:" Slave accounts of the literacy process, 1830–1865. *Phylon, 44*(3), 171–186. https://doi.org/10.2307/274930

Crenshaw, K. (1989). Demarginalizing the intersection of race and sex: A Black feminist critique of antidiscrimination doctrine, feminist theory and antiracist politics. *University of Chicago Legal Forum, 140*, 139–167. https://chicagounbound.uchicago.edu/cgi/viewcontent.cgi?article=1052&context=uclf

Crenshaw, K. (1995). *Critical race theory: The key writings that formed the movement.* The New Press.

Darling-Hammond, L., Schachner, A., & Edgerton, A. K. (with Badrinarayan, A., Cardichon, J., Cookson, P. W., Jr., Griffith, M., Klevan, S., Maier, A., Martinez, M., Melnick, H., Truong, N., & Wojcikiewicz, S.). (2020). *Restarting and reinventing school: Learning in the time of COVID and beyond.* Learning Policy Institute. http://learningpolicyinstitute.org/product/restarting-reinventing-school-covid

Delgado R., & Stefancic, J. (2000). *Critical race theory: The cutting edge* (2nd ed.). Temple University Press.

Delgado R., & Stefancic, J. (2001). *Critical race theory: An introduction.* NYU Press.

DePaoli, J. L., Hernández, L. E., Furger, R. C., & Darling-Hammond, L. (2021, March 16). *A restorative approach for equitable education* [Research brief]. Learning Policy Institute. https://learningpolicyinstitute.org/product/wce-restorative-approach-equitable-education-brief

Dixson, A. D., & Anderson, C. R. (2018). Where are we? Critical race theory in education 20 years later. *Peabody Journal of Education, 93*(1), 121–131. https://doi.org/10.1080/0161956X.2017.1403194

Esterberg, K. G. (2001). *Qualitative methods in social research.* McGraw-Hill.

Fields, J. F., Hunter-Childs, J., Tersine, A., Sisson, J., Parker, E., Velkoff, V., Logan, C., & Shin, H. (2020). *Design and operation of the 2020 Household Pulse Survey.* U.S. Census Bureau. https://www2.census.gov/programs-surveys/demo/technical-documentation/hhp/2020_HPS_Background.pdf

Gauthier, G. R., Smith, J. A., García, C., Garcia, M. A., & Thomas, P. A. (2021). Exacerbating inequalities: Social net-works, racial/ethnic disparities, and the COVID-19 pandemic in the United States. *Journals of Gerontology: Series B, 76*(3), e88–e92. https://doi.org/10.1093/geronb/gbaa117

Geertz, C. (1989). *Works and lives: The anthropologist as author.* Stanford University Press.

Herold, B. (2020, April 10). *The disparities in remote learning under coronavirus (in charts).* EducationWeek. https://www.edweek.org/technology/the-disparities-in-remote-learning-under-coronavirus-in-charts/2020/04

Hill, F. (2020, April 18). The pandemic is a crisis for students with special needs. *The Atlantic.* https://www.theatlantic.com/education/archive/2020/04/special-education-goes-remote-covid-19-pandemic/610231/

Holmes, A. G. D. (2020). Researcher positionality—A consideration of its influence and place in qualitative research—A new researcher guide. *Shanlax International Journal of Education, 8*(4), 1–10. https://doi.org/10.34293/education.v8i4.3232

Hsiung, P. (2008). Teaching reflexivity in qualitative interviewing. *Teaching Sociology, 36*(3), 211–226. https://doi.org/10.1177/0092055X0803600302

IDEA: Individuals With Disabilities Education Act, 20 U.S.C. § 1400 (2004).

Jenkins, S. (2021). Constructing ableism. *Genealogy, 5*(3), 66–81. https://doi.org/10.3390/genealogy5030066

Krezmien, M. P., Leone, P. E., & Achilles, G. M. (2006). Suspension, race, and disability: Analysis of statewide practices and reporting. *Journal of Emotional and Behavioral Disorders, 14*(4), 217–226. https://doi.org/10.1177/10634266060140040501

Kuhfeld, M., Soland, J., & Lewis, K. (2022). *Test score patterns across three COVID-19-impacted school years* (EdWorkingPaper: 22-521). Annenberg Institute at Brown University. https://doi.org/10.26300/ga82-6v47

Kuhfeld, M., Soland, J., Lewis, K., & Mortan, E. (2022, March 3). *The pandemic has had devastating impacts on learning. What will it take to help students catch up?* Brookings. https://www.brookings.edu/blog/brown-center-chalkboard/2022/03/03/the-pandemic-has-had-devastating-impacts-on-learning-what-will-it-take-to-help-students-catch-up/

Ladson-Billings, G. (2000). Fighting for our lives: Preparing teachers to teach African American students. *Journal of Teacher Education, 51*(3), 206–214. https://doi.org/10.1177/0022487100051003008

Ladson-Billings, G. (2015). Getting to Sesame Street? Fifty years of federal compensatory education. *The Russell Sage Foundation Journal of the Social Sciences, 1*(3), 96–111. https://doi.org/10.7758/rsf.2015.1.3.05

Lawrence-Lightfoot, S. (1994). *I've known rivers: Lives of loss and liberation.* Addison-Wesley.

Lawrence-Lightfoot, S., & Hoffman Davis, J. (2002). *The art and science of portraiture* (2nd ed.). Jossey-Bass.

Losen, D. J, & Gillespie, J. (2012). *Opportunities suspended: The disparate impact of disciplinary exclusion from school.* The Center for Civil Rights Remedies at The Civil Rights Project/Proyecto Derechos Civiles. https://escholarship.org/uc/item/3g36n0c3

Milner, H. R., IV, (2007). Race, culture, and researcher positionality: Working through dangers seen, unseen, and unforeseen. *Educational Researcher, 36*(7), 388–400. https://doi.org/10.3102/0013189X07309471

Montiel, D. A. (2014). *Predictors for the provision of publicly funded service for children with Autism Spectrum Disorder* (Publication No. 3625819) [Doctoral dissertation, Alliant International University]. ProQuest.

Morgan, E. H. (2021). *The developmental process of parent advocacy for Black mothers of children on the autism spectrum* [Doctoral dissertation, University of California Davis]. eScholarship. https://escholarship.org/uc/item/9x30v30x

Morris, T. D. (1996). *Southern slavery and the law, 1619–1860.* University of North Carolina Press.

Munir, F. (2021). Mitigating COVID: Impact of COVID-19 lockdown and school closure on children's well-being. *Social Sciences, 10*(10), 387–405. https://doi.org/10.3390/socsci10100387

Office for Civil Rights. (2021). *Education in a pandemic: The disparate impacts of COVID-19 on America's students.* U.S. Department of Education. https://www2.ed.gov/about/offices/list/ocr/docs/20210608-impacts-of-covid19.pdf

Perry, I., & Roy, A. (2020, May 1). *The pandemic is a portal.* Department of African American Studies, Princeton University. https://aas.princeton.edu/news/pandemic-portal

Proffitt, W. A. (2022). From "problems" to "vulnerable resources:" Reconceptualizing Black boys with and without disability labels in U.S. urban schools. *Urban Education, 57*(4), 686–713. https://doi.org/10.1177/0042085920972164

Pugh, A. J. (2013). What good are interviews for thinking about culture? Demystifying interpretive analysis. *American Journal of Cultural Sociology, 1*, 42–68. https://doi.org/10.1057/ajcs.2012.4

Sacha, J. O. (2017). Fighting feelings: The emotional labor of "old heads" in an amateur boxing gym. *Sociological Perspectives, 60*(1), 77–94. https://doi.org/10.1177/0731121415596083

Schwandt, T. A., Lincoln, Y. S., & Guba, E. G. (2007). Judging interpretations: But is it rigorous? Trustworthiness and authenticity in naturalistic evaluation. *New Directions for Evaluation, 2007*(114), 11–25. https://doi.org/10.1002/ev.223

Sebastian, M. L. (2021). *I don't have to stay here! The experiences of Black women, higher education administrators who experienced a professional transition and/or promotion to a historically white institution during the coronavirus pandemic* [doctoral dissertation, University of Northern Colorado]. Digital UNC. https://digscholarship.unco.edu/cgi/viewcontent.cgi?article=1815&context=dissertations

Silva, E. (2020, March 31). *What school closures mean for students with disabilities* [Blog post]. New America. https://www.newamerica.org/education-policy/edcentral/what-school-closures-mean-students-disabilities

Slavin, R. E., & Storey, N. (2020). The U.S. educational response to the COVID-19 pandemic. *Best Evid Chin Edu, 5*(2), 617–633. https://ssrn.com/abstract=3652585

Solórzano, D. G., & Yosso, T. J. (2001). Critical race and LatCrit theory and method: Counter storytelling. *International Journal of Qualitative Studies in Education, 14*(4), 471–495. https://doi.org/10.1080/09518390110063365

Sullivan, A. L., Van Norman, E. R., & Klingbeil, D. A. (2014). Exclusionary discipline of students with disabilities: Student and school characteristics predicting suspension. *Remedial and Special Education, 35*(4), 199–210. https://doi.org/10.1177/0741932513519825

Teasley, M. L., & Miller, C. R. (2011). School social workers' perceived efficacy at tasks related to curbing suspension and undesirable behaviors. *Children & Schools, 33*(3), 136–145. https://doi.org/10.1093/cs/33.3.136

Tushnet, M., & Lezin, K. (1991). What really happened in Brown v. Board of Education. *Columbia Law Review, 91*(8), 1867–1930. https://doi.org/10.2307/1123035

Wright, B. L., Cross, B. E., Ford, D. Y., & Tyson, C. (2022). When I think of home: Black families supporting their children during the COVID-19 pandemic. *Education and Urban Society.* https://doi.org/10.1177/00131245211065415

CHAPTER 4

THE DISRUPTION OF MENTORING FOR BLACK YOUTH DURING COVID-19

No One to Turn To

Jay Matthew
University of Houston

Detra D. Johnson
University of Houston

ABSTRACT

The 2020–2021 school year was a heavy storm that poured and poured, and however the raindrops of trouble continue to drizzle around us, there is a clearing in the distance. Meanwhile, educational leaders are looking for and finding ways to repair and prepare their students, both intellectually and emotionally, for now and the future. Understanding the effectiveness of mentoring, especially for Black male youth, is necessary for their overall academic, mental, social, emotional, personal, and professional development and growth. By providing appropriate school-based mentoring programs—

School–University–Community Research in a (Post) COVID-19 World, pages 63–81
Copyright © 2023 by Information Age Publishing
www.infoagepub.com
All rights of reproduction in any form reserved.

64 ▪ J. MATTHEW and D. D. JOHNSON

such as college and career readiness—schools can create alternate narratives for how Black male youth are rationalized through the lens of White social norms. More so, community organizations, churches, and nonprofit organizations can assist and support Black communities and Black male youth by addressing some of the school-related issues such as problem behaviors, social and personal well-being, and self-esteem that could impact academic achievement and success. Therefore, mentoring—regardless of the type of mentoring (e.g., individual, peer, group)—is pivotal for the positive development and growth of today's Black male youth to disrupt life inconsistencies that they may experience due to circumstances beyond their control—such as COVID-19.

BACKGROUND AND INSIGHTS TO MENTORING

The world's most recent pandemic—COVID-19—had a harsh impact on school communities. Through parenting and caregivers, students were able to transition from in-house schooling to online platform schooling. Parents and caregivers became "proxy educators" who provided educational support by expecting "to retain teaching knowledge, teach individual content, assess the emotional needs of students, and so on—all in addition to their existing responsibilities" (Davis et al., 2021, para. 2). Nevertheless, there were still some missing components to meet students' social needs. Mentoring programs nearly become nonexistent during the transition from in-house school to some form of virtual schooling (such as Zoom or Microsoft Teams). However, Black communities continued to show up for youth, especially Black male youth, who could easily have been forgotten casualties when their "normal" was so unexpectedly disrupted by COVID-19.

Historically, young Black males have received little guidance in today's society as they navigate their daily lives. As a race of enslaved foreigners in the 1500s and 1600s, Blacks were sold and physically shifted throughout the country for centuries (Deyle, 2006; Rosenthal, 2018). The constant shifting and moving after slavery resulted in missed opportunities, which has had consequential impacts on the progression of Blacks in America. Unfortunately, the constant moving and relocation created households and livelihoods that were unstainable. Later, unemployment, the redrawing of school district lines, and eventually, the increase in drug abuse in Black communities undermined the culture of achievement in Black American homes (Ferguson, 2011; Grunwald & Fagan, 2019). Although Blacks in America have had a disadvantage in the pursuit for economic freedom and equal opportunity, Black men in the last 50 years have created ways to sustain careers that have provided for their households; this, in turn, has positively improved Black family sustainability (Isom et al., 2022; Thernstrom & Thernstrom, 1998). Therefore, the primary role of the Black male patriarch was to protect the family. In addition, Black men have learned through their experience how to survive and prosper in America despite the fact that many opportunities in the job market, in education, and society were not available to them (Sider, 2007; Stoeffler et al., 2020).

Over time, efforts to create Black male groups that would support young male growth continued with organizations within the church, lodges, and through higher education with Greek fraternities (Hackett, 2000; Leak, 2018). Black Greek letter organizations (BGLOs) mostly started at historically Black colleges and universities (HBCUs) in the 1900s. Their primary purpose, particularly the fraternities (e.g., Alpha Phi Alpha, Kappa Alpha Psi, Omega Psi Phi, Phi Beta Sigma), was to generally provide individual voice, a sense of community, and a shared identity as Blacks matriculated through college (McGuire, 2020; Patton et al., 2011). These organizations supported Blacks as they struggled with the obstacles on college campuses. The first two BGLO began at historically White universities (Cornell University and Indiana University) and their focus was finding ways to create organizations so that they could gather as "colored-men" without being harassed or ridiculed for being an unauthorized assembly of coloreds (NAACP Connect, 2022). These groups served as a pillar of support, allowing young Black men to build community and to mentor the next generation of young Black men behind them. Not long after, other Black fraternities would be created at another HBCU, Howard University (NAACP, 2022).

Later, organizations such as the Young Men Christian's Association (YMCA), Boys and Girls Club, and 100 Back Men Organization began to focus directly on Black males (Woodard, 2015), giving birth to some of the first organizations that attended particularly to Black youth. These organizations have been pivotal in providing needed support, resources, and access to mentoring and opportunities for Black male youth. The development of these organizations has provided much needed support, resources, and access to opportunities for Black male youth (Woodard, 2015).

Mentoring programs can support young Black males within the community and in education. Mentoring programs are a great tool to help young Black males but most youths are not aware of or desire to participate in mentoring opportunities. This lack of awareness or intrinsic motivation may contribute to some of the ill-fated dilemmas that some of our Black youth's face. Dolberry (2020) asserted that Black males are not or have not been made aware of mentoring supports because the systems were not developed for Blacks. Though Blacks in America have created and sustained accomplished legacies and careers, we find that over 23% of Blacks in America live in poverty (Creamer, 2020). Studying the effect of mentoring young Black males can help uncover the tools needed to improve Black poverty and entrance rates for Black males into higher learning institutions. Mentoring programs in K–12 schools and higher education can positively impact

66 ▪ J. MATTHEW and D. D. JOHNSON

and deter the continual cycles of generational poverty. The opportunities for marginalized groups of people to disrupt unfortunate cycles can be achieved through supports systems of this nature.

According to Harper and Davis (2012), "Blacks experience schools as social institutions that reinscribe hegemonic power structures, and therefore, they resist academic success to protect a collective cultural identity" (p. 106). Some Black male students do not believe having a post-secondary degree will help their future, and this unbelief can become a large hurdle to overcome. Furthermore, the media exacerbates this unbelief by portraying young Black males throughout society as people who do not care about education. From an early age, young men are characterized negatively, and consequently, they begin to believe and embody the persona of one who disvalues the entire education system (Bettini et al., 2022; Solórzano & Yosso, 2002) and do not see the value in the education system offered to them in their schools. These examples of Black males disconnected from education suggest that the education system should look for ways to improve the acceptance of Black males into colleges and universities.

Faced with the need to address the college readiness of Black students, school districts are looking for ways to improve Black students' educational outcomes. This calls for a brief examination of the literature on the effectiveness of mentoring programs to help Black males gain access and acceptance into 2- or 4-year colleges and universities. Many of these study the effect of the mentoring program from the point of views of graduating participants and alumni. Understanding the reactions of young Black males to school-based mentoring provides a personal look and overview into the perceptions of a select group of young Black males on gaining acceptance into college.

According to the 2020 U.S. Census Bureau, of the four major demographic groups in America (i.e., White, Hispanic, African Americans, and Asian), the African American has the lowest annual household income average of $45,438 (Creamer, 2020). Low-income communities are often populated with single-parent homes; adults who grew up without a father; or abusive households due to depression, drugs, and/or mental illness (Radcliffe & Bos, 2011). In this environment, Black youth may not necessarily see the value of being mentored by Black men for whom they do not find respect or significance (Nasir et al., 2019). Therefore, it is critical that all groups of Black youth, particularly males who are identified as marginalized, be encouraged and mentored by Black men or men of color. Black youth may be influenced by popular music, social media, and outside negative forces, which can cause them to repeat the mistakes that can eventually lead to poverty, drugs, alcohol, jail, and even death (Alexander, 2020). This supports the need for ongoing efforts to find ways to mentor Black male youth no matter what. Yampolskaya et al. (2006) reported that "studies on mentoring have shown that failure to complete high school and poor academic performance can relate to serious adverse individual, social, and economic consequences" (p. 458). Effective policies and procedures put into place for mentoring programs are critical to meeting the needs of today's Black youth. These programs can play a part in the education system process and help improve the disparities that exist in Black America.

History of Mentoring From Africa and Asia

The overarching purpose of our chapter is to determine if mentoring of Black males as students can help improve their acceptance into colleges and universities. Throughout history, mentoring has played an integral part in the growth of families, villages, communities, militaries, and countries. The archetype of mentoring that is used today uses the name *mentor* from Greek mythology, but even before the use of the word mentor, other nations used their own forms of mentoring (Miller, 2019).

> According to Greek Mythology, there once existed a man named Mentor, who was friends with the famous Odysseus. When Odysseus went to war against Troy, he trusted his house under the care of Mentor. Mentor ended up becoming a guide to Odysseus's son Telemachus, giving him advice and [*sic*]. As a result, in modern times we still refer to trusted advisers as "mentors." (Mentoring Institute, 2014, p. 1).

Mentoring occurs when someone with experience in a certain field of endeavor supports and guides another person during their time of development (Dolberry, 2020). Many people who have accomplished great achievements acknowledge that they owe a large part of their growth and development to a person who served as their mentor (Nasir et al., 2019). Therefore, mentoring can be an essential component to the success of any community and especially important to the Black community.

Many traditions in African nations stressed the grooming of young African women through mentoring by their elders to become village and community leaders. Similarly, the young men were groomed to be warriors, religious leaders, or war leaders. The ancient civilization of Ghana had a strong history of mentoring their youth; mentoring was considered a major role in their communities. Ghana is especially known for its rich tradition to develop girls into women of valor and great influence within their society. Many African countries have had matriarchal societies for centuries (Farrar, 1997; Schiele, 2017).

More recently, in Ghanaian history, religious and secular rule became more common, which brought along the pantheon of Krobo deities, where Nana Kloweki is most important. It is associated with the Dipo festival, which celebrates the initiation of women. The Dipo festival in Ghana celebrates the initiation of young women who were mentored and groomed by the older women in the community (Baldwin et al., 2020; Wilson, 1987). This, in turn, produced young women that understood the traditions and were ready for womanhood at the proper age.

The evolution of the Krobo deities made way for the Okumo and Anikaka Council traditions or religious and secular traditions (Baldwin et al., 2020; Wilson, 1987). This council developed and expanded during the 16th and 17th centuries but stood heavily on traditions from their ancient forefathers. These traditions united the political and spiritual leadership, giving the nation a more cohesive approach to leading the nation while responding to outside trade and warfare.

Another thread in the history of mentoring comes from Asia. Around 200 A.D., more people from the continent of Asia began to travel east to an island with great and plentiful rice vegetation (Bowen & Bok, 2019). This island is today the country of Japan. The country began as peaceful groups and communities that harvested crops together but soon encountered predators and enemies that wanted their land. The ancient people of Japan soon realized that they would need to protect themselves and their land. Therefore, the most athletic and skilled fighters began to hone their craft in combat. They would then create a group of great warriors and defenders of the people.

The Samurais, an ancient Japanese warrior caste (Foust, 2015), have a culture of great discipline and loyalty. This philosophy of loyalty is known as *Bushido* (Foust, 2015). The code of Bushido is often referred to as the *Samurai virtues*. These virtues evolved through the years and are known today as the *Eight Virtues of the Samurai* (Nitobe, 2005, as cited in Clark, 2008). These virtues include: (a) rectitude or justice, (b) courage, (c) benevolence or mercy, (d) politeness, (e) honesty and sincerity, (f) honor, (g) loyalty, and (h) character of self-control. These values have been used for centuries to help mentor young Japanese men to become protectors, providers, and models for their families, community, and country. Although the political reign has passed, these practices of mentoring young men to have Bushido values still exist today (Clark, 2008).

The book, *The Spirit of the Samurai* (Nitobe, 2005), gives a detailed definition of the eight virtues that connect with the inner-being of a person and its connection to the spiritual realm. The teachers and the doers of the Samurai give their lives to the virtues. The young men who are mentored, do not approach the devout code of conduct as a punishment or restraint. Instead, they see it as a privilege and responsibility to their heritage. The great warriors and men honored and upheld the philosophy of loyalty, known as Bushido, and were responsible for keeping Japan safe through the centuries.

Mentoring in Ghana, Japan, and worldwide has been used to create progress and sustain communities and traditions. Therefore, mentoring has been proven to be an essential component to the success of every community, which is especially important to the Black community.

Identifying the Importance and Effectiveness of Black Male Youth Mentoring

The mentoring of Black male youth provides opportunities for mentors to invest and improve student social, academic, and emotional learning in multiple environmental contexts (i.e., schools, communities, churches, personal homes). For example, classroom and school settings can provide Black male youth with multiple opportunities for them to access academic content in a collaborative environment with peers. In addition, churches can offer kinship relationships among Black male youth; their peers and their communities can serve as a cultural norm and value, without a biblical relationship. More so, the homes and extended families of Black male youth can offer support in positively molding their identities by directly focusing on and encouraging youth to disregard stereotyping and negative views outside of their cultural and familial relationships. Effective mentoring could provide support in the abovementioned areas to meet the needs of Black male youth in their communities.

Identifying gaps in the areas of community, school, and home—and filling these gaps with intelligent and careful mentoring—will provide a bridge for the young Black male youth who lack the tools needed to make proper decisions that can and will change the trajectory of their entire life (Boykin & Allen, 2003). When these young men find out that there is no one to turn to, they create opportunities for themselves or someone else may see their lack of direction as an opportunity for them to be manipulated. This phenomenon often results in crime, imprisonment, and the destruction of poor, overlooked, Black communities.

Understanding Social Norms

Social norms are often referred to as common standards within a particular social group, most often a White social group, which may be deemed socially acceptable and/or appropriate behaviors in certain social situations. These White social norms inevitably become part of accepted standard practices and expectations in society and especially in our public schools. According to Johnson and Bornstein (2021), it is important to identify policies, practices, and curriculum that presume and privilege underlying

White norms and are thus implicitly biased. Hence, implicit bias as well as explicit bias can become evident in powerful structural racism across the school system.

Implicit and explicit bias should both be challenged by tackling policies and practices that appear to be impartial but are in fact predicated on holding White behavior as the expected social norm against which all students should be judged (Johnson & Bornstein, 2021). More so, social norms can be dictated and facilitated through school environments and other aspects of students' ecological systems which may impact students' identity, motivation, and sense of belonging. This speaks to the old adage that you are a product of your community. Therefore, it is pivotal to provide a different narrative that speaks to the capabilities of individuals to be successful in spite of biases and stereotypes.

For example, mentoring via peers and/or adults can offer opportunities for Black students to engage in an inclusive environment where they are valued and included while being empowered to succeed. Here, Black male youth can engage with like-minded people who help to facilitate deep connections and interactions that support a positive sense of self for Black youth. Sánchez et al. (2018) showed that peer mentoring led to close relationships and connectivity, which included safe spaces, mutual support, group identity, rapport-building activities, and trust. In addition, other research showed that cross-age peer mentoring is equally effective in providing reciprocal interactions for both mentors and mentees that can provide a sense of community for youth who may feel disconnected (St. Vil & Angel, 2018). Based on this information, effective mentoring, including peer mentoring, can disrupt the social norms that do not meet the needs of the Black male youth. These expected norms have been established by the White and European culture, which transcribe what is normal or not. And it is these expectations that systemically support and contribute to racism and discrimination in the Black communities and in society as a whole. More so, these norms may contribute so marginalized students of color do not receive the support and benefits needed for academic, emotional, and social achievement. Therefore, strong support systems and programs with various community partners can be indispensable for students in need (Rossiter et al., 2015). Peer and/or adult mentoring relationships are vital for students to feel safe and secure and to adequately address their need for a sense of belonging (Rossiter et al., 2015).

Preparing for College and Career Readiness

Career earning disparities exist beyond graduation due to the lack of college and career readiness preparation. Young Black adults continue to find

The Disruption of Mentoring for Black Youth During COVID-19 • **71**

themselves earning less full-time income compared to their White peers in most occupations in today's workforce (Kena et al., 2016). Comparatively, there is substantive evidence of academic disparities that have been measured in academic achievement performances and academic achievement outcomes such as test scores, graduation rates, dropout rates, college enrollment, and career earnings (Kena et al., 2016).

Therefore, the preparation for career and college readiness is critical to increasing Black male participation for college attendance; evidence shows that college enrollment rates have not changed since 2004 (Kena et al., 2016). The prospect of many young Black men with college degrees entering Black society is analogous to a domestic lion being placed back into the wild. Realistically, Black men may not receive the full value of the education that they may need. Career and college readiness in high school should be at the forefront of developing students, including Black youth, into productive members in post-secondary school. However, systemic and institutionalized barriers (i.e., racism, discipline and academic disparities, discrimination) limit the opportunities of Black youth and present challenges for students to engage in active learning necessary for them to be successful in both K–12 school systems and in higher education.

School-based mentoring (SBM) may overlap with college and career readiness, but there are also cases where the mentoring focus is on high school student achievement and behavioral issues. College and career readiness can be facilitated by a planned mentoring program. School-based mentoring programs can either bring in an outside entity to mentor students or use internal staff to promote multiple options such as college readiness, career readiness, academic improvement, and behavioral improvement. College and career readiness means something different to young Black males. They must wear a mask (while engaging with the social norms created by the systems in America) in order to lead struggling communities and marginalized people. The masks that Black men wear provide them the resources that are necessary for them to accomplish career goals.

More focus should be directed to college and career readiness for Black males. Relationship building can serve as a common thread throughout the efforts of improving college opportunities for Black males. Many of the programs do not change the students' performance in grades, behaviors, or new skill sets, but the most powerful outcome is often the seed planted into the students and future educators (Cates & Schaefle, 2019).

Cates and Schaefle (2019) were responsible for a quantitative study on the relationship between 6-year college preparation programs and college readiness for low-income and Hispanic students. The research focused on gaps in college enrollment, college-track course enrollment, and standardized testing preparation. However, the study also focused on some of the differences in two approaches to college preparation and found that both programs

72 • J. MATTHEW and D. D. JOHNSON

lacked effectiveness in post-program follow up (2019). Most programs that aimed at providing the best opportunities for student success seemed to falter after the implementation phase. Therefore, such programs should invest in the evaluation process to determine and address weaknesses.

Both Black and Latino youth experience common economic and academic constraints that may prevent them from being successful in schools and in higher education for long-term life improvement. Researchers have found that more than half of Latino households make less than $25,000 annually compared to 23% of White Americans households (Yampolskaya et al., 2006). These researchers focused on college-track course enrollment, standardized testing preparation, college plans, and elements of college preparation programs. Various tools, such as tutoring, mentoring, advising, college visits, summer programs, and educational field trips—combined with data information from Pearson Education—were used to help bring improvement. They were also very focused on attendance and participation. Most of their mentor guidance during these 6 years came from the Gaining Early Awareness and Readiness Program (GEAR UP). Using GEAR UP was helpful when planning college visits and field trips. The experiences of Black youth and Latino youth in this context are quite similar.

Enriching Black Communities

Successful academic achievement for Black male youth in mentoring programs is contingent upon the acceptance of mainstream values or White social norms, which are at times incongruent with the culturally rooted value systems that Black/African American students learn at home and in their communities (Boykin & Allen, 2003). Consequently, African American students may develop a disjointed and/or adverse perception of successful academic achievement (Ogbu, 1981). Therefore, it is imperative that Black male youth be exposed to culturally relevant support systems (e.g., mentoring programs, mentors, churches, organizations, schools) which strategically focus on enriching the lives of students of color.

Black communities (including parents, caregivers, churches and religious organizations, nonprofit organizations, and other community programs) have always stepped up for youth who need extra guidance and support. The strength within the Black community ensures that growth mindsets continue to thrive and that systemic and generational dysfunction ceases. Communities often reference the saying, it takes a village to raise children. Historically, Black communities have proven that statement to be true even during unprecedented events such as the COVID-19 pandemic. These communities made sure that the loss of interactions between peer and adult mentors were addressed.

The Disruption of Mentoring for Black Youth During COVID-19 ▪ **73**

LOSS OF INTERACTIONS IN MENTORING PROGRAMS FOR BLACK STUDENTS

Impact of COVID-19 on our Educational Systems

Ironically, the current pandemic has created ebbs and flows of access for students who are engaged in mentoring programs while attending our school systems on a daily basis. State and national resources for stakeholders (e.g., students, parents/caregiver, teachers, administrators, community members) have not yet proven to be consistent or readily available. Therefore, equity and access gaps continue to increase thus creating educational and academic disparities in our schools. Chevalier and Johnson (2020) reported that there has been limited research on the practices, responses, and experiences during the pandemic. Much consideration is primed on what the public is considering the crux of understanding and addressing the unique challenges of this pandemic. While the authors focused on access to technology during COVID-19, they also posed this perspective: "How are the decisions made to address equitable access to resources—that is, who is making sure that students get access to resources and how are they deciding who gets what resource?" (p. 67). This statement intersects with multiple issues of access and equity and includes opportunities for students to participate in mentoring programs.

The event of the pandemic affirmed that schools have an obligation to ensure that students' needs (i.e., academic, social-emotional) are being met regardless of their disability/ability, race, ethnicity, language, gender, or age. However, in the absence of special programs and services, the equity gap for students tends to increase. Mentoring programs could serve as a conduit for supporting students when our schools are not adequately equipped with the necessary resources that students, particularly, Black students, might need. Of course, we do not assert that only Black students need and should have access to opportunities. Nonetheless, the research continues to show equity gaps and deficiencies for students of color, and male students particularly. Consequently, this chapter speaks to the needs of Black male youths in our communities and how different programs centered on mentoring can support various equity and achievement gaps.

The Impact of School-Based Mentoring on the Academic Achievement Gap

Grey (2019) examined how various factors contribute to the achievement gap between African Americans and White Americans over a 15-month period and how the effective use of SBM might help improve African American achievement. Grey wanted to know if an SBM would significantly reduce the gap in academic achievement between African American and White students and, furthermore, if the mentor's race had any effect on the student's academic improvement. Data from a 2009 Institute of Education Sciences (IES), which evaluated federal school mentoring programs, provided information prior to the start of Grey's (2019) study. The IES study focused on student dropout rates and areas of delinquencies after school or graduation among a population of students with economic problems, behavioral issues, and family problems who lived in high crime or rural areas.

The 2009 IES study was a quantitative study that focused on 3,000 students in Grades 4–8 in two groups: a control group with students who did not receive mentoring and a treatment group for students who did receive mentoring. The entire student group in the IES study consisted of 39% African American, 30% Hispanic, and 21% White. In contrast, Grey's subset of students in Grades 6–8 was 46% male; 60.1% were African American and 39.9% White (Grey, 2019). The author concludes that the SBM in this project was only effective with African American males that received mentoring from other African American men; in contrast, White males benefitted when they were mentored by other races (Grey, 2019).

Closing the achievement gap for Black male students continues as a topic of great importance in schools. Mentoring, regardless of whether a school uses SBM or outside groups after school, is a tool that educators can use with few resources. If a school or a school district utilizes their community members as mentors, young Black men could possibly receive the encouragement and guidance that they need to become ready for college or university studies and they could possibly have the will to perform better in school.

An Impact Study of Big Brothers Big Sisters School-Based Mentoring

Herrera et al. (2011) examined the impact of the Big Brothers Big Sisters organization on school-related attitudes and performance, problem behavior in and outside of school, and social and personal well-being (including relationships with peers and adults and self-esteem). The population studied by the researchers involved 1,139 students in Grades 4–9. The data came from 71 schools, using 16 youth per school; all but five schools had 35 or fewer participating youth. Demographically, the sample group was 63% minority students with 23% Latino, 18% African American, and 13% multiracial youth. There were 554 mentors (Herrera et al., 2011). The study showed that initially the mentoring made impacts in student academic perspectives and the students were able to identify with an adult who became

The Disruption of Mentoring for Black Youth During COVID-19 • **75**

special in their lives. However, the newness of the program soon faded away for the students and while they gained a special person in their life, their academics and behavior became worse or stayed the same.

The Big Brothers Big Sisters organization continues to help schools and communities throughout the country. Their focus on all communities helps schools, churches, and families with improving the lives of all young people, including young Black young men and boys. Through their commitment to one-to-one mentoring, the program is changing one life at a time while creating relationships that bring focus and excitement to young Black males (Big Brothers Big Sisters of America, n.d.).

Church Mentoring: Boys 2 Men Mentoring

The Boys 2 Men Mentoring program was created at the Church Without Walls in Houston, Texas 12 years ago to fill a need that was found within the young males at the church. The youth lacked guidance and protection against the influence of the outside world. The young Black youth were seeking male encounters but were not finding them in the church. The Boys 2 Men program gave those young men a source to tap into. The program also gave parents additional help in raising young men oftentimes on their own in single parent homes. Church mentoring groups not only use spiritual guidance to lead their mentors, but these organizations also use wisdom to help young people make decisions that will have a lasting impact on their lives.

In church-based mentoring, men and women become lifelong mentors. Church mentoring gives people a common ground, with a similar belief system. This commonality can break down walls and create a continuous approach to mentoring. Church-based mentoring not only serves as a place where young men can receive guidance throughout their adolescent years, but it continues to play a part in their adult experience. Church mentoring comes in several forms: formal mentoring, informal mentoring, even speed mentoring (Conklin, 2020). Church-based mentoring is an asset to the Black community and plays an important role in the lives of young Black men who participate in those programs (Cozart, 2016).

The Impact of Houston's "First and Goal" Nonprofit Mentoring Program

Houston, Texas—as well as other cities throughout America—have several nonprofit organizations that provide mentoring and leadership opportunities for mature men and young men to work together with a goal of making a difference and a brighter future for themselves and their families. First and Goal is one of those organizations that is making a difference. Minister Tyrone Smith is the founder and leader of the organization, and he is dedicated to making a difference in the lives of young people that have been overlooked in society. His main focus is not solely on young men; he focuses on all those that need mentoring and guidance, but a large portion of his students are young Black youth (First and Goal, n.d.).

Nonprofit mentoring groups allow schools to help students in ways that are often discouraged. For example, Texas House Bill 4093 would not have allowed educational systems to specifically focus on race and gender (the bill was fortunately defeated; Texas HB4093, 2021). Educators and schools need resources, groups, and organizations to help young people who have little access to funds that could help them with their education. The community nonprofits play a large role in keeping young people connected and empowered. These organizations also played a huge role in communicating with young people during the pandemic, and they continue to find ways to stay connected.

The Impact of Mentoring Throughout the Greater Houston Area

Many mentoring programs throughout the Greater Houston Texas area closed during the pandemic (Macias & Rogalski, 2021). For example, during the 2020–2021 school year, the Katy Independent School District (ISD, outside Houston) paused communication and enrollment of new students and new mentor applicants (Kingdom K.E.Y.S. Mentoring, n.d.). Some mentors were able to reach out to their students through campus counselors, but due to the way their KEYS program was set up, no communication outside of Katy ISD staff supervision could be made between the mentor and the student. Therefore, students in Katy ISD did not receive any mentoring services during that school year (Kingdom K.E.Y.S. Mentoring, n.d.).

The closing of schools affected our communities, jobs, and several innocent students tragically. During the 2020–2021 school year, virtual middle and high school students failed courses at a higher rate than their classmates that attended in person. According to Macias and Rogalski (2021), of the students "across the 10 largest local school districts, 19 percent of middle and high school students failed at least one class in fall 2019. In the fall 2020 semester, the failure rate for secondary students rose to 32 percent" (p. 1). With failure rates increasing, and student attendance sinking, mentoring and adult guidance was in high demand, but it was not made available to most students during the 2020–2021 school year.

The lack of mentoring and positive adult interaction was noticed in several school districts throughout the 2020–2021 school year. School districts like Spring ISD saw this as an opportunity to help their students during this time of constant change and looked for ways to improve their mentoring efforts. In February 2021, the Vine program in Spring ISD publicly sought out community members who were willing to serve as mentors. Superintendent Rodney Watson went on record acknowledging that mentoring played a significant role in the nurturing of students' interactions with adults and assisting with their future success (Brol, 2021). Their program is now up and running, providing several opportunities for mentors to give back to students with programs, support, tools, and resources. The need to continue supporting Black male youth through mentoring is imperative to reducing generational dysfunction, the academic achievement gap, and other social-emotional disparities. Our current pandemic status has created opportunities for schools and communities to become innovative in ways to meet the needs of students.

CONCLUSION

The 2020–2021 school year was a heavy storm that poured and poured, and however the raindrops of trouble continue to drizzle around us, there is a clearing in the distance. Meanwhile, educational leaders are looking for and finding ways to repair their student's intellectually and emotionally by preparing for now and the future. Mentoring programs can serve as a tool to help educators travel down the long educational road ahead of them. Mentoring brings buy-in from the communities and gives community members a chance to play a role in the rebuilding of the schools and the students who attend them.

Since long ago, there has been a need to support Black youth. Understanding the effectiveness of mentoring, especially for Black male youth, is necessary for their overall academic, mental, social, emotional, personal, and professional development and growth. By providing appropriate SBM programs such as college and career readiness, schools can create alternative narratives for Black male youth who are rationalized through the lens of White social norms. More so, community organizations, churches, and nonprofit organizations can assist and support Black communities and Black male youth by addressing some of the school-related issues such as problem behaviors, social and personal well-being, and self-esteem, which could ultimately impact academic achievement and success. Therefore, mentoring, regardless of its form, is pivotal for the positive development and growth of today's Black male youth to disrupt life inconsistencies that they may experience, often due to circumstances beyond their control such as COVID-19.

REFERENCES

Alexander, M. (2020). *The new Jim Crow: Mass incarceration in the age of colorblindness.* The New Press.

Baldwin, K., Karlan, D., Udry, C. R., & Appiah, E. (2020). *How political insiders lose out when international aid underperforms: Evidence from a participatory development experiment in Ghana* (Working Paper 26930). National Bureau of Economic Research. https://doi.org/10.3386/w26930

Bettini, E., Cormier, C. J., Ragunathan, M., & Stark, K. (2022). Navigating the double bind: A systematic literature review of the experiences of novice teachers of color in K–12 schools. *Review of Educational Research, 92*(4), 495–542. https://doi.org/10.3102/00346543211060873

Big Brothers Big Sisters of America. (n.d.). *About us.* https://www.bbbs.org/about-us/

Bowen, W. G., & Bok, D. (2019). The shape of the river. In W. G. Bowen & D. Bok (Eds.), *The shape of the river: Long-term consequences of considering race in college and university admissions* (pp. xxix–xlvi). Princeton University Press. https://doi.org/10.2307/j.ctv36zppr.6

Boykin, A. W., & Allen, B. A. (2003). Cultural integrity and schooling outcomes of African American children from low-income backgrounds. In P. B. Pufall & R. P. Unsworth (Eds.), *Rethinking childhood* (pp. 104–120). Rutgers University Press. https://doi.org/10.36019/9780813558325-009

Brol, H. (2021, February 3). Spring ISD seeking community members to join new mentoring program. *Community Impact.* https://communityimpact.com/houston/spring-klein/education/2021/02/03/spring-isd-seeking-community-members-to-join-new-mentoring-program/

Cates, J. T., & Schaefle, S. E. (2019). The relationship between a college preparation program and at-risk students' college readiness. In E. G. Murillo Jr. (Ed.), *Critical readings on Latinos and education* (pp. 288–301). Routledge. https://doi.org/10.4324/9780429021206-19

Chevalier, T., & Johnson, D. D. (2020). Technology access and equity issues for students of color related to COVID-19: A case study in an urban school district. *The Journal of the Texas Alliance of Black School Educators, 5*(1), 65–85.

Clark, T. (2008). *The Bushido code: The eight virtues of the Samurai.* https://china.usc.edu/sites/default/files/forums/Samurai%20and%20the%20Bushido%20Code.pdf

Conklin, K. (2020, September 21). *The importance of mentors in the local church.* Focus on the Family. https://www.focusonthefamily.com/church/the-importance-of-mentors-in-the-local-church/

Cozart, H. (2016). *The impact of spiritual mentoring among African American males at Eastern Kentucky University* (Publication No. 10156651) [Doctoral dissertation, Asbury Theological Seminary]. ProQuest.

Creamer, J. (2020, September 15). *Poverty rates for Blacks and Hispanics reached historic lows in 2019.* United States Census Bureau. https://www.census.gov/library/stories/2020/09/poverty-rates-for-blacks-and-hispanics-reached-historic-lows-in-2019.html

The Disruption of Mentoring for Black Youth During COVID-19 • **79**

Davis, C. R., Grooms, J., Ortega, A., Rubalcaba, J. A. A., & Vargas, E. (2021). Distance learning and parental mental health during COVID-19. *Educational Researcher, 50*(1), 61–64. https://doi.org/10.3102/0013189x20978806

Deyle, S. (2006). *Carry me back: The domestic slave trade in American life.* Oxford University Press.

Dolberry, M. (2020). *Encouraging greatness: How boys and young men of color define high-quality mentoring for career and college readiness.* JP Morgan Chase and Co. http://files.eric.ed.gov/fulltext/ED605707.pdf

Farrar, T. (1997). The queenmother, matriarchy, and the question of female political authority in precolonial west African monarchy. *Journal of Black Studies, 27*(5), 579–597. https://doi.org/10.1177/002193479702700501

Ferguson, A. G. (2011). Crime mapping and the fourth amendment: Redrawing "high-crime areas." *Hastings Law Journal, 63*(1), Article 4. https://repository.uchastings.edu/cgi/viewcontent.cgi?article=1232&context=hastings_law_journal

First and Goal. (n.d.). *About us.* https://www.teamfirstandgoal.org/about-us/

Foust, M. A. (2015). Nitibe and Royce: Bushido and the philosophy of loyalty. *Philosophy East and West, 65*(4), 1174–1193. https://doi.org/10.1353/pew.2015.0099

Grey, L. (2019). The impact of school-based mentoring on the academic achievement gap. *Professional School Counseling, 23*(1). https://doi.org/10.1177/2156759x19890258

Grunwald, B., & Fagan, J. (2019). The end of intuition-based high-crime areas. *California Law Review, 107,* 345. https://scholarship.law.columbia.edu/faculty_scholarship/2317

Hackett, D. G. (2000). The prince hall masons and the African American church: The labors of grandmaster and Bishop James Walker Hood, 1831–1918. *Church History, 69*(4), 770–802. https://doi.org/10.2307/3169331

Harper, S. R., & Davis, C. H., III. (2012). They (don't) care about education: A counternarrative on Black male students' responses to inequitable schooling. *Educational Foundations, 26,* 103–120. http://files.eric.ed.gov/fulltext/EJ968820.pdf

Herrera, C., Grossman, J. B., Kauh, T. J., & McMaken, J. (2011). Mentoring in schools: An impact study of Big Brothers Big Sisters school-based mentoring. *Child Development, 82*(1), 346–361. https://doi.org/10.1111/j.1467-8624.2010.01559.x

Isom, D. A., Boehme, H. M., Cann, D., & Wilson, A. (2022). The White right: A gendered look at the links between "victim" ideology and anti-Black Lives Matter sentiments in the era of Trump. *Critical Sociology, 48*(3), 475–500. http://dx.doi.org/10.1177/08969205211020396

Johnson, D. D., & Bornstein, J. (2021). Racial equity policy that moves implicit bias beyond a metaphor for individual prejudice to a means of exposing structural oppression. *Journal of Cases in Educational Leadership, 24*(2), 81–95. https://doi.org/10.1177/1555458920976721

Kena, G., Hussar, W., McFarland, J., De Brey, C., Musu-Gillette, L., Wang, X., Zhang, J., Rathbun, A., Wilkinson-Flicker, S., Diliberti, M., Barmer, A., Bullock Mann, F., & Dunlop Velez, E. (2016). *The condition of education 2016* (NCES 2016-144). U.S. Department of Education, National Center for Education Statistics. https://nces.ed.gov/pubs2016/2016144.pdf

80 ▪ J. MATTHEW and D. D. JOHNSON

Kingdom K.E.Y.S. Mentoring. (n.d.). *Welcome to Kingdom K.E.Y.S. Mentoring.* https://www.kingdomkeysmentoring.org/

Leak, H. N. (2018). *Making bricks without straw: The Kresge HBCU Initiative and fundraising at historically Black colleges and universities* (Publication No. 10743128) [Doctoral dissertation, New York University]. ProQuest.

Macias, T., & Rogalski, J. (2021, May 27). School failure rates during pandemic double, triple at some Houston-area districts. *KHOU-11.* https://www.khou.com/article/news/investigations/school-failure-rates-during-pandemic-double-triple-some-local-districts/285-e00d44d1-92f8-4e17-8f24-fe7161
4c444b

McGuire, K. M., McTier, T. S., Jr., Ikegwuonu, E., Sweet, J. D., & Bryant-Scott, K. (2020). Men doing life together: Black Christian fraternity men's embodiments of brotherhood. *Men and Masculinities, 23*(3–4), 579–599. http://dx.doi.org/10.1177/1097184X18782735

Mentoring Institute. (2014, April 10). *The history of mentorship part 1.* The University of New Mexico. https://mentor.unm.edu/blog/post/12

Miller, N. K. (2019). When your friend is also a mentor: The mentrix identity. *Tulsa Studies in Women's Literature, 38*(2), 435–441. https://doi.org/10.1353/tsw.2019.0031

NAACP Connect. (2022). *From the burning sands of the divine nine.* The National Association for the Advancement of Colored People. https://www.naacpconnect.org/blog/entry/from-the-burning-sands-of-the-divine-nine

Nasir, N. S., Givens, J. R., & Chatmon, C. P. (Eds.). (2019). *"We dare say love": Supporting achievement in the educational life of Black boys.* Teachers College Press.

Nitobe, I. (2005). *Bushido: The spirit of the Samurai.* Shambhala Publications.

Ogbu, J. U. (1981). Origins of human competence: A cultural-ecological perspective. *Child Development, 52*(2), 413–429. https://doi.org/10.2307/1129158

Patton, L. D., Flowers, L. A., & Bridges, B. K. (2011). Effects of Greek affiliation on African American students' engagement: Differences by college racial composition. *College Student Affairs Journal, 29*(2), 113–123. https://eric.ed.gov/?id
=EJ969829

Radcliffe, R. B., & Bos, B. (2011). Mentoring approaches to create a college-going culture for at-risk secondary level students. *American Secondary Education, 39*(3), 86–107. https://eric.ed.gov/?id=EJ944163

Rosenthal, C. (2018). *Accounting for slavery; Masters and management.* Harvard University Press.

Rossiter, M. J., Hatami, S., Ripley, D., & Rossiter, K. R. (2015). Immigrant and refugee youth settlement experiences: "A new kind of war." *International Journal of Child, Youth and Family Studies, 6*(4–1), 746–770. https://doi.org/10.18357/
ijcyfs.641201515056

Sánchez, B., Pinkston, K. D., Cooper, A. C., Luna, C., & Wyatt, S. T. (2018). One falls, we all fall: How boys of color develop close peer mentoring relationships. *Applied Developmental Science, 22*(1), 14–28. https://doi.org/10.1080/
10888691.2016.1208092

Schiele, J. H. (2017). The Afrocentric paradigm in social work: A historical and future outlook. *Journal of Human Behavior in the Social Environment, 27*(1–2), 15–26. https://doi.org/10.1080/10911359.2016.1252601

The Disruption of Mentoring for Black Youth During COVID-19 • 81

Sider, R. J. (2007). *Just generosity: A new vision for overcoming poverty in America*. Baker Books.

Solórzano, D. G., & Yosso, T. J. (2002). Critical race methodology: Counter-storytelling as an analytical framework for education research. *Qualitative Inquiry*, *8*(1), 23–44. https://doi.org/10.1177/107780040200800103

St. Vil, C., & Angel, A. (2018). A study of a cross-age peer mentoring program on educationally disconnected young adults. *Social work, 63*(4), 327–336. https://doi.org/10.1093/sw/swy033

Stoeffler, S. W., Joseph, R., & Creedon, E. (2020). The community empowerment framework: A benchmark for Christian social work. *Social Work and Christianity, 47*(3), 50–65. http://dx.doi.org/10.34043/swc.v47i3.143

Texas HB4093 | 2021-2022 | 87th legislature. https://legiscan.com/TX/text/HB4093/id/2339789

Thernstrom, A., & Thernstrom, S. (1998, March 1). *Black progress: How far we've come, and how far we have to go*. Brookings. https://www.brookings.edu/articles/black-progress-how-far-weve-come-and-how-far-we-have-to-go/

Wilson, L. E. (1987). The rise of paramount chiefs among the Krobo (Ghana). *The International Journal of African Historical Studies, 20*(3), 471–495. https://doi.org/10.2307/219690

Woodard, E. D. (2015). *An analysis of the impact of the Boys and Girls Club program on sixth grade African American male students' achievement and parental perception* (Publication No. 3685929) [Doctoral dissertation, Arkansas State University]. ProQuest.

Yampolskaya, S., Massey, O. T., & Greenbaum, P. E. (2006). At risk high school students in the "Gaining Early Awareness and Readiness Program" (GEAR UP): Academic and behavioral outcomes. *Journal of Primary Prevention, 27*(5), 457–475. https://doi.org/10.1007/s10935-006-0050-z

CHAPTER 5

EDUCATIONAL AND MENTAL HEALTH CHALLENGES OF GRANDCHILDREN RAISED BY GRANDPARENTS DURING THE COVID-19 PANDEMIC IN SOUTH CAROLINA

Qualitative Results From a Community-Based Study

Theresa M. Harrison
University of South Carolina

Sue Levkoff
University of South Carolina

Yanfeng Xu
University of South Carolina

Ashlee A. Lewis
University of South Carolina

Patrice Forrester
University of Maryland

Gina M. Kunz
Independent Consultant

Karen Utter
University of South Carolina

School–University–Community Research in a (Post) COVID-19 World, pages 83–107
Copyright © 2023 by Information Age Publishing
www.infoagepub.com
All rights of reproduction in any form reserved.

ABSTRACT

Approximately 2.7 million grandparents in the United States raise their custodial grandchildren. In this research study, we identified educational and mental health challenges of grandchildren raised by grandparents during COVID-19 and explored the role of access to the Internet and technology in influencing grandchildren's educational and mental health challenges. We collaborated statewide on a community-based research study with K–12 school districts, state agencies, and community organizations with an interest in supporting grandparents raising grandchildren. Using a qualitative methodology, this study identified educational and mental health challenges faced by grandchildren during COVID-19 and further indicated the critical need for school personnel to better support grandfamilies with a focus on increasing access to the Internet and technology to address the educational and mental health concerns of students raised by grandparents. In this chapter, we describe the unique challenges faced by custodial grandparents and the need for coordination at both the local and state levels to positively impact grandfamilies. These efforts call for establishing reciprocal school–university–community relationships, which we utilized by engaging with our partners and study participants throughout this study to ensure that we met their needs. We hope our findings are not only informative for addressing custodial grandparents' and their grandchildren's concerns, but also instructive in how to build more sustainable partnerships with state and educational institutions.

Scholars define custodial grandparents as those who have assumed full responsibility for grandchildren aged 18 years or younger (Hayslip et al., 1998). Approximately 2.7 million grandparents in the United States live with their grandchildren in the absence of biological parents (U.S. Census Bureau, n.d.). In South Carolina alone, approximately 51,121 children live in a grandparent-headed household without either parent present ("Grandfacts," 2021). According to the National Survey of America's Families, 41% of custodial grandparent-headed families are White, 42% are Black, and 17% are from other racial and ethnic minorities (Lin, 2018). As such, grandparents from racial and ethnic minority groups are overrepresented in custodial grandparent-headed families relative to the general U.S. population (Chen et al., 2015).

Custodial grandparents step in to care for grandchildren primarily because parental neglect (related to parental substance abuse, incarceration, mental illness, military deployment, financial needs, or even death of the biological parents) and associated child maltreatment (Campbell et al., 2012; Generations United, 2021; Goodman et al., 2004; Hayslip & Kaminski, 2005; G. C. Smith et al., 2018). Due to childhood trauma and life transitions, grandchildren face additional challenges and related stress, such as physical health concerns; socioemotional, mental, and behavioral problems; and poor educational outcomes (Campbell et al., 2012; Generations United, 2021;

Goodman et al., 2004; G. C. Smith et al., 2018; Xu et al., 2022). Additionally, with the opioid crisis and COVID-19-related deaths, even more grandparents have stepped up to care for grandchildren (Dolbin-MacNab et al., 2022). Although the Supporting Grandparents Raising Grandchildren Act (2018) emphasized the importance of support at the policy level, custodial grandparents and their grandchildren are still under-resourced and underserved (U.S. Senate Special Committee on Aging, 2018).

The COVID-19 pandemic disproportionately affected the education and mental health of children in grandparent-headed families. Many schools temporarily replaced in-person instruction with a mix of synchronous and asynchronous instruction via web-based platforms (Hamilton et al., 2020; Harris et al., 2020). Unfortunately, approximately one third of all public school students lack adequate access to digital devices for virtual learning (Lieberman, 2020). Lack of digital access is even more prominent among grandparent-headed families due to poverty, low computer literacy, and lack of broadband Internet (Anderson & Perrin, 2017; Charalambides, n.d.). Furthermore, the lack of digital access meant that COVID-19 potentially exacerbated grandchildren's mental health problems, because they could not take advantage of telemental health services. Telemental health is the use of videoconferencing to conduct real-time mental health treatment between a clinician and patient. School personnel are typically unaware of the unique challenges grandfamilies face and are unprepared to effectively support students raised by grandparents, particularly during COVID-19 (Campbell et al., 2012; Dolbin-MacNab et al., 2022; Pelt, 2001). Given these issues, this study aimed to examine challenges influencing grandchildren's education and mental health during the COVID-19 pandemic in South Carolina and offer recommendations for better support.

REVIEW OF THE LITERATURE

Grandchildren's Educational Challenges

Grandchildren who are parented by their grandparents experience lower cognitive assessment scores, lower literacy and math scores, and elevated school dropout rates (Pilkauskas & Dunifon, 2016; Vandivere et al., 2012; Xu et al., 2022). The grandparents' lack of comfort navigating new technologies can further hinder their ability to provide academic support to their grandchildren (Brunissen et al., 2020). Additionally, prior studies demonstrated that custodial grandchildren tend to perform at a relatively lower academic level than their peers, and some need special education support and services (Cross & Day, 2008; Smithgall et al., 2009). The grandchildren's low educational performance is associated with grandparent characteristics such as low educational attainment, physical and mental health issues, a lack of understanding of the school curriculum, different educational expectations, outdated methods of learning, lack of communication with teachers, poor relationships with their adult children, scant support and financial resources, and low quality of parenting (Ingersoll-Dayton et al., 2020; Lee & Blitz, 2022; Nadorff et al., 2021; Peterson et al., 2019; Xu et al., 2022). The intersectional nature of the lived experiences of grandparents and the resulting effects on their grandchildren point to the need for further research. For instance, the low educational attainment of grandparents' leads to lower-paying jobs and consequent economic hardships, which preclude early childhood resources or tutoring services for their grandchildren. Despite these known challenges, grandparents often are ineligible to receive the same social service financial supports that might be extended to nonrelative foster caregivers, for example.

Grandchildren's Mental Health Challenges

Custodial grandchildren often experience significant adverse childhood experiences (Sprang et al., 2015). Prior studies have defined these experiences as physical, mental, or sexual abuse; emotional or physical neglect; domestic violence; parental substance abuse; exposure to parental mental illness; parental separation or divorce; and parental incarceration (Felitti et al., 1998). Therefore, custodial grandchildren tend to experience greater mental health problems, including depression and anxiety (Fruhauf et al., 2020; G. C. Smith et al., 2019); they are at greater risk of mental health challenges as compared to grandchildren raised by one or more biological parent (Brunissen et al., 2020; Pilkauskas & Dunifon, 2016; G. C. Smith et al., 2019; Vandivere et al., 2012; Xu et al., 2022). G. C. Smith et al. (2019) used a nationally representative sample to quantitatively compare the psychological or behavioral challenges of custodial grandchildren with other households with a single parent, both parents, or no biological parents; they found that elementary school-aged children (ages 4–12) raised by their grandparents had more psychological difficulties, regardless of race and gender.

Impact of COVID-19 on Educational and Mental Health Challenges

During the COVID-19 pandemic, children had to engage in online learning, which sometimes posed challenges (Goldschmidt, 2020). Absenteeism is a chronic problem in American education but is particularly prevalent when school buildings have closed and lessons are online, because students do not log on, do not check assignments, and miss more classes than ever (Goldstein et al., 2020). Data on learning loss during COVID-19 have been slow to emerge, with parents, educators, and policymakers often lacking the knowledge to make informed decisions to address these challenges (Kuhfeld et al., 2020). Research on the impact of COVID-19 and supplemental education (e.g., homeschooling, worksheets) has suggested that learning loss disproportionately affects families with lower socioeconomic status, which includes grandparent-headed families (Bacher-Hicks et al., 2021). Children who lack access to a computer may not be able to receive instruction or engage in educational activities online (Goldschmidt, 2020). Children may not receive support from caregivers who lack knowledge of computers or are unavailable while at work (Goldschmidt, 2020; Walters, 2020). Dolbin-MacNab et al. (2022) found in a mixed-methods study that grandchildren with preexisting learning disabilities or problems with socioemotional functioning were unmotivated or easily distracted and had difficulty learning online. This issue was further exacerbated during the pandemic because of a lack of mental, learning, or socioemotional support.

In addition to the effects on educational outcomes, COVID-19 has increased grandchildren's mental health problems. For instance, the closure of schools and separation from friends can cause stress and anxiety in children (Imran et al., 2020) and, in general, children can experience negative feelings during COVID-19 such as boredom, anger, and irritability (World Health Organization, 2020a; World Health Organization, 2020b). Existing findings have been mixed regarding mental health outcomes during COVID-19; some studies found that children experienced an increase in mental health disorders, whereas other studies found that children experienced a decrease due to greater support at home or less stress from in-person instruction at school (Rider et al., 2021). Some findings suggested that the pandemic led to increased mental health problems for grandchildren due to a lack of access to mental health services (e.g., telemental health or in-person services) and fear of contracting COVID-19, which prevented the use of such services in-person (Dolbin-MacNab et al., 2022; Xu et al., 2020).

Role of the Internet and Technology in Educational and Mental Health Challenges

Due to COVID-19, many schools switched to remote instruction hastily, transforming the delivery of education. According to the National Center for Education Statistics—which conducted a nationally representative survey in Spring 2021—31% of U.S. districts offered more than 5 hours of remote learning instruction for their fourth graders (Institute of Education Sciences, n.d.). Remote instruction effectively required households to have access to technology to support remote learning, but some grandparent-headed families had limited access to digital devices and stable Internet (Generations United, 2020) or lacked the skills and confidence to use the technology (Generations United, 2020), which may have affected their grandchildren's educational outcomes. Since most students and teachers also had little experience with online instruction prior to COVID-19, the full implications of moving to remote learning as the primary mode of instruction has yet to be determined (Kuhfeld et al., 2020). Many teachers reported having no contact with a significant portion of their students during the period of remote instruction (Lieberman, 2020).

Access to the Internet and technology has also affected how mental health support services were provided to children raised by grandparents. Even prior to the pandemic, communities with limited geographic access to health care disproportionately utilized technology (Jetty et al., 2018). For example, telemental health significantly reduces transportation barriers to treatment access (Nelson et al., 2017). However, low-income communities have been slow to engage in telemedicine, possibly due to cultural or political factors and differences in education (Cantor et al., 2021). The significant implications of providing telemental health were realized during shelter-in-place and physical distancing requirements, when people felt uncomfortable being in public during COVID-19 (Wright & Caudill, 2020).

Further, telemental health has been shown to be effective in treating children's general mental health challenges when compared to in-person treatment (Gloff et al., 2015). However, children with maltreatment histories or other adverse childhood experiences may struggle during telemental health sessions because of severe emotional regulation difficulties or challenges sustaining attention (Comer & Myers, 2016). Additionally, telemental health use for children lags behind that for adults due to, for example, differences in state licensing laws, gaps in insurance policy coverage (Goldschmidt, 2020), and a dearth of research documenting that such services can be implemented successfully with minoritized, underserved youth and families (Ralston et al., 2019). As a result, the mental health system and policy makers are playing catch up to make sure the needs of our most vulnerable populations are being met.

The Digital Divide

The phrase *digital divide* delineates the gap between Americans who use and have access to telecommunications and information technologies (e.g., computers, tablets, and Internet) and those who do not (Kruger & Gilroy, 2019). Even when teachers made themselves and their instructional materials available online, many students lacked the means to access online materials from home (Kuhfeld et al., 2020). According to an The Education Trust (2020) poll, nearly 50% of low-income families and 42% of families of color lacked sufficient devices at home to access distance learning. When schools provided families with such devices, not all families had access to the Internet. Schools inaccurately assumed that students had families who could assist them with this technology.

During the pandemic, connectivity was a necessity in education, not an amenity, because it affected children's ability to do homework and teachers' ability to connect with students and their parents. The three most common reasons for lack of Internet access in low-income, high-minority neighborhoods were lack of availability, high cost, and low user skill sets (e.g., lack of digital literacy or perceived irrelevance of broadband; Horrigan, 2010; Mossberger et al., 2017). For instance, although many companies and organizations offered free or low-cost Internet service during South Carolina's mandated quarantine period, rural areas of the state were still not equipped to take advantage of high-speed Internet. Unfortunately, rural deployment of broadband service infrastructure lags urban use regardless of the service levels (Federal Communications Commission, 2001).

Numerous mental health-related interventions are affected by the digital divide, including direct real-time interaction (e.g., videoconferencing), the ability to participate in online surveys, access to telephone hotlines, and use of online mental health educational materials (Simms et al., 2011). Some studies have shown the incorporation of complementary interventions such as smartphone applications have a moderate positive effect on some mental health disorders such as depression (Firth et al., 2017). However, when grandfamilies lack access to the Internet or up-to-date technology, they cannot take advantage of the resources available to other families to support their children. Although some schools are starting to see the benefits of attending to their students' mental health needs and are willing to use videoconferencing systems to allow families to access telemental health services (Simms et al., 2011; Stephan et al., 2016), this is not the case everywhere.

Study Purpose

This study aimed to understand grandchildren's educational and mental health challenges during the COVID-19 pandemic in South Carolina. More specifically, this study sought to answer the following research questions:

1. What are the educational and mental health challenges of grandchildren raised by grandparents during COVID-19?

90 • T. M. HARRISON et al.

2. How does access to the Internet and technology influence grand-children's educational and mental health challenges during CO-VID-19?

The ability to quickly assess the disparate impact on custodial grandchildren will be key in mitigating any potential adverse educational and mental health outcomes.

METHOD

Research Design

The present study was part of a large mixed-methods community-based research (CBR) project (Creswell, 2014). CBR is a form of action research that takes place in community settings and involves community members in the design and implementation of the research project, demonstrating respect for the contributions made by community partners and the principle of "doing no harm" to the communities involved (Strand et al., 2003). The first phase of this project was a survey for grandparents raising grandchildren, and the second phase was one-on-one or focus group interviews with grandparents. In this book chapter, we present qualitative findings from our interviews with grandparents.

As part of CBR, our research design and questions were reviewed by the Carolina Family Engagement Center (CFEC) Advisory Council, whose members represent students, parents, grandparents raising grandchildren, teachers, administrators, and business leaders across South Carolina. CFEC works extensively with schools and communities across the state to support vulnerable families, including custodial grandparents. The inclusion of community members' perspectives in how we structured our study ensured that their voice was represented in how questions were developed and what questions were asked. We developed interview guides, with a focus on identifying educational and mental health challenges, based on the literature and relevant feedback from the CFEC Advisory Council.

Data Collection

We purposefully selected custodial grandparents who expressed a desire to participate in qualitative interviews through their survey participation. Of the approximately 220 participants who completed the survey, 30 participants responded that they would be willing to participate in an interview. Of those 30, 11 accepted a follow-up invitation and completed the interview process. We took a multistep approach to recruitment. We initially reached out to some university–community partners (two state agencies and three community organizations) that work with grandparent populations, and they recruited participants for our study primarily via direct email or listservs. To recruit participants via schools, we reached out to 12 school districts, and personnel at three school districts recruited grandparents. To assist us in recruiting grandparents, we delivered a 30-minute PowerPoint presentation to potential partners (e.g., schools, state agencies, community organizations) to explain the study and shared flyers with research study information that could be disseminated via email and listservs. Once we selected grandparents and confirmed the date and time, we conducted all interviews via Zoom and then recorded and transcribed them verbatim. The interviews were semi-structured, lasting 30 to 60 minutes, and the questions posed to grandparents focused primarily on educational and mental health challenges facing their grandchildren during the pandemic. Even if grandparents were raising several grandchildren, we asked them to focus on one grandchild for the duration of the focus group or interview (i.e., one participant and two researchers), but they were welcome to discuss all their grandchildren. In the focus groups, we attempted to connect the points expressed among the grandparents to facilitate a conversation among grandparents. Grandparents received $25 Walmart e-gift cards for their participation in a focus group or interview.

The following are examples of interview questions we posed to participants:

1. As a grandparent raising grandchildren, what kinds of challenges and stressors have you experienced during COVID-19? Challenges might include remote learning or home-schooling stress (e.g., technology) and mental health concerns (e.g., insurance, access to physicians, affordability, mental health, telemental health).
2. What if any educational or behavioral problems have your grandchildren faced, if you are willing to share?
3. What kinds of support do you need the most?
4. What kinds of support do your grandchildren need the most?

Grandparents' and Grandchildren's Characteristics

Eleven grandparents participated in either a focus group or interview (see Table 5.1 for a comprehensive demographic description of all participants). The two focus groups had two and three grandparents in attendance, respectively. The remaining six grandparents participated in interviews. Most participants were women, with five identifying as Black, five

TABLE 5.1 Grandparents' and Grandchildren's Characteristics

Pseudonym	Grandparents						Grandchildren				
	Race	Gender	Age	Marital Status	Education	Income	Race	Gender	Age	Grade	Remote Learning in the Past
Avery	Black	Female	55	Married	Graduate or professional school	More than $80,000	Black	Female	11	Grade 5	Yes
Carol	White	Female	71	Married	Some college or 2-year degree	$40,001–60,000	White	Female	6	Kindergarten	Yes
Cecil	White	Female	62	Divorced	Some college or 2-year degree	$60,001–80,000	White	Female	7	Grade 1	Yes
Chloe	Black	Female	58	Separated	Graduate or professional school	$30,001–40,000	Black	Male	10	Grade 5	Yes
Emile	White	Female	57	Married	Bachelor's degree	$25,001–30,000	White	Female	9	Grade 3	Yes
Grace	Black	Female	48	Single	Bachelor's degree	$40,001–60,000	Mixed race	Male	4	Prekindergarten or kindergarten	No
Hazel	Black	Female	53	Single	Some college or 2-year degree	$15,001–20,000	Black	Female	5	Kindergarten	Yes
Sadie	Black	Female	64	Single	Some college or 2-year degree	$30,001–40,000	Black	Female	7	Grade 1	Yes
Sofia	Mixed race	Female	47	Single	Some college or 2-year degree	$20,001–25,000	Black	Female	4	Prekindergarten or kindergarten	Yes
Roman	White	Male	60	Married	Graduate or professional school	$40,001–60,000	White	Male	7	Grade 1	Yes
Riley	White	Female	67	Married	Some college or 2-year degree	$40,001–60,000	White	Male	9	Grade 3	Yes

Note: All participants were non-Hispanic or Latinx.

identifying as White, and one identifying as mixed race. In terms of marital status, 54% were married and 36% were single, with one grandparent identifying as being separated and one as divorced. All grandparents had some college education, with half indicating their income was more than $40,000 per year and half indicating they made less than $40,000 per year.

The demographics of the grandchildren they were raising aligned with their self-identified race. Grandparents identified seven grandchildren as female and four as male. The ages of the grandchildren were 4 to 11, representing prekindergarten to fifth grade. All grandchildren except one had participated in remote learning.

Data Analysis

During our data analysis process, we completed independent coding of a single interview transcript first and created an initial codebook. We then shared the codebook with three researchers, who independently coded the same transcript. We collaboratively added codes and modified existing codes to ensure the codebook reflected appropriate codes, was comprehensive, and reflected the perspectives of the entire research team. Once the codebook was developed, we reviewed the remaining transcripts by conducting thematic analysis using Dedoose software. Each researcher received specific transcripts to conduct initial coding; then additional coding was completed in a round-robin fashion for at least two more reviews. After each transcript had been coded by at least three researchers, we reconvened to share thoughts and analytic insights on overall themes that emerged during the coding process and finalized the coding. We also assigned pseudonyms to grandparents to protect participants' confidentiality.

RESULTS

Educational Challenges of Grandchildren During COVID-19

These interviews revealed a perceived lack of consistency in the educational expectations of schools for students during COVID-19. Several grandparents mentioned an apparent lack of school concern about whether students signed on to their online platforms on time or that their grandchildren seemed to demonstrate a lack of engagement while using the online platforms.

For instance, Emile, a 57-year-old White grandmother, acknowledged that in her grandchild's school district, it seemed fine for children to either sign in or skip their online class sessions. She stated:

94 • T. M. HARRISON et al.

> There was a lot of times that they were not signed in and you know, grades were still there... They were not being docked for not being there. So, I am just glad that they are now being taken to school.

Some grandparents said the lack of their grandchildren's engagement stemmed from their young age, whereas others attributed it to having multiple grandchildren who needed to access online classes at the same time. Additionally, grandparents said that the general lack of social engagement of grandchildren was problematic. For example, Carol, a 71-year-old White grandmother, stated:

> But it does hurt their education, being isolated in this house just around us and not being with their peers and you know, I have seen it affect their education... They are tired of their grandparents teaching them and they are tired of COVID. They are tired of us telling them what to do 24-hours a day.

One alternative that many schools used to supplement online education was take-home worksheet packets. Riley, a 67-year-old White grandmother, expressed, "He gets a paper packet. When it first started, the paper packets were just unbelievable. Being an adult, I had difficulty doing it myself, much less teaching him how to do it." The frustration expressed by this grandparent was reminiscent of many grandparents.

Mental Health Challenges of Grandchildren During COVID-19

Grandparents also became more aware of the mental health of their grandchildren during the pandemic. The impact of reduced socialization for grandchildren could be seen and heard in accounts from grandparents. For instance, Cecil, a 62-year-old White grandmother, stated that her 17-year-old grandson (a different grandchild than referenced in Table 5.1) could not see his friends; she was having a tough time with him because of that, so she sought out counseling services for him. She realized that the lack of interaction with his friends was affecting his social and emotional health and their relationship.

Access to mental health services during COVID-19 posed an issue for Avery's grandson as well. Avery, a 55-year-old Black grandmother, stated:

> I was having trouble getting mental health services.... The school did diagnose him, but I don't have a medical diagnosis, which is what they're telling me I need for him to get services. And to this day, I still cannot get anyone to see him so that is a barrier right there for him.

Schools often provide mental health services as part of a multitiered system of support. Apparently, poor communication between the school and this grandparent resulted in a delay in receiving treatment. These delays can lead to worsening mental health conditions that ultimately are both harder and more costly to treat (National Alliance on Mental Illness, n.d.).

Role of Access to the Internet and Technology in Mitigating Challenges

In terms of the role of access to the Internet and technology in assisting their grandchildren's education, Riley, a 67-year-old White grandmother, stated: "We're out in the country, and our Internet is not really great. I mean, you might get on it or you might not." Sadie, a 64-year-old Black grandmother, replied, "I got Internet services here, I will not say it is the best, but it is good Internet service."

The lack of access to the Internet and technology services affected the use of telemental health services during COVID-19, which led to concerns that these services, similar to the education services, did not seem to be as effective with grandchildren. Emile stated, "I do not like the tele because I do not think being in person on the phone with a psychiatrist is going to help anything. Because you need to be face-to-face with that person." Other grandparents expressed envy that one grandparent secured face-to-face counseling for her grandchild. Carol said, "I could only find the virtual, and I do not know how you found a face-to-face counselor. I wish I had a face-to face counselor." Cecil also commented:

> I was just wondering where she was meeting for in person, because I am having a difficult time finding somebody that will do it in person. They would rather do it over the phone, and being 7 and 13 [years old], that's difficult for them to be doing that over the phone.

Grandparents' Recommendations for Supporting Grandchildren Through COVID-19

Grandparents expressed a need for an increased quantity and quality of support to promote positive education and mental health outcomes for their grandchildren from schools and communities during and after COVID-19. Their grandchildren required more academic, social, and personal support. Sadie suggested that students raised by grandparents needed assistance after school through tutoring programs (that is, someone to sit with students and go over their homework with them). This recommendation addressed a concern expressed by many grandparents: They simply did not understand the homework their grandchildren brought home. Having someone knowledgeable about the school curriculum and willing to assist with homework would help alleviate grandparents' concerns. Riley shared a touching account of educators supporting students and their grandparents during COVID-19:

> His teacher was always available by text messaging so that I [could] ask her different things, and she always responded back. And she kept reassuring me, "Just do the best you can do, and we'll handle the rest." So, that's what I did.

Oftentimes, grandparents might have simply wanted reassurance that they were not alone, that they were in this (i.e., raising their grandchildren) together, whether with their spouse, family members, teachers, or church members. Perhaps even more importantly, grandchildren needed individualized support for their academic performance and mental health well-being.

Several grandparents suggested that having a support group for grandchildren being raised by grandparents would be beneficial and could even be offered simultaneously with a grandparent support group. Avery stated in regards to the grandchildren:

> I do believe that they do have a lot that they need to say. They are not going to say it to their grandparents. They are not going to say it to the teacher. But they will say it to other peers. You know, they will talk about it. And if they, like us as grandparents, get together with a group and try to help each other out, I think other kids can help each other out as well.

An adult peer support group could be in person or virtual, but grandparents may need additional support in accessing the Internet and technology to attend virtual peer support groups.

DISCUSSION

We conducted a CBR study on the educational and mental health challenges of grandchildren raised by grandparents during COVID-19. The reciprocal nature of our school–university–community partnership was evident throughout all phases of the study. The ability to confer with the CFEC Advisory Council and other stakeholders (e.g., school district leaders, state agencies, and community organizations) to get relevant and timely feedback on survey question topic choices and the length and format of the survey was invaluable. The research team made substantive changes to the survey and interview guide based on stakeholder feedback. Due to

CFEC's and research team members' extensive relationships with schools, state agencies, and community organizations, we also successfully navigated some missteps such as a glitch with our electronic link requiring information to be disseminated multiple times and the need to soften some of the racial disparity language in the recruitment materials to be more appealing to broader audiences.

Parent engagement coordinators from schools and community service representatives who regularly worked with grandparents acted as trusted brokers and gave heightened visibility to our research. Our research team would not have been as successful in recruiting grandparents statewide without our partners' persistence in outreach efforts. We reciprocated by strategically placing information about their agencies and organizations on our two-sided flyer used to recruit grandparents. Therefore, regardless of whether grandparents chose to participate in the study, they had information about resources they could access to assist them and their grandchildren.

This research makes a significant contribution to the limited literature on custodial grandchildren's educational and mental health challenges during COVID-19. Similar to the findings of prior studies (Brunissen et al., 2020; Dolbin-MacNab et al., 2022), being raised by aging individuals seemed to affect grandchildren's ability to rely on their grandparent for assistance with homework via navigating online platforms for school. Specifically, Brunissen et al. (2020) reflected on the lack of research regarding the extent to which barriers related to technology made it difficult for grandparents to effectively meet their grandchildren's educational needs; the caregivers' age was related to those barriers. This study contributes to our understanding of these issues. Further, although not all grandparents mentioned access to the Internet or technology being an issue, the experiences of two grandmothers, aged 62 and 67, reflected our findings on this topic. This age range is fairly young when considering grandparenthood, but with the pace of technological advancement, it is not surprising that baby boomers (i.e., those born from 1946 to 1964) might struggle with navigating online platforms.

Relatedly, several grandparents in our study mentioned struggling to ensure their grandchildren signed on to participate in academic instruction. Similarly, Goldstein et al. (2020) found that children during COVID-19 missed more classes by not logging on and not checking assignments. Our results are consistent with a recent study that found access to technology, adequate instructional support, and grandchildren's socioemotional difficulties all play a critical role in their engagement and success with remote instruction (Dolbin-MacNab et al., 2022).

Many grandparents in our study reported that their grandchildren experienced mental health challenges, which was substantiated in the literature

(Brunissen et al., 2020; Xu et al., 2022). However, they were also dissatisfied with the virtual mental health support services provided during COVID-19. Some grandparents had a hard time finding services in general for their grandchildren; others could not find their preferred mode of receiving services (e.g., face to face). These difficulties are highly problematic because mental illness that goes untreated or is inadequately treated has been shown to lead to high rates of school dropout, future unemployment, substance use, arrest, incarceration, and even early death (National Alliance on Mental Illness, n.d.).

Overall, in the era of COVID-19, few studies have examined remote learning and telehealth and mental health among grandparent-headed families and their grandchildren. Results from our study support findings from similar studies related to technology use (e.g., Comer & Myers, 2016; Kuhfeld et al., 2020) in education and mental health settings. One specific finding from our study was grandfamilies' difficulties accessing and using technology and their concerns with grandchildren using online platforms to access mental health services or as a primary mode of learning. Schools and communities have an opportunity to meet these challenges by working with families to increase their comfort level with accessing and using technology. Additionally, schools could assist families by allowing them to use videoconferencing technology in schools to access telemental health services. We still need more information on the effectiveness of telemental health services with vulnerable populations (Ralston et al., 2019); therefore, as more grandfamilies gain familiarity with virtual technologies, more research can be conducted to demonstrate the effectiveness, or lack thereof, of its use with this population.

Limitations

Our study participants were primarily Black and White due to the racial demographic composition of South Carolina; we still need more research with Latino and Asian American grandfamilies because they may experience different challenges (e.g., language, cultural practices). Further, our study included a small number of participants ($n = 11$) in one Southeastern state, which limits the broad application of our findings.

Additionally, we interviewed grandparents regarding their own perceptions of their grandchildren's mental health and educational challenges. These perceptions might be skewed for various reasons, such as a lack of open and honest communication in the home.

Finally, the COVID-19 protocols (e.g., physical distancing) severely limited access to grandparents for all our partner organizations. Grandparents in general have higher comorbidities (such as atherosclerotic cardiovascular disease, hypertension, and chronic pulmonary disease), which could deter their engagement with schools or social services more intentionally during our recruitment efforts.

Future Directions for Research

Despite these limitations, we have identified several potential directions for future research. To ascertain an accurate landscape, we need large-scale, multi-state studies of the schooling experiences and challenges of grandparents raising grandchildren, which would be more representative of this population. Future studies with a broader range of racial identities are warranted.

We intentionally conducted this study in a time-sensitive manner during the COVID-19 pandemic. Future studies should seek an understanding of which challenges and barriers have persisted post-pandemic for grandparents raising grandchildren, which have been resolved, and which, if any, have been exacerbated.

Although we recognize the challenges inherent in interviewing children, future research would benefit from obtaining firsthand accounts from grandchildren about their experiences being raised by grandparents. We need new studies to better understand how families with little or no Internet access meet new educational expectations. As the use of technology is increasingly prioritized in curricula development, educational policy, and mental health services, additional research must consider the disparate impact this might have on families without reliable access to the Internet. New research could help us understand and anticipate the potential negative impacts of mandated e-learning and lack of access to telemental health services on these families.

Recommendations

There is much to be gleaned from the impact of a nationwide emergency such as COVID-19. If anything, the pandemic has highlighted the need to have the proper infrastructure in place to meet the needs of low-income and rural areas. Our findings suggest that educational outcomes of grandchildren raised by grandparents during these COVID-19 years might be negatively affected by the lack of technological support available in the home or provided by schools. These challenges are compounded when access to telemental health services are also compromised. Sustained inequality in education negatively influences the academic trajectory of students due to lack of motivation to stay engaged in the educational system and limited career choices (Gamoran, 2001). Our results reflect how educational and mental health challenges facing grandchildren and their grandfamilies during COVID-19 are intimately interwoven, strongly suggesting these challenges should be addressed concurrently. Schools and community organizations such as public libraries should work together to provide access to and promote the use of free digital hotspots (i.e., Internet connection using special wireless equipment) for both educational and mental health purposes.

We suggest that researchers, practitioners, and community members invested in improving the mental health and educational outcomes of custodial grandchildren would benefit significantly from seeking opportunities for partnership. The expertise of both administrators and families should be incorporated in the development of trainings, workshops, and information sessions. For example, workshops for grandparents raising grandchildren might provide information on how to use technologies currently in place for children in school. During national crises, such as pandemics or other widespread disasters, extra attention and support for grandparents raising grandchildren would mitigate the time lost trying to engage their grandchildren on educational platforms. This is particularly recommended during school closures, when grandparents may feel isolated and lack intensive school support. Perhaps it would be beneficial to have grandparent support groups led by a teacher, social worker, or family engagement liaison in coordination with an information technology specialist whose sole focus is to check in with grandparents on Internet- and technology-related matters, including providing home visits to assist with technology setup if necessary.

Regarding mental health, we recommend that information regularly be provided through various means (e.g., school websites, paper flyers distributed to parents picking up their children, information sessions held at schools, etc.) on current and accessible mental health resources to reach a larger swath of caregivers. Although schools tend to provide a lot of professional development for teachers and support staff members on various issues such as mental health, similar efforts should be made to educate caregivers on signs and symptoms of mental health concerns in children. Grandchildren would benefit from in-person student support groups through their schools; the opportunity to interact with other children being raised by their grandparents would provide them a space to share their experiences and assist in destigmatizing mental health needs. If access to the Internet is an issue and telemental health is not a viable option, schools should work with their mental health staff (e.g., psychologists, social workers) to facilitate alternative in-person mental health services.

Although many schools have returned to in-person instruction, additional variants of the COVID-19 virus continue to spread, leaving many to wonder whether we are any more prepared to handle a new wave of school closures or another global pandemic. Administrators must be zealous in exploring how to better incorporate remote learning into their school's everyday service delivery methods. Practice in using virtual platforms would be an important step, not only for teachers and school personnel, but also students and their families. Furthermore, the prevention of widening achievement gaps between those separated by the digital divide will require better access to electronic devices and the Internet for all families, especially those most vulnerable to these education disruptions.

The policies and practices of our social institutions have a broad impact on how families are supported with financial and social resources, thus affecting students' educational and mental health outcomes. Policymakers can often be somewhat removed from the outcomes of the policy decisions they make; unintended negative consequences of policy decisions can prove detrimental to building trust. Researchers and practitioners should help legislators make informed decisions regarding policies that could mitigate the inequities due to COVID-19. For instance, when considering digital equity and universal service initiatives, public institutions such as schools and libraries are logical sites for investment (Strover, 2019). It is imperative that we reach out now to key stakeholders, such as legislators and state agencies, while these challenges are at the forefront of everyone's minds, lest we miss this moment and fall back to business as usual.

CONCLUSION

In conclusion, a final responsibility of the CBR researcher is to report the findings to participants and community partners. We plan to host several virtual community feedback sessions, to which we will invite all statewide participants and stakeholders (e.g., grandparents, K–12 school districts, state agencies, community organizations). After presenting the study findings, we will elicit additional feedback, particularly regarding directions for future research and implications for policy and practice in the educational community. If we want to succeed in addressing systemic barriers, we must disseminate our conclusions and reflections broadly with the extended community and those in a position to advocate for change. Following the advice of L. T. Smith (2021) that researchers should share "the theories and analyses which inform the way knowledge and information are constructed and represented" (p. 17), we intend to ensure that community members have the opportunity and skills to share in future knowledge production. We hope that through the dissemination of our research findings to school administrators, state agencies, and community organizations, we accurately convey the concerns related to grandchildren's education and mental health during the COVID-19 crisis and show what can be done to help alleviate the problems. Finally, we expect that this study will empower

102 · T. M. HARRISON et al.

grandfamilies in our state to offer feedback to local, state, and federal agencies and organizations regarding where and in what format services (e.g., Internet connectivity, mental health support) are most useful and how financial and technical assistance might help. We expect that this advocacy will improve educational and mental health outcomes for all students.

AUTHOR NOTE

Funding statement: This research was supported by the University of South Carolina's Office of the Vice President Research Racial Justice and Equity Research Fund (Grant number: USCIP 80004043).

REFERENCES

Anderson, M., & Perrin, R. (2017, May 17). *Technology use among seniors*. Pew Research Center. https://www.pewresearch.org/internet/2017/05/17/technology-use-among-seniors/

Bacher-Hicks, A., Goodman, J., & Mulhern, C. (2021). Inequality in household adaptation to schooling shocks: Covid-induced online learning engagement in real-time. *Journal of Public Economics, 193*, 104345. https://doi.org/10.1016/j.jpubeco.2020.104345

Brunissen, L., Rapoport, E., Fruitman, K., & Adesman, A. (2020). Parenting challenges of grandparents raising grandchildren: Discipline, child education, technology use, and outdated health beliefs. *GrandFamilies: The Contemporary Journal of Research, Practice and Policy, 6*(1), 16–33. https://scholarworks.wmich.edu/grandfamilies/vol6/iss1/6

Campbell, L., Carthron, D. L., Miles, M. S., & Brown, L. (2012). Examining the effectiveness of a case management program for custodial grandparent families. *Nursing Research and Practice, 2012*, 124230. https://doi.org/10.1155/2012/124230

Cantor, J. H., McBain, R. K., Pera, M. F., Bravata, D. M., & Whaley, C. M. (2021). Who is (and is not) receiving telemedicine care during the COVID-19 pandemic. *American Journal of Preventive Medicine, 61*(3), 434–438. https://doi.org/10.1016/j.amepre.2021.01.030

Charalambides, A. (n.d.). *Promoting digital literacy and active ageing for senior citizens: The GRANKIT project—grandparents and grandchildren keep in touch*. Emphasys Centre: Centre for Education, ICT Training and Research. https://conference.pixel-online.net/ICT4LL/files/ict4ll/ed0008/FP/1952-SLA1219-FP-ICT4LL8.pdf

Chen, F., Mair, C. A., Bao, L., & Yang, Y. C. (2015). Race/ethnic differentials in the health consequences of caring for grandchildren for grandparents. *Journals of Gerontology, Series B, 70*(5), 793–803. https://doi.org/10.1093/geronb/gbu160

Comer, J. S., & Myers, K. (2016). Future directions in the use of telemental health to improve the accessibility and quality of children's mental health services.

Challenges of Grandchildren Raised by Grandparents During COVID-19 ▪ **103**

Journal of Child and Adolescent Psychopharmacology, 26(3), 296–300. https://doi
.org/10.1089/cap.2015.0079

Creswell, J. W. (2014). *A concise introduction to mixed methods research* (1st ed.). SAGE.

Cross, S. L., & Day, A. G. (2008). American Indian grand families: Eight adolescent and grandparent dyads share perceptions on various aspects of the kinship care relationship. *Journal of Ethnic & Cultural Diversity in Social Work, 17*(1), 82–100. https://eric.ed.gov/?id=EJ898579

Dolbin-MacNab, M. L., Jeanblanc, A. B., Musil, C. M., Infurna, F. J., & Smith, G. C. (2022). Supporting grandchildren's remote instruction during COVID-19: Experiences of custodial grandmothers. *Psychology in the Schools, 60*(5), 1560–1580. https://doi.org/10.1002/pits.22714

Federal Communications Commission. (2001). *Inquiry concerning deployment of advanced telecommunications capability to all Americans in a reasonable and timely fashion* (16 FCC Rcd 15515 (21)). https://www.fcc.gov/document/inquiry-concerning-deployment-advanced-telecommunications-capability-3

Felitti, V. J., Anda, R. F., & Nordenberg, D., Williamson, D. F., Spitz, A. M., Edwards, V., Koss, M. P., & Marks, J. S. (1998). Relationship of childhood abuse and household dysfunction to many of the leading causes of death in adults: The adverse childhood experiences (ACE) study. *American Journal of Preventive Medicine, 14*(4), 245–258. https://doi.org/10.1016/S0749-3797(98)00017-8

Firth, J., Torous, J., Nicholas, J., Carney, R., Pratap, A., Rosenbaum, S., & Sarris, J. (2017). The efficacy of smartphone-based mental health interventions for depressive symptoms: A meta-analysis of randomized controlled trials. *World Psychiatry, 16*(3), 287–298. https://doi.org//10.1002/wps.20472

Fruhauf, C. A., Mendoza, A. N., Bishop, P., Engel, G., & Hetchler, S. (2020). Utilizing a community-university partnership to meet grandfamilies' needs: Development and evaluation of a grandchildren-mentoring program. *GrandFamilies: The Contemporary Journal of Research, 6*(1), 34–46. https://scholarworks.wmich.edu/grandfamilies/vol6/iss1/7

Gamoran, A. (2001). American schooling and educational inequality: A forecast for the 21st century. *Sociology of Education, 74*, 135–153. https://doi.org/10.2307/2673258

Generations United. (2020). *Facing a pandemic: Grandfamilies living together during COVID-19 and thriving beyond.* State of Grandfamilies 2020. https://www.gu.org/app/uploads/2020/10/2020-Grandfamilies-Report-Web.pdf

Generations United. (2022). *Grandfamilies and kinship families: Strengths and challenges fact sheet.* https://www.gu.org/app/uploads/2022/10/General-Grandfamilies-Fact-Sheet-2022-FINAL-UPDATE.pdf

Gloff, N. E., LeNoue, S. R., Novins, D. K., & Myers, K. (2015). Telemental health for children and adolescents. *International Review of Psychiatry, 27*(6), 513–524. https://doi.org/10.3109/09540261.2015.1086322

Goldschmidt, K. (2020). The COVID-19 pandemic: Technology use to support the wellbeing of children. *Journal of Pediatric Nursing, 53*, 88–90. https://doi.org/10.1016/j.pedn.2020.04.013

Goldstein, D., Popescu, A., & Hannah-Jones, N. (2020, April 6). As school moves online, many students stay logged out. *The New York Times.* https://www.nytimes.com/2020/04/06/us/coronavirus-schools-attendance-absent.html

Goodman, C. C., Potts, M., Pasztor, E. M., & Scorzo, D. (2004). Grandmothers as kinship caregivers: Private arrangements compared to public child welfare oversight. *Children and Youth Services Review, 26*(3), 287–305. https://doi.org/10.1016/j.childyouth.2004.01.002

Grandfacts: State Fact Sheets for Grandfamilies: South Carolina. (2021). Grandfactsheets.org. https://www.grandfamilies.org/Portals/0/State%20Fact%20Sheets/South%20Carolina%20GrandFacts%20State%20Fact%20Sheet%202021%20Update.pdf

Hamilton, L. S., Grant, D., Kaufman, J. H., Diliberti, M., Schwartz, H. L., Hunter, G. P., Setodji, C. M., & Young, C. J. (2020). *COVID-19 and the state of K–12 schools: Results and technical documentation from the Spring 2020 American Educator Panels COVID-19 surveys.* RAND Corporation. https://www.rand.org/pubs/research_reports/RRA168-1.html

Harris, D. N., Liu, L., Oliver, D., Balfe, C., Slaughter, S., & Mattei, N. (2020, July 13). *How America's schools responded to the COVID crisis.* National Center for Research on Education Access and Choice; Education Research Alliance for New Orleans. https://www.edworkingpapers.com/sites/default/files/COVID%20Tech%20Report%20Merged%20Complete%20Final%20Working.pdf

Hayslip, B., Jr., & Kaminski, P. L. (2005). Grandparents raising their grandchildren: A review of the literature and suggestions for practice. *The Gerontologist, 45*(2), 262–269. https://doi.org/10.1093/geront/45.2.262

Hayslip, B., Jr., Shore, R. J., Henderson, C. E., & Lambert, P. L. (1998). Custodial grandparenting and the impact of grandchildren with problems on role satisfaction and role meaning. *The Journals of Gerontology, Series B, 53*(3), S164–S173. https://doi.org/10.1093/geronb/53B.3.S164

Horrigan, J. B. (2010, March). *Broadband adoption and use in America: Results from an FCC survey.* Broadband.Gov National Broadband Plan; Federal Communications Commission. https://transition.fcc.gov/DiversityFAC/032410/consumer-survey-horrigan.pdf

Imran, N., Zeshan, M., & Pervaiz, Z. (2020). Mental health considerations for children & adolescents in COVID-19 pandemic. *Pakistan Journal of Medical Sciences, 36*(COVID19-S4), S67–S72. https://doi.org/10.12669/pjms.36.COVID19-S4.2759

Ingersoll-Dayton, B., Tangchonlatip, K., & Punpuing, S. (2020). A confluence of worries: Grandparents in skipped-generation households in Thailand. *Journal of Family Issues, 41*(2), 135–157. https://doi.org/10.1177/0192513X19868836

Institute of Education Sciences. (n.d.). *School responses to COVID-19.* U.S. Department of Education. https://ies.ed.gov/schoolsurvey/

Jetty, A., Moore, M. A., Coffman, M., Petterson, S., & Bazemore, A. (2018). Rural family physicians are twice as likely to use telehealth as urban family physicians. *Telemedicine and e-Health, 24*(4), 268–276. https://doi.org/10.1089/tmj.2017.0161

Kruger, L. G., & Gilroy, A. A. (2019, October 25). *Broadband internet access and the digital divide: Federal assistance programs.* Congressional Research Service. https://sgp.fas.org/crs/misc/RL30719.pdf

Kuhfeld, M., Soland, J., Tarasawa, B., Johnson, A., Ruzek, E., & Liu, J. (2020). Projecting the potential impact of COVID-19 school closures on academic achievement. *Educational Researcher, 49*(8), 549–565. https://doi.org/10.3102/0013189X20965918

Lee, Y., & Blitz, L. (2022). 'Kufunika kwa mtundu/fuko' (Family circle): Understanding experiences of grandparents raising grandchildren in Malawi. *International Social Work, 65*(4), 773–786. https://doi.org/10.1177/0020872820959360

Lieberman, M. (2020, June 29). A third of K–12 students aren't adequately connected for remote learning, report says. *Education Week.* https://www.edweek.org/technology/a-third-of-k-12-students-arent-adequately-connected-for-remote-learning-report-says/2020/06

Lin, C.-H. (2018). The relationships between child well-being, caregiving stress, and social engagement among informal and formal kinship care families. *Children and Youth Services Review, 93*, 203–216. https://doi.org/10.1016/j.childyouth.2018.07.016

Mossberger, K., Tolbert, C. J., & Anderson, C. (2017). The mobile Internet and digital citizenship in African-American and Latino communities. *Information, Communication, & Society, 20*(10), 1587–1606. https://doi.org/10.1080/1369118X.2016.1243142

Nadorff, D. K., Scott, R., & Griffin, R. (2021). Custodial grandchildren and foster children: A school performance comparison. *Children and Youth Services Review, 131*, 106253. https://doi.org/10.1016/j.childyouth.2021.106253

National Alliance on Mental Illness. (n.d.). *Mental health in schools: Where we stand.* Retrieved May 14, 2022, from https://www.nami.org/Advocacy/Policy-Priorities/Improving-Health/Mental-Health-in-Schools

Nelson, E. L., Cain, S., & Sharp, S. (2017). Considerations for conducting telemental health with children and adolescents. *Child and Adolescent Psychiatric Clinics of North America, 26*(1), 77–91. https://doi.org/10.1016/j.chc.2016.07.008

Pelt, P. (2001). Grandparents raising grandchildren: A school nurse perspective. *Reflections, 7*, 98–104.

Peterson, T. L., Scott, C. B., Ombayo, B., Davis, T., & Sullivan, D. (2019). Biggest concerns of school personnel about students raised by grandparents. *Children and Youth Services Review, 102*, 201–209. https://doi.org/10.1016/j.childyouth.2019.05.004

Pilkauskas, N. V., & Dunifon, R. E. (2016). Understanding grandfamilies: Characteristics of grandparents, nonresident parents, and children. *Journal of Marriage and Family, 78*(3), 623–633. https://doi.org/10.1111/jomf.12291

Ralston, A. L., Andrews, A. R., III, & Hope, D. A. (2019). Fulfilling the promise of mental health technology to reduce public health disparities: Review and research agenda. *Clinical Psychology: Science and Practice, 21*(1), e12277. https://doi.org/10.1111/cpsp.12277

Rider, E. A., Ansari, E., Varrin, P. H., & Sparrow, J. (2021). Mental health and wellbeing of children and adolescents during the covid-19 pandemic. *BMJ, 374*(1730). https://doi.org/10.1136/bmj.n1730

Simms, D. C., Gibson, K., & O'Donnell, S. (2011). To use or not to use: Clinicians' perceptions of telemental health. *Canadian Psychology /Psychologie canadienne, 52*(1), 41–51. https://doi.org/10.1037/a0022275

Smith, G. C., Hayslip, B., Jr., Hancock, G. R., Strieder, F. H., & Montoro-Rodriguez, J. (2018). A randomized clinical trial of interventions for improving well-being in custodial grandfamilies. *Journal of Family Psychology, 32*(6), 816–827. https://doi.org/10.1037/fam0000457

Smith, G. C., Hayslip, B., Jr., & Webster, B. A. (2019). Psychological difficulties among custodial grandchildren. *Children and Youth Services Review, 104,* 104390. https://doi.org/10.1016/j.childyouth.2019.104390

Smith, L. T. (2021). *Decolonizing methodologies: Research and indigenous peoples.* Bloomsbury.

Smithgall, C., Mason, S., Michels, L., LiCalsi, C., & Goerge, R. (2009). Intergenerational and interconnected: Mental health and well-being in grandparent caregiver families. *Families in Society, 90*(2), 167–175. https://doi.org/10.1606/1044-3894.3869

Sprang, G., Choi, M., Eslinger, J. G., & Whitt-Woosley, A. L. (2015). The pathway to grandparenting stress: Trauma, relational conflict, and emotional well-being. *Aging & Mental Health, 19*(4), 315–324. https://doi.org/10.1080/13607863.2014.938606

Stephan, S., Lever, N., Bernstein, L., Edwards, S., & Pruitt, D. (2016). Telemental health in schools. *Journal of Child and Adolescent Psychopharmacology, 26*(3), 266–272. https://doi.org/10.1089/cap.2015.0019

Strand, K., Cutforth, N., Stoeker, R., Marullo, S., & Donohue, P. (2003). *Community-based research and higher education: Principles and practices.* Jossey-Bass.

Strover, S. (2019). Public libraries and 21st century digital equity goals. *Communication Research and Practice, 5*(2), 188–205. https://doi.org/10.1080/22041451.2019.1601487

Supporting Grandparents Raising Grandchildren Act, Pub. L. 115-196 (2018). https://www.congress.gov/115/plaws/publ196/PLAW-115publ196.pdf

The Education Trust. (2020, June 1). *Parents overwhelmingly concerned their children are falling behind during school closures.* https://edtrust.org/ca-ny-parents-overwhelmingly-concerned-their-children-are-falling-behind-during-school-closures/

U.S. Census Bureau. (n.d.). Why we ask questions about . . . Grandparents as caregivers. Retrieved May 6, 2022, from https://www.census.gov/acs/www/about/why-we-ask-each-question/grandparents/

U.S. Senate Special Committee on Aging. (2018, February 28). *Collins, Casey bill to support grandparents raising grandchildren unanimously passes HELP Committee.* https://www.aging.senate.gov/press-releases/collins-casey-bill-to-support-grandparents-raising-grandchildren-unanimously-passes-help-committee-

Vandivere, S., Yrausquin, A., Allen, T., Malm, K., & McKlindon, A. (2012). *Children in nonparental care: A review of the literature and analysis of data gaps.* U.S. Department of Health and Human Services, Office of the Assistant Secretary for Planning and Evaluation. https://aspe.hhs.gov/reports/children-nonparental-care-review-literature-analysis-data-gaps-0

Walters, A. (2020). Inequities in access to education: Lessons from the COVID-19 pandemic. *The Brown University Child and Adolescent Behavior Letter, 36*(8), 8. https://doi.org/10.1002/cbl.30483

World Health Organization. (2020a). *Mental health and psychosocial considerations during the COVID-19 outbreak.* https://www.who.int/docs/default-source/coronaviruse/mental-health-considerations.pdf

World Health Organization. (2020b, March 30). *Coronavirus disease 2019 (COVID-19) situation report—70.* https://www.who.int/docs/default-source/coronaviruse/situation-reports/20200330-sitrep-70-covid-19.pdf

Wright, J. H., & Caudill, R. (2020). Remote treatment delivery in response to the COVID-19 pandemic. *Psychotherapy and Psychosomatics, 89*(3), 130–132. https://doi.org/10.1159/000507376

Xu, Y., Wang, Y., McCarthy, L. P., Harrison, T., & Doherty, H. (2022). Mental/behavioural health and educational outcomes of grandchildren raised by custodial grandparents: A mixed methods systematic review. *Health and Social Care in the Community, 30*(6), 2096–2127. https://doi.org/10.1111/hsc.13876

Xu, Y., Wu, Q., Levkoff, S. E., & Jedwab, M. (2020). Material hardship and parenting stress among grandparent kinship providers during the COVID-19 pandemic: The mediating role of grandparents' mental health. *Child Abuse & Neglect, 110*(2), 104700. https://doi.org/10.1016/j.chiabu.2020.104700

SECTION II

PERSPECTIVES ON LEARNING

CHAPTER 6

STUDY BUDDY

An Online Individualized Tutoring Program for Racialized, Indigenous, and Immigrant Students

Wendy Cukier
Ted Rogers School of Management

Bincy Wilson
Ted Rogers School of Management

Donna Fradley
Ted Rogers School of Management

Aaron Smajda
Toronto Metropolitan University
(Formerly Ryerson University)

Stefan Karajovic
Ted Rogers School of Management

School–University–Community Research in a (Post) COVID-19 World, pages 111–134
Copyright © 2023 by Information Age Publishing
www.infoagepub.com
All rights of reproduction in any form reserved.

ABSTRACT

The COVID-19 crisis has affected all segments of Canadian society with the impacts being particularly severe for equity-deserving groups. Families were challenged by the convergence of multiple stresses, specifically with schools being closed. When K–12 education was disrupted, the uneven approaches to supporting remote students caused opportunity gaps among students and increased the burden on families. Families from equity-deserving communities were concerned about their children falling behind in learning outcomes. Using a combination of the social innovation theory and the ecological model, the Diversity Institute developed a project to address these challenges by bringing different stakeholders (e.g., families, communities, individual students, community services and education institutions, etc.) together with one solution—the Study Buddy program. This chapter presents a case study of this innovative program which supported students from equity-deserving groups both during and after the pandemic. The program provides a platform to support parents by connecting them to teacher candidates from universities across Ontario who provide free online individualized tutoring services to their children. In so doing, the program helps teacher candidates gain first-hand tutoring experience while also counting towards their practicum hours. Since launching in May 2020, the program has enrolled 684 students and serviced 451 families with the help of 331 tutors who have delivered over 12,800+ individualized tutoring sessions across K–12 teachable subjects. The case study findings present evidence of the impacts the program has had on participating students and their families. Namely, the findings suggest that targeted efforts to address systemic challenges in education faced by equity-deserving communities have resulted in increased well-being of these children and their families.

The COVID-19 pandemic has had a significant impact on all segments of the Canadian society (Statistics Canada, 2022; Turcotte & Hango, 2020) with impacts being particularly severe for equity-deserving groups[1] in terms of financial insecurity, unemployment, education, and health related outcomes among others (Alello, 2020; Burt, 2020; Mo et al., 2021; Statistics Canada, 2022). Students from equity-deserving groups faced the greatest challenges as the pandemic contributed to widening inequities in education, mental health, and well-being (Alello, 2020; Ng & Badets, 2020). However, the transition of tutor training programs into the digital space due to restrictions presented an opportunity to address the gap in learning outcomes and well-being for students from equity-deserving communities (Gallagher-Mackay et al., 2022), while also helping the teacher candidates fulfill their mandatory practicum hours to graduate. This book chapter attempts to understand how individualized tutoring programs, such as Study Buddy, addressed the well-being of equity-deserving children and families amidst the educational disruption caused by the COVID-19 pandemic.

The purpose of our research was to uncover how a financially accessible, online tutoring program targeting children from equity-seeking groups can help improve academic and life outcomes, particularly during periods of online study (as was seen during the COVID-19 pandemic). As such, the following two central research questions guided this study:

1. To what extent is our program serving the intended participants and what are their (a) needs around tutoring and (b) expectations of the Study Buddy program?
2. What are parents' perceptions of the program and how might it be improved for future cohorts?

Before outlining our methodology and presenting our findings, we begin by overviewing the relevant literature, presenting an original theoretical framework, and describing the Study Buddy program as well as the broader context within which it operates. We conclude the chapter with a discussion that both answers our research questions and outlines the implications of this study for ongoing program development and future research.

GAPS IN EDUCATIONAL OUTCOMES FOR EQUITY-DESERVING GROUPS: HOW ONLINE TUTORING PROGRAMS CAN HELP

The COVID-19 pandemic brought to light multiple longstanding structural inequalities present in Canadian society, particularly within our education system. Research shows that students from equity-deserving communities face a number of systemic barriers in schools that result in negative academic and long-term economic outcomes (Cukier, Middleton, et al., 2021). Black community members as well as parents and students from other equity-deserving groups have long protested the detrimental impacts of racism and structural inequalities that have contributed to a crisis within the education system (James, 2017). A study investigating the experiences of Black people in the Greater Toronto Area found that about half of Black students felt that being Black presented them with challenges that were not faced by other students (Environics Institute et al., 2017). Student achievement data collected by the Toronto District School Board (TDSB), the largest and most diverse school board in Canada,[2] serves as a useful reference. The board's data showed persistent gaps in achievement, as high as 30%, between populations on the basis of race and socioeconomic status with students of Latin American, Middle Eastern, Black, and Indigenous backgrounds among the populations most negatively impacted by the achievement gap (Shah, 2018). According to TDSB data, Black students make up about 12% of high school students but they were less likely to pursue post-secondary studies than their non-Black and non-racialized peers.

A recent investigation into the Peel District School Board (PDSB), Canada's second largest school board, revealed similar inequities leading to poorer educational outcomes for Black children (Chadha et al., 2020). Further research showed that teachers generally have lower expectations of Black students (compared to Asian or White students) and tend to discipline Black students more harshly than their non-Black peers. For example, 42% of Black students are suspended at least once during their schooling compared to 18% of White students. Furthermore, 48% of all expulsions in TDSB schools in 2017 were of Black students, compared to just 12% levied against White students (James & Turner, 2017). Additionally, teachers often negatively stereotype Black students, preemptively assuming they will underperform in school (James & Turner, 2017; Shizha et al., 2020). As such, systemic barriers often deny Black youth access to higher education and employment in specific fields, forcing them into industries with "limited and narrowly defined opportunities" (Briggs, 2019, p. 12).

Additionally, there is a lack of positive Black influence in the curriculum, with few Black teachers and role models. All of these factors lead to feelings of isolation and marginalization for Black students in the public education system (James & Turner, 2015). Black students are also twice as likely to come from low-income households as non-Black students. This often leads Black students to feel as if they do not belong in school (DasGupta et al., 2020). Another TDSB study (James & Turner, 2017) found that just 69% of Black students graduated high school, compared to 84% of White students and 87% of other racialized students. The study also found that Black students have a dropout rate of 20% which is more than double the rate of other racialized students (9%).

Many scholars have drawn attention to the fact that achievement gaps are affected by opportunity gaps which speak to the uneven distribution of resources and learning opportunities for students from equity-deserving groups (Downey & Condron, 2016; Gamoran & Long, 2007; Gorski, 2017). For example, students from equity-deserving communities tend to be over-represented in lower-level academic streams which, research shows, is disadvantageous to the educational and life trajectories of such students. The longstanding practice of streaming students from equity-deserving groups into non-academic programs, more punitive disciplinary practices towards Black students, the absence of Indigenous, Black, and other racialized people in class materials and curricula, preconceived negative stereotypes, and lower expectations for racialized students by teachers constitute systemic barriers within the education system (James & Turner, 2017; Shizha et al., 2020).

Youth who are not in education, employment, or training (NEET) run the risk of becoming excluded from society as participation in society is tied to one's employment status, and racialized youth are overrepresented in this group (Government of Canada, 2017). Census data from 2006 to 2016 revealed intersectional effects between race and gender in postsecondary attainment outcomes. For instance, Black men were nearly twice as likely as other young men to be NEET in 2016. This gap decreased but remained significant after socioeconomic factors were considered. Conversely, there was no difference between young Black women and other young women, after factoring in family and socioeconomic characteristics (Turcotte, 2022).

When it comes to newcomer youth in Canada, research shows that this group faces a number of systemic barriers in school. Some of the most common barriers faced by newcomer youth include (a) underfunded settlement services, (b) lack of diversity in the curriculum, and (c) a lack of adequate English-language instruction (Nichols et al., 2020). A recent study of Somali youth in Ottawa identified five common concerns: (a) barriers to accessing post-secondary education, (b) barriers to accessing job placements and training programs, (c) barriers to securing employment, (d) a need for a Somali-focused employment resource center, and (e) a need for Somali youth mentors (van de Sande et al., 2019). Insufficient family resources (both financial and social) are considered a key barrier to pursuing higher education among Filipino immigrant youth, for example, and students and parents feel underserved by overwhelmingly White institutions (Kelly, 2014).

One of the last frontiers for addressing the student achievement gap in schools is to provide resources and supports for the home environment so that racialized and newcomer families can adopt a positive posture towards education for their children. This said, little systematic research exists on the coverage, organization, and design of tutoring programs in Canada, especially those programs and initiatives focused on meeting the needs of equity-deserving students. Likewise there is no common forum or community of stakeholders in place to support the improvement and expansion of tutoring initiatives in Canada (Cukier, 2022). Research suggests that tutoring can be effective at bridging these learning gaps (Nickow et al., 2020). In fact, not only does tutoring improve educational outcomes more quickly and effectively than most other interventions, it also offers emotional benefits to both the students and families (Carlana & La Ferrara, 2021).

In targeting students from racialized, newcomer, and low socioeconomic backgrounds, community-based tutoring programs can address gaps in access to education by connecting these students with teacher candidates. A program that offers a free, individualized tutoring platform focused on the academic curriculum and the individual needs of the students provides critical support to (a) K–12 students with high-quality, individualized, academic instruction and (b) parents from equity-deserving communities who are struggling to balance the responsibilities of work with ongoing disruptions to their children's learning. Research demonstrates that individualized tutoring attention can help students strengthen their comprehension of subject matter, boost confidence, and build on important learning skills (Zhang et al., 2021).

As a consequence of COVID-19, and the resulting school closures around the world, tutoring programs began to emerge as an important mechanism for addressing the widening gaps in educational outcomes associated with the pandemic (Nickow et al., 2020). A meta-analysis reviewing over 100 tutoring programs found that tutoring had significant positive impacts on learning outcomes for students with the results holding true across different programs. Tutoring has been identified as one of the most impactful tools available for improving student learning and there is consistent evidence that one-on-one or one-on-three tutoring can be highly beneficial for students (Nickow et al., 2020; Oreopoulos et al., 2017). A 2016 study of Black middle school students in the United States found that tutoring programs resulted in significant improvements in academic grades, perceived educational commitment and attainment, and perceived support from the school for the student. Ultimately, tutoring was found to help these students smoothly transition to high school (Somers et al., 2016).

A number of studies were conducted during the COVID-19 pandemic specifically. One study of middle school students found that online tutoring during the pandemic significantly improved students' academic performance, socio-emotional skills, aspirations, and psychological well-being. The effects were strongest for students from low-income households and for newcomers (Carlana & La Ferrara, 2021). Online tutoring programs are, importantly, a low-cost solution as well, overcoming supply restraints by allowing students to connect to tutors from anywhere in the country. A single tutor can meet with multiple students without the need for facilities, transportation, or other costs associated with one-on-one meetings (Kraft et al., 2022).

Access to traditional tutoring programs tends to be unequally distributed, often benefiting only the wealthy and leaving behind students from equity-deserving communities (Mahnken, 2020). In addition, prior studies on digital tutoring indicated that students from equity-deserving populations face a number of systemic barriers that often prevent their participation in these sessions (Chi et al., 2001; Goslee & Conte, 1998; Merril et al., 1992; UNESCO, n.d.). The digital divide also limits the reach of virtual tutoring programs. A recent study (Cukier, Middleton, et al., 2021) found that students living in low-income neighborhoods in Toronto, which usually have highly racialized populations, have lower rates of access to high-speed internet and devices for connecting to the internet. This makes it more difficult for these students to connect to online resources such as tutoring programs.

THE STUDY BUDDY PROGRAM

In March 2020, with the onset of COVID-19, the Diversity Institute put together a program, funded by the Future Skills Centre, which would help lighten the burden on equity-deserving families hit hardest by the pandemic, while also providing the next generation of teachers with an opportunity to virtually enter the homes of these families (Cukier, 2022). The Study Buddy program paired teacher candidates with K–12 students across Ontario (Greater Toronto Area, Kingston, and Sudbury) in one-on-one, online, subject-specific, free tutoring sessions. In exchange, teacher candidates would receive hours toward their practicum placements at their respective universities, addressing the issue of teacher candidates not being able to enter classrooms to complete their practicum requirements. As such, participation in the Study Buddy program served as a work-integrated learning (WIL) opportunity. WIL offers students the opportunity to put their theoretical skills to use in a real-world workplace setting. WIL has been framed as a solution to the present "skills mismatch" that often exists between students and employers and is seen as a way to smooth university graduates' transition into the labor market (Cukier et al., 2018).

We piloted the program during the initial stages of the pandemic lockdown as an emergency response to the educational challenges that equity-deserving groups were facing. Funded largely through existing programming by the Diversity Institute and supported by volunteers, this innovative program provided a new approach to a seemingly intractable problem. Applying an ecological model approach, the Diversity Institute worked with universities, communities, and schools to develop the program and address the gaps in education.

The program relied heavily on community partners identifying equity-deserving families who would benefit most from the services offered. We recruited these families through partner community organizations such as the Lifelong Leadership Institute and the Jean Augustine Center for Young Women's Empowerment. To ensure the Study Buddy program was supporting racialized and newcomer families, prospective participants completed an intake survey. The students were accepted based on tutor availability and subject matching. Students who participated in the program could expect up to three hours per week of free tutoring with subject-specific support from Ontario teacher candidates. After having received tutoring support for several months, families were given a satisfaction survey to complete that included questions on their child's overall improvements in anxiety, well-being, and confidence. Families were also given the opportunity to provide suggestions on how to improve the program.

We pitched the program as an opportunity for teacher candidates to complete their practicum requirements during a time of school closures, as well as being an opportunity to provide much needed individualized support to equity-deserving groups. We recruited teacher candidates through partnerships with Laurentian University, Nipissing University, Queen's University, Ontario Tech University, the University of Toronto, and Lakehead University; some non-practicum tutors came from Toronto Metropolitan University. Being teacher candidates, they were already subject matter experts, having completed (or were concurrently completing) a bachelor's degree in a teachable area. While with Study Buddy, the majority were also completing courses with their respective faculties of education in pedagogical strategies, ministry guidelines, and curricular expectations. As part of tutor onboarding, all teacher candidates participated in an Anti-Black racism workshop prepared by the Diversity Institute. To receive hours toward their practicum placements, we required the teacher candidates to submit detailed, bi-monthly reports on their activities, which were audited to ensure compliance.

Given the widely varying schedules of teacher candidates and families, our solution to scheduling sessions was to seek out an already existing and successful tutoring platform. Our networking and market research identified a university tutor scheduling platform; they offered to host the program at no cost. We matched tutors and students according to student subject needs and tutor availability. The meetings occurred in an interactive "whiteboard space" with video and audio functionality. However, with the growth of the program, we migrated in January 2021 to a paid SAAS (software as a service) tutoring business management platform. At the time of scheduling, an email was sent to the tutor and parent with a link to the lesson space where the tutor and student would meet. During sessions, tutors and students interacted through video, audio, screen sharing, and an interactive whiteboard. Once a tutor and student met for the first session, they could both decide if they would like to continue working together. Tutors then communicated directly with parents to schedule future tutoring sessions. Exact figures on students, tutors, sessions, and hours are provided in Table 6.1.

TABLE 6.1 Study Buddy Program Highlights	
	Total Numbers
Total Number of Students	684
Total Number of Families	451
Total Number of Tutors	331
Total Number of Sessions	12,800+
Total Number of Hours	8,600+

Note: Numbers are accurate as of May 2022.

EVALUATION FRAMEWORK

In designing the criteria for evaluating the Study Buddy program, we utilized the Universal Evaluation Toolkit for Academic Tutoring Programs developed by Proulx and colleagues (2022). This approach seeks to help organizations answer the following question about their tutoring programs:

1. Are we reaching the most vulnerable children, youth, and families?
2. What difference are we making?
3. What is working well?
4. How can we improve?

This method begins by developing a logic model to describe the tutoring program, followed by formulation of an evaluation plan, and evidence gathering. Finally, the findings are communicated and any lessons learned are shared. A logic model provides a visual overview of the tutoring program, highlighting inputs, tutoring activities, and expected outcomes. Importantly, it also provides a common understanding of how the program creates change. In our case, the focus was on the expansion of tutoring programs to children from equity-deserving groups who may not otherwise have been able to afford access to such programs. The toolkit suggested that both student outcomes and process outcomes should be examined. However, due to the longitudinal nature of many academic outcomes, this study only focused on process outcomes, gauging such things as attendance and satisfaction with the program. A detailed overview of the methodology follows in the next section.

METHODS

In an effort to measure the effectiveness of the Study Buddy program and answer the research questions posed earlier, our study employed two primary methods of data collection: a pre-program registration questionnaire and a post-program satisfaction survey. We collected data using these two methods at different time points from four program cohorts between June of 2020 and December of 2021. The registration questionnaire, which was administered to parents prior to the start of the program using Qualtrics, consisted of 44 closed-ended questions aimed at better understanding participants and their motivations for enrolling in the Study Buddy program. Specifically, the questionnaire asked respondents to report on student and family demographics (e.g., age, gender, ethnicity, immigration status, education, income, place of residence, etc.) as well as their access to technology, tutoring needs, and prior experiences with the program.

120 ▪ W. CUKIER et al.

We then sent a satisfaction survey, together with a letter of invitation and consent form, to the parents of participating students via email after the completion of the program. The survey comprised 21 closed-ended questions which, in addition to gathering data on student and family demographics and both their comfort levels with and access to technology, assessed respondents' overall satisfaction with the program—including both child and parental experiences with their assigned tutors and the tutoring platform used—by asking them to rate their level of agreement to several statements about the program on a 5-point Likert scale. A further seven open-ended survey questions asked parents to elaborate on some of their responses and sought their insights for ongoing program improvement.

We subsequently subjected the quantitative data, collected via both the registration questionnaires and satisfaction surveys across four program cohorts, to standard descriptive and bivariate analyses in SPSS. Meanwhile, we used an inductive thematic approach to qualitative content analysis (Gioia et al., 2013; Thomas, 2006) to analyze parents' qualitative survey comments. Among other steps, this entailed conducting multiple close readings of the text, generating initial codes, coding the raw data, searching for themes, and both refining and naming key themes. We used checks of interrater reliability in an effort to assess the trustworthiness of the data analysis (Lincoln & Guba, 1985).

We could not conduct a pre- and post-test analysis of the data gathered because a unique code was not generated to identify respondents on the registration questionnaire or the satisfaction survey. Thus, rather than capturing change at an individual level, our findings present the average participant experience. Additionally, certain demographic data (e.g., level of education and income) were not uniformly collected across cohorts at the time of registration, preventing analysis of some of the demographic data gathered and, thus, are not reported here. Further, any missing cases in Likert scale variables have been excluded from the analysis with only the valid percentage values reported herein.

REGISTRATION QUESTIONNAIRE AND SATISFACTION SURVEY FINDINGS

Parent Registration Questionnaire Findings

A total of 451 parents across four cohorts completed the registration questionnaire. The registration data revealed that, during the study period, 59% of parents had enrolled one child ($n = 266$) in the program while 30% of parents had enrolled two children ($n = 137$), and a further (11%) had enrolled three children ($n = 48$) for a total of 684 children. Roughly 68% of parents (n = 308) indicated that they were registering their child/children in the program for the first time while the remaining 32% (n = 143) reported having enrolled their child/children sometime in the past. The majority (73%) of parents reported English as being the primary language that was spoken at home. The remaining 27% reported a wide range (n = 16) of other languages spoken in the household (e.g., French, Russian, Mandarin, Arabic, Tamil, etc.).

Of the 684 children that were serviced by the program, 56% were girls (n = 380), 44% (n = 302) were boys, and 0.3% (n = 2) did not specify their gender. The vast majority of children were identified by their parents (88%, n = 395) as being racialized. A further 103 were identified as belonging to another equity-deserving group. Specifically, 15% (n = 72) had immigrated to Canada within the last five years, 5% (n = 23) had a disability, 1% (n = 5) were Indigenous, and another 1% (n = 3) identified as belonging to the 2SLGBTQ+ community. Importantly, some families identified their children as belonging to more than one equity-deserving group.

Given that the four cohorts under study were participating in the program during the height of the COVID-19 pandemic, it is perhaps unsurprising that the majority of children (62%) were simultaneously enrolled in either online or blended learning models at their respective schools. Irrespective of whether participating children attended school in person or virtually, all families reported having access to both computers and the internet at home. Most children were enrolled at the secondary school (high school) level (60%), with 25% at the elementary school level and 15% at the middle school level. A little over half of all high schoolers reported seeking tutoring support in STEM subjects (i.e., math, science, computer science). Other areas of tutoring support at this level included both English language and French, albeit to a lesser extent. The majority of elementary school-aged children sought general tutoring support across a range of curricular subject areas. At the middle school level, meanwhile, children primarily sought tutoring support in math and science which was followed by English, social studies, and French.

Parent Satisfaction Survey Findings

A total of 141 parents completed the post-program satisfaction survey. When asked to rate the effects of the program experience on their child's learning (Figure 6.1), all parents either agreed or strongly agreed with all 11 response options provided. Specifically, 93% said that, as a result of participating, their children became more comfortable with online learning, 91% indicated that their child grew more confident in their schoolwork, while another 90% reported their children having learned important skills. Parents

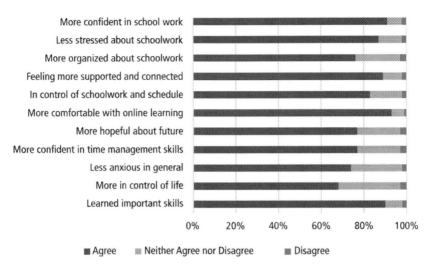

Figure 6.1 Impact of Study Buddy on student learning.

also agreed that the program had a positive effect on their child's sense of connectedness to school while helping to both reduce their stress around schoolwork and increase their ability to manage their workload and schedule.

Several parents revealed that their children's confidence rose following sessions with Study Buddy tutors, which was attributable to the tutors being able to devote one-on-one attention to the child versus the group classes they were a part of in school. As one parent said,

> I see a complete 180 degree positive change in my daughter's attitude towards her studies and life since being homeschooled. Her voice was very quiet when she started out with her tutor last month. I noticed this month she is more confident as she speaks and asks questions of her tutor.

And this parent reported:

> My son has had only one session. He was not confident at the beginning, he didn't want support; however, after the session, he told me that his tutor explained even better than the teacher, and that he is thankful to me to get him help that makes him feel comfortable and not ashamed of not knowing a subject very well.

When asked to rate their child's overall experience with the Study Buddy program (Table 6.2), an overwhelming majority of the families agreed that their child's experience was useful, helpful, and enjoyable for them, and met their needs. With respect to providing students the opportunity

Study Buddy · **123**

TABLE 6.2 Parent Perception of Student Experience With the Study Buddy Program

	Agree	Neither Agree nor Disagree	Disagree
Provided them with opportunity to gain experience in problem-solving and decision-making skills	85	13	2
Provided them with opportunity to gain experience in technology skills	79	16	5
Provided them with opportunity to gain experience in teaching and learning skills	76	19	5
Provided them with opportunity to gain experience in interpersonal skills	82	14	4
Was stressful for them	9	15	76
Provided them with ongoing supports	84	14	2
Was useful for them	94	5	1
Provided them with appropriate training	89	11	0
Provided them with new skills	85	13	2
Was difficult	9	18	73
Met their needs	91	5	4
Was helpful	94	4	2
Was enjoyable	92	6	2

to gain experience in various skills, most parents agreed that the program resulted in an increase in new skills, problem-solving and decision-making skills, interpersonal skills, and provided the children appropriate training, and ongoing support to handle the educational disruption caused by the pandemic. Similarly, more than two-thirds of the families agreed that the program resulted in an increase in teaching and learning skills, and technology skills in their children. Parents widely agreed that the program was neither stressful nor difficult for their child.

When asked to rate their own experiences with the Study Buddy program (Table 6.3), an overwhelming majority of parents revealed that the program was helpful and met their needs. Most of the parents credited the program with reducing their personal stress, anxiety, and overall family stress. Ultimately, they reported that the program made them feel more hopeful about the future.

Additionally, parents' qualitative comments revealed a number of key benefits. A recurring theme among parents was gratitude for having access to tutors for their children that they would not otherwise be able to afford. Moreover, a number of parents commented on how having access to a tutor

124 ▪ W. CUKIER et al.

TABLE 6.3	Parent Experiences With the Study Buddy Program		
	Agree	Neither Agree nor Disagree	Disagree
Was stressful	4	14	82
Was difficult	4	12	84
Met the needs of our family	90	6	4
Made me feel more hopeful about the future	86	12	2
Reduced overall family stress	81	14	5
Reduced my stress	84	12	4
Reduced my anxiety	80	16	4
Was helpful	94	4	2

enabled them to get other work done (either employment or house work and childcare). One parent wrote,

> The experience for me and my husband was positive. I would not have been able to afford tutoring and this eased the financial stress. It also lightened my work load as far as assisting with homework. This freed me up to get other things completed like cooking and cleaning. Thank you for this opportunity.

Another key benefit noted by parents was how much more engaged their children were with their tutors versus their school teachers during the pandemic. Because Study Buddy sessions were one-on-one, children were able to ask questions and receive tailored instruction. One parent noted,

> We only leveraged the Study Buddy program for one of my two children, and only for a specific area—math. I feel that the relationship between my child and tutor is fantastic, and would love to explore more tutoring, more subject areas, and add my younger child (going into Grade 5) to the program if possible. This is a program that my child looked forward to—eager to get to the computer and get started on days tutoring was booked, and was much more engaged in this program than regular school work during the pandemic.

Another parent noted that the participation in the program had helped improve their child's psychological and emotional well-being. As this parent observed,

> The overall experience of the Study Buddy program has been life altering for both my daughter and I. And, I am not talking about the intellectual work, while that saw significant improvement for us too. I am talking about the psychological, emotional, and social gains that I have seen in my daughter.

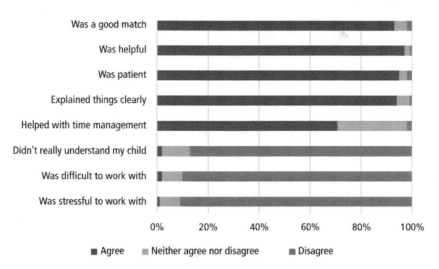

Figure 6.2 Student experiences with their tutors.

When asked to rate their child's overall experience with their tutor (Figure 6.2), the overwhelming majority of responses were positive. Over 93% of participants found that their child's tutor was patient, helpful, and a good match. Similarly, very few parents found that their child had a difficult time working with their tutor, with under 11% of parents reporting any sorts of issues. It was only with respect to helping their child with time management that a larger percentage (27%) of parents were not sure that the tutor was helpful.

Parents' qualitative comments about their children's experiences with their tutor(s) revealed that the hands-on nature of the tutoring sessions tended to elicit enthusiasm for learning from the children. This mother wrote,

> My girls look forward to their time with each tutor. My youngest is in Grade 1 and I don't have to argue to get her on. She willingly goes on each day and does her work. I have seen tremendous growth in both my girls. My eldest is loving math which hasn't happened in a long time. She said that her tutors use so many hands on tools so she is able to visualize what is being taught.

When asked to rate their child's experiences with the Study Buddy program online platform (Table 6.4), the overwhelming majority of parents agreed that the platform was easy to use and conducive to learning. Agreement was slightly lower when asked if the platform contained helpful subject matter (81%) and whether the platform helped students refine technology skills (78%).

126 ▪ W. CUKIER et al.

TABLE 6.4 Student Experiences With the Study Buddy Online Platform			
	Agree	Neither Agree nor Disagree	Disagree
Contained helpful subject matter/content	81	15	4
Was helpful for scheduling appointments with students	87	8	5
Was easy to navigate and find things	84	7	8
Line communication skills	86	11	2
Provided an opportunity to refine technology skills	78	20	2
Provided an opportunity to learn new technology skills	84	15	2
Met my needs overall	93	6	2
Enabled effective tutor/student match	87	7	7
Was easy to use overall	87	8	5
Was easy to learn overall	90	4	6

When asked to rate their own experiences with the Study Buddy program online platform (Table 6.5), parents reported similar experiences to those of their children.

Parents' qualitative comments about the Study Buddy program platform revealed that, although generally easy to use, there were still some minor technical hiccups along the way, but that support was easy to access. As this parent noted,

> We had issues with our microphone a month into our sessions. After some troubleshooting with [name redacted], we figured out, well, [name redacted]

TABLE 6.5 Parent Experiences With the Study Buddy Online Platform			
	Agree	Neither Agree nor Disagree	Disagree
Contained helpful subject matter/content	81	12	7
Was helpful for scheduling appointments with tutor	88	4	8
Was easy to navigate and find things	87	6	8
Line communication skills	78	17	6
Provided an opportunity to refine technology skills	76	18	6
Provided an opportunity to learn new technology skills	81	14	5
Met my needs overall	97	0	8
Enabled effective tutor/student match	85	7	8
Was easy to use overall	91	3	7
Was easy to learn overall	89	3	8

let me know that the Wizedemy platform is more compatible with Chrome, as opposed to Safari. I was using Safari. We're good now.

One parent also noted that using the Study Buddy program platform made her child more prepared for using their school's online platform. She wrote,

I think that having to use the Study Buddy platform helped to reinforce the technology aspects of learning online, which complemented her having to learn online for her regular school class platforms.

A recurring piece of feedback from parents was that the program could use better session availability. Most respondents were cognizant of the fact that tutors were students or full-time workers themselves and that they were providing this service for free. Nonetheless, the lack of sessions available at more convenient times was sometimes an impediment to accessing the program. This parent explained:

My feedback is not something that can necessarily be fixed so I guess it's [*sic*] more of an observation based on our experience ... but one of the things I was often confronted with was lack of consistent availability for sessions from week to week. I say this is something that can't necessarily be fixed because I know the tutors are students themselves and only have a handful of hours to allocate to the program per week AND there are other people vying for their time and also booking so slots fill up fast. That in turn meant there were some weeks one or both of the kids didn't have a session.

An examination of differences in satisfaction based on families' self-identification with various equity-deserving groups (see Table 6.6) revealed some notable findings. Families where children identified as being persons with disabilities (67%) and newcomers to Canada (20%) were more likely to find the experience stressful, compared to those who identified themselves as being racialized (8%) or having another intersectional identity (9%). Similarly, parents who identified themselves as newcomers (20%) were more likely to experience Study Buddy as being difficult compared to those who were racialized (1.4%).

Finally, we also consulted with the teachers to see what their experiences were like with the program, and to determine if any meaningful skill development occurred. The following quotes illustrate some of the skills that the teachers developed through this work-integrated opportunity.

Professionally, it has given me valuable experiences that I will be able to take with me and implement as I am teaching ... I have learned a new platform, I have learned new ways to engage students virtually, I have become a lot more well-versed in the curriculum, and I have developed new skills to differentiate

128 ▪ W. CUKIER et al.

TABLE 6.6 Differences in Satisfaction Based on Identification With Equity-Deserving Groups

Level of Agreement With Each Statement	Racialized Group/ Visible Minority	Newcomer to Canada (arrived within last 5 years)	Persons With Disabilities	Inter- Sectional Experience
Study Buddy experience was stressful for the child	8.0%	20%	67%	9%
For me (parent) the Study Buddy experience was difficult	1.4%	20%	0%	0%

instruction. Not to mention every opportunity to teach and interact with students is beneficial to my teaching career and will only benefit me as an educator.

The Study Buddy program has definitely opened my eyes to the personal and academic struggles my students may face. Often students would tell me that they didn't understand something in class, but the teacher had to move for whatever reason. After you miss one thing, particularly in science, the rest of the lesson becomes unintelligible and students would check out. I want to make sure I teach lessons that are digestible with questions along the way to check understanding. I also truly understand the value of one-on-one help. I want to ensure that I am available to help my students, and may even consider tutoring in the future.

I am more aware of the difficulties that students of color and new immigrants to Canada face in the education system. Through taking both the Deepening the Divide and Anti-Racism workshops as well as my own experience tutoring, I have really come to understand how students' educational experiences differ based on their race and where they are from. This has made me a more aware and conscientious teacher. I will take this knowledge with me and apply it to my future teaching situations with the goal of providing extra support for marginalized students so as to ensure their success in school.

DISCUSSION OF KEY FINDINGS BY RESEARCH QUESTION

Students

After their engagement with the program the students were observed to be more confident, organized, and in control of schoolwork instead of being stressed and anxious. They reported being more supported and connected to school and comfortable with online learning during COVID-19. Their involvement in the program met their needs, provided them appropriate training and important skills such as problem solving, decision-making, experience in technology, teaching and learning, and interpersonal skills. There was an increased confidence in being able to manage time and hopefulness about the future. A vast majority identified the experience in the program as being enjoyable, helpful, and useful. Given the reported increase in mental-health related emergency department visits for youth between January to October 2020 (Leeb et al., 2020), seeing this improvement in student well-being was particularly encouraging. Although due to government regulations with regard to sharing of information about student grades, the quantitative improvements in learning outcomes were not captured, anecdotal feedback from parents suggests a positive impact on student achievement as a result of participation in the program.

Our findings showed that newcomer children and children with disabilities were more likely to experience stress and difficulty in the program than their Canadian-born and/or non-disabled counterparts (albeit the overall numbers of participants experiencing stress and other difficulties were low). Thus, it is imperative to collect intersectional data in order to better understand the needs of these two (and other) equity-deserving groups in future research. Such research would be used to create programs that better support the unique needs of members of these groups.

Furthermore, capturing changes in the students' experiences at an individual level by conducting pre- and post-tests would provide more information about the impact of the program on various equity-deserving groups. Longitudinal data capturing the academic outcomes of students participating in the program would also provide a more complete picture of the effectiveness of the program.

Parents

For most parents, the program resulted in a reduction in stress and anxiety, and feeling more hopeful as the program met the needs of the family and was helpful. The findings evidently reflect that the program has been immensely useful for families that identified as racialized or had intersectional background.

Although parents saw the program as having an overwhelmingly positive impact on their child's academic success, a number of improvements were suggested. Chief among them was a need for more flexible scheduling. Because the tutors are volunteers who are themselves full-time students, and who may also be working to pay for their studies, they may not be able to provide families with as many time slots as they would like. As such, some families reported having to drop out of the program due to not being able to find tutors with compatible schedules. This concern highlights a limitation of offering a service such as this for free. Because the tutors are not employed by the service provider, the time they can provide to the program

130 • W. CUKIER et al.

is limited. If the program were to grow, the potential volunteer pool would need to be expanded, possibly to additional universities across the province and/or country.

Tutors

Finally, for tutors, the findings revealed that the program was of value for teacher candidates. One goal of the Study Buddy program was to provide teacher candidates a work-integrated learning opportunity. Specifically, teacher candidates were exposed to a new online platform and gained valuable experience teaching online. Teachers also got a firsthand look at the difficulties faced by students of equity-deserving groups, an insight that may not have arisen in their studies or during large-group teaching sessions.

CONCLUSION

A collaborative effort of university, community, and schools coming together resulted in the creation of Study Buddy, the individualized online tutoring program that impacted not only students from equity-deserving communities but also their parents. The COVID-19 pandemic presented families of school-aged children with unique and pressing challenges, which had a compounding effect on equity-deserving communities. The Study Buddy program responded to this need by adopting a multifaceted approach that connected families from equity-deserving groups to one-on-one interactive online tutoring supports, while working to remove barriers to high quality, individualized education for K–12 students in Ontario. This case study demonstrates how such social innovations adopted in education can result in improved outcomes for students from equity-deserving families. Although there is scope for improvement by exploring ways to increase the engagement of students from equity-deserving groups, such as Indigenous Peoples and those living in rural and remote parts of Northern Canada, or addressing the technological challenges that might impede student participation, this program lays the groundwork for creating an inclusive and equitable educational environment for all students.

NOTES

1. For the purposes of this chapter, equity-deserving groups include those identifying as: racialized, Black, and/or people of color ("visible minorities"), people with disabilities (including invisible and episodic disabilities), 2SLG-

BTQ+ and/or gender and sexually diverse individuals, and "Aboriginal" and/or Indigenous Peoples. The Study Buddy program and participants recognize First Nation Peoples, Métis Nation, and Inuit as founding Peoples of Canada.
2. School Boards are also known as school districts in Canada.

REFERENCES

Alello, R. (2020, October 28). *Canada's top doctor calls for 'structural change' to address COVID-19 inequities.* CTV News. https://www.ctvnews.ca/health/coronavirus/canada-s-top-doctor-calls-for-structural-change-to-address-covid-19-inequities-1.5164415

Briggs, A. Q. (2019). "We had support from our brothers": A critical race counter-narrative inquiry into second-generation Black Caribbean male youth responses to discriminatory work pathways. *Journal of Education and Work, 32*(4), 377–392. https://doi.org/10.1080/13639080.2019.1624696

Burt, M. (2020, March 23). *Most vulnerable to be hardest hit by the COVID-19 economic downturn.* The Conference Board of Canada. https://www.conferenceboard.ca/insights/blogs/most-vulnerable-to-be-hardest-hit-by-the-covid-19-economic-downturn

Carlana, M., & La Ferrara, E. (2021). *Apart but connected: Online tutoring and student outcomes during the COVID-19 pandemic* (IZA Discussion Papers, No. 14094). Institute of Labor Economics. https://www.econstor.eu/bitstream/10419/232846/1/dp14094.pdf

Chadha, E., Herbert, S., & Richard, S. (2020, February 28). *Review of the Peel District School Board.* Ministry of Education, Government of Ontario. https://files.ontario.ca/edu-review-peel-dsb-school-board-report-en-2023-01-12.pdf

Chi, M. T., Siler, S. A., Jeong, H., Yamauchi, T., & Hausmann, R. G. (2001). Learning from human tutoring. *Cognitive science, 25*(4), 471–533. https://doi.org/10.1207/s15516709cog2504_1

Cukier, W. (2022). *An innovative online individualized tutoring program to minimize educational disruption among racialized, Indigenous and immigrant students during COVID-19,* EDULEARN22 Proceedings, 4077. http://doi.org/10.21125/edulearn.2022.0981

Cukier, W., Adamu, P., Wall-Andrews, C., & Elmi, M. (2021). Racialized leaders leading Canadian universities. *Educational Management Administration & Leadership, 49*(4), 565–583. https://doi.org/10.1177/17411432211001363

Cukier, W., Campbell, M., & McNamara, L. (2018). *Ensuring equitable access to work-integrated learning in Ontario.* Diversity Institute. https://www.torontomu.ca/diversity/reports/Ensuring_Equitable_Access_to_Work-Integrated_Learning_in_Ontario.pdf

Cukier, W., Middleton, C., Elmi M., & Parkin, A. (2021). *Toronto's deepening digital divide: Impact on families and children.* Future Skills Centre, Environics Institute, Diversity Institute. https://www.toronto.ca/legdocs/mmis/2021/ex/comm/communicationfile-126455.pdf

DasGupta, N., Shandal, V., Shadd, D., & Segal, A. (2020, December 14). *The pervasive reality of anti-Black racism in Canada: The current state, and what to do about it.*

Boston Consulting Group. https://www.bcg.com/en-ca/publications/2020/reality-of-anti-black-racism-in-canada

Downey, D. B., & Condron, D. J. (2016). Fifty years since the Coleman Report: Rethinking the relationship between schools and inequality. *Sociology of Education, 89*(3), 207–220. https://doi.org/10.1177/0038040716651676

Environics Institute, Diversity Institute, United Way of Greater Toronto and York Region, YMCA of Greater Toronto, & Jean Augustine Chair in Education, Community & Diaspora. (2017). *The Black experience project in the GTA: Overview report.* https://www.torontomu.ca/content/dam/diversity/reports/black-experience-project-gta—1-overview-report.pdf

Gallagher-Mackay, K., Mundy, K., Feitosa de Britto, T., & Asim, M. (2022, March). *The evidence for tutoring to accelerate learning and address educational inequities during Canada's pandemic recovery.* Diversity Institute; Future Skills Centre; Ontario Institute for Studies in Education; Wilfrid Laurier University. https://www.torontomu.ca/content/dam/diversity/reports/The_Evidence_for_Tutoring.pdf

Gamoran, A., & Long, D. A. (2007). Equality of educational opportunity a 40 year retrospective. In R. Teese, S. Lamb, M. Duru-Bellat, & S. Helme (Eds.), *International studies in educational inequality, theory and policy* (pp. 23–47). Springer.

Gioia, D. A., Corley, K. G., & Hamilton, A. L. (2013). Seeking qualitative rigor in inductive research: Notes on the Gioia methodology. *Organizational Research Methods, 16*(1), 15–31. https://doi.org/10.1177/1094428112452151

Gorski, P. C. (2017). *Reaching and teaching students in poverty: Strategies for erasing the opportunity gap.* Teachers College Press.

Goslee, S., & Conte, C. (1998, June). *Losing ground bit by bit: Low-income communities in the information age. What's Going on Series.* Benton Foundation, National Urban League. https://eric.ed.gov/?id=ED424333

Government of Canada. (2017). *13 ways to modernize youth employment in Canada – Strategies for a new world of work.* https://www.canada.ca/en/employment-social-development/corporate/youth-expert-panel/report-modern-strategies-youth-employment.html

James, C. (2017, August). *Towards race equity in education: The schooling of Black students in the Greater Toronto area.* York University. https://edu.yorku.ca/files/2017/04/Towards-Race-Equity-in-Education-April-2017.pdf

James, C., & Turner, T. (2015). *Fighting an uphill battle: Report on the consultations into the well-being of Black youth in Peel Region.* F.A.C.E.S. of Peel Collaborative. https://youthrex.com/report/fighting-an-uphill-battle-report-on-the-consultations-into-the-well-being-of-black-youth-in-peel-region/

James, C. E., & Turner, T. (2017). *Towards race equity in education: The schooling of black students in the Greater Toronto Area.* York University https://youthrex.com/report/towards-race-equity-in-education-the-schooling-of-black-students-in-the-greater-toronto-area/

Kelly, P. (2014, February). *Understanding intergenerational social mobility: Filipino youth in Canada* (IRPP Study 45). Institute for Research on Public Policy. https://irpp.org/wp-content/uploads/assets/research/diversity-immigration-and-integration/filipino-youth/kelly-feb-2014.pdf

Kraft, M. A., List, J. A., Livingston, J. A., & Sadoff, S. (2022, May). Online tutoring by college volunteers: Experimental evidence from a pilot program. *AEA Papers and Proceedings, 112*, 614–618. https://doi.org/10.1257/pandp.20221038

Leeb, R. T., Price, S., Sliwa, S., Kimball, A., Szucs, L., Caruso, E., & Lozier, S. G. (2020). COVID-19 trends among school-aged children—United States, March 1–September 19, 2020. *MMWR Morbidity and Mortality Weekly Report, 69*(39), 1410–1415. https://doi.org/10.15585/mmwr.mm6939e2

Lincoln, Y., & Guba, E. (1985). *Naturalistic inquiry.* SAGE.

Mahnken, K. (2020, September 30). *Using tutors to combat COVID learning loss: New research shows that even lightly trained volunteers drive academic gains.* The 74. https://www.the74million.org/using-tutors-to-combat-covid-learning-loss -new-research-shows-that-even-lightly-trained-volunteers-drive-academic -gains/

Merrill, D. C., Reiser, B. J., Ranney, M., & Trafton, J. G. (1992). Effective tutoring techniques: A comparison of human tutors and intelligent tutoring systems. *Journal of the Learning Sciences, 2*(3), 277–305. https://doi.org/10.1207/ s15327809jls0203_2

Mo, G. Y., Cukier, W., Atputharajah, A., Itano Boase, M., & Hon, H. (2021). Differential impacts on diverse groups during COVID-19 in Canada. *Academy of Management Proceedings, 2021*(1), 13936. https://doi.org/10.5465/ ambpp.2021.13936abstract

Ng, E., & Badets, N. (2020, August 27). *COVID-19 IMPACTS: Youth well-being in Canada.* The Vanier Institute of the Family. https://vanierinstitute.ca/covid -19-impacts-youth-well-being-in-canada/

Nichols, L., Ha, B., & Tyyskä, V. (2020). Canadian immigrant youth and the education-employment nexus. *Canadian Journal of Family and Youth, 12*(1), 178–199. https://doi.org/10.29173/cjfy29497

Nickow, A., Oreopoulos, P., & Quan, V. (2020, July). *The impressive effects of tutoring on PreK-12 learning: A systematic review and meta-analysis of the experimental evidence* (Working Paper 27476). National Bureau of Economic Research. https:// doi.org/10.3386/w27476

Oreopoulos, P., Brown, R. S., & Lavecchia, A. M. (2017). Pathways to education: An integrated approach to helping at-risk high school students. *Journal of Political Economy, 125*(4), 947–984. https://doi.org/10.1086/692713

Proulx, K., Mundy, K., Asim, M., & Gallagher-Mackay, K. (2022, March). *Universal evaluation toolkit for academic tutoring programs.* Diversity Institute, Future Skills Centre, Ontario Institute for Studies in Education, Wilfrid Laurier University. https://www.torontomu.ca/diversity/reports/universal-evaluation-toolkit -for-academic-tutoring-programs/

Shah, V. (2018). Different numbers, different stories: Problematizing "Gaps" in Ontario and the TDSB. *Canadian Journal of Educational Administration and Policy, 187*, 31–47. https://journalhosting.ucalgary.ca/index.php/cjeap/article/view/43198

Shizha, E., Abdi, A. A., Wilson-Forsberg, S., & Masakure, O. (2020). African immigrant students and postsecondary education in Canada: High school teachers and school career counsellors as gatekeepers. *Canadian Ethnic Studies, 52*(3), 67–86. https://doi.org/10.1353/ces.2020.0025

Somers, C. L., Wang, D., & Piliawsky, M. (2016). Effectiveness of a combined tutoring and mentoring intervention with ninth-grade, urban Black adolescents. *Journal of Applied School Psychology, 32*(3), 199–213. https://doi.org/10.1080/15377903.2015.1136719

Statistics Canada. (2022, March 10). *COVID-19 in Canada: A two-year update on social and economic impacts.* https://www150.statcan.gc.ca/n1/pub/11-631-x/11-631-x2022001-eng.htm

Thomas, D. R. (2006). A general inductive approach for analyzing qualitative evaluation data. *American Journal of Evaluation, 27*(2), 237–246. https://doi.org/10.1177/1098214005283748

Turcotte, M. (2022). *Results from the 2016 Census: Education and labour market integration of Black youth in Canada.* Statistics Canada. Accessed 25 September 2022: https://www150.statcan.gc.ca/n1/pub/75-006-x/2020001/article/00002-eng.htm

Turcotte, M., & Hango, D. (2020, May 28). *Impact of economic consequences of COVID-19 on Canadians' social concerns.* Statistics Canada. https://www150.statcan.gc.ca/n1/pub/45-28-0001/2020001/article/00025-eng.htm

UNESCO. (n.d.). *Education: From school closure to recovery.* https://www.unesco.org/en/covid-19/education-response

Van de Sande, A., McWhinney, T., Occhiuto, K., Colpitts, J., Hagi-Aden, I., Hussein, A., & Feder, Z. (2019). Identifying barriers faced by Ottawa Somali youth in accessing post-secondary and vocational opportunities: An example of community-based participatory research. *Engaged Scholar Journal: Community-Engaged Research, Teaching, and Learning, 5*(1), 1–20. https://doi.org/10.15402/esj.v5i1.67846

Zhang, L., Pan, M., Yu, S., Chen, L., & Zhang, J. (2021). Evaluation of a student-centered online one-to-one tutoring system. *Interactive Learning Environments,* 1–19. https://doi.org/10.1080/10494820.2021.1958234

CHAPTER 7

"IF YOU EVER DID NEED THE HELP, IT WOULD BE THERE IN A SECOND. NO QUESTIONS ASKED"

A Study of Perceived Impact of Out-of-School STEM Programs During COVID-19

Christopher J. Fornaro
Drexel University

Kimberly Sterin
Drexel University

Katrina Struloeff
Drexel University

Alonzo M. Flowers III
The University of Texas at San Antonio

School–University–Community Research in a (Post) COVID-19 World, pages 135–153
Copyright © 2023 by Information Age Publishing
www.infoagepub.com
All rights of reproduction in any form reserved.

ABSTRACT

This study examined four administrators and four instructors from an out-of-school time (OST) summer science, technology, engineering, and mathematics (STEM) program as they made the transition from an in-person to a virtual program early in the COVID-19 pandemic in the Summer of 2020. The summer STEM program is one branch of an organization called Pathways which provides in- and out-of-school programming for Grades 5 through students during the academic year and over the summer; our study focused on students in Grades 5–9. Through semi-structured interviews, each participant was able to share supports that they found to be valuable during this transition. Additionally, Fornaro triangulated these findings with document analysis and observations as they were in an instructional role in the summer STEM program. The supports fell into the three themes: teaching supports, operational supports, and both teaching and operational supports. We share implications for other OST programs and virtual programming along with ideas for future research.

Despite being 2 years removed from the start of COVID-19 in the United States, the educational impact of the pandemic continues for students, teachers, administrators, and families. At one time or another, many classrooms have needed to shift from their typical in-person plan to a virtual setting. Inequalities in school funding can make the shift to a virtual space more difficult for some schools and programs (Darling-Hammond, 2010; Haelermans et al., 2022). School communities have been keeping the bus moving by allowing for flexible accountability (understanding that everyone is faced with new challenges) and prioritizing open communication as the shift to a virtual space is made (Brelsford et al., 2020; O'Connell & Clarke, 2020). While classrooms face their own hurdles, out-of-school time (OST) science, technology, engineering, and math (STEM) programs transitioning their programming to a virtual space often have additional challenges with attendance and engagement (Abouhashem et al., 2021; Hallett & De, 2020). This study bridges the gap between established research on OST STEM programs (Cohen, 2018) and instructor needs in the time of COVID-19 (Lee & Campbell, 2020). The findings of this work will benefit administrators of OST STEM programs, instructors, and/or school administrators who need to create virtual programming. We address the supports that were offered to instructors in the Summer of 2020 and how those supports were perceived by administrators and instructors for a summer STEM program that worked with fifth–ninth graders for approximately 5 weeks even as administrators and instructors were still learning how to best work in a virtual environment and students were adjusting to this new modality of learning.

BACKGROUND

OST STEM programs can be effective at incorporating integrated STEM curricula (Gates, 2017; Kelley & Knowles, 2016). By using project- or problem-based learning, inquiry-based models, or working alongside community partners, OST programs have demonstrated improved academic and behavioral factors for students such as content knowledge, opportunities and access, and student engagement (Cutucache et al., 2018; Gates, 2017; Mac Iver & Mac Iver, 2019; Roberts et al., 2018). In addition, OST programs can occur in a variety of spaces such as a school, library, or museum. Programs that take place outside the classroom can be rich experiences that drive interest in STEM for students by providing time for hands-on projects not easily achieved in the classroom (Gates, 2017; Roberts et al., 2018). However, OST programs are not without their challenges. OST programs can struggle with attendance (due to students being enrolled in multiple programs), logistical issues, or lack of student interest in the program (Moreno et al., 2016). Strong, interesting programming that engages students can help keep them enrolled. Thus, it is important that OST STEM instructors feel they have the knowledge and skills required to engage their students in programming that targets real world problems.

Those instructors who lead OST STEM programming are also unique. They are not necessarily classroom certified STEM teachers, which means they may lack formal pedagogical training and STEM content knowledge (Brady et al., 2014). Furthermore, they may not be content experts in any of the STEM disciplines, which could lead to discomfort with the programs they are expected to lead. For example, they could be classroom teachers of a different discipline, a dedicated volunteer, or a community leader (Cohen, 2018). To mitigate some of this discomfort, a strong OST STEM program needs to support instructors, which could help improve the overall program. A few ways to support instructors in this space are offering professional development opportunities, bringing in community partners to assist with programming and/or real world experiences, and fostering STEM-instructional practices, all which could lead to instructors feeling more successful with OST STEM programming (Christensen et al., 2015; Cohen, 2018; Margot & Kettler, 2019). Professional development can focus on the curriculum to be delivered (Christensen et al., 2015; Mac Iver & Mac Iver, 2019), integration of various STEM disciplines (Guzey et al., 2014), or rely on an engineering design to be implemented (Bartholomew & Strimel, 2017). While no one form of professional development will work for all instructors, a clear focus on professional development in the form of content, delivery of curricula, and/or integrating the disciplines can help with eventual programming. Community partners, such as professionals with a background in STEM or OST program mentors, are experts in their field who can provide real-world experiences that link to the STEM curriculum (Gates, 2017). Ensuring that instructors of OST STEM programs are familiar with the material is an important factor in successful OST STEM programming.

Transitioning instruction and programming to a virtual space can be difficult. The lack of access to technology, quality training on how to incorporate technology into classroom activities, and specific to transition from an in-person class to a virtual space is an ongoing issue for teachers that predates the COVID-19 pandemic (García & Weiss, 2019, 2020). Furthermore, issues of funding between high and low-wealth districts compound this challenge; opportunities provided to teachers, funding for professional development, and resources to implement new skills can vary widely (Darling-Hammond, 2010; García & Weiss, 2019). During the pandemic, teachers were often put in a position of finding technology applications that worked for their specific context, simultaneously learning and teaching their students how to use the applications, and still ensuring quality instruction was being provided (Bacher-Hicks et al., 2021; García & Weiss, 2020). While there was some programming aimed at assisting regular teachers with transitioning their classrooms to a virtual space, OST STEM instructors could be stepping into their virtual classroom for the first time. The sudden nature of the COVID-19 pandemic merely compounded the existing issues of inequity and teacher training.

PURPOSE

The purpose of this research was to describe the support structures that had a positive impact in the shift from an in-person to the virtual learning environment. Additionally, we examine the ways that the perceived impact of support structures is similar or different between administrators and instructors.

1. What support structures were described as having a positive impact on the virtual learning environment by administrators and instructors?
2. In what ways, similar or different, did the administrators and instructors perceive the impact of various support structures on the virtual learning environment?

METHODS

This phenomenological study utilized participant-as-observer observations (Billups, 2020), semi-structured interviews (Cohen et al., 2007; Merriam

"If You Ever Did Need the Help, It Would Be There in a Second." ▪ **139**

& Tisdell, 2016), and document analysis (Merriam & Tisdell, 2016). We observed weekly meetings and conducted semi-structured one-on-one interviews with four administrators and four instructors via Zoom. We performed document analysis on relevant documents. We triangulated the observations and document analysis with the semi-structured interviews to increase the trustworthiness of the study (Lincoln & Guba, 1985). In all, we performed three rounds of coding: open, axial, and values coding (Saldaña, 2015). While the data collection was primarily done by the lead author (Fornaro) with the support of my advisor (Flowers), the whole team was a part of the coding and analysis for this project.

Site and Participants

Pathways was the overarching non-profit for the site of this research project. Pathways has multiple branches of programming to provide in- and out-of-school STEM opportunities for multiple grade levels both during the school year and in the summer. The specific branch of Pathways studied in this project brought together approximately 100 fifth–ninth grade students from across a large urban Northeastern city to participate in a summer STEM program. Typically, the summer STEM program occurs in person and is taught by educators who are certified teachers, teachers on an emergency certification, or undergraduates. Pathways has been running programming for approximately 20 years. Additionally, some Pathways employees are former students of the program who are brought back as they have a better understanding of student experiences in the program. Unfortunately, due to COVID-19, the summer STEM program was transitioned to a virtual space during the period of this study (Summer 2020). The students participating in this summer STEM program took up to three classes throughout their day. While all students must take a mathematics course for their upcoming grade level, the other classes focused on electives such as journalism, engineering, and entrepreneurship.

Prior to COVID-19, this program was held in classroom settings at schools or local colleges. Grade levels were consolidated in neighboring classrooms so collaboration could happen between classrooms. Additionally, administrators and instructors were encouraged to engage with students over breakfast for about half an hour in the morning and they could attend extracurricular activities, such as cooking or recess, with the students. While the in-person program was academically focused, there were also field trips during the week, instructors were encouraged to utilize spaces outside of their classes for learning, and a portion of every Friday was spent working on capstone projects. After the transition to a virtual space, students, instructors, and administrators were provided with laptops and internet

140 ▪ C. J. FORNARO et al.

connections if they needed them. However, technology was frequently an issue throughout the summer and administrators worked with teachers to help fix issues by providing replacement computers or contacting internet service providers for families. Instructors and administrators frequently contacted parents if students were not in a session and did so collaboratively throughout the day. For example, students would log in for homeroom but not log on 10 minutes later for their first period. The overall school day was shortened for students from 6 hours down to approximately 4 hours. This decision by administrators allowed for extra planning time for instructors and time for administrators to contact families; it also encouraged students to log off of their computer and step away from screen time.

The eight adult participants in this study were members of the administrative team and instructors for the Pathways' summer STEM program. The administrative roles included deans, grade team leads, and individuals at the director level. These administrators included full-time employees of Pathways, teachers stepping into a leadership role for the summer, and administrators at other schools during the regular school year. In an attempt to preserve participant confidentiality, descriptions of the participants are not provided.

As lead author, I was an instructor in the program as well. There were concerns that confidentiality could not be upheld since I was a participant in the summer STEM program as an educator. As such, I individually solicited potential participants, utilized a password-protected folder for research documents, and stripped away identifying information identifiers from transcription data. Finally, I digitized all of the observational data and removed names, using instead a general identifier of instructor or administrator with a number attached.

Data Collection

We collected three forms of data for this research project. While semi-structured interviews drove the findings for this project, the document analysis and observations allowed us to triangulate the findings based on participant responses, programmatic delivery, and observations of the support process during professional development throughout the summer.

As lead researcher, I conducted semi-structured interviews with four administrators and four instructors of the summer STEM program. Interviews allowed for participants to explain their experiences regarding the shift to an online setting due to COVID-19 in the summer of 2020. I created an interview protocol to allow for the "lived experiences and the meaning they make of that experience" (Seidman, 2019, p. 9) to be explored. Furthermore, the use of a semi-structured framework allowed for follow-up

"If You Ever Did Need the Help, It Would Be There in a Second." ▪ **141**

questions and extensions on important vignettes that emerged throughout the interview (Merriam & Tisdell, 2016). We used the interviews as another data point for the purposes of triangulation during data analysis.

The observations allowed us to see participant delivery of programmatic supports and helped with triangulation. It is important to observe participants in their natural setting to compare what is said in interviews and what is said during a programmatic meeting in their own space (Billups, 2020). Since I was also an instructor in the summer STEM program, I recorded all the questions I asked during meetings to allow reflection on how my presence could impact the meetings.

The document analysis allowed me to compare observation and interview data with what was sent out to instructors over the summer. For example, I reviewed programmatic emails, the summer handbook, and weekly newsletters to improve triangulation of the data (Merriam & Tisdell, 2016). The document analysis was important to connect what was provided to all instructors versus individual support. Furthermore, I kept a weekly reflective journal to increase the trustworthiness of the study (Lincoln & Guba, 1985).

Data Analysis

I digitally recorded the interviews and transcribed them verbatim, unitizing the transcriptions sentence-by-sentence to allow for the smallest possible unit of analysis while still retaining meaning (Lincoln & Guba, 1985). However, during this process there were some sentences that could not stand alone, and these were combined at my discretion. I kept notes of when this was done and the rationale behind it to keep an audit trail (Merriam & Tisdell, 2016). Our team then used three rounds of coding, open, axial, and values, to analyze the unitized data to ensure participant voices were heard throughout the process (Billups, 2020; Saldaña, 2015). Specifically, I performed the initial open coding and the two other researchers addressed the axial and values coding based on their background in education having roles as classroom teachers or administrators. Through coding, we identified nine support categories from the initial 30 codes; then we further consolidated these into three themes of teaching supports; operational supports; and teaching and operational supports.

While the semi-structured interviews drove the analysis of this project, I (Fornaro) used the document analysis and observational data to triangulate the findings. For example, if a participant mentioned a professional development session or other meeting, I was able to look back on my notes from that meeting to see what was discussed with the team and if it took place with the full staff or certain teachers.

142 ▪ C. J. FORNARO et al.

Trustworthiness

In order to ensure the trustworthiness of this study, our research team addressed credibility, confirmability, dependability, and transferability following Lincoln and Guba (1985). I used a member check of initial findings, where the participants of the study reviewed the initial findings and gave feedback to increase credibility (Cohen et al., 2007; Merriam & Tisdell, 2016). This provided me with feedback on the participant's thoughts on the themes and initial findings. I then addressed confirmability by utilizing an audit trail (Merriam & Tisdell, 2016), journaling at each step to explain decisions that were made during the research process. An example of an audit trail was recording instances where sentences were combined during data analysis. We triangulated data from the semi-structured interviews, observations, and document analysis to increase the dependability of the findings (Merriam & Tisdell, 2016). My thick description (Geertz, 1973) of the interview and observation data addressed the transferability of findings, thus allowing readers to better understand the experiences of the participants.

Researcher Positionality

As first author of this study (Fornaro), I am a middle-class, White male in my late 30s. Being aware of the privilege that comes with the researcher's background was important as my presence during interviews and observations could have an impact on participants. Additionally, I align with a postpositivist research stance but I utilized a constructivist approach for this study. While I believe that there is value in large data, I know that it cannot tell the full story. Diving into the experiences of instructors and administrators experiencing COVID-19 and teaching online in the moment could only be done through the participants. Before the observations, interviews, and throughout data analysis I refreshed my understanding of the constructivist paradigm to better represent the lived experiences (Lincoln & Guba, 1985) of participants. Professionally, I have been a STEM student, STEM educator, and administrator who has participated in and led STEM programming. While I worked to create best practices for STEM programming as a department chair and educator, I reduced bias by reflecting throughout the process on my own experiences versus those of the participants. Constantly reflecting on the process helped me differentiate between my own bias and participants' experiences. Lastly, as an educator in the summer STEM program, it was important to be transparent with potential participants throughout the summer by also identifying myself as a researcher.

As second author (Sterin), I am racialized as White, of Jewish heritage, gendered as a cis-gendered female, and able-bodied. I am a dedicated scholar-activist who aims to bridge gaps between research, policy, and practice in education. I have 7 years of experience as a public school English teacher in both the middle and high school settings. During this time I sponsored multiple extra-curricular activities and taught in several OST summer programs.

As third author (Struloeff), I identify as a queer, cis-gendered woman racialized as White. I am a critical researcher with an eye toward intersectionality and feminism, particularly in leadership and policy. I have experience in K–12 urban education both as an out-of-school educator for STEM and arts programming and as a school administrator. Through these roles, I have been both an administrator and instructor for educational programming for over 15 years. Prior to education, I worked in non-profit operations, educational program design, development, and communications engaging with communities across the United States.

As faculty supervisor and the final author of this study (Flowers), I am a Black male who is a tenured associated professor at a predominantly White institution. Recognizing the context of institutions is important for unpacking one's position. Particularly, as a scholar who centers his work around critical race theory (CRT), I recognize that justice-oriented education is quite broad, and even amongst the cadre of scholars, the meanings, characteristics, and contexts of justice-oriented are varied. As a Black male scholar in higher education, my worldview is informed by the intersection of my various identities, thus, informing the lens by which I approach my research and training of doctoral students. CRT as a philosophical orientation allows me to unmask and critically evaluate systems of oppression. In addition, CRT offers me a lens to interrogate ways in which social structures can produce entrenched power and marginalization; I use this lens to seek ways to challenge the injustices that often lie within organizational structures. At the core of advising students, the goal is to allow them to self-reflect on their qualitative research as an instrument for social change. Combined with praxis, qualitative research should be a form of liberation to create a more equitable society. As a faculty member, the alignment of my teaching, scholarship, and service resonate deeply with a clear social justice philosophy that supports my professional framework as a scholar-advocate.

FINDINGS

Instructors and administrators described support structures that had a positive impact on the virtual learning environment which emerged in three

144 ▪ C. J. FORNARO et al.

overarching themes: (a) teaching supports, (b) operational supports, and (c) supports that bridged both teaching and operational support categories. While all three of these themes were viewed as positive by both administrators and instructors, their perceived impact varied between the two groups.

Teaching Supports

During the interviews, both administrators and instructors described the positive influence of teaching support structures which included the sub-themes of curricular support, instructional support, and virtual instruction support. These support structures directly targeted teaching practices meant for the specific OST STEM program during the immediate shift to the virtual environment.

Teaching Supports: Administrator Perspective

Through this shift to an online environment, administrators attempted to provide additional teaching support to instructors through curricular, instructional, and virtual instruction support. The latter, virtual instruction supports aimed to give guidance to improve instruction in the virtual classroom such as suggesting videos for higher student engagement. One administrator (Admin_2) recommended a number of games, techniques, and tools to instructors as well as resources such as Nearpod, online drawing games (quick draw), and features on the learning management system for the distribution of work. One administrator noted the positive elements of virtual learning for instructional support in the following statement:

> When you're online, also, you have a better idea of how the class went versus when you're in person. So we were able to have some really good conversations about this happened then and different things we could do next time, versus in person, I feel like sometimes when you're a new teacher, you're in kind of a blur where sometimes you don't remember what happened after the lesson's over and you can't really be as reflective as when we're online. (Admin_1)

Additionally, administrators highlighted how the virtual environment provided space for curricular support in the moment of instruction, much like in a traditional in-person environment, but with the use of online tools they felt were more mobile. Below an administrator describes one perspective:

> But online it's the same thing, except I would just direct message the teacher and be like, "Hey, such and such is going on." Or there was an added help that I could help mute their class and control the chat. So I think a lot of the

"If You Ever Did Need the Help, It Would Be There in a Second." • **145**

instructor supports were similar as the school year, but I think the most helpful were probably lesson plan feedback and then the ability to just hop in any
class and help out with stuff. (Admin_1)

Overall, administrators felt positively about the teaching supports they were
able to offer to their instructors during this shift to virtual learning and
felt that the teaching supports made a difference in the instructors' online
classrooms.

Teaching Supports: Instructor Perspective

When asked about various support structures put in place during their
time working at the OST STEM program during the pandemic, the instructors interviewed named similar instructional supports as the administrators. Overall, the instructors found that the curricular materials provided
to them, the instructional feedback, and suggestions for engagement strategies in the virtual environment were very helpful. In regard to curricular
support, one teacher discussed the versatility of the lesson plan rubrics:

> So the lesson plan rubric included . . . is a Google doc one, and it was already
> pre-made for each individual career class, which made it not only easy for
> the career teachers to write their curriculum. But if for any reason you had
> to cover another class, you weren't kind of confused by looking at someone
> else's lesson plan format. (Instructor_3)

According to this instructor, the pre-made lesson plan rubrics eased both
collaboration between instructors as well as when class coverage may have
been needed.

The instructors also found the administrators to be very supportive when
it came to instruction. When discussing a specific instructional resource,
one instructor explained how responsive the administrators were to questions about instructional delivery:

> So they're very supportive if I had a question. Or how do you want this pre-
> sented? Or do you just want me to touch on this? They were really supportive
> in anything I had a question about, as far as how they wanted material pre-
> sented. (Teacher_3)

The instructors found that the administrators were receptive to questions
and supportive when it came to instructional needs.

Instructors also found the suggestions for how to best engage students
while in the virtual environment to be a meaningful support. One teacher
spoke to the usefulness of incorporating visuals and videos in the virtual
environment:

146 • C. J. FORNARO et al.

> I know in person it's not very, not very highly recommended to show a lot of videos in the class cause it takes away from the whole teaching element, but virtually it was extremely helpful to just throw in, there's a two minute video on how to find a credible source versus possibly me cutting in and out. (Teacher_3)

Instructors found the supports that were tailored specifically to the virtual environment to enhance their teaching practice during this time.

Operational Supports

The second theme identified in the analysis was operational supports. Both administrators and instructors described the positive impacts of certain support structures which were put in place to help the behind-the-scenes operations of the OST STEM program. This theme includes two sub-themes: non-teaching support and well-being support. Non-teaching support often consisted of supporting areas outside of the instructional setting or logistical components that allowed for instruction to go more smoothly. Well-being support included direct attention to personal needs such as mental health. Both administrators and instructors found an increased need and appreciation for well-being supports in the context of the ongoing global pandemic.

Operational Supports: Administrator Perspective

To provide the operational supports, administrators had to focus attention and dedicate time to communicate with stakeholders, ensure technology was working, and engage with instructors. They also ensured that all staff were trained on the technology tools prior to engaging with classes and students. An administrator noted the positive impact of these non-teaching supports through this statement:

> The number of staff available to call kids, run computers to kids, just troubleshoot the problems that will come up ... I think that that's a really positive support that parents echoed, teachers echoed and students echoed to the program. (Admin_4)

Additionally, the administrators focused on ensuring the well-being of instructors and students throughout the program. These well-being supports ranged from ensuring logistical components like the above were provided; allowing instructors to be comfortable in their personal spaces and attire; to ensuring fun and engaging activities for the students including book clubs, performances, and celebrations on Fun Fridays. In particular, the well-being supports were designed to create community and to support the

"If You Ever Did Need the Help, It Would Be There in a Second." • **147**

instructors as whole people in the midst of a pandemic, not just as a role in the summer program. One administrator summarized their attempts at well-being support as:

> I think the main thing that I tried to focus on this summer was prioritizing people's mental health. I think that right now when we're online ... It's different during the school year because if I need to talk to an instructor, I can just stop him in the hallway and talk to him. Or if I need to talk to an instructor, I can just really quickly go in her class. But in the summer, and I was definitely feeling this from the school year, so I tried to make it a priority in the fall, there's just lots of emails and there's lots of action items, and there's a million things you need to get done all the time really fast when you're virtual, because you can't do in person check-ins. (Admin_1)

In summary, the operational supports included non-teaching supports such as technology and staffing assistance, and a focus on well-being supports which, from the administration's view, positively impacted not only the instructors and students, but also themselves in being able to maintain a smooth program and finding connection within the OST STEM program community.

Operational Supports: Instructor Perspective

The instructors also spoke to the benefits of the non-teaching and well-being components of the operational supports throughout the OST STEM program. For example, one instructor noted the advantage of the approximately 40 hours of paid time, double the regular amount, the administration allotted for them to prepare specifically for the virtual environment:

> The time that I got in May, that 10 hours or something that we were given, I think that was very helpful, especially because we had just gotten into the virtual space, just rethinking. Because I had taught, towards the end I found a lot of resources that I could use. I think that's what started me on finding those resources. (Teacher_2)

Instructors stated that the OST STEM program's built-in preparation time was a key non-teaching support, especially within the crisis context of the pandemic.

In addition to the non-teaching, operational supports, instructors emphasized the importance of how the administration provided them with support for their personal well-being.

Some instructors spoke about the ways the administration made efforts to foster community amongst all of the staff, and how that was adapted for the virtual environment. Some instructors also highlighted well-being supports that were tailored specifically to their needs. Because the OST STEM program was taking place in the virtual environment without much time to

148 ▪ C. J. FORNARO et al.

prepare, some instructors found themselves in need of new resources to be able to teach effectively. One instructor mentioned how important it was to their experience that the administration was able to address their need for headphones:

> Giving me anything that I asked for, as far as like, "Okay, well, I really need some different headphones." And that was key for me. It may seem small, but working from home, I have my kids going, just regular traffic. And for example, my kids were doing online stuff. So the headphones were important because it blacked out a lot of the outside stuff that was going on . . . It's small, but it was huge for me in my environment. (Teacher_1)

The instructors expressed that the administrators were supportive of their well-being which contributed to a successful flow of OST STEM program operations even within the unforeseen pandemic context. Overall, both administrators and instructors shared a similar view for the value of the operational supports enacted during the OST STEM program.

Wrap Around Supports

Through the analysis, there were four types of supports that were identified to bridge both teaching and operational supports by their nature, including proactive supports, staffing supports, teaching assistant supports, and technology supports. These supports were people-centered and were touted as having positive impacts in the transition to virtual programming.

While both administrators and instructors mentioned the benefits of all four themes of these supports during the interviews, their emphasis varied. Findings revealed that administrators emphasized proactive support and teaching assistant support, whereas instructors more heavily emphasized staffing support. We found that administrators and instructors perceived the positive value of technology support more equally.

Wrap Around Supports: Administrator Perspective

Because the pandemic hit just months before administrators were to provide the OST STEM program, they did not have a lot of time to prepare. One administrator highlighted how the administrative team attempted to meet the challenge of providing proactive support in this context:

> So always up against the clock, timing was always a thing. So we didn't have a ton of time training around Canvas or just around the virtual space in general. I sought out some [university]-sponsored webinars to see what people were saying, what people were doing online . . . So he held some trainings and then before you know it, we were online. (Admin_2)

Administrators expressed that although they experienced the pressure of time, they understood the need and value of proactive support to help their instructors be prepared for teaching in the virtual environment.

Administrators also highlighted the positive impacts of teaching assistant support as "one of the big things... have another adult in the room for all the classes" (Admin_3). Conceptually these teaching assistants were other adults in the virtual classroom to support instruction and learning by monitoring the chat, troubleshooting with individual students, and engaging with students in small groups through breakout rooms. Administrators reported that the staff felt that teaching assistants were able to assist in activities both in and out of the classroom, such as calling home (Admin_3). Teaching assistants were teachers in training or content specialists that were hired to support instructors in their virtual classrooms by making phone calls, hosting break out rooms, or helping teach mini lessons.

Furthermore, administrators viewed the additional staffing that was provided by deans who could engage with students and families one-on-one, if needed, and provide targeted support to be very beneficial. The number of staff allowed for pop-ins in classrooms to offer instructors student support and personal support, especially in the cases of technology malfunctions or student disengagement.

Wrap Around Supports: Instructor Perspective

Similarly, the instructors referred to support structures that could be described as both instructional and operational supports. Multiple instructors emphasized how supports to staff—such as the accessibility to administrator feedback, the speed of their response, and the frequency of their presence—were key to their success in the virtual environment. One instructor shared:

> Whenever there was an issue in the class during the summer, a quick text and not maybe a minute later, somebody within the class... the awareness for the kids that somebody on the administration team was there definitely helped. And of course the just reassurance that if you ever did need the help, it would be there in a second if no questions asked. (Teacher_3)

The instructors asserted that the presence of administration in their virtual classrooms served as an important support to them in the OST STEM program.

Additionally, instructors identified the administration's support for the use of technology as critical to their success during the summer program. One instructor expressed gratitude that the administrators exposed them to a specific virtual tool and described how integral it became to their teaching:

I didn't know anything about Nearpod, which was like my bread and butter on virtual learning and it will be my bread and butter this school year. So, I mean, I know they didn't create Nearpod, but they [Admin] exposed me to it. (Teacher_4)

Instructors reported that the ways the administration both exposed them to new technology and provided them with support for their ongoing use of it supported their virtual teaching experiences.

DISCUSSION

Administrators and instructors were given the time and space in this study to share the supports that were found to be beneficial at the start of the COVID-19 pandemic. Overall, administrators and instructors were flexible in their delivery and use of supports in the summer session. Additionally, focus on people first was a theme woven throughout the various supports. As the regular school year came to a close, the administrators provided time for the instructors to familiarize themselves with the new virtual environment and to plan with a curriculum, and they provided tools for instructors to build their virtual classroom. Instructors received funding and support during this time before the start of the summer program. Additionally, instructors shared on numerous occasions that the well-being and professional supports that they received in the summer STEM program made their transition to a virtual space in the uncertain time of COVID-19 easier. Whether it was the added support during the virtual summer of administrators popping into their class, teaching assistants, or the understanding that life happens during this time, instructors felt that there was a unified team working together to tackle problems. Overall, administrators and instructors found common supports to be beneficial, which ensured that the team provided a better overall OST STEM program for students throughout the summer in a time of otherwise uncertain educational experiences.

SIGNIFICANCE AND IMPLICATIONS

Building on the current research of supporting STEM instructors and providing best practices in OST STEM programs (Cohen, 2018; Francom et al., 2021) and the needs in a virtual space (Lee & Campbell, 2020), this study shares ideas for other OST STEM programs on incorporating virtual learning in their practices and programming. Furthermore, school districts may adopt virtual instruction which has an impact on OST STEM programs for instructors, administrators, and students. The transition to a virtual setting

"If You Ever Did Need the Help, It Would Be There in a Second." ▪ **151**

for these administrators and instructors were built around trust, support, and being flexible. This scholarship provides educational administrators of OST STEM programs ideas on providing virtual support to instructors for new types of activities. Furthermore, some of this work could broadly apply to virtual programming that is being adopted across various educational settings. For example, the context of this study focused on students' in the middle grades where it could apply to elementary or high school students.

IDEAS FOR FUTURE RESEARCH

Thinking towards the future, school and program shut-downs due to COVID-19 will hopefully subside over time. However, thinking of ways to provide rich virtual programming to students who cannot physically be in a space could be the logical next step for this research. Furthermore, some of the supports provided in this summer program could persist as the program transitions back to in-person. Flexibility can be difficult for the flow of an individual classroom but is often necessary as the school year progresses. Whether the issue is students moving during lunch periods, staff out for the day, or catching students up who have not been in class, it is beneficial for everyone to understand that "life happens." Three avenues for future research might include: (a) re-interviewing administrators and teachers to determine which supports have continued back to in-person programming; (b) investigating other virtual OST STEM programs to see if these, or other, supports are currently being utilized; and (c) developing a survey to gather broad Likert-scale data around the favorability or utilization of the supports found in this study across a wider network of OST STEM programs that transitioned to a virtual space during COVID-19.

REFERENCES

Abouhashem, A., Abdou, R. M., Bhadra, J., Siby, N., Ahmad, Z., & Al-Thani, N. J. (2021). COVID-19 inspired a STEM-based virtual learning model for middle schools—A case study of Qatar. *Sustainability, 13*(5), 2799. https://doi.org/10.3390/su13052799

Bacher-Hicks, A., Goodman, J., & Mulhern, C. (2021). Inequality in household adaptation to schooling shocks: Covid-induced online learning engagement in real time. *Journal of Public Economics, 193*, 104345. https://doi.org/10.1016/j.jpubeco.2020.104345

Bartholomew, S. R., & Strimel, G. J. (2017). The problem with assessing open-ended problems. *Techniques: Connecting Education & Careers, 92*(3), 44–49. https://www.researchgate.net/publication/316990538_Assessing_Open-ended_Design_Problems

152 ▪ C. J. FORNARO et al.

Billups, F. D. (2020). *Qualitative data collection tools: Design, development, and applications.* SAGE.

Brady, T., Salas, C., Nuriddin, A., Rodgers, W., & Subramaniam, M. (2014). Make-Ability: Creating accessible makerspace events in a public library. *Public Library Quarterly, 33*(4), 330–347. https://doi.org/10.1080/01616846.2014.970425

Brelsford, S. N., Camarillo, E. E., Garcia, A. S., Garcia, G., Lopez, V. R., Montoya, C. P., Mora III, R., Olvera, Z., Ramirez, A., Wicker, F., & Merchant, B. (2020). Keeping the bus moving while maintaining social distance in a COVID-19 world. *International Studies in Educational Administration, 48*(2), 12–20. http://cceam.net/wp-content/uploads/2020/08/ISEA-2020-48-2.pdf

Christensen, R., Knezek, G., & Tyler-Wood, T. (2015). Alignment of hands-on STEM engagement activities with positive STEM dispositions in secondary school students. *Journal of Science Education and Technology, 24*(6), 898–909. https://doi.org/10.1007/s10956-015-9572-6

Cohen, B. (2018). Teaching STEM after school: Correlates of instructional comfort. *The Journal of Educational Research, 111*(2), 246–255. https://doi.org/10.1080/00220671.2016.1253537

Cohen, L., & Manion, L., & Morrison, K. (2007). *Research methods in education* (6th ed.). Routledge. https://doi.org/10.4324/9780203029053

Cutucache, C., Boham, T., Luhr, J., Sommers, A., Stevenson, N., Sointu, E., Mäkitalo-Siegl, K., Kärkkäinen, S., Valtonen, T., Grandgenett, N., & Tapprich, W. (2018). NE STEM 4U afterschool intervention leads to gains in STEM content knowledge for middle school youth. *Cogent Education, 5*(1), 1558915. https://doi.org/10.1080/2331186X.2018.1558915

Darling-Hammond, L. (2010). *The flat world and education: How America's commitment to equity will determine our future.* Teachers College Press.

Francom, G. M., Lee, S. J., & Pinkney, H. (2021). Technologies, challenges and needs of K–12 teachers in the transition to distance learning during the COVID-19 pandemic. *TechTrends, 65*(4), 589–601. https://doi.org/10.1007/s11528-021-00625-5

García, E., & Weiss, E. (2019, July 17). *The role of early career supports, continuous professional development, and learning communities in the teacher shortage.* Economic Policy Institute. https://www.epi.org/publication/teacher-shortage-professional-development-and-learning-communities/

García, E., & Weiss, E. (2020, September 10). *COVID-19 and student performance, equity, and US education policy: Lessons from pre-pandemic research to inform relief, recovery, and rebuilding.* Economic Policy Institute. https://www.epi.org/publication/the-consequences-of-the-covid-19-pandemic-for-education-performance-and-equity-in-the-united-states-what-can-we-learn-from-pre-pandemic-research-to-inform-relief-recovery-and-rebuilding/

Gates, A. E. (2017). Benefits of a STEM collaboration in Newark, New Jersey: Volcano simulation through a glass-making experience. *Journal of Geoscience Education, 65*(1), 4–11. https://doi.org/10.5408/16-188.1

Geertz, C. (1973). *The interpretation of cultures.* Basic Books.

Guzey, S. S., Harwell, M., & Moore, T. (2014). Development of an instrument to assess attitudes toward science, technology, engineering, and mathematics

(STEM). *School Science and Mathematics, 114*(6), 271–279. https://doi.org/10.1111/ssm.12077

Haelermans C., Korthals R., Jacobs M., de Leeuw S., Vermeulen S., van Vugt L., Aarts, B., Prokic-Breuer, T., van der Velden, R., van Wetten, S., & de Wolf, I. (2022). Sharp increase in inequality in education in times of the COVID-19-pandemic. *PLoS ONE, 17*(2), e0261114. https://doi.org/10.1371/journal.pone.0261114

Hallett, J., & De, S. (2020). Effects of COVID-19 on education in healthcare and STEM. *AIJR Preprints, 275*(1). http://dx.doi.org/10.13140/RG.2.2.36137.21607

Kelley, T. R., & Knowles, J. G. (2016). A conceptual framework for integrated STEM education. *International Journal of STEM Education, 3*(11). https://doi.org/10.1186/s40594-016-0046-z

Lee, O., & Campbell, T. (2020). What science and STEM teachers can learn from COVID-19: Harnessing data science and computer science through the convergence of multiple STEM subjects. *Journal of Science Teacher Education, 31*(8), 932–944. https://doi.org/10.1080/1046560x.2020.1814980

Lincoln, Y. S., & Guba, E. G. (1985). *Naturalistic inquiry.* SAGE.

Mac Iver, M. A., & Mac Iver, D. J. (2019). "STEMming" the swell of absenteeism in the middle years: Impacts of an urban district summer robotics program. *Urban Education, 54*(1), 65–88. https://doi.org/10.1177/0042085915618712

Merriam, S. B., & Tisdell, E. J. (2016). *Qualitative research: A guide to design and implementation* (4th ed.). Jossey-Bass.

Moreno, N. P., Tharp, B. Z., Vogt, G., Newell, A. D., & Burnett, C. A. (2016). Preparing students for middle school through after-school STEM activities. *Journal of Science Education and Technology, 25*(6), 889–897. https://doi.org/10.1007/s10956-016-9643-3

O'Connell, A., & Clarke, S. (2020). A school in the grip of COVID-19: Musings from the principal's office. *International Studies in Educational Administration, 48*(2), 4–11. https://shorturl.at/js257

Roberts, T., Jackson, C., Mohr-Schroeder, M. J., Bush, S. B., Maiorca, C., Cavalcanti, M., Schroeder, D. C., Delaney, A., Putnam, L., & Cremeans, C. (2018). Students' perceptions of STEM learning after participating in a summer informal learning experience. *International Journal of STEM Education, 5*(35). https://doi.org/10.1186/s40594-018-0133-4

Saldaña, J. (2015). *The coding manual for qualitative researchers.* SAGE.

Seidman, I. (2019). *Interviewing as qualitative research: A guide for researchers in education and the social sciences* (5th ed.). Teachers College Press.

CHAPTER 8

REMOTE INSTRUCTIONAL COACHING DURING THE COVID-19 PANDEMIC

An Exploration of Coaching Moves and Teacher Reflection

Jeanna R. Wieselmann
Southern Methodist University

Marc T. Sager
Southern Methodist University

ABSTRACT

A unique opportunity to study remote instructional coaching emerged when COVID-19 necessitated a shift to remote teaching and professional development. Prior evidence suggested that the provision of a STEM curriculum unit and remote coaching supported a first-year science teacher in improving his instructional practices. This study utilized a single case study design with interaction analysis methods to explore coaching moves implemented by three university-based STEM instructional coaches in a remote coaching environ-

School–University–Community Research in a (Post) COVID-19 World, pages 155–177
Copyright © 2023 by Information Age Publishing
www.infoagepub.com
All rights of reproduction in any form reserved.

ment, and to identify those moves that prompted teacher reflection. Findings highlight the range of coaching moves utilized and the unique approaches to coaching that were adopted by the three coaches. Further, we identify the coaching moves that most frequently preceded teacher reflection. In addition to explicit prompts for reflection, we found that affirming the teacher, focusing on how students learn, discussing pedagogical approaches, and emphasizing science content knowledge also prompted teacher reflection. Implications for remote instructional coaching are discussed.

The COVID-19 pandemic caused many aspects of teaching to shift to remote modalities. K–12 teachers delivered remote instruction to students, and, in turn, these teachers received much of their professional development (PD) remotely. This created new opportunities to consider the strengths and limitations of remote approaches to teacher PD. Reflective practice has long been recognized as a key to teacher PD and growth (e.g., Killion & Todnem, 1991; Knight, 2007; Schön, 1987). Teacher reflection has been associated with improved teaching practices (e.g., Borrego & Henderson, 2014; Bubnys & Zavadskienė, 2017; Sellars, 2012), and instructional coaching is one means of promoting reflective practice among teachers (Desimone & Pak, 2017; Knight, 2007). However, while web-based, virtual approaches have been recommended to increase access to high-quality coaching (Kraft et al., 2018), researchers have called for studies of online and remote PD approaches and raised concerns about their quality and effectiveness (e.g., Dede et al., 2009). For example, a meta-analysis of science, technology, engineering, and mathematics (STEM) PD revealed significantly smaller positive effects with online compared to in-person PD (Lynch et al., 2019). However, there is great variety within online PD experiences; teachers may encounter synchronous and/or asynchronous components, which were intentionally developed for online implementation (i.e., online PD) or simply be adaptations of in-person programs (i.e., remote PD), and their instruction could be guided by a range of learning theories. Thus, there remains a need for research that considers outcomes associated with specific and well-detailed online and remote PD approaches (Dede et al., 2009; Lynch et al., 2019). With COVID-19 necessitating online and remote PD, this study fills a gap in the literature to further explore how remote instructional coaching can be used to promote teacher reflection.

In our previous study of teaching practices, we found that the provision of an integrated STEM curriculum unit along with remote instructional coaching supported a first-year teacher in utilizing research-based practices for teaching within the COVID-19 context (Wieselmann et al., 2022). The present study seeks to better understand the nature of the remote coaching that supported this teacher and addresses the research questions:

1. What coaching moves do STEM instructional coaches implement in a remote coaching environment?
2. What remote coaching moves prompt a first-year teacher to reflect on their instructional practices?

LITERATURE REVIEW

Research–Practice Partnerships

There has been a continued attempt to bridge the gap between research and practice in education through innovations in pedagogy, technology, and methodology (Anderson & Shattuck, 2012; Koehler et al., 2007). One area of research and partnership aims to bridge this divide through research-practice partnerships (RPPs). RPPs are intentionally designed to investigate problems of practice and support collaborative problem-solving among researchers and practitioners (Coburn et al., 2013). They are characterized by being long-term, focusing on problems of practice, maintaining a commitment to mutualism, using intentional strategies to foster partnership, and producing original data analyses (Coburn et al., 2013; Coburn & Penuel, 2016). Existing literature recognizes a range of challenges associated with RPPs, including developing and maintaining trust between partners, maintaining mutualism, balancing local relevance with scalability (Coburn et al., 2013), and potentially excluding critical partners from the table (Booker et al., 2019).

Despite these challenges, RPPs can be a powerful tool in improving teaching practice and student outcomes. For example, Yarnall et al. (2006) found positive effects for teachers' assessment and accountability goals in science classrooms using technology-supported assessment interventions developed through an RPP. Scharber et al. (2021) used creative risk-taking measures to promote teacher learning by normalizing failure, facilitating reflection, and providing supportive collaborative environments through an RPP. RPPs and their supports for practitioners are also associated with improved student outcomes on standardized tests and measures of content knowledge (Booth et al., 2015; Geier et al., 2008). For example, Fishman et al. (2003) found positive effects on improving student scores in science through curriculum implementation associated with the RPP. Based on these previous studies, RPPs serve as a challenging, yet beneficial approach to bridging the research–practice gap to improve teaching practices and student outcomes.

Teacher Reflection

Teacher reflection can be used to promote professional growth and learning among teachers (Killion & Todnem, 1991). Through metacognition and reflection, teachers can "restructure strategies of action, understandings of phenomena, or ways of framing problems" (Schön, 1987, p. 28), with the ultimate goals of deeper knowledge of self and students, as well as improved instructional practices (Sellars, 2012). Killion and Todnem (1991) discussed the idea of reflection for practice, which supports the notion that teachers further their understanding of pedagogical knowledge and pedagogical content knowledge (PCK) to inform future practice. Further, Borrego and Henderson (2014) suggested that frequent reflection on teaching practice can result in modifications and improvements to instruction. Reflective practice can also shift attention to student thinking and learning, as teachers translate their own use of reflective inquiry into their approach to teaching students (Bubnys & Zavadskienė, 2017); in turn, this supports students' development of skills such as problem-solving and critical thinking (Attard et al., 2010).

Researchers have identified and studied a range of methods to promote teacher reflection. For example, written reflections allow teachers to develop a deeper understanding of themselves (Holly, 1989), and structured PD workshops and conferences can be used to develop teachers' reflective practice and inquiry into their own teaching (Campbell, 2012). Teacher participation in learning communities prompts reflection, which can broaden teachers' understanding of different disciplines, cultures, and approaches to teaching (Borrego & Henderson, 2014). Shulman's (1987) notion of PCK emphasized in-the-moment reflection as teachers consider both what is taught and how it is taught. Finally, Desimone and Pak (2017) suggested that instructional coaching allows for multiple cycles of reflection and action to promote teacher learning. While teacher reflection is an established approach to professional growth and improved instructional practices, there is a need to further consider how instructional coaching can be used to support teacher reflection. This phenomenon has been largely unexplored within remote instructional coaching environments (Kraft et al., 2018).

Professional Development and Instructional Coaching

PD programs often fail to result in improvement in instructional practice or student achievement despite a range of approaches (Garet et al., 2016; Glazerman et al., 2010; Harris & Sass, 2011; Randel et al., 2011). This is particularly true of traditional approaches that involve teachers as passive recipients of information; such approaches are characterized by low impacts on teacher practice (Knight, 2007). In considering the weak relationship between PD and desired outcomes, Desimone (2009) explored a broad range of longitudinal, cross-sectional, quasi-experimental, and qualitative studies and identified five critical features of effective PD. First, quality PD should have a content focus and be matched to specific subject matter and how students learn those topics. Second, it should include active learning, with the teachers actively participating in observation, analysis, and discussion. Third, PD efforts should be coherent and aligned with the broader school and district goals, as well as teacher knowledge and beliefs. Fourth, PD should have a sustained duration, including 20 or more hours of contact time across the school year. Finally, quality PD includes elements of collective participation, developing an interactive learning community with groups of teachers working together. Unlike other PD approaches, those that are characterized by these features show promise for improving teacher practice and student outcomes (Scher & O'Reilly, 2009).

Instructional coaching was introduced to overcome the shortcomings of traditional PD approaches by offering opportunities for instructional coaches to work specifically with teachers to help them implement research-based instructional practices in their classrooms (Knight, 2007). This is a versatile approach to teacher PD that can be used for any content or strategy (Sprick & Knight, 2018). Instructional coaching is characterized by ongoing observation and debrief cycles with the coach and teacher as co-participants (Desimone & Pak, 2017; Joyce & Showers, 1981; Knight, 2011). The job-embedded nature of this PD allows for meaningful and relevant learning that can translate directly to classroom practice (Deussen et al., 2007; Nolan & Hoover, 2010). Instructional coaches can take on a variety of roles and responsibilities (e.g., Denton & Hasbrouck, 2009), but supporting teacher reflection is central (Knight, 2007). One of the key goals of this reflective practice is for teachers to think critically about their own instruction, considering what went well and what could be improved, so they can identify areas for instructional improvement (Schön, 1987).

While some researchers (e.g., Kamil, 2006) have questioned the evidence base for instructional coaching, recent studies suggest it is a promising strategy. Desimone and Pak (2017) considered the alignment of instructional coaching with Desimone's (2009) tenets of quality PD, concluding that instructional coaching has strong potential to be high-quality. In a meta-analysis of 60 studies of teacher coaching programs that used causal research designs, Kraft et al. (2018) found large positive effects of coaching on teachers' instructional practices as well as positive effects on student academic achievement. They also found that providing teachers with instructional resources and materials, such as curriculum units, resulted in greater gains. Although they explored differences in outcomes based on whether coaching was conducted in person or virtually, Kraft et al. (2018) did not identify significant differences; however, they noted that even moderately sized differences would have been impossible to detect given the large standard errors. Thus, further exploration of virtual instructional coaching is warranted.

THEORETICAL FRAMEWORK

Situated cognition theorists (e.g., Brown et al., 1989) posit that learning is intricately linked to the activity, context, and culture in which it occurs. Our study is grounded in Putnam and Borko's (2000) conceptualization of teacher learning as (a) situated in particular contexts; (b) social in nature; and (c) distributed across the individual, other people, and tools. This sociocultural view of learning emphasizes the specific context and purpose of the learning (Gee, 1997), which for teachers, requires their classroom context to be central to learning efforts. Without the careful integration of the teaching context (e.g., characteristics of the student population, academic standards, required curricula, pacing expectations, administrative support, teacher background, and experience), learning opportunities may not translate to real-world application. This is particularly important in considering equitable access to and outcomes from PD opportunities; teachers' school and personal contexts must be considered and intentionally incorporated into the PD design to achieve meaningful learning.

In this study, three university-based coaches worked with a first-year teacher who was implementing an integrated STEM curriculum with his students for the first time. The coaching meetings centered on the teacher's actual students and instructional practices, providing a clear opportunity for him to put new pedagogical strategies into action. Knowledge was distributed across the teacher and the coaches, emphasizing the social and collective nature of knowledge construction (Hutchins, 1996; Zhang & Patel, 2006). Further, reflection played a central role in the coaching process (Knight & Cornett, 2009).

ANALYTICAL FRAMEWORK

Within this study, we adopted the reflective cycle developed by Gibbs (1988) to identify instances of teacher reflection in our analysis. Noting that debriefings following an experience are often superficial in nature, Gibbs (1988) recommended six stages to compose a full reflective cycle:

1. Description: What happened?
2. Feelings: What were your reactions and feelings?
3. Evaluation: What was good or bad about the experience?
4. Analysis: What sense can you make of the situation?
5. Conclusions: What can be concluded, either generally or in relation to you specifically, about the experience and your analysis?
6. Personal Action Plan: What would you do differently in this type of situation next time?

While Gibbs (1988) encouraged working through these steps sequentially if time allows, we utilized a less rigid approach and did not adhere to a strict sequential approach. However, in considering what constituted teacher reflection for the purposes of this study, we required that the teacher go beyond description (Stage 1) and comment on at least one of the other stages of the reflective cycle.

RESEARCH DESIGN

We utilized a single case study (Yin, 2014) design to explore the potential of remote instructional coaching to support a teacher's implementation of an integrated STEM unit and prompt teacher reflection. This method was selected because of the need for in-depth exploration of a social phenomenon and how it works. Turns of speech served as the units of analysis in this descriptive study. By utilizing speech turns, we were able to consider the fluid and dynamic nature of the coaching discussions, including instances where conversation was continuous versus those where the topic shifted (Sacks et al., 1974).

Context and Participants

This study built upon an existing RPP among a university, an urban school district, a Fortune 100 company, and the local community in the Southwestern United States. These partners worked together to design an innovative STEM school with an overarching goal of equity through education and wraparound community services. Three coaches, two of whom are the authors of this chapter, developed an integrated STEM curriculum unit that focused on physics concepts of force and motion and included an engineering challenge of designing a helmet to withstand a collision (for more information on the curriculum unit, see Wieselmann et al., 2022). Prior to adopting the unit as part of the STEM school curriculum, it was piloted in a seventh-grade classroom by Nick (pseudonym). Nick was a first-year teacher who identified as a White male and taught predominantly Latinx and Black students. He had completed an alternative teacher certification program the previous summer. With his undergraduate studies focusing on biology and chemistry, this summer program was the only teacher training Nick had received at the time he started teaching. He was implementing an integrated STEM unit for the first time and desired coaching to support his understanding of the curriculum materials and to facilitate his learning of STEM instructional strategies.

The three university-based coaches all had prior science teaching experience and varying degrees of coaching experience. I (Jeanna Wieselmann, Coach 1) am an assistant professor of STEM education. My teaching experience was primarily at the elementary school level in another state, and I have extensive knowledge of integrated STEM curriculum and instruction. I utilized this knowledge in formally appointed coaching positions throughout my graduate studies and have continued supporting teachers in my position as an assistant professor. Coach 2 was a first-year doctoral student. Her teaching experience included middle school science instruction in the state in which the study occurred, and she had informal coaching experience as a mentor to peer teachers. Marc Sager (Coach 3) was a first-year doctoral student. His teaching experience included secondary agricultural science education and integrated STEM curriculum development in the state in which the study occurred. He had informal coaching experience as a mentor to peer agricultural science teachers.

Data Collection and Analysis

The integrated STEM unit was taught over the course of five class periods, each of which was 90 minutes long. Prior to each class period, we coaches and the teacher met on Zoom to discuss the day's lesson plan; these meetings were referred to as planning meetings. We then observed the teacher's implementation of the lesson via Zoom. Finally, we all met again following the lesson in a debrief meeting focused on promoting reflection and considering any modifications that needed to be made to the lessons moving forward. The planning and debrief meetings were guided by a protocol intended to prompt teacher reflection but were designed to be informal and responsive to the topics of conversation that arose in each meeting.

We recorded and transcribed all of the Zoom planning and debrief meetings for analysis. Utilizing interaction analysis methods described by Jordan and Henderson (1995), we used collaborative viewing of the meeting videos to develop a codebook and code the data. We paused the video after each turn of speech and used inductive process coding (Saldaña, 2015) to capture the coaching moves evident in each speech turn. This inductive and collaborative approach to coding was critical in helping to reduce bias (Jordan & Henderson, 1995). As disagreements among coders emerged, we modified our codebook definitions to reach consensus. These discussions helped refine the codes and ensure that we were equally calibrated in their use (Wasser & Bresler, 1996). The final codebook included 24 codes (see Table 8.1).

Once collaborative coding was complete, we conducted code frequency counts for each coach in each Zoom meeting. These frequency counts were

Remote Instructional Coaching During the COVID-19 Pandemic ▪ **163**

TABLE 8.1	Codebook	
Abbreviation	**Code**	**Description**
AFF	Affirming	Providing positive feedback about something the teacher said or what was done in the classroom
AGEN	Attending to student agency and choice	Emphasizing opportunities for students to make choices in their learning
ANEC	Sharing anecdote from another classroom or person	Like PERS, but instead of personal experience as a teacher, this is secondhand experience or information
CURR	Supporting teacher in using curriculum materials	Walking through curriculum materials (slides, inquiry activities, lesson plans, etc.)
DATA	Focusing on student data	Discussing student assessment results (formative and summative)
DESC	Describing what happened	Objectively describing, without judgment, what happened in the classroom
DISC	Attending to student discourse	Emphasizing opportunities for students to contribute to small group or whole class discourse
EQUIT	Attending to equity	Emphasizing the need to ensure all students have access to the content and activities
FEED	Providing feedback	Providing a critique of teaching or suggesting improvement; must be tied directly to a specific instance or event
IMP	Planning for classroom implementation	Developing plans for how the lesson will be implemented
IMP-log	Attending to logistics of classroom implementation	Focusing on logistics of implementation (timing, materials, etc.)
IMP-troub	Troubleshooting classroom implementation	Addressing previous or anticipated challenges related to classroom implementation
LP	Developing/revising lesson plans	Building on or making changes to the existing lesson plans
MOD	Modeling	Explicitly modeling approaches to teaching, including specific phrasing, as if talking to students
PCK	Focusing on pedagogical content knowledge	Sharing teaching strategies or processes specific to the topic of instruction
PERS	Sharing personal experience	Describing relevant experiences from one's own teaching
PK	Focusing on pedagogical knowledge	Sharing general teaching strategies or practices
REF	Promoting reflection	Explicitly prompting the teacher to think about practices, students, etc.

(continued(

TABLE 8.1 Codebook (continued)

Abbreviation	Code	Description
REV	Revoicing	Restating an idea shared by the teacher or another coach
RW	Raising real-world connections	Emphasizing the real-world relevance of the lesson and content, including career connections
SCI	Focusing on science content	Emphasizing the importance of science concepts and building to deepen student understanding
STUD	Focusing attention on how students learn	Emphasizing student thinking and learning processes
STUD-online	Focusing attention on online student learning	Recognizing unique elements of student thinking and learning within the remote or hybrid context
TECH	Focusing on integrating technology	Discussing approaches to technology integration, including specific technology tools

used to calculate the percentage of coaching moves each code accounted for. This highlighted the relative frequency of each coaching move for a given coach and illustrated key differences in coaching moves across the three coaches. We also examined the temporal relationship between codes to determine which coaching moves preceded the teacher's reflective practice.

FINDINGS

In this section, we share the key findings related to the two research questions. First, we share the coaching moves and the frequencies with which they were utilized in the remote coaching environment. Next, we highlight the remote coaching moves that prompted Nick to reflect on his instructional practices, achieving the goal of promoting reflection through remote instructional coaching.

Coaching Moves

Our interaction analysis revealed that the coaches used a range of coaching moves within the remote coaching environment (see Figure 8.1). Most frequently (77 occasions), these focused on pedagogical knowledge, describing general, content-agnostic teaching strategies or practices with Nick. Given his unique pandemic-related experiences as a first-year teacher, Nick desired support on everything from approaches to distributing materials to monitoring small groups, and the coaches provided this type of feedback. The second most frequent coaching move was attending to the logistics of unit implementation (62 occasions). This included discussions about pacing and timing to ensure the lesson goals were accomplished within the class period, as well as supply logistics, such as ensuring that all students (both remote and in-person) had access to the necessary materials to complete the activities. A class COVID-19 exposure caused a shift from hybrid (with both remote and in-person students) to fully remote in the middle of the unit, so these discussions of logistics became even more frequent at that point.

The coaches also frequently focused attention on student thinking and how students learn (60 occasions) by referring to specific moments in the lessons when student thinking was revealed, or not revealed, through discussions or formative assessments. While Nick considered his own actions, the coaches pushed him to think critically about what students were taking away from the lessons and how their learning could be better supported. The coaches also recognized Nick's strengths and affirmed his decisions and instructional practices when they aligned with research-based practices for integrated STEM instruction (59 occasions). As Nick considered how to best implement the lessons in the hybrid or fully remote context, discussions of technology integration were frequent (51 occasions). These conversations included the consideration of the specific technology tools available as well as how to use these most effectively with students. The coaches also worked

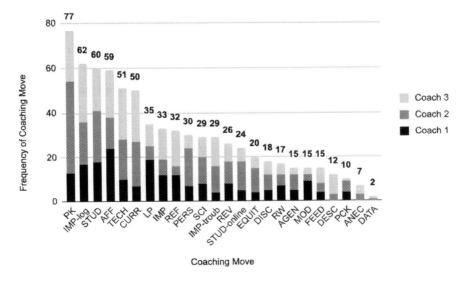

Figure 8.1 Frequency of coaching moves.

to ensure that Nick was familiar with all the instructional materials, walking through the slides, lesson plans, and inquiry-based activities (50 occasions).

When combined, these six coaching moves accounted for 49.3% of the 728 total moves that were utilized across all the planning and debrief meetings. The remaining interactions included 18 additional coaching moves, all of which had frequencies of 35 or fewer (see Figure 8.1).

In addition to considering the overall frequency of each code, we also considered each coach's unique approach to coaching. I (Wieselmann, Coach 1) performed a total of 202 coaching moves. I used my prior knowledge and expertise to provide an affirmation-rich approach to coaching, with 11.9% of my coaching moves centered around affirming Nick for his pedagogical and science content knowledge during the planning and debrief meetings. I also suggested revisions to the lesson plans (9.4% of my coaching moves), focused attention on student learning (8.9%) attended to logistics of classroom implementation (8.4%), and addressed pedagogical knowledge (6.4%).

Coach 2 performed a total of 265 coaching moves and used her expertise surrounding the content and the state standards to focus on pedagogical knowledge (15.5% of her coaching moves) and how students learn (8.7%). She also supported Nick in using the curriculum materials (7.6%), attended to logistics of classroom implementation (7.2%), and shared her personal teaching experiences (6.4%).

Marc Sager (Coach 3) performed a total of 261 coaching moves and employed his expertise surrounding integrated STEM curriculum design and the learning sciences to focus on the logistics of classroom implementation (9.9% of his coaching moves), integrating technology (8.9%), and pedagogical knowledge (8.9%). He also supported Nick's use of the curriculum materials (8.9%), provided affirmations to Nick (8.1%), and attended to student learning (7.3%).

Teacher Reflection

Nick reflected on his practice and student thinking on 36 distinct occasions. Because of the unit of analysis focusing on speech turns, it was possible for more than one coaching move to be used in the speech turn preceding teacher reflection. As expected, reflection was often preceded by a coach explicitly prompting this reflection (16 occasions; see Figure 8.2). However, even in the absence of explicit prompting, Nick reflected on 20 additional occasions. In analyzing the coaching moves that preceded these occasions of reflection that were not explicitly prompted, several moves were most frequent. In descending order of frequency, these coaching moves included affirming the teacher (12 occasions), focusing on how students learn (8

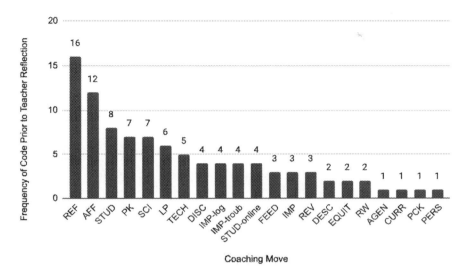

Figure 8.2 Coaching moves that preceded teacher reflection.

occasions), focusing on pedagogical knowledge (7 occasions), focusing on science content (7 occasions), developing or revising lesson plans (6 occasions), and focusing on integrating technology (5 occasions). Interestingly, providing Nick with feedback on his instructional practices only prompted reflection on three occasions.

Nick reflected on a range of topics during the planning and debrief meetings with the coaches. For example, in the Lesson 2 debrief, I prompted Nick to reflect on why he chose to elaborate on a science concept beyond what was included in the original lesson plan and why he used a free body diagram to explain this concept to his students. Nick reflected:

> It seemed that they needed a visualization of the directions, and I thought that free body diagrams, their essence, is for them to depict simple forces. I shouldn't have done it on a ramp, that was too much. I probably should have done just a flat surface, but I still think a free body diagram, and that example would have been made more powerful if we did the PhET simulation, but I think having some visualization of the concept of force [was important].

Nick recognized that providing students with a way to visualize forces acting upon an object was important to their understanding; however, he recognized that adding an inclined plane into the free body diagram resulted in the visualization being more complex than what some students were ready for. Being prompted to consider his instructional choices and their impact on student thinking pushed Nick to reflect and identify both the affordances and limitations of his choices.

Nick continued to reflect on student thinking and understanding of the central science concepts throughout the unit. In the Lesson 5 debrief, Marc prompted Nick to consider an egg drop activity in relation to the desired learning outcomes. Nick reflected:

> There were two ways students could have approached this. They could have really dug deep into the physics behind it and been like, "Why are we making the decisions that we're making?" And then there's the "Let's put something together and see if it works" approach. And I think some scaffolded short-answer questions to get the students to interrogate the reasons behind the design choices they may or may not make would have been helpful...and would get them to engage with the conceptual problem they were working with instead of the material problem they were working with. Because I think a lot of them were working on, "How do I keep this egg from cracking?" and not a lot were working on, "How do I dissipate the energy?" And I think that's the best way to frame the problem.

This recognition that students could be successful on the design challenge without actually having a conceptual understanding of the science that underpinned the challenge made Nick consider how he could ensure greater alignment between the physics concepts and the engineering design tasks.

Nick also considered student engagement through his reflections. For example, in the Lesson 1 debrief, I acknowledged the challenging circumstances Nick faced in the lesson, including facilitating his first hands-on activity with students, managing both in-person and remote students, and coordinating industry guest speakers who spoke to the class via Zoom. Following my affirmation of Nick's effort and perseverance despite these challenges, Nick went on to reflect on this lesson (as compared to his typical, more traditional approach to teaching). He said, "It was definitely the most engaged [students have been], and that was the most fun I've had teaching." This recognition that hands-on, integrated STEM activities could be appealing to both students and himself had the potential to positively influence Nick's teaching practices moving forward.

Nick further reflected on some of his challenges related to classroom management. For example, in the Lesson 2 debrief, Marc provided feedback to Nick, pointing out that he called on a particular student more often than others, sometimes to the full exclusion of students in the class discussion. After receiving this feedback, Nick reflected:

> I have a problem with [student]. He loves talking, and I don't want to squash that. And also, he is slightly addicted to video games, so I have to sit him in a specific location so I can see his screen, which also means he was sitting there

[at the front of the classroom] today. It is hard to ignore when he is like [raising his hand] up, up, up. .

In this reflection, Nick acknowledged the tension between maintaining student participation and ensuring that all students have a chance to contribute.

In addition to these illustrative examples, Nick reflected on many aspects of instruction, including eliciting and building upon students' initial ideas, ensuring the development of conceptual understanding of science through engineering activities, incorporating students' lived experiences into instruction, and increasing student engagement. However, it is important to note that Nick did not spontaneously reflect on his instruction. Rather, these instances of reflection were always prompted by a specific coaching move or moves. While some instances were prompted by an explicit request for reflection and others were not, no discernable differences in the topic or depth of reflection were identified based on the type of prompt that resulted in teacher reflection.

DISCUSSION

In this study, we considered the potential for remote instructional coaching to support teacher reflection. As described in the previous section, a variety of remote coaching moves pushed Nick to reflect on his instructional practices and choices on 36 distinct occasions across 5 days of instruction. In informal communications following the study, Nick shared that this type of coaching support far exceeded the support he had previously received in his first year of teaching, despite the fact that he had three individuals assigned to him as mentors or coaches. Given the potential for reflection to result in improved teaching practices (e.g., Borrego & Henderson, 2014), it is particularly important that early-career teachers are supported in this way. Our previous analysis of Nick's instructional practices in the integrated STEM unit and a comparison unit using a validated observation protocol revealed that the provision of the curriculum materials and coaching support further translated to improved teaching practices (Wieselmann et al., 2022), illustrating the potential for remote instructional coaching to promote deep reflection and improved instruction.

It is important to note that specific contextual features likely impacted the range and frequency of the coaching moves utilized in this study. As a first-year teacher, Nick wanted and needed support in basic pedagogical strategies that may not have been needed for a more experienced teacher. The coaches also recognized the challenging COVID-19-related circumstances he faced in his first year of teaching and made efforts to provide affirmations to Nick on a regular basis. As a result, the most frequently used coaching moves included affirmations and focusing on pedagogical knowledge. Further, because of the hybrid and remote teaching context necessitated by COVID-19, a significant amount of time was dedicated to discussing implementation logistics and technology. While these factors may limit the ability to generalize findings from this study to a broader population, they also emphasize the situated nature of teacher learning within a particular context (Gee, 1997; Putnam & Borko, 2000). Without attending to the immediate contextual factors and teacher needs, the remote instructional coaching likely would have failed to achieve the intended outcomes of supporting a first-year teacher in implementing an integrated STEM unit in hybrid and remote contexts, while also promoting the teacher's reflection and growth in teaching.

With reflection being one of the key elements of instructional coaching (Knight & Cornett, 2009), it is critical to consider how teacher reflection was prompted and supported in the remote coaching setting. While explicit prompts for reflection (e.g., "What would you do differently if you taught this lesson again, and why would you make those changes?") were effective in eliciting reflection, the teacher also reflected in the absence of such prompts. Interestingly, the coaching move of affirming the teacher was the most frequent prompt that led to reflection outside of explicit prompting. It is possible that Nick felt more comfortable critiquing his own instructional practices when he had already been affirmed by the coaches. This study demonstrates that teacher reflection can be prompted by a range of coaching moves, including explicit requests for reflection as well as more general discussion of instruction.

In considering which coaching moves most frequently preceded teacher reflection, it became apparent that two of the six most frequent moves (supporting the teacher in using curriculum materials and focusing on the logistics of implementation) never prompted Nick to reflect on his instruction. This seems to suggest that the frequent use of these moves may have been a less effective use of coaching time. While PD should have a designated purpose (Gee, 1997), it is also important to recognize that instructional coaching is a versatile approach to teacher learning that can be used for a variety of purposes (Sprick & Knight, 2018). In this study, the coaching aims were twofold: supporting a first-year teacher in implementing an integrated STEM unit for the first time and promoting reflection on teaching practices. Thus, it is unsurprising that some coaching moves were more focused on the first goal rather than the second. In designing the planning and debrief meetings, we originally envisioned a clear separation of purpose and focus, with the planning discussions dedicated to helping Nick navigate the curriculum materials and attending to implementation logistics, and the debrief discussions focused specifically on reflection. In practice, this distinction became less apparent, as Nick reflected and raised logistical questions or concerns across both types of meetings. Although reflection was more frequent in debrief meetings, it also occurred in planning meetings, illustrating the intertwined nature of the coaching aims. Although it is important to maintain a clear purpose, we found that it was possible to simultaneously work toward multiple goals through remote instructional coaching.

While there was overlap in the coaching moves used by the three coaches, each coach also adopted a distinct coaching style in the remote environment. As the most senior coach, I adopted a coaching approach that emphasized the positive aspects of the teacher's practices through affirmations. This may have served to make the teacher more comfortable with being observed and open to discussing his teaching practices. Coach 2 drew heavily upon her knowledge of general pedagogical strategies, offering suggestions for everything from classroom management to ensuring equitable participation by using a random name generator. Given her recent classroom teaching experience in the same state and district, these suggestions were highly relevant. Marc Sager had extensive experience with technology integration and was able to share specific advice related to the hybrid format of instruction with both remote and in-person learners. Each coach leveraged their position and distinct set of experiences in unique ways in developing the coaching relationships. Previous studies have shown that coaches differ in the extent to which they focus on teacher reflection, with some being more directive and others being more reflective and responsive, involving teachers in exploring the thinking behind their practices (Deussen et al., 2007; Ippolito, 2010). This study illustrates that even within the same context, individual differences across coaches are important to consider.

Situated within an RPP context, this study also offers insight into the affordances of instructional coaching within an RPP. Nick intentionally sought support related to integrated STEM instruction in hybrid and remote modalities, and our shared interest in his problem of practice presented a mutual and collaborative context for learning by all of us (Coburn et al., 2013; Coburn & Penuel, 2016). The clear framing of the problem of practice and the shared goals of the RPP allowed for a consistent focus on supporting teacher reflection and practice in integrated STEM instruction. This consistency in focus may have led to success in instructional coaching, as previous studies have demonstrated that competing priorities can shift the focus of instructional coaching. For example, Wieselmann et al. (2021) found that literacy and STEM coaching were combined into a single position in an effort to accomplish dual initiatives. Blazar and Kraft (2015) found that over time, the coaching emphasis shifted from instructional delivery to behavior management, and this shift was associated with less positive outcomes related to teacher practices. The RPP structure provided helpful parameters for focusing the coaching efforts while also ensuring

LIMITATIONS

As previously described, this study was situated within a specific context at a specific point in time, so caution should be taken in generalizing these findings. In particular, COVID-19 caused significant shifts in PD and instructional approaches used with students, which impacted the nature of coaching in this study. However, the codebook we have developed may prove to be useful across contexts as remote instructional coaching is further explored. Additional studies that compare remote, intentionally designed online, and in-person instructional coaching are needed in order to draw conclusions about the relative effectiveness of each approach.

We also note that teacher reflection may be impacted by factors in addition to the coaching moves that are implemented. For example, across the three coaches in this study, I implemented the fewest coaching moves but prompted reflection more than the other coaches. While this could be a result of my specific coaching moves, it could also result from personal factors. For example, Nick had a longer professional relationship with me than the other coaches, and he may have responded differently to my prompts given my status as an assistant professor, in comparison to Coaches 2 and 3, who were doctoral students. As situated cognition theorists note, it is impossible to separate teacher learning from the context and social interactions among the individuals (e.g., Putnam & Borko, 2000). Thus, we are unable to draw definitive conclusions about the relative impact of the individual versus the coaching moves.

IMPLICATIONS AND CONCLUSION

Situated within a community-based RPP, this study explored the interactions between a classroom teacher and university-based instructional coaches. In light of the COVID-19 context, a remote approach to instructional coaching was utilized to achieve two aims: supporting a first-year teacher in implementing an integrated STEM unit for the first time (see Wieselmann et al., 2022) and promoting teacher reflection on instructional practices. The ability to achieve these aims despite numerous challenges, including shifts in instructional format throughout the unit, a combination of in-person and fully remote students, and a lack of access to resources for some students, illustrates the potential for remote instructional coaching to support improved instruction.

While limited in scope, this study provides a practical codebook for use in future studies. It also reveals promising opportunities for remote instructional coaching. Given the evidence of improved teaching practices (Wieselmann et al., 2022) and the range of coaching moves that prompted teacher reflection, findings from this study can be used to inform instructional coaching decisions. Further, this study has implications for providing more equitable access to high-quality, integrated, STEM education within historically under-resourced communities, which may not have access to in-person instructional coaches.

ACKNOWLEDGMENTS

This material is based upon work supported by the Toyota USA Foundation under grant numbers G001740 and G002017. Any opinions, findings, conclusions, or recommendations expressed in this material are those of the author(s) and do not necessarily reflect the views of the Toyota USA Foundation.

REFERENCES

Anderson, T., & Shattuck, J. (2012). Design-based research: A decade of progress in education research? *Educational Researcher, 41*(1), 16–25. https://doi.org/10.3102/0013189X11428813

Attard, A., Di Iorio, E., Geven, K. M., & Santa, R. (2010). *Student-centered learning: Toolkit for students, staff and higher education institutions.* Education International; European Students' Union. https://esu-online.org/?publication=student-centred-learning-toolkit-students-staff-higher-education-institutions

Blazar, D., & Kraft, M. A. (2015). Exploring mechanisms of effective teacher coaching: A tale of two cohorts from a randomized experiment. *Educational Evaluation and Policy Analysis, 37*(4), 542–566. https://doi.org/10.3102/0162373715579487

Booker, L., Conaway, C., & Schwartz, N. (2019). *Five ways RPPs can fail and how to avoid them: Applying conceptual frameworks to improve RPPs.* William T. Grant Foundation. https://wtgrantfoundation.org/wp-content/uploads/2019/06/Five-Ways-RPPs-Can-Fail.pdf

Booth, J. L., Cooper, L. A., Donovan, M. S., Huyghe, A., Koedinger, K., & Pare-Blagoev, E. J. (2015). Design-based research within the constraints of practice: AlgebraByExample. *Journal of Education for Students Placed at Risk, 20*(1–2), 79–100. https://doi.org/10.1080/10824669.2014.986674

Borrego, M., & Henderson, C. (2014). Increasing the use of evidence-based teaching in STEM higher education: A comparison of eight change strategies. *Journal of Engineering Education, 103*(2), 220–252. https://doi.org/10.1002/jee.20040

Brown, J. S., Collins, A., & Duguid, P. (1989). Situated cognition and the culture of learning. *Educational Researcher, 18*(1), 32–42. https://doi.org/10.3102/0013189X018001032

Bubnys, R., & Zavadskienė, L. (2017). Exploring the concept of reflective practice in the context of student-centered teacher education. *SOCIETY. INTEGRATION. EDUCATION. Proceedings of the International Scientific Conference, 1*, 91–101. http://dx.doi.org/10.17770/sie2017vol1.2250

Campbell, C. (2012). Professional learning—Reflective practice in science education. In C. Campbell & W. Jobling (Eds.), *Science in early childhood* (pp. 177–189). Cambridge University Press. https://doi.org/10.1017/cbo9781139197007.013

Coburn, C. E., Penuel, W. R., & Geil, K. E. (2013). *Research practice partnerships: A strategy for leveraging research for educational improvement in school districts.* William T. Grant Foundation. https://wtgrantfoundation.org/wp-content/uploads/2015/10/Research-Practice-Partnerships-at-the-District-Level.pdf

Coburn, C. E., & Penuel, W. R. (2016). Research–practice partnerships in education: Outcomes, dynamics, and open questions. *Educational Researcher, 45*(1), 48–54. https://doi.org/10.3102/0013189X16631750

Dede, C., Jass Ketelhut, D., Whitehouse, P., Breit, L., & McCloskey, E. M. (2009). A research agenda for online teacher professional development. *Journal of Teacher Education, 60*(1), 8–19. https://doi.org/10.1177/0022487108327554

Denton, C. A., & Hasbrouck, J. (2009). A description of instructional coaching and its relationship to consultation. *Journal of Educational and Psychological Consultation, 19*(2), 150–175. https://doi.org/10.1080/10474410802463296

Desimone, L. M. (2009). Improving impact studies of teachers' professional development: Toward better conceptualizations and measures. *Educational Researcher, 38*(3), 181–199. https://doi.org/10.3102/0013189X08331140

Desimone, L. M., & Pak, K. (2017). Instructional coaching as high-quality professional development. *Theory Into Practice, 56*(1), 3–12. https://doi.org/10.1080/00405841.2016.1241947

Deussen, T., Coskie, T., Robinson, L., & Autio, E. (2007). *"Coach" can mean many things: Five categories of literacy coaches in Reading First* (Issues & Answers Report, REL 2007–No. 005). U.S. Department of Education, Institute of Education Sciences, National Center for Education Evaluation and Regional Assistance, Regional Educational Laboratory Northwest. https://ies.ed.gov/ncee/edlabs/regions/northwest/pdf/REL_2007005_sum.pdf

Fishman, B. J., Marx, R. W., Best, S., & Tal, R. (2003). Linking teacher and student learning to improve professional development in systemic reform. *Teaching and Teacher Education, 19*(6), 643–658. https://doi.org/10.1016/s0742-051x(03)00059-3

Garet, M. S., Heppen, J. B., Walters, K., Parkinson, J., Smith, T. M., Song, M., Garrett, R., Yang, R., & Borman, G. D. (2016). *Focusing on mathematical knowledge: The impact of content-intensive teacher professional development* (NCEE 2016-4010). National Center for Education Evaluation and Regional Assistance, Institute of Education Sciences, U.S. Department of Education. https://files.eric.ed.gov/fulltext/ED569154.pdf

Gee, J. P. (1997). Thinking, learning, and reading: The situated sociocultural mind. In D. Kirshner & J. A. Whitson (Eds.), *Situated cognition: Social, semiotic, and psychological perspectives* (pp. 235–259). Routledge. https://doi.org/10.4324/9781003064121-9

Geier, R., Blumenfeld, P. C., Marx, R. W., Krajcik, J. S., Fishman, B., Soloway, E., & Clay-Chambers, J. (2008). Standardized test outcomes for students engaged in inquiry-based science curricula in the context of urban reform. *Journal of Research in Science Teaching, 45*(8), 922–939. https://doi.org/10.1002/tea.20248

Gibbs, G. (1988). *Learning by doing: A guide to teaching and learning methods.* Oxford Further Education Unit.

Glazerman, S., Isenberg, E., Dolfin, S., Bleeker, M., Johnson, A., Grider, M., & Jacobus, M. (2010). *Impacts of comprehensive teacher induction: Final results from a randomized controlled study* (NCEE 2010-4028). National Center for Education Evaluation and Regional Assistance, Institute of Education Sciences, U.S. Department of Education. https://ies.ed.gov/ncee/pubs/20104027/pdf/20104028.pdf

Harris, D. N., & Sass, T. R. (2011). Teacher training, teacher quality and student achievement. *Journal of Public Economics, 95*(7–8), 798–812. https://doi.org/10.1016/j.jpubeco.2010.11.009

Holly, M. L. (1989). Reflective writing and the spirit of inquiry. *Cambridge Journal of Education, 19*(1), 71–80. https://doi.org/10.1080/0305764890190109

Hutchins, E. (1996). *Cognition in the wild.* MIT Press. https://doi.org/10.7551/mitpress/1881.001.0001

Ippolito, J. (2010). Three ways that literacy coaches balance responsive and directive relationships with teachers. *The Elementary School Journal, 111*(1), 164–190. https://doi.org/10.1086/653474

Jordan, B., & Henderson, A. (1995). Interaction analysis: Foundations and practice. *Journal of the Learning Sciences, 4*(1), 39–103. https://doi.org/10.1207/s15327809jls0401_2

Joyce, B. R., & Showers, B. (1981). Transfer of training: The contribution of "coaching." *Journal of Education, 163*(2), 163–172. https://doi.org/10.1177/002205748116300208

Kamil, M. (2006). What we know—and don't know—about coaching? A conversation with Professor Michael Kamil. *Northwest Education, 12*, 16–17. https://permanent.access.gpo.gov/lps3359/2006-fall.pdf

Killion, J. P., & Todnem, G. R. (1991). A process for personal theory building. *Educational Leadership, 48*(6), 14–16. https://files.ascd.org/staticfiles/ascd/pdf/journals/ed_lead/el_199103_killion.pdf

Knight, J. (2007). *Instructional coaching: A partnership approach to improving instruction.* Corwin.

Knight, J. (2011). *Unmistakable impact: A partnership approach for dramatically improving instruction.* Corwin. https://doi.org/10.4135/9781452219721

Knight, J., & Cornett, J. (2009, April 16). *Studying the impact of instructional coaching* [Paper presentation]. American Educational Research Association Conference, San Diego, California. https://resources.corwin.com/sites/default/files/Studying%20the%20Impact%20of%20Instructional%20Coaching%204.0.doc

Koehler, M. J., Mishra, P., & Yahya, K. (2007). Tracing the development of teacher knowledge in a design seminar: Integrating content, pedagogy and technology. *Computers & Education, 49*(3), 740–762. https://doi.org/10.1016/j.compedu.2005.11.012

Kraft, M. A., Blazar, D., & Hogan, D. (2018). The effect of teacher coaching on instruction and achievement: A meta-analysis of the causal evidence. *Review of Educational Research, 88*(4), 547–588. https://doi.org/10.3102/0034654318759268

Lynch, K., Hill, H. C., Gonzalez, K. E., & Pollard, C. (2019). Strengthening the research base that informs STEM instructional improvement efforts: A meta-analysis. *Educational Evaluation and Policy Analysis, 41*(3), 260–293. https://doi.org/10.3102/0162373719849044

Nolan, J., Jr., & Hoover, L. (2010). *Teacher supervision and evaluation* (3rd ed.). Wiley.

Putnam, R. T., & Borko, H. (2000). What do new views of knowledge and thinking have to say about research on teacher learning? *Educational Researcher, 29*(1), 4–15. https://doi.org/10.3102/0013189X029001004

Randel, B., Beesley, A. D., Apthorp, H., Clark, T. F., Wang, X., Cicchinelli, L. F., & Williams, J. M. (2011). *Classroom assessment for student learning: Impact on elementary school mathematics in the central region* (NCEE 2011-4005). National Center for Education Evaluation and Regional Assistance, Institute of Education Sciences, U.S. Department of Education. https://files.eric.ed.gov/fulltext/ED517969.pdf

Sacks, H., Schegloff, E. A., & Jefferson, G. (1974). A simplest systematics for the organization of turn-taking for conversation. *Language, 50*(4), 696–735. https://doi.org/10.2307/412243

Saldaña, J. (2015). *The coding manual for qualitative researchers* (3rd ed.). SAGE.

Scharber, C., Peterson, L., Baskin, K., Cabeen, J., Gustafson, D., & Alberts, J. (2021). A research–practice partnership about K12 technology integration: Technology as a catalyst for teacher learning through failure and creative risk-taking. *TechTrends, 65*(4), 626–635. http://dx.doi.org/10.1007/s11528-021-00621-9

Scher, L., & O'Reilly, F. (2009). Professional development for K–12 math and science teachers: What do we really know? *Journal of Research on Educational Effectiveness, 2*(3), 209–249. https://doi.org/10.1080/19345740802641527

Schön, D. A. (1987). *Educating the reflective practitioner: Toward a new design for teaching and learning in the professions.* Jossey-Bass.

Sellars, M. (2012). Teachers and change: The role of reflective practice. *Procedia–Social and Behavioral Sciences, 55*, 461–469. https://doi.org/10.1016/j.sbspro.2012.09.525

Shulman, L. S. (1987). Knowledge and teaching: Foundations of the new reform. *Harvard Educational Review, 57*(1), 1–23. http://dx.doi.org/10.17763/haer.57.1.j463w79r56455411

Sprick, R., & Knight, J. (2018). Involving teachers in schoolwide behavior policy. *Educational Leadership, 76*(1), 48–53. https://www.ascd.org/el/articles/involving-teachers-in-schoolwide-behavior-policy

Wasser, J. D., & Bresler, L. (1996). Working in the interpretive zone: Conceptualizing collaboration in qualitative research teams. *Educational Researcher, 25*(5), 5–15. https://doi.org/10.3102/0013189X025005005

Wieselmann, J. R., Roehrig, G. H., Ring-Whalen, E. A., & Meagher, T. (2021). Becoming a STEM-focused school district: Administrators' roles and experiences. *Education Sciences, 11*(12), 805. https://doi.org/10.3390/educsci11120805

Wieselmann, J. R., Sager, M. T., & Binford, L. (2022). A school–university partnership for integrated STEM learning: Curriculum modifications and considerations for emergency remote teaching. *PDS Partners: Bridging Research to Practice, 17*(2), 95–116. https://eric.ed.gov/?id=EJ1349028

Yarnall, L., Shechtman, N., & Penuel, W. R. (2006). Using handheld computers to support improved classroom assessment in science: Results from a field trial. *Journal of Science Education and Technology, 15*(2), 142–158. https://doi.org/10.1007/s10956-006-9008-4

Yin, R. K. (2014). *Case study research: Design and methods* (5th ed.). SAGE.

Zhang, J., & Patel, V. L. (2006). Distributed cognition, representation, and affordance. *Pragmatics & Cognition, 14*(2), 333–341. https://doi.org/10.1075/pc.14.2.12zha

SECTION III

TWIN EPIDEMICS

CHAPTER 9

YOUTH CURATION AS COLLECTIVE DISRUPTION

Making in Museums During the COVID-19 Pandemic

Kristina M. Stamatis
University of Nebraska Omaha

Joseph L. Polman
University of Colorado Boulder

José Rogelio Manriquez-Hernandez
University of Colorado Boulder

ABSTRACT

The COVID-19 pandemic offered opportunities to recreate frameworks for participation. This chapter examines a possible future for youth learning in museums through community curation that arose from the constraints imposed by the pandemic. Historically, youth have been invited into museum contexts as consumers rather than curators. However, the changes in edu-

School–University–Community Research in a (Post) COVID-19 World, pages 181–205
Copyright © 2023 by Information Age Publishing
www.infoagepub.com
All rights of reproduction in any form reserved.

cational engagement, alongside systems of oppression and inequity emphasized during COVID-19, point to the ways that youth must be engaged as critically literate participants in the creation of historical narratives. During the 2020–2021 school year, a small group of educators, university researchers, and Latino students partnered to create a youth-curated museum exhibit intended to showcase the narratives of Latino youth as they navigated their experiences in a small city in the mountain west. While our project began as an attempt to disrupt the dominant narratives by asking youth to recount their own lived experiences, the COVID-19 pandemic shed new light on systemic inequities faced by historically marginalized community members and added a sense of urgency and justice to the work of our youth partners. We present the experiences of several young people as they navigated the creation of a museum exhibit in a hybrid learning format. Our analysis illustrates the potential for youth-community curation sponsored by community museums in partnership with schools and universities as spaces for learning and engagement during a period when so many other educational spaces were faced with extreme limitations.

In October 2020, six collaborators sat around the lobby of the museum in masks, each perched on modular vinyl seating in six-foot increments, separated for safety from COVID-19. A small, pressed pine table held curated objects—feathers and leaves and iPads with images of things too large to bring back to the museum—that we had found as we explored the surrounding neighborhood. It was the first day of *Viviendo Aquí*, a partnership between researchers from a large university, an educator at a local history museum, and a group of Latino teenagers who had volunteered to lead a community curation project to represent the stories and experiences they felt were missing from the museum's exhibits. While our meeting had started with a tour of the museum, COVID-19 pandemic mandates dictated that we should spend as much time outside as possible. We took advantage of the late-afternoon sun and walked around the neighborhood together, taking pictures and finding objects that could serve to help us get to know one another and our relationships to the city. Walking through the residential streets, we talked about our experiences. It was nearly Halloween, and the teens laughed as we walked past decorated houses, sharing stories of their own traditions for Día de los Muertos. As the light faded, we returned to the museum lobby and laid out our treasures.

Each of us (teen participants, museum educator, researcher, and undergraduate collaborator) presented mini exhibits, a collection of three objects or sounds that told a story about our experiences in our city. Telema (all participant names are pseudonyms), a ninth-grade student at a local high school, went first, laying out her objects and images. Through her mask, she explained that she wanted to hear how others would interpret her display. Uriel, Telema's older brother, pointed to a picture Telema had taken of a sign that stated "Justice." He noted that they spent a lot of time marching for social justice with their mom, a local advocate for women's rights. Maggie, the museum educator, drew our attention to how Telema seemed to collect textures rather than artifacts that told a definitive story. Telema agreed and explained that the objects she collected both reminded her of home in Mexico and of life in our city. "It's good to remember that people can see our stories when we, like, share them," she said.

After the activity, Jose, an undergraduate researcher and author on this paper who collaborated on the project's implementation, agreed. "Having someone else explain what we collected felt productive because they explained it through a different lens. It helped us see how other people experience things and how they explain things differently than us." Maggie agreed and pointed out that the activity was also unique because we never would have left the museum if not for the pandemic. "It will be interesting to see how this experience none of us wanted might actually shape our exhibit," she said, referring to the required masks, distancing, and limited group gatherings that were mandated because of the pandemic that began in 2020.

In this chapter, we explore the ways a partnership between a local museum educator, a university-based research team, and a group of 41 secondary students resulted in the design and development of a museum exhibit during the COVID-19 pandemic. The project, entitled *Viviendo Aquí*, took place over the 2020–2021 school year in three phases. First, an undergraduate facilitator (Jose), museum educator (Maggie), and graduate student researcher (Kristina) met with three teens from local middle and high schools to discuss the potential for a museum exhibit that could add their stories to the dominant narratives often present in this local history museum and more broadly in their city. Next, educators and youth, whom the museum called the Teen Corps, developed digital workshops to support local classes of primarily Latino[1] middle and high school students in creating shadow boxes that extended participation in the exhibit. Finally, the Teen Corps worked with Maggie to design and curate the exhibit, using the stories collected from themselves, their families, and other local secondary students who participated in digital workshops with the team.

Throughout this chapter, we take a sociocritical approach to learning (e.g., Gutiérrez et al., 2019; Vossoughi & Gutiérrez, 2017), which helps us understand the ways young people develop identities as they engage in acts of representation and restorying (Stamatis, 2021; Stornaiuolo & Thomas, 2018) through making and creating (Shannon, 2015; Sheridan et al., 2014). We understand the museum context as one that is both underrepresented in educational research and rich in possibilities for youth to explore what it means to assert agency through acts of public representation (Tobelem,

2013). Amid the dual pandemics of COVID-19 and racism in the United States (de Royston et al., 2020), and particularly in the context of the political rhetoric that was used to vilify Latino people during the 2016 and 2020 elections (e.g., Phillips, 2017), our project was designed to center Latino youth and the stories they deemed missing from the dominant narratives in their community.

The collaborative nature of this project meant that youth, educators, and researchers mutually contributed to reimagining the kinds of engagement that can happen in museum settings. The teen corps and participants across the project took advantage of the set of available and emerging tools and practices for adjusting to the needs for remote and hybrid education, and in the process of combining these tools with the aims of community curation and existing educational practices, created a new set of possibilities for cross-institutional learning.

BACKGROUND

Curation in Museums

Historically, museums have been spaces that draw upon curatorial interpretations to represent "relationships between people and documents" (Latham & Simmons, 2019, p. 102), or as Stránský (1987) wrote, "the specific relation between man and reality" (p. 295). However, in the United States, these representations have been primarily interpreted by White museum professionals—in 2015, 76% of staff museums across the United States were White (American Alliance of Museums, 2019). While museums in the 21st century have made concerted efforts to increase representation of Black, Indigenous, and people-of-color engaged in programming, the survival of museums as cultural institutions depends upon their ability to become more representative of and relevant to the diverse peoples in their communities (Simon, 2010; Yarrow et al., 2008). For curators, this work has led to reconsidering the role of Whiteness in preservation (Debono, 2014), raising questions about who is curating, for what purpose, and to preserve which lived histories?

These questions have pushed some museum professionals to consider how to develop practices positioning diverse communities as curators, rather than consumers, which has led to trends in collaborative exhibit-building to disrupt hegemonic portrayals of groups through the usurpation of artifacts and the interpretation of exhibits through the mostly White lenses of museum professionals (Debono, 2014). As museums acknowledge how White supremacy has shaped understandings of history, some curators have questioned how to restory narratives that have centered Whiteness (e.g., Shannon,

2015). Community curation—community members and museum professionals collaborating to curate exhibits—has emerged as common practice for museums seeking decolonization (Ferguson & Renner, 2019; Simon, 2010). However, discrepancies exist in how community members are positioned (Tobelem, 2013). Boundaries between traditional curation and community-oriented efforts raise questions about how collaborations can support justice rather than marginalization (Black, 2010).

Community Curation

Beyond the curatorial work of professionals, research in museum studies has also demonstrated the continued need for community-based approaches to shift how diverse communities engage and to broaden representation in exhibits if museums are to continue growing their audiences (e.g., Hill & Douilette, 2014; McCarthy & Herring, 2015). Several museums in the United States have created models to address the ways that collaborative efforts in museums can honor the traditions and perspectives of participants while upholding the curatorial integrity of museum spaces. For example, a Community Curation Program at one Smithsonian Museum supports the "preservation and sharing of community history and culture" (National Museum of African American History & Culture, 2022, para. 1) by offering digitization services to participants to simultaneously preserve family histories and extend understandings of U.S. history through the intentional inclusion of Black family stories. Where the physical museum offers "parallel examinations of African and European societies as they encounter one another on the coast of Africa in the early fifteenth century" (Melish et al., 2017, p. 145), the digitization project expands understandings of Black history in America by creating space for families to share their own stories, artifacts, and understandings.

Some prior efforts toward community curation, such as the Missouri History Museum's exhibit *Through the Eyes of a Child: Growing Up Black in St. Louis 1940–1980*, similarly engaged community oral history efforts with exhibit development. In recent years, these kinds of oral history projects for museum collections and public display have made use of online platforms to provide public archives of the stories they collect. Additionally, several museums have begun to seek the expertise of staff who embody the identities of the people their artifacts depict; for example, the Metropolitan Art Museum hired Native American curator Patricia Marroquin Norby in 2020. However, even as efforts have been made to reexamine the ways that communities might support more authentic curation of historically marginalized stories, issues of sovereignty and cultural property remain (Vamanu, 2020).

Further, despite these moves toward community curation, barriers to participation—including lack of representative staff, lack of information about accessible tickets for low-income families, and lack of bilingual programming—have kept historically marginalized communities from seeing their histories accurately represented in museums (Black, 2010; Debono, 2014). Engaging diverse patrons is particularly urgent for museums that are considering how to develop new generations of museum goers. As technology makes information more accessible, there is often less need for patrons to travel to museums to gain perspectives on the content of museums. This lack of patron engagement has led to museum professionals exploring ways to leverage technology toward public engagement. The COVID-19 pandemic presented yet another urgent opportunity for museums to explore what Yarrow et al. (2008) described as the rich possibilities for including patrons—in the telling and interpretation of the multiple stories embedded in artifacts—by leveraging technology to engage participants who may have never before had opportunities to attend museum exhibits (McQuade, 2020).

Youth and Museum Education Programs

While generations of school children have visited history, science, and art museums on fieldtrips, cuts to school funding have shifted the availability of these kinds of experiences for young people (Harackiewicz et al., 2016). However, museum education programs have a pivotal role to play in supporting youth to actively and critically examine the world. Hein (2011) explained that as history museums have become institutions whose missions often center on "social responsibility" (p. 342), education in museums has had to become more active as opposed to a passive absorption of information. One example is the development of exhibits, which are either displayed at the school or—less often—at a partner museum site (e.g., Cornish et al., 2021; Wylder et al., 2014). Social studies and history classes have most often engaged in such museum exhibit development, frequently around local history or family history (e.g., Boardman et al., 2021; Levstik & Barton, 1997). These projects aim to develop youths' historical thinking by challenging students to put stories they have heard in interviews of family members or community elders in historical context; the exhibitions often simultaneously provide a means for teachers to assess what students have learned during a school project (Barton & Levstik, 2004). Less often, the creation of exhibits in school allows learners to provide a service to others by educating the public about important issues for democracy (Achiam, 2020; Barton & Levstik, 2004; Boardman et al., 2021).

In recent years, researchers have partnered with museums to examine the overlap between the personal curation embedded within social media and the ways that museum professionals curate exhibits. For example, Shapiro and Hall (2018) used video, audio, and social media to follow the physical and digital movements of 22 visitor groups as they engaged in a museum gallery space. Their analysis illustrated the ways that museum visitors use personal curation through their own devices to shape networked understandings of cultural heritage and pointed to the ways that museums can leverage visitors' use of social media to build engagement. Still others have taken this idea of curative media outside museums. Taylor and colleagues' work on learning "on the move" (e.g., Leander et al., 2010; Taylor, 2017) similarly leveraged social media technologies to chart the hidden histories and stories of local spaces. These kinds of curatorial projects illustrate the potential for young people to participate in building historical records and capturing hidden histories.

Finally, museum educators have begun to explore the ways that young people can be engaged in the curatorial process. For example, the Failure Lab at the Museum of Contemporary Art Denver (https://mcadenver.org/teens/failure-lab) invites local high school students to apply to become interns, working with museum staff and professional artists to plan events, organize exhibitions, and develop a creative community. The New Bedford Whaling Museum in New Bedford, MA has an apprenticeship program through which low-income students participate in a museum internship while also receiving tutoring and test-preparation intended to support their success in high school and college (Rose, 2016). While many of these programs have been aimed at engaging youth in museum processes, questions remain about how to reposition youth in museums as content creators, rather than assistant curators (Achiam, 2020). In this project, our goal was to not only engage youth in the process of museum curation, but to also acknowledge the ways that Latino youth were historical actors (Gutiérrez et al., 2019) whose stories were embedded in the fabric of the city's history and were shaping its future.

THE VIVIENDO AQUÍ PROJECT

The Viviendo Aquí project began in 2019 as a collaboration between a local history museum and the two lead authors of this chapter. Through Summer and Fall 2019, we met with Maggie, a museum educator, and other museum administrators to consider ways the museum might engage young people in the museum through exhibit design and curation. Meanwhile, students and activists at the university had begun efforts to use community-developed art installations on the university grounds to acknowledge local acts of violence against Mexican American students and community members in the 1970s. The museum had also begun a partnership with a local Latino history project to better depict the histories of the towns' Latino peoples. All these efforts created a rich space to engage youth voices in the representation of their own stories. When I (Kristina) approached Maggie about a partnership to engage Latino teens in a narrative project, the trends in both educational spaces were already pointing to the necessity of diverse stories as vehicles for learning.

By January of 2020, our partnership was set to recruit young people for a summer session of the museum's Teen Corps, a group who would lead the design and development of their own museum exhibit that would become part of a larger community exhibit on Latino history in the city and region. However, as the COVID-19 pandemic closed local schools and businesses in the Spring of 2020, we decided to push the project to Fall 2020 in the hopes of meeting in person. We also recognized that in our mostly White, wealthy town, the Latino population was being disproportionately impacted by the pandemic. According to the county government, while Latino people made up approximately 14% of the town's population in 2020, they accounted for one-third of all COVID-19 related hospitalizations and 25% of all COVID-19 related deaths in our city. As the pandemic stretched through the late spring, we began to question what we might reasonably be able to do while ensuring the safety of young people and their families. With the release of vaccinations, we decided we would work to engage a small, core group of teens in the early fall who would be able to lead a larger group of teenagers the following spring.

By October of 2020, we had three young people who had agreed to act as our core design group: two high school students (brother and sister, Uriel and Telema) who had immigrated from Mexico, and one middle school student, Lela, who identified as Mexican American. We had also engaged Jose as an undergraduate research assistant and collaborator. Jose, whose reflections feature prominently in the subsequent sections of this chapter, acted as both a mentor and facilitator for the teen corps and as an integral part of the research team. As an upper-level undergraduate who was studying leadership/community engagement and history, and as someone who identified as Chicano and valued sharing his family's stories, Jose was uniquely qualified to support and guide the otherwise White-identifying researchers and museum educators in building culturally responsive representations with youth. While we were aware of the ways our own White, socioeconomically privileged positionalities and our limited Spanish proficiency did not allow us to fully understand the stories of our participants, we also had to grapple with the constraints of a mostly White, monolingual museum staff and the limits that COVID-19 placed on the size of the project team. We worked to engage several Latino community members, including leaders from a local Latino history project, activists, and teachers to combat the lack of adult representation offered to our young participants.

After struggles with recruitment during the fatigue and fear brought on by the pandemic, the Viviendo Aquí Teen Corps held our first meetings in person at the museum in October of 2020. That fall, the city had maintained strict masking and school closure policies, so the three teens who formed the Teen Corps were enthusiastic about meeting in person, particularly in the mild fall months when we could be outside. Kristina, Jose, Maggie, and the teens met for 2 hours each week in the museum lobby, an outdoor exhibit area, and the makerspace (a small lab with a laser printer that had been donated by a local technology company). Our initial goals were to engage with the core group of teens to design the museum exhibit and then to recruit smaller groups of teens to join us at the museum to build out the exhibit and populate it with their own stories and artifacts. However, in November, schools went back to in-person meetings, and it became more and more difficult to gather because of the increased likelihood of COVID-19 exposure. By January 2021, we were still seeking ways to engage additional youth and had begun to move our meetings online to accommodate the teen corps and their families.

In March of 2021, as we should have been moving toward production of the exhibit, the Teen Corps agreed to keep meeting for an additional 4 weeks beyond the initial timeframe of the project. The museum offered the project a large exhibit space, and our group of participants collaborated with Maggie to reimagine the activities and stories they had created as models for other teens to be the primary components of the exhibit. We also decided to partner with two public school teachers (one middle and one high school) who taught heritage classes at local city schools. These heritage classes included 24 middle school students and 15 high school students who were able to participate in at least one remote exhibit design workshop (see Table 9.1 for descriptions of all project participants). As we looked toward extending the project to engage students remotely, Uriel suggested we use shadow boxes, to which he had been introduced during a previous Teen Corps experience with the museum. Maggie, who had been concerned about the lack of representation in the exhibit, lit up at the suggestion of personal curation as a means of engaging young people remotely in the exhibit design. She worked with Uriel and the others to imagine the possibilities of these small, curated spaces and the team used them as the basis for engaging the school-based teen groups in the making of the physical exhibit.

The exhibit, which Jose and the Teen Corps members had named Viviendo Aquí, to represent a sense of belonging in the city, as well as an acknowledgement of the multiple meanings of home, opened in April of 2021 and ran at the museum for 45 days. During this time, the museum recorded more than 1,500 visitors to the exhibit. Figure 9.1 shows a panoramic view

TABLE 9.1	Viviendo Aquí Participants, Roles, and Self-Identifications	
Name	Role	Self-Identification
Kristina	Graduate student researcher	White, female; former secondary teacher and project designer
Joe	University professor & researcher	White, male; advisor for the project
Jose	Undergraduate student researcher	Chicano, male; undergraduate student and Teen Corps leader
Maggie	Museum educator	White, female; project design lead for the museum
Uriel	Teen Corps participant	Mexican, male; 15-year-old immigrant to the U.S. and sophomore in high school; Telema's brother
Telema	Teen Corps participant	Mexican, female; 14-year-old immigrant to the U.S., freshman in high school; Uriel's sister
Lela	Teen Corps participant	Mexican American, female; 13-year-old born in U.S., spent 2 months participating online from her family's home town in Mexico
24 middle school students	Online participants from a local school between 11 and 13 years old	Students self-identified as Latino. The project did not collect identifiable data on students other than first names and what was shared in their shadow boxes.
15 high school students	Online participants from a local school between 15 and 18 years old	

Figure 9.1 *Viviendo Aquí* exhibit.

of the exhibit; Figure 9.2 shows the shadow boxes. The exhibit was bilingual, with everything printed and recorded in both English and Spanish. In their reflections on the experience, one high school student who had contributed shadow boxes explained, "I hope that this [exhibit] means there is more people who know what others have gone through and how that makes each one of us who we are." Others similarly expressed feeling that the experience of contributing their stories to the museum exhibit had

Figure 9.2 *Viviendo Aquí* shadow boxes.

made them feel "part of something," what Jose described in fieldnotes as a sense of belonging, particularly within a city where they "would normally feel left out." Another student stated, "I feel like this project made me dig deeper into my experiences and how it's made me the person who I am today. It's also a great opportunity to use my creativity." The exhibit, created through a co-design process with youth, also became a model and a set of tools through which the museum was able to engage patrons in a larger community curation project featuring stories of the city's history and contributions of Latino community.

THE CONSTRAINTS AND AFFORDANCES OF UNIVERSITY–MUSEUM PARTNERSHIP DURING COVID-19

Historically, university–community–school partnerships have been characterized by relational work to build understandings of partners' contexts and skills (e.g., Farrell et al., 2023). These kinds of research–practice partnerships have often been used to democratize educational research, planning, and engagement, offering a venue for researchers and practitioners to work together to develop new tools and understandings of the possibilities for learning (Coburn & Penuel, 2016). However, during the COVID-19 pandemic, many of these partnerships were either put on hold or were forced to scale down their engagements for partners to cope with the trauma of collective loss and the ways that the pandemic had shifted their ability to collaborate in schools (Farrell et al., 2023). As described above, the Viviendo Aquí project began as a university–community–school partnership, intended to engage young people who identified as Latino to explore their own history and tell the stories of their lives and families in our city. Our project was an opportunity for young people to add to the narratives constructed about themselves and their families (a move toward more equitable representation of narratives in our predominantly White city) while also learning how to engage in museum contexts. This is akin to what Gutiérrez et al. (2019) termed "youth as historical actors" who are simultaneously participating in an education initiative designed to add to their repertoire of skills and knowledge while also enabling them to enact transformative agency (Stetsenko, 2019) in their community. As the pandemic created constraints that meant we could no longer bring large groups of young people together in the museum setting, we were forced to reimagine the ways that we might equitably engage youth in these goals with digital tools.

Adapting to the Pandemic

COVID-19 Constraints Meant a More Intimate Project Setting

When we first envisioned the Viviendo Aquí workshops and exhibit, we assumed we would meet with 10–12 youth participants over the course of 12 sessions. The pandemic forced us to rethink the ways that we could bring youth participants together. Rather than meeting with the same group of young people each week, we were pushed to reimagine the different kinds of roles that exist in these research–practice partnerships and the tools that could facilitate engagement across institutional boundaries. Where we initially designed the Teen Corps to meet weekly in-person and build the exhibit through hands-on activities, COVID-19 requirements stretched our partnership design to include a very small core group of teen designers who could co-design new online workshops for their peers across the city. This kind of layered participation, though initially frustrating for the Teen Corps participants whose social experiences had been severely limited by the pandemic, also led us to imagine a new model of museum participation where community members could engage with museum curation across multiple sites.

In October 2020, as we began to meet with the Teen Corps, Uriel, Telema, and Lela expressed excitement about the possibility of engaging with peers in-person. The pandemic had taken away a lot of their social activities, particularly because the three of them lived in multi-generational households with elders who were at heightened risk of health complications from COVID-19. Uriel and Telema were especially eager to return to the museum as part of the Teen Corps. They had initially been engaged in the museum when their mother, Astrid, an activist from Northern Mexico whose work focused on Indigenous women's rights, had moved them from their city in Mexico to our city. They explained that Astrid had been especially interested in providing better educational opportunities for them and their older

Youth Curation as Collective Disruption • **193**

brother and had engaged in the museum to get them involved with the city and its stories. Maggie had specifically recruited them because "they seem to grow so much when they engage in [museum programming]." She went on to explain that Uriel had learning differences that his school in Mexico was unable to address. Astrid had homeschooled him prior to deciding to pursue a wider range of educational opportunities in the United States. She was his greatest advocate and had engaged Maggie as an ally in her children's education. Maggie felt a sense of responsibility to ensure these young people had opportunities to engage in meaningful and expansive ways. She wanted to offer them the social experiences that they were no longer able to have in school.

However, as we worked to recruit other Latino students during the Summer and Fall of 2020, we continued to hear from parents and teachers that young people across the city were experiencing such high degrees of burnout and trauma from the effects of the pandemic that few wanted to engage in any kind of extracurricular activity, even those that offered in-person engagement. Added to this trauma was the caution many Latino families were taking because of medical complications and their fears due to lack of documentation and the political rhetoric surrounding the Trump presidency. We also found that families were traveling extensively to Central and South America because youth were able to participate in school online instead of in person. As a result, we struggled to find participants who could commit to even part of the 12-week program. We continued to encounter difficulties with recruitment, even after the museum offered to pay participants for their engagement with the program. For a time, the barriers the pandemic created to the collaborative work appeared nearly insurmountable. Lela, whose parents and grandparents had emigrated from Central Mexico before she was born in the United States, was the one exception who was willing to join the program in person.

As we explained our difficulties in recruitment, Uriel, Telema, and Lela were at first enthusiastic about the potential of acting as leaders for small groups of young people to engage for more limited amounts of time to develop the exhibit. However, a few weeks into the project—as the pandemic appeared to be escalating in the Winter of 2020—the project team (youth and adult members) decided to just accept the limitations to in-person participation and move instead toward new online models of engagement to broaden our co-design team. In a group interview, the Teen Corps members voiced their conflicting feelings about the small design group. "It would be nice to have more people and more ideas," Telema explained. Uriel echoed her but also said, "Yes, but it's cool to have *our* ideas." This tension arose for the teens throughout the project. The members were enthusiastic about the ways that their ideas were expressed and emerged as the central part of the exhibit design, while missing opportunities to engage with a larger group of Latino young people whose stories resembled their own.

Despite the disappointment, Maggie observed that a small Teen Corps afforded the young people we were working with the opportunity to engage in the design process of the exhibit in ways that felt different from her previous attempts at collaborative engagement. She explained, "You know, in a previous project, they were just helping us to think through one element about accessibility; this is the first time they've gotten to design the exhibit content." This move toward content design became a driving element in our workshops with the Teen Corps. During one of the first design sessions, the teens worked individually with Maggie, Jose, and Kristina to explore the ways that the five senses defined their stories in the city. Sensory exploration took us almost immediately toward stories of food. Telema recounted, with poignant detail, memories of her uncle's laughter as her family shared *cemitas*—"giant sandwiches with poblano," she explained—on Sundays when they were in Mexico together. "I was so little and the *cemitas* were bigger than my head," she said, laughing. Uriel joined her story, adding details of his own. The two then set out to create a mock exhibit to tell the story, using clay to craft a giant sandwich on a tiny table. After that session, Maggie remarked that in a larger group it would be almost impossible to garner the kind of intimate family details that the teens were sharing. The pandemic's constraints on the workshops were also leading to a kind of sharing that she had not previously experienced in teen workshops (where between 10 and 20 young people came together to rapidly support the installation of an exhibit that had already been designed).

During the 8 weeks of workshops, the Teen Corps followed models of products, created during the program by Jose, to develop and share their own mini-exhibits. Jose told stories of his family and their history, sharing how his parents had emigrated from Mexico to seek more opportunity in the United States. In turn, Teen Corps members also examined their family stories, sharing intimate details about how their parents came to the United States, and the ways that they themselves had come to understand their lives in two places (their ancestral homes in Mexico and their lives in our city). The Teen Corps began to find themes that connected their experiences, such as the way that they always returned to recounting meals together when asked to think about stories of home in both Mexico and the United States. Where a larger group may have had difficulties pulling their disparate stories together, the small design team was able to make connections and create stories that were personal rather than generically representative.

In December 2020, just before the school winter break, we asked the Teen Corps to summarize what they wanted their audience to take away from the exhibit and the stories that defined their lives and cultures in our city. Telema explained that she kept coming back to stories about gathering with her family and eating *cemitas* in her city in Mexico because

> thinking of living in [our city] is kind of hard because when I think of the stories [that define me] I think of my family and they're in Mexico...but then I think of my friends and I'm wondering, like, if they know about me, or how much they know about my culture, and I do want people to see what they can tell from the exhibit about me...if they can see my identity in my exhibit.

For Telema, the experience of sharing a meal with family was integral to her identity; this experience was missing from her current life, both because her family was far away and because the pandemic had made it so difficult to gather with people she loved outside of her immediate household. After this session, Maggie explained to the research team that although she had been searching for ways to create broad stories to represent a lot of Latino experiences, she wanted to shift toward a more intimate exhibit experience that simply showcased the stories the Teen Corps members kept repeating. She once again remarked on the ways these intimate stories may not have been possible if we had a larger group of young people on the design team, but also wondered about engaging other youth.

Creating a Hyflex Informal Learning Environment

Much of the educational research literature on environments that seek to create "third spaces" that hybridize youth and educator priorities and perspectives (Gutiérrez, 2008) is characterized by youth and educators gathering to participate in "meaningful activity [that] builds on the learner's initiative or interest or choice" (Rogoff et al., 2016, p. 356). However, few of these projects have engaged in "hyflex" environments—educational experiences that take place simultaneously online and in physical spaces, where participants are flexible at moving back and forth between modalities (Liu & Rodriguez, 2019). By the third week of workshops with the Teen Corps, we recognized that the realities of the pandemic were going to require new means of participation, even within our small group of designers. The young people in the Teen Corps were allowed to return to their schools shortly after we began the project. While Telema and Uriel decided to continue attending school remotely through the fall semester, Lela returned to in-person classes, but soon learned that she had been exposed to COVID-19. We recognized that if we wanted to continue to host Teen Corps, we also needed to offer them options for the ways that they would engage each week. However, we were hesitant to move our workshops entirely online because of our participants' limited access to technology and reliable Internet. While each of our participants received a digital device (most frequently a Chromebook or iPad) from their schools, the capacity of these devices to run programs was limited (Garcia et al., 2022). This capacity was further constrained by the lack of technology support and lack of consistent Internet access frequently experienced by students with lower socioeconomic status and in under-funded schools during the pandemic (Starr et al., 2020).

Because exhibit design so often involves building physical models (Smithsonian Exhibits, n.d.) and because of the limitations on our participants' technology access, we needed to ensure that participation was not based solely on online capacity. To ensure that the Teen Corps, and later, the other students from classrooms across the city, were able to fully participate, we chose to work toward a hybrid, hyflex workshop model using tools accessible with minimal Internet and 10-year old technology. These tools included the Google suite (reimagined to become museum spaces; see Figure 9.3), paper and pencil, or physical materials that the teens could pick up from the museum. We never knew who would make it to the museum to meet in person, who would have consistent Internet access, and who would be well enough to attend the entire workshop each week, so we worked to adjust each 2-hour workshop with a purpose that could be collaboratively developed or individually explored.

In any given week, we (the authors)—Maggie, Telema, Uriel, and Lela—would join in-person or online in different combinations. Maggie and Kristina would present a few possible directions for design, the teens would comment, and then we would plan moments to share and trade ideas. In this way, the young people in the Teen Corps were able to simultaneously adapt to the realities of their family's needs during COVID-19 while also continuing to engage in the exhibit design process in ways that felt meaningful to them.

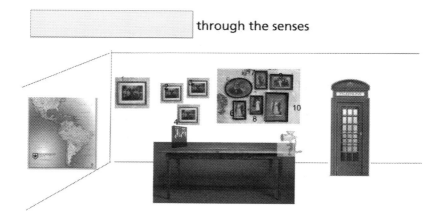

Figure 9.3 Sample exhibit in google slides.

Youth Curation as Collective Disruption • **197**

For example, when Lela's parents chose to go to Mexico for the winter break to visit extended family from whom they had been separated for nearly 2 years, Lela continued to engage with the project by collecting photos and stories from her extended family, addressing the longing they felt in being separated from each other. Because she still had the option of engaging in both school and the museum remotely, Lela explained that she, for the first time, felt connected to both places her family lived. At the end of the project, she reflected, "I never noticed how different my culture is, like how many parts there are . . . It was cool to see how my family and my experience in Mexico is similar and different [from other people's] . . . and to get to share those with other people." She attributed her recognition and excitement about her culture to having an opportunity to engage with the group, even when she could not attend in person.

Shadow Boxes as Tools for Remote Making

Perhaps the most salient tool that emerged from this collaboration were shadow boxes—glass-front, wood-framed boxes that had space for found and created art or objects. In February, the design team had begun to design the final exhibit, but continued to discuss ways to include additional stories beyond those of Jose and the Teen Corps. During one rapid design session where the teens created prototypes of the visual displays of their stories, Uriel explained that he missed being in the city's makerspace and suggested using shadow boxes, which he had learned about there. Maggie emphasized Uriel's idea, explaining that she had been struggling to imagine how to fully engage community members in the making of exhibits long term. She explained, "The shadow boxes totally solve something I've been puzzling over: How do we have families participate in curation without asking to risk their heirlooms? These would allow for pictures and individual curation in a way that is totally doable from a museum point of view."

The following week, Maggie developed kits for the shadow boxes—full of clay, double-sided tape, foam board, tacks, and twine, as well as the frames—and delivered them to the design team. Jose and the Teen Corps members created their own shadow boxes, along with process descriptions, for their personal curation work. In the next meeting, they shared their boxes and then worked on recording narratives to explain their curation to an outside audience. These audio recordings were connected to QR codes (a machine-readable code that linked to a webpage with the youths' recordings and writing), which were displayed alongside the boxes in the museum exhibit. The QR codes added a level of interactivity that allowed audiences to hear the creators' voices, adding what the teens called "a more personal experience" to the exhibit.

Blurring Institutional Boundaries

Maggie's enthusiasm for the shadow boxes also created momentum for new ways to engage additional Latino youth across the city. Maggie reached out to several teachers who taught Latino heritage classes in a local school district; in lieu of the yearly field trips that she typically hosted, the project team would be happy to lead digital workshops to make shadow boxes. Two secondary classes—one high school class of 15 students and one middle school class of 24 students all of whom identified as having heritage speakers from Central or South America—agreed and then coordinated to have the shadow box kits delivered to the schools. We then collaborated with Maggie to lead a series of workshops to create shadow boxes aligned with the Teen Corps designs for the exhibits. The school-based youth participants also recorded their own corresponding audio diaries. We then invited them to contribute to the Viviendo Aquí exhibit with assurances that they could retrieve their boxes after the exhibit closed in May 2021.

The shadow boxes, along with the digital design of the workshops, blurred the museum's boundaries by inviting young people to be part of the museum through making and tinkering with their own stories. The use of Zoom and Google Meet applications, as well as video conferencing platforms, shifted what felt possible during the pandemic and changed the museum's educational programming to be more inclusive of participants' homes, families, and classrooms. The young people explained that this kind of representational activity felt different: simultaneously more personal and more authentic than their previous experiences in museums.

While only 15 classroom participants chose to have their shadow boxes included in the museum exhibit, surveys showed that 31 of the 39 students saw the workshops and shadow boxes as valuable, shared their products with family members, and were moved to think about themselves and their stories in new ways in relation to our city. Blurring the boundaries of the museum ultimately meant that in a time of extreme restriction, more young people had opportunities to share their own experiences and ideas with each other and with their community in a hybrid space that was neither solely museum field trip nor school classroom.

Youth (and Family) Access to Museums as Community Resource

Community curation is one way that museums are working to engage visitors and develop new audiences, but little research explores the ways that historically marginalized youth and their families might act as community resources, providing foundational knowledge and first-person accounts of

Youth Curation as Collective Disruption • **199**

their own history. Initially, we understood our work to be that of engaging youth in designing their own stories and discovering their own histories as part of a community-curation effort. However, as the pandemic shifted our engagement with the Teen Corps and other young people toward hybrid ecologies with homes and schools, we also found that family members' knowledges became prevalent in these designs.

For example, during one meeting on Zoom, we asked Lela a question about the *posole* she shared with her family each holiday. She was unsure of the recipe, so she immediately called out to her mother in the kitchen. Off camera, we could hear the family trading memories of their favorite meal before Lela returned to Zoom. Being on Zoom with the Teen Corps while also at home gave Lela simultaneous access to her mother's knowledge, enabling Lela to engage with her in a way not possible at the museum. Such shared, extended memory became characteristic of our work with the youth and was reflected in the artifacts they included in shadow boxes, videos, and audio recordings. In fact, families often appeared as a network of active relations for youth that would not have been as easily engaged without the constraints of the pandemic.

Ingrid, a student at the local high school with whom we partnered, designed a shadow box that highlighted the ways family became a resource for sense-making and storytelling in the exhibit. In her audio recording, she described her shadow box, explaining:

> I came to the U.S. when I was 4 years old. The scorpion represents where I come from because [my city] is the "land of the scorpions"... The graduation hat means how important education is for my family and I; it also represents one of the main reasons my parents came to the United States. We came to the U.S. because my parents wanted a better future for us and a thing that my parents have always told my sisters and I [*sic*] is to work hard and graduate so we can be successful and have a better life than what they had. As a Latina, our family is important in our culture because we all look out for each other and personally my family and I are very close. I wanted to represent this by making the figures of people. There are six people. It represents my parents, my three sisters, and I [*sic*] ...

For Ingrid, as for many of our participants, depicting her culture and her own life was not an individual endeavor but an act of honoring her family and their collective values. We came to recognize that their participation was a new kind of partnership that extended into their collective consciousness, community, family, and memories (Wertsch, 2002).

In the final weeks of the project, Jose reminded us about his initial concerns that Viviendo Aquí would not be an exhibit driven by the Latino community because of the presence of White curators and researchers. However, he noted both in fieldnotes and in a final reflection that these worries were allayed as the project team worked to honor his expertise, experience, and perspectives. In reviewing fieldnotes, interviews, and artifacts, he noted that Teen Corps members and school-based participants had remarked on the respect they felt was given to their work and their stories. He wrote, "Each student had the freedom to express their culture and story the way that they wanted to and they could add any items they felt expressed who they are, giving the students freedom to express what it means to be a Latino person in our city." This comment is a testament to the importance of "creating space for agency" (Verhoeven et al., 2021, p. 125) by cultivating a community that emphasizes social relations beyond just museum content.

DISCUSSION AND SIGNIFICANCE

The success of Viviendo Aquí acted as a catalyst for a larger community curation exhibit in partnership with adult community members and the local Latino history project. Images and selected artifacts from Viviendo Aquí were included in the larger exhibit, which opened in February 2022, is scheduled to run through 2023, and has been featured nationally as a model of community curation efforts. In many ways, Viviendo Aquí became a prefiguration of the larger community exhibit; prefiguration, in this context, refers to projected ideal futures with regards to acts of politics and power (Curnow, 2016; Uttamchandani, 2021). This project was designed for Latino youth as a means to question and disrupt dominant narratives in a community museum. Too often, projects trying to engage historically marginalized youth simply reinforce hegemonic structures that silence their stories (McLaren, 1997). The context of the dual pandemics of COVID-19 and institutional racism could have shifted our project toward more traditional modes of community engagement, but instead, they offered opportunities to reimagine the tools that young people use to engage in exhibits and the boundaries that have framed their participation.

This new hybrid educational ecology acted as a kind of third space (Gutiérrez, 2008), a co-constructed means for youth to engage in project activities across physical environments and in collaboration with their families. This space countered old museum participation models, with museums as sole physical sites for community curation, and offered instead a more networked model with nodes of activity in the museum, schools, and homes. Along with the affordances of the shadow boxes as a compact and relatively easily transportable, curated, exhibit component, the digital engagement presents opportunities for different kinds of scale-making. Scale-making here refers to "the systems of temporal, social, and spatial relations in which [a] thing exists and has meaning" (Jurow & Shea, 2015, p. 287). Acknowledging the pitfalls present in entrenched systems of inequity, we recognize that this start is modest and tenuous, but also promising. In this project, a key part of that promise lies in the fact that youth participants' engagement in depicting experiences was collective, dependent upon shared understandings of their contexts, backgrounds, languages, and families. The shadow boxes illustrated not only the youth participants' interpretation of their lives in our city, but also the values imbued into those places and stories with, by and for their families. These depictions of collective experiences are different from the historical interpretations of traditional museum exhibits often translated individually or by a small team of mostly white exhibit designers.

Possible Futures for Youth Community Curation and Partnership Work

Community curation has the potential to be not only a means of engaging new participants in the museum setting, but a new network of extended active relations, with both youth and their families, that did not previously exist. As Jose explained, developing the museum exhibit was not just about creating something for the museum, but turning the museum into a new space, a place in which he and the youth participants felt they belonged. If this model could be sustained over time as an alternative or supplement to large school-based field trips to the museum, with genuine openness to modifications to process and content from stakeholders at schools, families' homes, the museum, and the local university, the opportunities for transformation are myriad.

Viviendo Aquí points to the possibilities of engaging youth to develop justice-oriented hybrid practices in museum education. It also suggests that when diverse youth are engaged as participants in community–university partnerships, they have potential to draw upon not only their own sets of knowledge and experiences, but also the histories and knowledges of their families and communities. When we consider the aims of research–practice partnership work as moving toward more democratic and just models of research and practice (Farrell et al., 2022), community curation has potential to support youth to act agentically in building out their own stories and representations. However, to meet these aims, institutional partners must make moves to attend to the lessons of the pandemic, shifting modalities of engagement to accommodate a new paradigm of hybrid interactions that blurs the boundaries between institutions and homes. Further, we recognize the potential for these kinds of projects to reinforce hegemonic notions of participation, or worse, to invade and usurp the stories that historically marginalized youth and their families have worked to keep out of reach of the White gaze (Tuck & Yang, 2012). To navigate these turbulent and at times dangerous waters, partnerships spanning these institutions must commit to an ethic of reciprocity that attends to the historic injustices often perpetuated in these spaces. We expect that this continuing work may include explorations of the trajectories of identifications young people take (Polman & Miller, 2010) as they engage in making with material, ideational, and relational resources (Nasir & Cooks, 2009) alongside museum experts.

NOTE

1. We use Latino throughout this chapter to reflect the term preferred by the young people with whom this collaborative design study took place. While each young person identified differently, they concluded that Latino would be the appropriate term to refer to the project group as a whole.

REFERENCES

Achiam, M. (2020). Reflections on empowering youth in science museums. In H. McLaughlin & J. Diamond (Eds.), *Science museums in transition: Unheard voices* (pp. 44–48). Routledge.

American Alliance of Museums. (2019, January 28). *Latest art museum staff demographic survey shows increases in African American curators and women in leadership roles*. https://www.aam-us.org/2019/01/28/latest-art-museum-staff-demographic-survey-shows-increases-in-african-american-curators-and-women-in-leadership-roles/

Barton, K. C., & Levstik, L. S. (2004). *Teaching history for the common good*. Erlbaum.

Black, G. (2010). Embedding civil engagement in museums. *Museum Management and Curatorship, 25*(2), 129–146. https://doi.org/10.1080/09647771003737257

Boardman, A. G., Garcia, A., Dalton, B., & Polman, J. L. (2021). *Compose our world: Project-based learning in secondary English Language Arts*. Teachers College Press.

Coburn, C., & Penuel, W. (2016). Research–practice partnerships in education. *Educational Researcher, 45*(1), 48–54. https://doi.org/10.3102/0013189x16631750

Cornish, C., Driver, F., Nesbitt, M., & Willison, J. (2021). Revitalizing the school museum: Using nature-based objects for cross-curricular learning. *Journal of Museum Education, 46*(3), 334–347. https://doi.org/10.1080/10598650.2021.1953324

Curnow, J. (2016). Towards a radical theory of learning: Prefiguration as legitimate peripheral participation. In S. Springer, R. White, & M. Lopes de Souza (Eds.), *The radicalization of pedagogy: Anarchism, geography and the spirit of revolt* (pp. 27–49). Rowman and Littlefield.

Debono, S. (2014). MUŻA: Rethinking national art museums and the value of community curation. *Malta Review of Educational Research, 8*(2), 312–320. http://www.mreronline.org/wp-content/uploads/2014/12/MRERv8V2P7.pdf

de Royston, M. M., Lee, C., Nasir, N. S., & Pea, R. (2020). Rethinking schools, rethinking learning. *Phi Delta Kappan, 102*(3), 8–13. https://doi.org/10.1177/0031721720970693

Farrell, C. C., Penuel, W. R., Allen, A., Anderson, E. R., Bohannon, A. X., Coburn, C. E., & Brown, S. L. (2022). Learning at the boundaries of research and practice: A framework for understanding research–practice partnerships. *Educational Researcher, 51*(3), 197–208. https://doi.org/10.3102/0013189X211069073

Farrell, C. C., Singleton, C., Stamatis, K., Riedy, R., Arce-Trigatti, P., & Penuel, W. R. (2023). Conceptions and practices of equity in research-practice partnerships. *Educational Policy, 37*(1), 200–224. https://doi.org/10.1177/0895 9048221131566

Ferguson, M., & Renner, K. (2019). A museum without walls: Community collaboration in exhibition development. *Theory and Practice, 2.* http://articles.themuseumscholar.org/tp_vol2fergusonrenner

Garcia, A., Kelly, M. R., & Stamatis, K. (2022). When technology goes unnoticed: Teacher beliefs and assumptions about technology use in three 9th grade English classrooms. *Pedagogies: An International Journal, 17*(1), 54–75. https://doi.org/10.1080/1554480X.2020.1781638

Gutiérrez, K. D. (2008). Developing a sociocritical literacy in the third space. *Reading Research Quarterly, 43*(2), 148–164. https://doi.org/10.1598/rrq.43.2.3

Gutiérrez, K. D., Becker, B. L. C., Espinoza, M. L., Cortes, K. L., Cortez, A., Lizárraga, J. R., Rivero, E., Villegas, K., & Yin, P. (2019). Youth as historical actors in the production of possible futures. *Mind, Culture, and Activity, 26*(4), 291–308. https://doi.org/10.1080/10749039.2019.1652327

Harackiewicz, J. M., Smith, J. L, & Priniski, S. J. (2016). Interest matters: The importance of promoting interest in education. *Policy Insights From the Behavioral and Brain Sciences, 3*(2), 145–161. https://doi.org/10.1177/2372732216655542

Hein, G. (2011). Museum education. In S. Macdonald (Ed.), *A companion to museum studies* (pp. 340–352). Blackwell Publishing.

Hill, R., & Douillette, J. (2014). Teens, new media and contemporary art: Expanding authority in the museum context. *Journal of Museum Education, 39*(3), 250–261. https://doi.org/10.1080/10598650.2014.11510817

Jurow, A. S., & Shea, M. (2015). Learning in equity-oriented scale-making projects. *Journal of the Learning Sciences, 24*(2), 286–307. https://doi.org/10.1080/105 08406.2015.1004677

Latham, K. F., & Simmons, J. E. (2019). Whither museum studies? *Journal of Education for Library and Information Science, 60*(2), 102–117. https://doi.org/10.3138/jelis.2018-0050

Leander, K. M., Phillips, N. C., & Taylor, K. H. (2010). The changing social spaces of learning: Mapping new mobilities. *Review of Research in Education, 34*(1), 329–394. https://doi.org/10.3102/0091732X09358129

Levstik, L. S., & Barton, K. C. (1997). *Doing history: Investigating with children in elementary and middle schools.* Routledge. https://doi.org/10.4324/9781315818108

Liu, C.-Y. A., & Rodriguez, R. C. (2019). Evaluation of the impact of the Hyflex learning model. *International Journal of Innovation and Learning, 25*(4), 393–411. https://doi.org/10.1504/IJIL.2019.099986

McCarthy, C., & Herring, B. (2015). *Museum & community partnerships: Collaboration guide for museums working with community youth-serving organizations.* National Informal STEM Education Network. https://www.nisenet.org/collaboration-guide

McLaren, P. (1997). Decentering whiteness. *Multicultural Education, 5*(1), 4–11. https://digitalcommons.chapman.edu/education_articles/153/

McQuade, C. (2020, June 15). *Online exhibits versus bricks-and-mortar exhibits, part 1.* https://www.caitlinmcquade.com/post/online-exhibits-v-bricks-and-mortar-exhibits

Melish, C., Chatelain, M., & Jeffries, H. K. (2017). Smithsonian National Museum of African American History & Culture, Washington, D.C. *The Journal of American History, 104*(1), 145–161. https://doi.org/10.1093/jahist/jax009

Nasir, N. S., & Cooks, J. (2009). Becoming a hurdler: How learning settings afford identities. *Anthropology & Education Quarterly, 40*(1), 41–61. https://doi.org/10.1111/j.1548-1492.2009.01027.x

National Museum of African American History & Culture. (2022). *The community curation program.* Smithsonian. https://nmaahc.si.edu/explore/initiatives/family-history-center/community-curation-program

Phillips, A. (2017, June 16). 'They're rapists.' President Trump's campaign launch speech two years later, annotated. *Washington Post.* https://www.washingtonpost.com/news/the-fix/wp/2017/06/16/theyre-rapists-presidents-trump-campaign-launch-speech-two-years-later-annotated/#annotations:12172391

Polman, J. L., & Miller, D. (2010). Changing stories: Trajectories of identification among African American youth in a science outreach apprenticeship. *American Educational Research Journal, 47*(4), 879–918. https://doi.org/10.3102/0002831210367513

Rogoff, B., Callanan, M., Gutiérrez, K. D., & Erickson, F. (2016). The organization of informal learning. *Review of Research in Education, 40*(1), 356–401. https://doi.org/10.3102/0091732X16680994

Rose, S. W. (2016). Museum–university partnerships transform teenagers' futures. *Journal of Museum Education, 41*(4), 286–292. https://doi.org/10.1080/10598650.2016.1232510

Shannon, J. (2015). Artifacts of collaboration at the National Museum of the American Indian. *New Proposals: Journal of Marxism and Interdisciplinary Inquiry, 7*(2), 37–55. https://ojs.library.ubc.ca/index.php/newproposals/article/view/186172

Shapiro, B. R., & Hall, R. (2018). Personal curation in a museum. *Proceedings of the ACM on Human-Computer Interaction, 2*(158), 1–22. https://doi.org/10.1145/3274427

Sheridan, K., Halverson, E. R., Litts, B., Brahms, L., Jacobs-Priebe, L., & Owens, T. (2014). Learning in the making: A comparative case study of three makerspaces. *Harvard Educational Review, 84*(4), 505–531. https://doi.org/10.17763/haer.84.4.brr34733723j648u

Simon, N. (2010). *The participatory museum.* Museum 2.0.

Smithsonian Exhibits. (n.d.). *A guide to exhibit development.* http://exhibits.si.edu/wp-content/uploads/2018/04/Guide-to-Exhibit-Development.pdf

Stamatis, K. M. (2021). *Seeking stories: Throughlining in 9th grade English language arts* (Publication No. 28543865) [Doctoral Dissertation, University of Colorado Boulder]. Proquest. https://www.proquest.com/openview/5f8914976669a7e1343e783e6f3ff136/1.pdf?pq-origsite=gscholar&cbl=18750&diss=y

Starr, D., Hayes, J., & Gao, N. (2020). *The digital divide in education.* Public Policy Institute of California. Retrieved October 1, 2022, from https://www.ppic.org/publication/the-digital-divide-in-education/

Stetsenko, A. (2019). Radical-transformative agency: Continuities and contrasts with relational agency and implications for education. *Frontiers in Education, 4*(148), 1–13. https://doi.org/10.3389/feduc.2019.00148

Stornaiuolo, A., & Thomas, E. E. (2018). Restorying as political action: Authoring resistance through youth media arts. *Learning, Media and Technology, 43*(4), 345–358. https://doi.org/10.1080/17439884.2018.1498354

Stránský, Z. Z. (1987). La muséologie est-elle une conséquence de l'existence des musées ou les précède-t-elle et détermine [-t-elle] leur avenir? [Is museology a consequence of the existence of museums or does it precede them and determine [does] their future?] *ICOFOM Study Series, 12,* 295.

Taylor, K. H. (2017). Learning along lines: Locative literacies for reading and writing the city. *Journal of the Learning Sciences, 26*(4), 533–574. https://doi.org/10.1080/10508406.2017.1307198

Tobelem, J.-M. (2013). The arts and culture: Financial burden or a way out of the crisis? *ENCATC Journal of Cultural Management and Policy, 3*(1), 52–60. https://www.encatc.org/media/2689-encatc_journal_vol3_issue_1_20135361.pdf

Tuck, E., & Yang, K. W. (2012). Decolonization is not a metaphor. *Decolonization: Indigeneity, Education & Society, 1*(1), 1–40. https://clas.osu.edu/sites/clas.osu.edu/files/Tuck%20and%20Yang%202012%20Decolonization%20is%20not%20a%20metaphor.pdf

Uttamchandani, S. (2021). Educational intimacy: Learning, prefiguration, and relationships in an LGBTQ+ youth group's advocacy efforts. *Journal of the Learning Sciences, 30*(1), 52–75. https://doi.org/10.1080/10508406.2020.1821202

Vamanu, I. (2020). Indigenous museum curatorship in the United States and Canada: Roles and responsibilities . *Libri, 70*(1), 65–79. https://doi.org/10.1515/libri-2018-0155

Verhoeven, M., Polman, J. L., Zijlstra, B. J. H., & Volman, M. (2021). Creating space for agency: A Conceptual framework to understand and study adolescents' school engagement from a funds of identity perspective. *Mind, Culture, and Activity, 28*(2), 125–137. https://doi.org/10.1080/10749039.2021.1908363

Vossoughi, S., & Gutiérrez, K. D. (2017). Critical pedagogy and sociocultural theory. In I. Esmonde & A. N. Booker (Eds.), *Power and privilege in the learning sciences: Critical and sociocultural theories of learning* (pp. 139–161). Taylor & Francis Group. https://doi.org/10.4324/9781315685762

Wertsch, J. V. (2002). *Voices of collective remembering.* Cambridge University Press. https://doi.org/10.1017/CBO9780511613715

Wylder, V. D. T., Lerner, E. B., & Ford, A. S. (2014). Elementary reflections: Case study of a collaborative museum/school curatorial project. *Journal of Museum Education, 39*(1), 83–95. https://doi.org/10.1080/10598650.2014.11510798

Yarrow, A., Clubb, B., & Draper, J.-L. (2008). *Public libraries, archives and museums: Trends in collaboration and cooperation* (No. 108). International Federation of Library Associations and Institutions. https://archive.ifla.org/VII/s8/pub/Profrep108.pdf

CHAPTER 10

LEVERAGING UNIVERSITY PARTNERS AS BROKERS TO NAVIGATE RESEARCH– PRACTICE PARTNERSHIPS DURING INTERTWINED GLOBAL PANDEMICS

Holly Plank
University of Pittsburgh

Eleanor R. Anderson
University of Pittsburgh

Cassie Quigley
University of Pittsburgh

School–University–Community Research in a (Post) COVID-19 World, pages 207–231
Copyright © 2023 by Information Age Publishing
www.infoagepub.com
All rights of reproduction in any form reserved.

ABSTRACT

While the intertwined global pandemics of racial oppression and COVID-19 have been significantly influencing the field of education at large, research–practice partnerships (RPPs) have continued their dramatic rise in popularity. The role of brokering in RPPs has become more critical as diverse educational stakeholders look to the promise of RPPs as a mechanism to solve complex problems of practice collaboratively. In this chapter, we chronicle the launch of the Museum+School RPP, a unique partnership forged across formal and informal education organizations, by members with multiple complex roles. Drawing together our experiences in this RPP with recent literature, here we elucidate new possibilities for imagining the role of RPP brokers in spanning across multiple types of boundaries. We document in particular the power of university-based educators to serve as brokers to support the visions of new and existing RPPs. As our world transitions from pandemic to endemic concerns related to COVID-19, we argue that greater attention to diverse forms and sources of brokerage can serve a critical role in pursuing more equitable and just outcomes.

This is a story about the launch of an unusual partnership. It begins with an urban public charter school and a city museum, each with their own distinct learning culture, who came together to launch the Museum+School research–practice partnership (a pseudonym). Facing challenges in navigating multiple intersecting lines of difference—organizational, professional, racial, and more—the museum and school leaders decided to include members of a local university research team as brokers to support their collaboration and evolving vision. In a surprise turn that is by now a familiar part of so many stories, as the global pandemic of racial oppression intertwined with the novel coronavirus pandemic in March 2020, the landscape and challenges facing the museum+school research–practice partnership (Museum+School RPP) rapidly shifted. Thus, throughout the extended launch of this unique collaboration, teachers, school leadership, museum educators, museum researchers, and the university-based team—including the first and third author of this chapter—all took on roles both familiar and novel, navigating challenges never before seen and also deeply rooted in history.

This is also a story about what unusual partnerships convened in unusual times can teach us about common dynamics we might otherwise overlook. In this chapter, we draw on the story of the Museum+School RPP to explore the possibilities and necessities of brokering not only across boundaries of research and practice but across multiple lines of difference. Synthesizing across existing frameworks for knowledge brokering (Wentworth et al., 2021; see also Davidson & Penuel, 2019; Glegg & Hoens, 2016; Ward et al., 2009), research–practice partnerships (RPPs; Farrell et

Leveraging University Partners as Brokers During Intertwined Global Pandemics • **209**

al., 2022; Farrell et al., 2021; see also Coburn et al., 2013), and organizational theories (Akkerman & Bruining, 2016; see also Akkerman & Bakker, 2011), we critically analyze the creation of the Museum+School RPP to reveal and reimagine potential roles for university-based educators as RPP brokers. We argue that this story offers us broader lessons about creative ways to build on the promise of RPPs, dismantle systems of oppression, and strengthen pathways for transformative school–university–community research in a (post) COVID-19 world.

RESEARCH–PRACTICE PARTNERSHIPS

Collaborations among researchers and educational stakeholders outside of the academy are increasingly common (Arce-Trigatti et al., 2018). In their recent report on the state of the field, Farrell and colleagues (2021) defined RPPs as "long-term collaboration[s] aimed at educational improvement or equitable transformation through engagement with research" (p. 4). Farrell et al. specifically noted that RPPs are also "intentionally organized to connect diverse forms of expertise and shift power relations in the research endeavor to ensure that all partners have a say in the joint work" (p. 4). Penuel and colleagues (2015) offered a similar perspective, arguing that RPPs are "a form of joint work requiring mutual engagement across multiple boundaries" (p. 182).

While collaborations that shift power and cross boundaries hold great potential, they can also be highly challenging to enact. The organizational and sociocultural differences among partners can cause incoherence in joint work and can be challenging to reconcile quickly (Akkerman & Bakker, 2011; Wegemer & Renick, 2021). When there is incoherence in joint work, it can be difficult for partners to communicate, build and maintain trust, center equity in decision-making, and overcome inevitable challenges associated with launching and maintaining RPPs. In the short term, this may slow down the planning and implementation of joint activities, but in the long term it interferes with reciprocity, the long-term health and sustainability of the partnership, and it can ultimately thwart efforts to close the research–practice gap (Wentworth, Khanna, et al., 2021).

Lines of Difference in Research–Practice Partnerships

The negotiation of boundaries within RPPs has garnered significant research attention, particularly negotiation of the boundary between researchers and practitioners (e.g., Farrell et al., 2022; Penuel et al., 2015; Wentworth, Khanna, et al., 2021). Indeed, closing the research–practice

210 • H. PLANK, E. R. ANDERSON, and C. QUIGLEY

gap is a common argument for the creation of RPPs in education as well as other social science fields (Bell et al., 2015; Coburn et al., 2013). Boundaries between research and practice can be based on differences in institutional values, practices, culture, language, identity, experience, and epistemological beliefs between research-based and practice-based organizations (Akkerman & Bruining, 2016).

While often highly salient, the boundary between research and practice is not the only important boundary that often needs to be navigated in RPPs. Organizational affiliation, training and professional identity, positional power, and racial identity also represent important lines of difference that can significantly impede the development of effective, sustainable, and mutually beneficial partnerships if not attended to carefully. While research–practice boundaries may, at times, align with these other lines of difference, we argue it is valuable to tease these distinctive dimensions apart.

The organizational affiliations of RPP members shape several factors that can influence how collaboration in an RPP unfolds. These factors include organizations' mission/vision, approach to research, training, hierarchical structure, composition, and funding sources (Farrell et al., 2021). Most RPPs described in the extant literature involve partner organizations that are categorized as either knowledge producers and research-based, or knowledge users and practice-based (Bell et al., 2015; Farrell et al., 2021). Research-side organizations are often universities or university-affiliated research institutes. In contrast, practice-side organizations might include individual schools, nonprofit educational service providers, cultural organizations, school districts, or state education agencies. However, not all researchers work for universities, and not everyone affiliated with a university is a researcher or expected only to prioritize traditional research. Researchers in an RPP might instead be affiliated with a private research or consulting firm or operate as independent scholars (e.g., Denner et al., 2019). Similarly, practice organizations often have members who specialize in research or even an official research division (Wentworth, Conaway, et al., 2021). Thus, lines of difference based on organizational affiliation may or may not align with divisions based on primary orientation to either research or practice.

Likewise, the current professional role of the individuals in a RPP may or may not align with their training and professional identity (Akkerman & Bruining, 2016). For example, university faculty are typically both researchers and educators. Particularly among university-affiliated education researchers, many also have years of experience and strong professional identities as teachers. The varied knowledge, skills, and mindsets associated with training for practitioners and researchers serve as important lines of difference in RPPs complicated by wide-ranging organizational structures

Leveraging University Partners as Brokers During Intertwined Global Pandemics • **211**

and cultures that may not fit neatly into a research or practice label (Akkerman & Bruining, 2016; Denner et al., 2019).

In addition to differences that may exist across organizational or industry boundaries within the ecosystem, important boundaries also exist within individual organizations in an RPP. These include explicit and implicit hierarchies that can dictate positional power (Davis & Harrison, 2013). For example, a school has important role distinctions of principal and classroom teacher which parallel the role of management and frontline workers in other organizations. This is an example of an explicit hierarchy where the principal has positional power over classroom teachers. In a research organization, this might look like a tenured university faculty member and a graduate student researcher in the same RPP (Ghiso et al., 2019). Implicit hierarchies are less obvious and indicated by titles, management roles, and salary, but they nevertheless influence the dynamics of an RPP.

Finally, the various identities of RPP participants serve as possible lines of difference. Given the existence of structural racism and institutional racism in education and research organizations, racial identity is a salient line of difference. Racial identity and the power differentials associated with it, represent a boundary that can be at play in any RPP configuration, and may or may not align with the boundaries and power differentials most often written about between research and practice. Vakil et al. (2016) offered powerful contrasting cases in their analyses of the process of developing and maintaining a sense of politicized trust—trust based on shared commitments to racial justice goals—across different configurations of racial and professional boundaries. While politicized trust required extensive work to develop and maintain for a White researcher working with Black and Latino youth, a Black researcher and her Black practitioner partner were able to work from a shared sense of politicized trust from the outset—yet other lines of difference proved more troublesome for their efforts at collaboration. Tanksley and Estrada (2022) pointed out that researchers of color, particularly women of color, and especially those who have less positional power within their own organizations due to their role as graduate students, are vulnerable to micro- and macro-aggressions from practitioner partners who hold positions of relative social privilege due to their being White, male, credentialed, and so on. Gonzales and Shotton (2022) illustrated how bridging boundaries of race and positioning within structures of colonialism and domination required intentionality and purposeful effort, even for colleagues within the university.

Recognizing the immense influence these boundaries often have on the ability for RPP members to collaborate, recent literature on RPPs has highlighted the processes by which such boundaries are crossed, spanned, or brokered.

Crossing Lines of Difference Through Brokering

RPP brokering is a "key function that helps start, support, and maintain partnerships" (Wentworth, Conaway, et al., 2021, p. 2). In the RPP literature, authors often refer to those who take on the role of helping RPPs navigate boundaries as boundary spanners, boundary crossers, boundary workers, intermediaries, or knowledge brokers (Wegemer & Renick, 2021; see also Akkerman & Bruining, 2016; Farrell et al., 2022; Wentworth, Conaway, et al., 2021). Here, we use the terms "broker" and "brokering" to refer to all these roles, for the sake of consistency. Brokers support RPPs in negotiating their structure, communication strategies, partner roles, evaluation tools, organizational routines, and collaborative focus (Wentworth et al., 2021). This role is often undervalued due to the "behind the scenes" nature of the work. This critical connector role, however, can be the difference between RPPs overcoming challenges or falling apart.

Ward et al. (2009) identified five functions performed by those in knowledge brokering roles, including information manager, linking agent, capacity builder, facilitator, and evaluator (see also Glegg & Hoens, 2016; Wentworth, Conaway, et al., 2021). Wentworth, Conaway, et al. (2021) further divided RPP brokerage activities into (a) brokering to strengthen partners and (b) brokering to strengthen the partnership. The "partners" in this framework are the individuals and organizations on both the research and practice sides of the partnership. The "partnership," is the ongoing, collaborative relationship between partners. These distinct brokerage activities can be connected to any of the five functions discerned by Ward et al. (2009) and nurture different facets of the RPP in relation to both research and practice differences but also with respect to other lines of difference like organizational affiliation, professional identity, power dynamics, and racial identity.

Brokering to Strengthen Partners

Wentworth, Conaway, et al. (2021) divided brokers' work to strengthen partners into three categories: competencies, relationships, and research-use. In thinking about a broader array of lines of difference that may need to be crossed, we argue that a focus on competencies is particularly useful. These competencies include the skills and knowledge needed to engage in joint work as well as self-knowledge competencies needed to build trust and form beneficial relationships. Developing individual competencies promotes the long-term sustainability of the RPP, perhaps without the ongoing need for independent brokerage. While the necessary knowledge, skill, and mindset development will vary depending on the nature of the RPP, building capacity for effective communication and centering equity are crucial, particularly for

Leveraging University Partners as Brokers During Intertwined Global Pandemics • **213**

partnerships where lines of racial difference are to be crossed (Booker et al., 2019; Diamond, 2021; Patel, 2015; Ryoo et al., 2015).

A key aspect of navigating across racial lines of difference in ways that center equity is the individual work that partners undertake to understand themselves and how they are situated in their local context (Tanksley & Estrada, 2022; Vakil et al., 2016; see also Milner, 2007). Brokers can strengthen partners' capacity to act in ways that center equity and sustain the partnership by building awareness through sensemaking activities. Individual self-knowledge and knowledge of one's own historical, social, and organizational positioning makes the process of learning about others' perspectives more meaningful (Gonzales & Shotton, 2022; see also Milner, 2007). Brokers can also prompt partners to engage in critical analysis of the ways in which identity, cultural differences, values, norms, power structures, and systems of domination influence partnership development (Diamond, 2021; Milner, 2007; Tanksley & Estrada, 2022). Effective brokers are both strong coaches and facilitators. They challenge assumptions and unearth implicit biases in ways that empower partners to continue to engage in self-work on their own. This supports the process of building trust, buy-in, and mutual respect between and among partners (Wentworth, Conaway, et al., 2021). Brokering activities that strengthen partners set up RPP members for success, which can be further supported by brokering activities to strengthen the partnership (Wentworth, Conaway, et al., 2021). However, activities for strengthening partners may also occur concurrently with activities designed to strengthen the partnership.

Brokering to Strengthen Partnerships

Brokers use different skills to strengthen the partnership itself. Wentworth, Conaway, et al. (2021) argued that these skills fall into three categories: governance and administration, assessment and continuous improvement, and process and communication. We suggest that a focus on facilitating joint activities across the three categories and negotiating norms and routines for process and communication is particularly useful, because such joint activities set the foundation for further collaboration between partners.

Governance and administration joint activities include negotiating the collaborative focus of the RPP and negotiating researcher roles (Bell et al., 2015; Denner et al., 2019). Facilitating joint activities related to assessment and continuous improvement can include creating data-driven decision-making procedures and designing methods for assessing the partnership. Assessment in RPPs is meant to be used as a tool for continuously improving the partnership rather than simply evaluating it (Wentworth, Conaway, et al., 2021; see also Henrick et al., 2017). Brokers can use RPP frameworks (e.g., Henrick et al., 2017) together with more detailed indicators of effectiveness to engage partners in purposeful reflection and to encourage them to commit themselves to formative self-assessment of their own work.

Joint activities related to process and communication allow partners to negotiate norms and routines for communication that can make the partnership more resilient. RPP partners must be able to communicate relentlessly and maintain productive social structures (Booker et al., 2019; Wentworth, Conaway, et al., 2021). Brokers can support the construction of routines for communication, conflict resolution, approaching difficult conversations and critical feedback, and ongoing, intentional reflection about the partnership (Booker et al., 2019; Wentworth, Conaway, et al., 2021). Once effective routines and structures are in place, they may become a largely invisible part of the RPP environment that can be maintained by the partners.

RPP Brokerage Configurations

Given the many lines of difference that can be at play in RPPs and the multiple components of actions serving to strengthen both partners and partnerships, brokerage plays a highly valuable role in RPPs. It is also a process that can be configured in a variety of ways. While Wentworth, Conaway, et al. (2021) focused on formal brokerage roles played by actors outside the partner organizations, RPP members within a partner organization can also broker across lines of difference, and brokerage activities can even occur within a single organization. We argue that any actor who engages in brokering activities within or between organizations (see Ward et al., 2009)—whether the formal title of "broker" is a negotiated role in the RPP or not—is an RPP broker. The nature of the brokerage will depend on the kinds of different boundaries that are relevant to the context of the RPP.

Broker Positioning and Functions

Building on the Wentworth, Conaway, et al. (2021) perspective on the kinds of brokerage activities that occur in an RPP and the Ward et al. (2009) functions of knowledge brokers, we illustrate the positioning and functions played by brokers within common RPP configurations in Figures 10.1 and 10.2.

Figure 10.1 represents one of the most common configurations of RPPs with brokers, which we refer to as internal brokerage. Recognizing that unidimensional distinctions between research and practice can be problematic, for the sake of simplicity here, Figure 10.1 represents RPP partners as including members from one practice-based organizational partner and one research-based organizational partner. In this configuration,

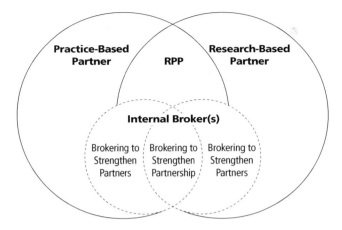

Figure 10.1 RPP with internal broker(s) configuration.

the RPP brokerage comes from an internal source—from within either the research-based or practice-based organizations in the partnership. Often, they are a member of the research team or a school district employee with a background in research or equity and justice facilitation (Penuel et al., 2015). Ideally, the brokering to strengthen partners' activities is facilitated with the broker's own organization as well as for their partner organization. When this type of brokering occurs within the broker's own organization, the brokering activities to manage information, make connections, build capacity, facilitate, and evaluate across lines of difference tend to be less noticeable since the broker is already embedded in the organization.

Figure 10.2 illustrates another common configuration of the broker(s) in an RPP in which the brokerage originates outside the partner organizations. We refer to brokers in this configuration as external brokers. They represent third-party consultants or facilitators who engage in brokering to strengthen the partners and the partnership from outside the partnership itself.

While, as we have argued, conceiving of the boundaries in RPPs as only separating research and practice is not sufficient, multiple lines of difference often are inseparable within specific cases, causing other analytic distinctions to get subsumed within the research–practice divide. In recognition of this common challenge, we focus here on the Museum+School RPP, an unusual partnership where these lines of difference are more empirically distinguishable and salient. We propose that understanding the Museum+School RPP makes it easier to comprehend the dynamics of brokering that occur across a wide range of other RPPs.

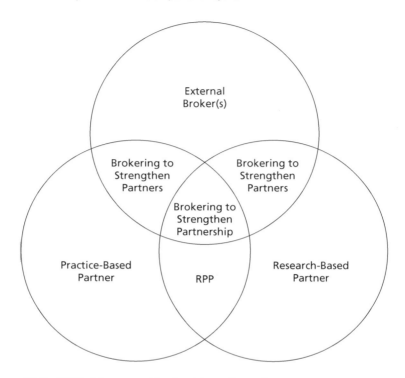

Figure 10.2 RPP with external broker(s) configuration.

METHODS AND DATA

We approached our analysis of the Museum+School RPP using an adaptation of Stake's (1994) framework for case study. As participants in the Museum+School RPP launch (Plank & Quigley), and active stakeholders in educational research and practice in our communities (all authors), we care deeply about understanding this partnership. Our primary purpose was to understand both the Museum+School RPP launch and the opportunities this particular RPP afforded for better understanding diverse forms of brokerage activities. Table 10.1 provides a list and description of our data sources.

To analyze the data, we worked iteratively among interviews, field notes, meeting transcripts, and artifacts, our reflections about the project, and literature on relevant concepts. We sought to categorize what we discerned in terms of how salient lines of difference impacted joint work, brokering strategies, and the configuration of the RPP.

Leveraging University Partners as Brokers During Intertwined Global Pandemics ▪ **217**

TABLE 10.1	Museum + Scool RPP Data Sources
Data Source	**Description**
Interviews	Semi-formal and informal interviews with members of the RPP working group, museum researchers, museum teaching artists, school leaders, and classroom teachers. Interviews were transcribed and coded to understand themes and inform brokerage activities.
Observations	Field notes and recordings of in-person and virtual observations of practitioners in the museum and school, including daily work, advisory board meetings, and biweekly working group meetings.
Organizational Artifacts	Early partnership documents that captured the evolution of the RPP from before we joined as brokers.
Brokerage Activity Artifacts	Artifacts from all brokering activities including participant surveys, photos/videos from collaborative activities, meeting minutes, participant responses in learning modules, reflections, etc.
Reflections	Ongoing, iterative reflective conversations and writing about the effectiveness of brokering activities, the health of the partnership, and next steps.

THE CASE OF THE MUSEUM+SCHOOL RPP

To deepen our understanding of brokering across lines of difference in RPPs, we return to the story of the launch of the Museum+School RPP. The impetus for the formation of the Museum+School RPP was the merging of an existing city museum and a public charter school into a newly remodeled physical space starting in the 2018/2019 school year. The city museum was growing and planning to renovate a historic building to expand hands-on learning opportunities for middle school-aged youth. The school was also growing and needed a new space for students in middle school. Both organizations wanted to learn from each other and partner to empower the youth in the shared space. However, the learning environments of the two organizations were markedly different, both in terms of focus and racial composition. The school's mission/vision centered on social justice and prioritized project-based learning. The school was led by mostly Black and African American faculty and served Black and African American students. The museum's robust research branch focused on innovation, learning sciences, and collaborative informal and formal learning efforts. At the inception of the Museum+School RPP, the museum was led by primarily White staff and served a largely White population.

The leaders of both the museum and school resolved to implement an RPP as the presumptive best way to achieve their goal to create a shared space where prominent learning scientists, educators, and designers could come together to reimagine education and test innovative approaches oriented to promoting youth learning in the shared space and beyond. Planning for the launch of the Museum+School RPP began in the Fall 2018 in anticipation of the impending move into the shared space in the Fall 2019.

Given the anticipated challenges of working across various lines of difference and effectively collaborating in a shared space, the Museum+School RPP working group decided to invite the university-based team (Plank—a PhD student—and Quigley—Plank's advisor) as temporary partners. The mid-level leaders from the museum and the school in the working group had previous relationships with us as educational researchers on a different grant-funded project. Leaders from each organization valued our relatively high status and neutral positioning as university-based educators/researchers. They also wanted the Museum+School RPP to be sustained for the foreseeable future while weathering challenges like shifts in funding and personnel turnover. While both holding White racial identities, we brought extensive experience working within organizations led by and predominantly serving people of color—aspects of our positionality that proved relevant as our work unfolded. The leaders of both school and museum knew that we could offer temporary support to launch the RPP and they tasked us with designing sustainable systems that would endure transition after our contract expired.

The main goals of the Museum+School RPP were to (a) grow the capacity of museum educators, designers and researchers, and partner-school teachers and administrators, to engage in mutually beneficial partnership work; and (b) lay the foundation for continuous collaborative research activities that (i) facilitate partners' capacity to address problems of practice and achieve local improvement goals, and (ii) influence and promote field-wide conversations about learning theory, practice, and policy. These goals were negotiated before we stepped in as RPP brokers and our goal was to facilitate the development of the requisite RPP infrastructure such as routines, roles, procedures, and protocols to achieve them (Anderson & Colyvas, 2021; Penuel, 2019).

Just as we joined the partnership, the building that housed the two organizations closed indefinitely due to the emergence of the second of the intertwined global pandemics: COVID-19! Like many schools during the height of the COVID-19 pandemic, the public charter school went through periods of complete shutdown, virtual learning, and hybrid instruction. The school was not able to remain open consistently until Spring 2022 semester. The museum was closed until the Summer of 2021 and most of the teaching artists (museum practitioners) were furloughed. We were also restricted in our ability to conduct research or collaborate due to closures and restrictions on in-person meetings and research throughout the pandemic.

After months of standing empty of young people, students returned to the school building intermittently in early 2021. However, the museum could not reopen its spaces until Summer 2021. The COVID-19 pandemic prolonged disruptions through 2022 as infection rates in the city continued to fluctuate. See Figure 10.3 for a visual timeline of the Museum+School RPP.

Leveraging University Partners as Brokers During Intertwined Global Pandemics • 219

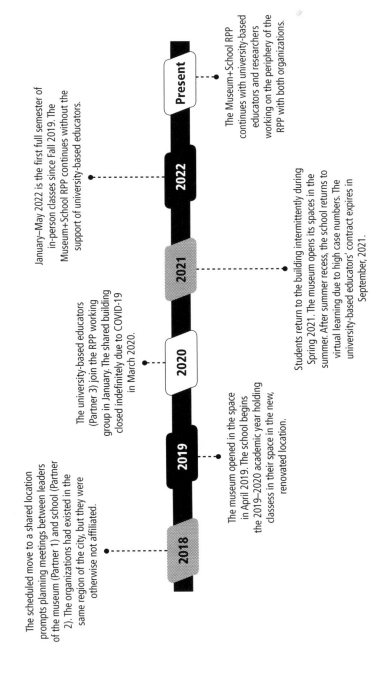

Figure 10.3 Museum+school RPP timeline.

BROKERING IN THE MUSEUM+SCHOOL RPP

Despite these challenges, we worked closely with both school- and museum-based members of the Museum+School RPP to broker across lines of difference as best we could. We began by seeking to understand what had already happened before and during the initial launch of the RPP through artifact analysis and semi-formal interviews with representatives from the teaching artists, classroom teachers, school administration, museum administration, and museum research division. We analyzed existing organizational structures and spent time observing various practitioners and contexts within the shared space. We also used a critical lens to interpret each organization's understanding of equity, hierarchies, and power dynamics, as well as systems of oppression that influenced trust building.

Superficially, the Museum+School RPP resembled the external broker configuration (Figure 10.2). However, the existence of both researchers and practitioners within the museum complicated the configuration so that it more closely resembled that shown in Figure 10.4. (Our role as brokers was intended to be temporary—as represented by the dotted line.) The RPP existed before and after the addition of us as external brokers, so the RPP itself exists at point 3 in Figure 10.4.

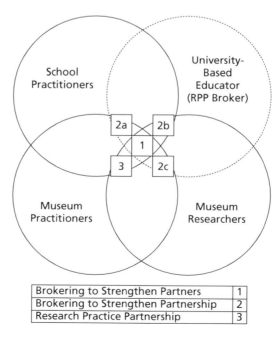

Figure 10.4 Museum+school RPP configuration.

Leveraging University Partners as Brokers During Intertwined Global Pandemics • **221**

As the COVID-19 pandemic intertwined with the ongoing pandemic of racial oppression, we were forced to reimagine how university-based educators as RPP brokers could navigate the unprecedented circumstances of this partnership. In doing so, we identified multiple salient axes of difference in the Museum+School RPP context, including research and practice, racial identity, organizational affiliation, and positional power within the organization. We sought to bridge each of these boundaries using multiple types of brokering activities, some of which proved more successful than others.

We describe these activities below by the types of boundaries they were intended to span, where they existed in the Museum+School RPP configuration, and whether they were meant to serve to strengthen partners (labeled 1 in Figure 10.4) or strengthen the partnership (labeled 2 in Figure 10.4). As we analyzed each salient line of difference to design and facilitate brokering activities, we also considered ways in which the work would be sustained and sought to strengthen the potential for brokerage roles within each partner organization as well as internal brokerage across the partners.

Research and Practice Line of Difference

While RPPs have traditionally involved one research-based organization and another that is practice-based, for the Museum+School RPP, lines of difference between research and practice did not align with organizational boundaries. Some personnel from both the school and the museum were in roles focused on educational practice. The practice partners from the school included classroom teachers, instructional coaches, and school leadership members. Practice partners from the museum side included teaching artists (specializing in out-of-school learning contexts) who worked at a similar hierarchical level as a classroom teacher in a school context. The museum was also positioned as the research-side partner, given the expertise of the staff in their robust, in-house research division.

Brokering to Strengthen Partners
In brokering across the divides of research and practice, the strands of our work to strengthen partners and to strengthen the partnership were often intertwined with one another. We worked primarily with a small working group comprised of both researcher and practitioner members that met online during the height of the COVID-19 pandemic. To strengthen partners' ability to collaborate across the research–practice line of difference and iteratively address meaningful problems of practice, we needed to build the capacity for each partner to engage in mutually beneficial research at point 1 in Figure 10.4. To support the museum- and school-based educators in this goal, we designed interactive, asynchronous, online

modules on a shared Google Site that introduced the knowledge and skills needed to engage in research comprehension and production as practitioners through design thinking. To support the museum researchers, we also designed interactive online modules focused on understanding how to engage practitioners in research that iteratively addressed meaningful problems of practice. As the museum researchers explored different types of research methods appropriate for an RPP, they became particularly interested in participatory design.

Brokering to Strengthen the Partnership

After tailoring distinct supports to support researchers and educators in building capacity around the research–practice line of difference, we facilitated joint activities to apply the learning to the Museum+School RPP. First, the working group studied a selection of reflections from the Google Site modules to understand the perspectives of other RPP members on issues related to the research–practice boundary. For example, school practitioners shared reflections on prior challenges with research implementation, which indicated a need to strengthen the partnership through information management, capacity building, linking, and facilitating at point 2b in Figure 10.4.

From there, we leveraged the five functions of brokers (Ward et al., 2009) to strengthen partnerships at point 2a between the school and museum practitioners and points 2b and 2c between practitioners and researchers. We facilitated activities designed to share relevant information from research and practice, build mutual trust, set a collective vision, imagine possibilities through design thinking protocols, create effective routines for collaboration, and negotiate high leverage problems of practice for the RPP.

Racial Identity Line of Difference

In addition to differences that crossed organizational boundaries, differences between the two organizations in relation to race were also quite apparent. During Fall 2019, Museum+School RPP members made a renewed effort to address what we have since characterized as the ongoing pandemic of racial oppression. The members of both museum and school expressed their desire to work collectively towards racial justice. Before we joined the team as brokers, and before the partners moved into the shared space, they jointly pursued professional development that addressed the impact of race and racism in education to inform their co-design research cycles. However, the line of difference between the racial composition of the museum and the school led to difficult conversations in the absence of either a foundation of mutual trust or the tools to facilitate productive engagement.

Leveraging University Partners as Brokers During Intertwined Global Pandemics • **223**

The difficult conversations about race and power from the perspectives of two very different institutions—each with entrenched cultures—raised questions, generated misunderstandings, and created tensions both within and between the school and museum. Such conversations presented a new challenge for the Museum+School RPP but the inequities they exposed are deeply rooted in the history of the two organizational types. Museums have a long history of patterns of inequitable access along the lines of race and class (Akiva et al., 2021; Hecht, 2021). Both K–12 and higher education organizations serving minoritized students and families have also served as both sites of organizing for collective liberation, as well as sites of racialized oppression in their own right (Love, 2019). Heightened tensions exacerbated the difficulties of building trust across boundaries of research and practice, organizational lines, and race.

Brokering to Strengthen Partners

Our brokering activities across lines of race were much more sharply differentiated in terms of activities to strengthen partners and the partnership. We strategically provided separate spaces for individuals to engage with self-identity work and to process the challenges that surfaced during the earlier attempts at joint work across racial identity lines of difference.

We perceived that the needs of the museum and school were very different. For example, the school team needed a chance to process what was going on in the world and how it was showing up in the RPP. They felt burdened by the early-stage ponderings of White RPP members who were wrestling with equity issues for the first time. As White educators ourselves, we were well positioned to support the museum research team in the self-work needed to learn how to work across lines of difference in terms of racial identity. Our shared Google Site housed a directory of shared resources for RPP brokering activities that centered on equity and justice and an evolving equity and justice syllabus for RPP members who were seeking to educate themselves. We focused on building awareness of how previous interactions caused harm and enhanced the capacity of individuals to analyze how systems of domination influenced the Museum+School RPP. Finally, we invited individuals to aspire to act as co-conspirators (Love, 2019).

Brokering to Strengthen the Partnership

After providing differentiated support depending on partner needs, we brought teams from both organizations together to address harm, restore trust, and build on what they learned separately to strengthen the partnership. The partners decided we needed to build a common vision that centered on equity and justice. We worked to support the development of this vision in a way that articulated the identity and culture of the partnership without losing the individual identity and culture of the partners. To do so,

224 • H. PLANK, E. R. ANDERSON, and C. QUIGLEY

we adapted established broker methods and tools from the research+practice collaboratory (researchandpractice.org) as well as activities from our varied experiences as formal and informal educational leaders. However, we also understood a vision to be an artifact that is meant to evolve over time, setting the partnership up for further growth in the future.

Organizational Affiliation Line of Difference

Despite the emphasis on educating youth shared by the Museum+School RPP partners, the distinct professional training and associated practices embedded in formal vs informal educational settings proved salient as well. For example, classroom teachers facilitated project-based learning that was aligned to content and skills mandated in state academic standards. Museum teaching artists, on the other hand, designed exhibits and learning experiences based on the interests of museum patrons. In our observations and interviews, we also noticed contrasting values and practices when it came to building and maintaining learning environments in the shared space. Classroom teachers felt that they were "on the hook" for managing student behavior and protecting learning resources owned by the museum. Meanwhile, teaching artists valued learning in environments that could be perceived as "messy" or chaotic to an outside observer. These lines of difference originated not only from the values of the organizations when it comes to what learning looks like for youth, but also from the way the practitioners were trained to design and facilitate learning experiences.

Brokering to Strengthen Partners

To broaden partners' horizons, our shared Google site included modules designed to facilitate partners' understanding of the strengths of their counterparts' approaches to learning. The learning modules included artifacts from the formal and informal education training described to us during interviews. Partners also had the opportunity to engage in video or synchronous virtual observations of each other in instructional settings using a protocol that allowed them to analyze the strengths of each other's approach. We hoped that in-person instructional observation opportunities would be made available once the shared space reopened after the height of the COVID-19 pandemic.

We also helped practitioners process their experiences with learning in their counterparts' organization to discern perceived boundaries that would need to be addressed to strengthen the partnership. For example, the school practitioners felt burdened by the responsibility of ensuring their students' safety and protecting expensive museum equipment. They envied the teaching artists' freedom to center student interests over state-mandated standards. Museum practitioners, on the other hand, confessed that they were intimidated by the structure and urgency of standards-driven learning at the school despite its emphasis on transdisciplinary, project-based learning.

Brokering to Strengthen the Partnership

To strengthen the partnership across lines of formal and informal education and the associated different training and approaches, we prioritized shifting from deficit-based to asset-based ways of understanding these differences. In the learning modules, we encouraged museum practitioners and school practitioners to imagine possibilities emerging from working within a different paradigm. To foster collaboration based on shared interests, we planned for frequent events including shared meals and collaborative making activities. We had to innovate to meet these goals during quarantine, so we planned virtual events like digital escape rooms over a shared meal that was delivered to each partner's home. The Google site also housed a space for co-generated research and artifacts to address equity-focused problems of practice. Our intention was that the Google site could serve as a tool to capture institutional knowledge and allow the RPP to grow through internal brokerage in the future.

Positional Power Line of Difference

The individual members of the Museum+School RPP also differed in terms of the positional power they held within each organization. In the museum context, the research team had positional power over the museum teaching artists—signified by differences in credentials, pay, and authority within the organization. In the school, administrators had positional power over classroom teachers, for whom they often served as managers. While these differences existed within each organization, they created challenges to resolving logistical issues that emerged across organizational boundaries.

A primary challenge concerned obstacles to collaboration related to scheduling. Both classroom teachers and teaching artists had to comply with top–down directives that constrained their time while also being expected to find time to collaborate with one another. In order to maintain after school and evening hours, the arrival time of teaching artists was much later than classroom teachers. Classroom teachers found it very difficult to prioritize collaboration with their museum counterparts during their limited planning time that was often used for collaboration with other classroom teachers who shared the same students, individualized education plan (IEP) meetings, family engagement, mandatory professional development, coverage for teachers who were absent, and so forth. There was an overlap in the practitioner schedules after school, but that tended to be the busiest time of the day for teaching artists who were tasked with running after-school clubs and engaging with patrons. In interviews, the teaching artists shared feelings of resentment that they were expected to work outside their normal schedule to collaborate while they perceived classroom teachers' time as more "protected."

Brokering to Strengthen Partners

While these challenges were at the forefront of the classroom teachers' and teaching artists' minds, they were not necessarily visible to higher level leadership in either context. This boundary was a difficult challenge for us to bridge, given the differences in how the school and museum operated. However, we tried by leveraging our knowledge of both types of contexts, and our positions outside of the positional hierarchies of both organizations.

Drawing on our confidential interviews with practitioners in both organizations, we highlighted the concerns of the teaching artists and classroom teachers, naming positional power as a barrier and offered potential solutions to leadership in both organizations. For example, drawing on our experiences with innovative master scheduling at schools across the country, we proposed alternative ways of organizing the limited flexible time available to teachers. Similarly, in pursuing possibilities for teaching artists to be available outside of their regular hours, we explored possibilities for securing grant funding to pay for their time. Our brokering efforts in this regard were particularly impacted by COVID-19 as the teaching artists were furloughed, and then the museum experienced significant turnover when it reopened.

Brokering to Strengthen the Partnership

We also worked to bridge this boundary through joint tools that engaged the Museum+School RPP members across both internal and cross-organizational boundaries. In addition to the vision development activities, we also designed other RPP infrastructure like a shared calendar, school and museum schedules, a virtual yearbook to connect practitioners and researchers, community agreements, frequently asked questions documents about the shared space, bi-weekly working group meetings, routines for developing a shared agenda for meetings, protocols for collaboration and conflict resolution, and so forth. Through facilitating activities to collaboratively create routines and RPP infrastructure, we were able to take a step towards building agency for classroom teachers and teaching artists as well as somewhat diminishing the conflicts across differences in positional power that were negatively impacting the RPP.

Sustaining the Museum+School RPP

Knowing that our funding was transitory, we focused our brokering activities on building towards sustainability. We believed that if we built a strong foundation, necessary competencies, and routines for effective collaboration, the Museum+School RPP would be able to rely on more informal, internal brokering from the museum and school partners—rather than relying on designated external brokers—to collaborate effectively across various lines of difference. Our greatest challenge was that, even though we had designated internal brokers to sustain the work after our departure, turnover associated with the COVID-19 pandemic made this line of succession problematic.

DISCUSSION AND IMPLICATIONS

For an RPP to solve problems of practice effectively and enjoy long-term sustainability, partners need to be able to collaborate in creative ways across multiple lines of difference within and between their organizations. The Museum+School RPP exhibited lines of difference that were more empirically distinguishable and salient than many. As such, the story of the Museum+School RPP can help us deepen our understanding of the brokering roles and dynamics at play in a broad array of research–practice partner configurations.

A key lesson is that being aware of research and practice boundaries is critical, but insufficient. Although the research–practice boundary was present in the Museum+School RPP, it was not the most challenging. As brokers, we needed to discern multiple lines of difference and nurture the RPP in relation to boundaries related to organizational affiliation, professional identity, power dynamics, and especially racial identity, as well.

The story of Museum+School RPP highlights that facilitating activities to strengthen partners is particularly important for brokering across lines of racial difference. There are growing bodies of literature on RPPs that discuss racial lines of difference (Gonzales & Shotton, 2022; Tanksley & Estrada, 2022; Vakil et al., 2016) and boundary spanning or brokering (Wentworth, Conaway, et al., 2021; see also Akkerman & Bruining, 2016; Farrell et al., 2022; Wegemer & Renick, 2021). We see this case study as drawing these distinct lines of research together. Our experiences highlight the important role that brokers can play in building partners' capacity to engage with difficult conversations, understand racial identity development, and engage in independent self-work.

Given our positions as university-affiliated researchers who also served as brokers of the Museum+School RPP, this case also highlights for us the importance of RPP participants being flexible in the roles and responsibilities they take on. Despite the emphasis on non-traditional divisions of labor in the RPP literature, university-affiliated RPP participants are typically positioned as a research-based partner, along the lines of Figure 10.3. The configuration that we exemplified in this chapter, with university-based educators positioned as external RPP brokers, is much less common. Despite the many challenges we encountered in this role, we contend that university partners are uniquely positioned to engage in RPPs as brokers outside of or in addition to their work as researchers. In addition to weighing-in on research, engaging in evaluations, or investigating data and artifacts produced by the RPP, university educators often bring understandings of theories of learning and organizational structure and dynamics, as well as classroom teaching experience. These experiences allow university-affiliated researchers to connect with RPP members positioned across various lines of difference and develop strategic approaches to strengthening both partners and the partnership.

Recognizing that research universities expect tenure-stream faculty and graduate students to maintain robust research agendas, researchers in these roles may approach brokerage as a contract outside the scope of university responsibilities or seek service recognition by their university for brokerage work. However, there are many university-affiliated educators who are clinical, teaching, or other appointment-stream faculty for whom being in a brokerage role in an RPP may be viable long term.

Moreover, in the Museum+School RPP, our role as brokers was a temporary arrangement designed to support the launch of the long-term RPP. In our case, this situation came about spontaneously in response to the very specific needs of partners in a particular time and place. Nonetheless, we contend that there may be a useful role for short-term external brokers in many partnerships. While challenges particular to the COVID-19 pandemic created unique obstacles in our case, external brokers can act strategically, as we tried to do, building the capacity of potential brokers from both organizations who can eventually transition into the role of continuously strengthening partners and the partnership through internal brokerage. The transitory nature of such short-term external brokering may also make it possible for more university educators to engage in RPP in a brokerage capacity.

As RPPs become increasingly commonplace, the role of RPP brokers will become even more important in launching new partnerships and sustaining existing ones. RPP brokerage offers an innovative way for university-based partners to impact the field while also contributing to ongoing research on the potential of this distinctive collaborative dynamic. Meanwhile, even as our world transitions from a pandemic to an endemic COVID-19 context, the pandemic of racial oppression rages. While the Museum+School RPP has helped us to take small steps forward, more research is needed to understand and scale ways RPP brokers may play a role in dismantling systems of oppression that hinder learning organizations of all kinds at intrapersonal, interpersonal, and organizational levels.

REFERENCES

Akiva, T., Hecht, M., & Osai, E. (2021). Arts learning across a city: How ecosystem thinking helps shape understanding of Black-centered and Eurocentric arts programming. *Urban Education*, 1–29. https://doi.org/10.1177/00420859211063434

Akkerman, S. F., & Bakker, A. (2011). Boundary crossing and boundary objects. *Review of Educational Research, 81*(2), 132–169. https://doi.org/10.3102/0034654311404435

Akkerman, S., & Bruining, T. (2016). Multilevel boundary crossing in a professional development school partnership, *Journal of the Learning Sciences, 25*(2), 240–284. https://doi.org/10.1080/10508406.2016.1147448

Anderson, E. R., & Colyvas, J. A. (2021). What sticks and why? A MoRe Institutional Framework for education research. *Teachers College Record, 123*(7). https://www.tcrecord.org/library/abstract.asp?contentid=23785

Arce-Trigatti, P., Chukhray, I., & López Turley, R. N. (2018). Research–practice partnerships in education. In B. Schneider (Ed.), *Handbook of the sociology of education in the 21st century* (pp. 561–579). Springer International Publishing. https://doi.org/10.1007/978-3-319-76694-2_25

Bell, P., Rhinehart, A., & Peterman, T. (2015, December 17). *Negotiating researcher roles within a research–practice partnership*. Research + Practice Collaboratory. http://researchandpractice.org/negotiating-researcher-roles

Booker, L., Conaway, C., & Schwartz, N. (2019, June 6). *Five ways RPPs can fail and how to avoid them: Applying conceptual frameworks to improve RPPs*. William T. Grant Foundation. https://wtgrantfoundation.org/five-ways-rpps-can-fail-and-how-to-avoid-them-applying-conceptual-frameworks-to-improve-rpps

Coburn, C. E., Penuel, W. R., & Geil, K. E. (2013). *Research–practice partnerships: A strategy for leveraging research for educational improvement in school districts*. William T. Grant Foundation. https://rpp.wtgrantfoundation.org/wp-content/uploads/2019/10/Research-Practice-Partnerships-at-the-District-Level.pdf

Davidson, K., & Penuel, W. R. (2019). The role of brokers in sustaining partnership work in education. In K. L. Davidson & W. R. Penuel (Eds.), *The role of knowledge brokers in education: Connecting the dots between research and practice* (pp. 154–167). https://doi.org/10.4324/9780429462436-11

Davis, T., & Harrison, L. M. (2013). *Advancing social justice: Tools, pedagogies, and strategies to transform your campus*. John Wiley & Sons.

Denner, J., Bean, S., Campe, S., Martinez, J., & Torres, D. (2019). Negotiating trust, power, and culture in a research–practice partnership. *AERA Open, 5*(2). https://doi.org/10.1177/2332858419858635

Diamond, J. B. (2021, July 19). *Racial equity and Research practice partnerships 2.0: A critical reflection*. William T. Grant Foundation. http://wtgrantfoundation. org/racial-equity-and-research-practice-partnerships-2-0-a-critical-reflection

Farrell, C. C., Penuel, W. R., Allen, A., Anderson, E. R., Bohannon, A. X., Coburn, C. E., & Brown, S. L. (2022). Learning at the boundaries of research and practice: A framework for understanding research–practice partnerships. *Educational Researcher, 51*(3), 197–208. https://doi.org/10.3102/0013189X211069073

Farrell, C. C., Penuel, W. R., Coburn, C. E., Daniel, J., & Steup, L. (2021, July 19). *Research–Practice Partnerships in education: The state of the field*. William T. Grant Foundation. https://wtgrantfoundation.org/wp-content/uploads/2021/07/RPP_State-of-the-Field_2021.pdf

Ghiso, M. P., Campano, G., Schwab, E. R., Asaah, D., & Rusoja, A. (2019). Mentoring in research–practice partnerships: Toward democratizing expertise. *AERA Open, 5*(4), 1–12. https://doi.org/10.1177/2332858419879448

Glegg, S. M., & Hoens, A. (2016). Role domains of knowledge brokering: A model for the health care setting. *Journal of Neurological Physical Therapy, 40*(2), 115–123. https://doi.org/10.1097/NPT.0000000000000122

Gonzales, L. D., & Shotton, H. (2022). Coalitional refusal in a neoliberal academy. *International Journal of Qualitative Studies in Education, 35*(5), 1–13. https://doi.org/10.1080/09518398.2022.2025472

Hecht, M. (2021). Creating cultural refugia to transform the boundaries of science. *Cultural Studies of Science Education, 16*, 549–556. http://doi.org/10.1007/s11422-020-10010-y

Henrick, E. C., Cobb, P., Penuel, W. R., Jackson, K., & Clark, T. (2017). *Assessing research–practice partnerships: Five dimensions of effectiveness*. William T. Grant Foundation. https://rpp.wtgrantfoundation.org/wp-content/uploads/2019/09/Assessing-Research-Practice-Partnerships.pdf

Love, B. L. (2019). *We want to do more than survive: Abolitionist teaching and the pursuit of educational freedom*. Beacon Press.

Milner, H. R., IV (2007). Race, culture, and researcher positionality: Working through dangers seen, unseen, and unforeseen. *Educational Researcher, 36*(7), 388–400. https://doi.org/10.3102/0013189X07309471

Patel, L. (2015). *Decolonizing educational research: From ownership to answerability*. Routledge. https://doi.org/10.4324/9781315658551

Penuel, W. R. (2019). Infrastructuring as a practice of design-based research for supporting and studying equitable implementation and sustainability of innovations. *Journal of the Learning Sciences, 28*(4–5), 659–677. https://doi.org/10.1080/10508406.2018.1552151

Penuel, W. R., Allen, A.-R., Coburn, C. E., & Farrell, C. (2015). Conceptualizing research–practice partnerships as joint work at boundaries. *Journal of Education for Students Placed at Risk, 20*(1–2), 182–197. https://doi.org/10.1080/10824669.2014.988334

Ryoo, J. J., Choi, M., & McLeod, E. (2015). *Building equity in research–practice partnerships*. Research+Practice Collaboratory. http://researchandpractice.org/wp-content/uploads/2015/10/BuildingEquity_Oct2015.pdf

Stake, R. E. (1994). Case study: Composition and performance. *Bulletin of the Council for Research in Music Education, 122*, 31–44. https://www.jstor.org/stable/40318653

Tanksley, T., & Estrada, C. (2022). Toward a critical race RPP: How race, power, and positionality inform research practice partnerships. *International Journal of Research & Method in Education, 45*(4), 397–409. https://doi.org/10.1080/1743727X.2022.2097218

Vakil, S., McKinney de Royston, M., Suad Nasir, N., & Kirshner, B. (2016). Rethinking race and power in design-based research: Reflections from the field. *Cognition and Instruction, 34*(3), 194–209. https://doi.org/10.1080/07370008.2016.1169817

Ward, V., House, A., & Hamer, S. (2009). Knowledge brokering: The missing link in the evidence to action chain? *Evidence Policy, 5*(3), 267–279. https://doi.org/10.1332/174426409X463811

Wegemer, C. M., & Renick, J. (2021). Boundary spanning roles and power in educational partnerships. *AERA Open*, 1–14. https://doi.org/10.1177/23328584211016868

Wentworth, L., Conaway, C., Shewchuk, S., & Arce-Trigatti, P. (2021). *RPP brokers handbook: A guide to brokering in education Research-Practice Partnerships*. National Network of Education Research–Practice Partnerships. https://nnerpp.rice.edu/rpp-brokers-handbook/

Wentworth, L., Khanna, R., Nayfack, M., & Schwartz, D. (2021). Closing the research–practice gap in education. *Stanford Social Innovation Review, 19*(2), 57–58. https://doi.org/10.48558/eh5b-y819

SECTION IV

REFLECTIONS AND ROADMAPS

CHAPTER 11

VIDEO DOCUMENTATION OF THE INTERNATIONAL RURAL SCHOOL LEADERSHIP PROJECT

A Retrospective Case Study of University–School–Community Collaboration

Jerry D. Johnson
East Carolina University

Hobart L. Harmon
Kansas State University

ABSTRACT

Collaborative actions enabled production of a documentary video chronicling the International Rural School Leadership Project. Following a visit by one of the U.S. collaborators to Queensland Australia, the project emerged

---

School–University–Community Research in a (Post) COVID-19 World, pages 235–257
Copyright © 2023 by Information Age Publishing
www.infoagepub.com
All rights of reproduction in any form reserved.

235

organically and took on structure and intentionality as it evolved in response to (a) external constraints imposed by the COVID-19 pandemic, and (b) insights and opportunities gained through collaboration among stakeholders representing university, school, and community constituencies on two continents. Guided by three research questions, a retrospective case study analysis of the project by two of the project collaborators reveals 21 key collaboration activities occurred during the almost 2-year project timeframe, determines how nine essential elements of public-sector collaboration applied to university–school–community stakeholder involvement, and identifies seven key activities as critical incidents for success. Following presentation of study results, a discussion section gives meaning to findings by explaining and elaborating on the key elements of collaboration and/or critical incidents that are perceived, in retrospect, as important to project success and video development. Based on study results, retrospective reflection of the International Rural School Leadership Project, and more than 50 years of combined engagement in rural education research and practice, the authors offer a list of 10 general research questions as examples of topics for advancing the study of collaboration in rural contexts.

Little did we know that a 3-week visit to Queensland Australia in Fall 2019 would turn into an almost 2-year collaboration opportunity—thanks to the COVID-19 pandemic. What started as invitations to present at Australia's national rural education conference, discuss education innovations with faculty at a major university, and tour rural schools subsequently inspired the International Rural School Leadership Project. The pandemic caused world shutdown of schools in early Spring 2020 and its varied challenges created opportunities for extending, broadening, and deepening the work and the relationships that evolved out of that initial visit. Ultimately, this led to the development of a video documentary that both captured the school–university–community collaboration that was occurring and leveraged that school–university–community collaboration as part of the development process.

This chapter presents results from a systematic reflection and subsequent analysis of the process. As such, it serves two primary purposes: (a) documenting the work that occurred among varied stakeholders across international settings in order to highlight how collaboration as an activity and a guiding principle contributed to both the end results of this particular project and to the ongoing partnerships that were built through the work, and (b) unpacking the collaborative activities that occurred to better understand how and why the project evolved as it did and produced what it did. The first purpose contributes to the literature by providing a coherent narrative of a collaboration process that breathes life into organizational activities and offers a case for examination and consideration by practitioners who may be engaged in work that would benefit from collaboration. The second purpose contributes to the work by assessing the sequencing

Video Documentation of the International Rural School Leadership Project ▪ **237**

and relative importance of *collaboration elements* within the context of a particular process and a particular organizational and socio-historical context (thus illustrating the idea that collaboration is not a one-size-fits-all set of steps/procedures but rather a multi-faceted process that—to be effective—must be attentive to context). Results related to this second purpose extend lines of inquiry related to partnerships and collaborative leadership.

REVIEW OF RELEVANT LITERATURE

Though widely used as a key strategy in conducting research in research-practice partnerships (Bevan & Penuel, 2017; Penuel & Gallagher, 2017) and similar research alliances (Scher et al., 2018), the development of collaboration theory is in its infancy and not clearly understood (Morris & Miller-Stevens, 2016). Scholarship on rural education, however, reveals applications of school–university–community collaboration in implementing innovations (e.g., see Reardon & Leonard, 2018a) and in determining impact of outcomes of educational practices (e.g., see Reardon & Leonard, 2018b). Moreover, collaboration and collaborative leadership are foundational to forming and fostering partnerships that seek solutions to educational challenges in rural contexts (Harmon, 2017).

Changing rural teaching practices (Harmon et al., 2007), understanding dynamics of social class and race in rural places (Hess et al., 2014), and achieving mutually-beneficial goals of rural schools and communities (Harmon & Schafft, 2009) require leaders with collaboration expertise. Collaboration support from universities can occur in numerous research activities and/or services (e.g., Johnson et al., 2009; Ohlson et al., 2018). Increasingly, the power of storytelling using short-format video is being recognized in communicating research and science (Finkler & Leon, 2019). Furthermore, the elements of collaboration are found among the essential steps in producing a documentary video. As Bernard (2007) points out in the book *Documentary Storytelling: Making Stronger and More Dramatic Nonfiction Films*:

> A film's author is the person (or people) with primary responsibility for the film's story and structure, which often means that person is the producer and/or director, working as or in tandem with a writer and editor. It's unfortunate that many documentary festivals have adopted the practice, more common to dramatic features, of attributing a film to its director. Unless a film is produced, written, and directed by a single person, it is misleading to credit the director as the author. Films are invariably collaborative, and they begin with ideas and stories that often originate with producers and/or writers. (p. 7)

In this study we investigate how collaborative actions enabled production of a documentary video chronicling the International Rural School

238 ▪ J. D. JOHNSON and H. L. HARMON

Leadership Project (https://www.youtube.com/watch?v=wpIMno6Ns10). The project emerged organically but took on structure and intentionality as it evolved in response to (a) external constraints imposed by the COVID-19 pandemic, and (b) insights and opportunities gained through collaboration among stakeholders representing university, school, and community constituencies on two continents.

PURPOSE AND RESEARCH QUESTIONS

We investigate the evolution and ultimate outcomes of the process using a retrospective case study approach with a conceptual framework drawn from applied models of collaboration in the literature (e.g., Mattesich & Johnson, 2018) and the evolving state of knowledge in collaboration (Morris & Miller-Stevens, 2016). Three primary research questions guided the inquiry:

1. What patterns and variations in collaboration elements are present across the evolution of the documentary video project?
2. What patterns and variations in collaboration elements are present among the primary stakeholder groups involved in the process resulting in the documentary video (university, school, and community)?
3. What *critical incidents* (Chell, 1998) are perceived to be most salient to the process and/or impactful to the success of the documentary video project?

Following the presentation of results, the discussion section gives meaning to those results by explaining and elaborating on key elements of collaboration and/or critical incidents that are perceived, in retrospect, as important to project success and video development. We then revisit the study results and project experiences to present recommendations for future study of collaboration in rural contexts.

Design, Methods, and Data

A retrospective case study design (Mills et al., 2010) was utilized as the foundational structure for the analysis. This approach allows for revisiting and reflecting on past events with the advantages of a systematic collection and organization of extant data and the strategic use of a relevant conceptual framework to guide and refine the reflective process. Data sources included planning documents, archived transcripts of zoom sessions (both group forums and individual interviews), journal entries of one project leader, and email correspondences between and among the project leadership, university staff, and school and community stakeholders. Mayer and Kenter's (2016) typology of nine prevailing elements of public-sector collaboration served as the primary conceptual framework: communication, consensus decision-making, diverse stakeholders, goals, leadership, shared resources, shared vision, social capital, and trust.

Using the above-described data, we employed a two-cycle thematic coding process (Saldana, 2021) with *a priori* codes based on the conceptual framework and key stakeholder categories (university, school, community) to answer research questions one and two. In the first coding cycle, we focused on identifying relevant data excerpts aligned to the nine collaboration elements identified by Mayer and Kenter (2016). In the second coding cycle, we focused on identifying which of the three stakeholder groups (university, school, or community) were involved in each of the 21 collaboration activities that collectively comprised the process being investigated. Results of the two coding cycles were used to generate tentative themes which were then tested using multiple credibility techniques: negative case analysis, triangulation, and member checking (Lincoln & Guba, 1985).

To answer research question three, we employed a critical incident technique (Chell, 1998). The 5-step process (establish aims, specify plans and conditions, collect critical incidents or facts, analyze data, interpret outcomes) allows for reviewing related activities that occur over an extended period to determine which are most salient to the larger set of activities as a whole and/or to outcomes identified at the conclusion of those activities. In the context of this study, the technique allowed us to identify which from among the 21 specific activities were especially helpful to the collaboration process and/or contributed most to the successful outcome of a documentary video that captured university–school–community collaboration. Results of the analysis using the critical incident technique were then tested using multiple credibility techniques: negative case analysis and member checking (Lincoln & Guba, 1985).

RESULTS

Collaboration Elements Across the Evolution of the Project

The first research question addressed patterns and variations in collaboration elements as they presented across the evolution of the project. Table 11.1 provides an overview of the 21 major activities and the collaboration elements identified in each.

TABLE 11.1 Major Activities With Timeframe and Collaboration Element(s) Reflected

Timeframe	Activity	Element
Aug 2018	Attending ISFIRE; introduction and initial discussions	COM, G, SV, SC, T
Aug–Nov 2018	Negotiating invitation to present at SPERA	COM, G, SV, SC, T
Oct 2019	Participating in SPERA conference	COM, DS, G, SV, SC, T
Oct 2019	Visiting schools and CLAW	COM, DS, G, L, SV, SC, T
May 2020	Brainstorming about "give-back" opportunities	COM, G, L, SV, SC, T
May 2020	Seeking collaborators	COM, G, L, SV, SC, T
June 2020	Planning forum sessions	COM, CDM, DS, G, L, SR, SV, SC, T
July 2020	Holding forums	COM, DS, G, L, SR, SV, SC, T
July 2020	Proposing documentary	COM, G, L, SR, SV, T
July 2020	Engaging videographers	COM
July 2020	Developing video plan	COM, CDM, G, L, SR, SV, SC, T
July 2020	Reviewing Zoom recordings of forums	COM, CDM, G, L, SR, SV, SC, T
Jul–Oct 2020	Conducting additional interviews	COM, DS, G, SR, SV, SC, T
Aug–Nov 2020	Collecting community information and visuals	COM, DS, G, SR, SV, SC, T
Aug–Nov 2020	Producing draft video	COM, CDM, G, L, SR, SV, SC, T
Sept 2020	Obtaining informed consent from participants	COM, L, SR, T
Feb–Mar 2021	Editing video and determining credits	COM, G, L, SR, T
March 2021	Conducting final review of video	COM, L
April 2021	Making decisions about release of video	COM, G, L, SR
April 2021	Making decisions about video dissemination	COM, CDM, G, L, SR, SV, T
April 2021	Making decisions about use of video database	COM, CDM, G, L, SR, SV, T

Note: COM = communication, CDM = consensus decision-making, DS = diverse stakeholders, G = goals, L = leadership, SR = shared resources, SV = shared vision, SC = social capital, T = trust

Results from the analysis suggest five broad interpretations that collectively describe how the collaboration elements manifested throughout the process:

1. All nine elements were present somewhere within the overall process.
2. Some elements were consistently present across all or nearly all phases of the project.

Video Documentation of the International Rural School Leadership Project • **241**

3. Some elements were present only after the process was underway and some preliminary phases had been completed.
4. Some elements were more prominent early in the process and received less emphasis later.
5. Major activities in the process included all or nearly all of the nine elements.

Over the course of the 21 activities documented in the data and analyzed for the study (see Table 11.1), all nine elements of collaboration described by Mayer and Kenter (2016) were identified as present: communication ($n = 21$), consensus decision-making ($n = 6$), diverse stakeholders ($n = 6$), goals ($n = 18$), leadership ($n = 15$), shared resources ($n = 13$), shared vision ($n = 16$), social capital ($n = 13$), and trust ($n = 18$). At least one of the nine collaboration elements was identified within each of the 21 activities with an average of six identified elements per activity (67%).

The three elements identified in all or nearly all activities (communication, goals, and trust) appear to be foundational to the process and—especially germane to this investigation—act as affordances (Gibson, 1975) for the interaction and collaborative action among the principal stakeholders from the university, school, and community contexts. Examples of communication as a foundational element include the principal university stakeholders from the United States and Australia being introduced at the International Symposium for Innovation in Rural Education (ISFIRE) and engaged in a dialogue about common interests that led to additional engagement with an Australian stakeholder from the school context and discussion of the possibility of the U.S. stakeholder traveling to Australia to present at the Society for the Provision of Education in Rural Australia (SPERA) conference. Notably, the three foundational collaboration elements did not just operate in isolation but *interacted* in ways that refined each element individually and produced a compounding effect on the overall process (e.g., common goals among the individual stakeholders helped to make the communication more focused and more intentional; open and extensive communication among stakeholders about shared interests and commitments helped to build trust early in the process). Additionally, the engagement of university and school stakeholders with these foundational elements created opportunities to engaging with the third stakeholder group (community)—for example, when the U.S. university stakeholder made the trip to Australia to present at SPERA, the Australian school stakeholder took steps to ensure ample and substantive opportunities for engagement with school and community stakeholders. Being a first-time traveler to Australia, the U.S. stakeholder, while in Brisbane, visited an open air market, a supermarket, retail venues, a local library, the Brisbane Botanic Gardens, Queensland University of Technology (QUT), and the

242 • J. D. JOHNSON and H. L. HARMON

Gold Coast Region—visits and observations that created meaningful opportunities to both gain cultural and economic perspectives and to engage with community members.

The centrality of the three foundational elements continued throughout the process. Communication was key to every collaborative activity, common goals continued to frame and refine activities, and trust grew in strength and extended to additional individuals and organizations that became part of the process. One key example involved the collecting of information about the communities in Kansas, Pennsylvania, and Queensland served by the school leaders participating in the International Rural Principal Collaborative Leadership Forum sessions. The effort required extensive communication, but it also required a high level of trust (not just to ask individual school and community leaders to share their valuable time during a very difficult period, but also to open up about their communities and about their challenges and successes during that difficult period), and a common goal (specifically, to represent the varied rural communities in ways that were open and transparent but also respectful). One further example of these foundational elements in action was witnessed in the collaborative production of the video documentary, an effort that again involved much communication (both within the production team and externally with participants who provided a form of *member checking* [Lincoln & Guba, 1985] as part of the vetting process).

Additional collaboration elements (specifically, consensus decision-making and shared resources) were notably absent in the early activities but became central to the process in the later phases. Some of this pattern of evolution no doubt resulted from the nature of the specific activities required in the various phases (i.e., when and where within the process do decisions need to be made and resources need to be allocated to meet video production timelines). We observed, however, that these collaboration elements emerged and grew stronger and more salient to the process after relationships had been established and a shared vision (another element identified by Mayer & Kenter [2016] that occurred just outside the top three elements that we identified as present in all or nearly all activities) had been established and clarified. An example here would be planning the two International Rural Principals Collaborative Leadership Forum sessions. The planning process involved important logistical decisions (e.g., participant numbers; format, structure, and agenda; dates and times for accommodating participants in time zones up to 15 hours apart) and made achieving consensus easier by the fact that the project leadership had by this time evolved into a team with solid relationships built on trust and a shared vision for how rural school and community leaders can learn with and from each other. Planning the forum sessions was also the first collaboration activity in the larger process that necessitated the allocation of resources (i.e., material resources in the form of the technology platform and human resources in the form of technology support and time to maintain necessary communications). Here too, the established relationships and shared vision facilitated the sharing of resources among institutions.

Other collaboration elements (specifically, trust and social capital) were more pronounced in early activities and became less central later in the process. These elements wane in the latter phases of the process (with the consent activity being a notable exception) because they had served their primary purpose and were no longer directly implicated in the activities (e.g., trust, once established, is maintained through the collaborative process without much direct consideration; social capital grows less relevant once a core set of university, school, and community stakeholders is established). An example here is the social capital created from the initial introduction of the U.S. university stakeholder and the Australian university and school stakeholders. That introduction and subsequent dialogue led to the creation of the social network of university and school stakeholders in Kansas, Pennsylvania, and Queensland that enabled conduct of the two International Rural Principals Collaborative Leadership Forum sessions and eventual production of the video documentary. In the later stages of the process, however, the work turned outward to public dissemination of the results of what was produced—at which stage social capital was less directly relevant. Similarly, in the latter phases of the process as the project leadership was conducting final reviews of the video and making decisions about release, trust within the group was implicit. However, high dependence on relationships and trust was necessary in achieving final consent of key stakeholders in Australia.

A final observed pattern is that the major activities within the process (specifically, planning the forum sessions, holding the sessions, producing the draft video) involved all or nearly all of the nine collaboration elements. As an example, all nine elements were identified as present within the work of planning the International Rural Principals Collaborative Leadership Forum sessions. Communication was both central and varied, with considerable investment of time for communication both within the project leadership and with external stakeholders involved in the activity. Communication needs varied in content (e.g., planning Zoom interviews, assessing logistical needs, recruiting participants, maintaining technical consults), in structure (one-to-one, small groups, larger groups), and in format (email, Zoom, in person).

Consensus decision-making on matters related to key implementation activities took place within the project leadership team. As noted previously, the decisions to be made were not inconsiderable and the consensus-reaching process was greatly enhanced by the initial trust that had been achieved and the agreed upon common outcome goal (i.e., video documentary) that

244 ▪ J. D. JOHNSON and H. L. HARMON

had been identified. Diverse stakeholders representing the varied school sites (in Kansas, Pennsylvania, and Queensland) and varied constituent groups (schools, university, regional and state administrative offices, national interest groups) provided input to the planning process. The common goal of bringing together rural school leaders from diverse settings to learn with and from each other was a touchstone that gave focus and direction to key elements of the collaboration process in producing the video documentary. Leadership largely involved operationalizing the social capital that had been built (to identify and recruit participants) and addressing logistical and technical matters. Shared resources were evident in the acquisition, allocation, and investment of material and human assets.

A shared vision was achieved through deliberations of the project leadership team, and through consistent and clear communication of the vision to other stakeholders within the university, school, and community stakeholder groups that facilitated the involvement of varied individuals and organizations. Social capital enabled the project leadership to bring together a diverse set of university, school, and community stakeholders as participants and observers. Finally, trust within the project leadership and among the larger group of participants was the basis for the commitment of time, energy, and expertise (notably, voluntary and unpaid commitments) that made each of the activities successful.

Collaboration Elements Among the Stakeholder Groups

The second research question addressed patterns and variations in collaboration elements as they were presented among the three stakeholder groups (university, school, and community). Table 11.2 provides an overview of the 21 major activities and participating stakeholder groups for the process that ultimately resulted in the documentary and formed the basis for the investigation reported here.

Results from the analysis suggest four broad interpretations that collectively describe how the collaboration elements manifested among the three groups:

1. The university stakeholder group was involved in every phase of the process, while the involvement of the other stakeholder groups was more limited (the school stakeholder group was directly involved in 18 of 21 activities, and the community stakeholder group was involved in eight of 21 activities).
2. The university stakeholder group was operating alone (or operating as the central decision maker) in the more technical activities within the process.

Video Documentation of the International Rural School Leadership Project • **245**

3. A recurring pattern involved some form of technical activity within the university followed by outreach to school and/or community stakeholder groups for input and refining, with schools and communities providing context for that technical work and facilitating its implementation.
4. The university played a primary role throughout as a *connector* (Johnson et al., 2009; Morse, 2004).

Since the institutional affiliation for three of the four members of the project leadership team represented the university stakeholder group, university involvement in all of the collaboration activities was expected. However, a close examination of the activities reveals that it was more than just the project leaders' affiliations. Many of the activities relied on assets and infrastructure that were not immediately available to individuals or groups outside of

TABLE 11.2   Major Activities With Timeframe and Participating Stakeholder Groups

Timeframe	Activity	Stakeholders
Aug 2018	Attending ISFIRE; introduction and initial discussions	U, S
Aug–Nov 2018	Negotiating invitation to present at SPERA	U, S
Oct 2019	Participating in SPERA conference	U, S, C
Oct 2019	Visiting schools and CLAW	U, S, C
May 2020	Brainstorming about "give-back" opportunities	U, S, C
May 2020	Seeking collaborators	U, S
June 2020	Planning forum sessions	U, S, C
July 2020	Holding forums	U, S, C
July 2020	Proposing documentary	U, S
July 2020	Engaging videographers	U
July 2020	Developing video plan	U, S, C
July 2020	Reviewing Zoom recordings of forums	U, S
Jul–Oct 2020	Conducting additional interviews	U, S, C
Aug–Nov 2020	Collecting community information and visuals	U, S, C
Aug–Nov 2020	Producing draft video	U
Sept 2020	Obtaining informed consent from participants	U, S
Feb–Mar 2021	Editing video and determining credits	U, S
March 2021	Conducting final review of video	U, S
April 2021	Making decisions about release of video	U
April 2021	Making decisions about video dissemination	U, S
April 2021	Making decisions about use of video database	U, S

Note: U = university, S = school, C = community

a university setting (e.g., access to a professional videography team). In this sense, the university operated as a hub for the collaboration, with university-based stakeholders leveraging the scale, scope, and resources to support non-university stakeholders and move forward the collaborative process.

Secondly, we observed that the university operated independently (or, at the very least, was the lead entity in decision-making and plan implementation) for the more technical phases of the process (e.g., creating the Zoom sessions for the forums and the database of recorded Zoom interviews with stakeholders). This directly reflected the fact that, among the three stakeholder groups, the university had the most substantial technological resources and the most substantial infrastructure for deploying such resources (e.g., the American university had access to a technology center and staff as well as the videography team). Moreover, one of the university stakeholders on the project leadership had budget authority within their university and so was able to readily direct resources to the project.

A pattern observed throughout the process involved (a) a university-based technical activity or decision occurred within the project leadership team (of which three of four were university stakeholders), followed by (b) outreach to other stakeholder groups for the purpose of either obtaining input for refining the vision and direction or for support with implementation. One example of such outreach was the decision by the project leadership team to include in the video documentary a brief overview of the setting and context for the individual schools and the communities they served; in this instance, project leadership team members reached out to school and community stakeholders for assistance in collecting information and capturing video for use in the documentary. While the technical matters of video production and related activities were centered at the university, and the material and human resources needed to enact those matters were under the control of the university, full and effective implementation would not be possible without the assistance of collaborative partners outside the university in the schools and communities.

In this kind of collaborative process, the university served as a source of resources and provided leadership; just as importantly, however, the university served as a *connector* (Johnson et al., 2009; Longo, 2007; Morse, 2004), facilitating relationships between collaboratively determined objectives and external assets with the potential to contribute. This kind of collaboration dynamic reflected an essential component of successful collaboration as defined by Mayer and Kenter (2016): collaboration partners understand and appreciate the varied assets that each brings to the table and they leverage those assets to achieve common objectives, taking a lead role at times and playing a support role at other times based upon required capacity and expertise.

Critical Incidents

The third research question sought to identify critical incidents (Chell, 1998) perceived to be most salient to the collaboration process and/or impactful to the success of the video documentary. Our analysis produced a total of seven: (a) the invitation to present at SPERA and QUT, (b) visits to rural schools in Queensland, (c) the International Rural Principals Collaborative Leadership Forum sessions, (d) the decision to produce a video, (e) university engagement, (f) follow-up and additional interviews, and (g) obtainment of informed consent from participants.

The invitation to present at SPERA and QUT was critical to the larger process and outcomes because it reflected the relationship-building that occurred at the beginning of the process and represented the point at which the initial engagement among individuals who would become project leaders moved to concrete collaborative activities. The early relationship-building was crucial to the success of the collaborative activities that followed, because it allowed for establishing common interests, demonstrating mutual respect, and building trust. The invitation to travel to Australia and subsequent presentations would not have happened without that initial relationship-building, and the larger collaborative process would not have been possible without the invitation that moved the relationship to a concrete operational level.

Visits by the U.S. university stakeholder to rural schools in Queensland (guided by the Australian school stakeholder who was one of the project leaders) was crucial in establishing the cultural and educational context, which enabled insights that guided major activities and shaped the overall process. To clarify, the recognition of similarities and differences among rural schools in the United States and Australia informed the process by calling attention to the potential for rural school leaders to learn from the successes of those in different settings. Additionally, the visits helped establish credibility for the U.S. stakeholder among Australian school leaders and built social capital that would later contribute to the activities of recruiting participants for the forums and the follow-up interviews.

The International Rural Principals Collaborative Leadership Forum sessions were critical in that they brought to life and clarified mutual interests and benefits among rural school leaders as well as among senior leaders in the governance and administration of schools in the two countries. Forum participants reported coming away from the experience with greater insight and appreciation for their colleagues in other rural settings, and several participating principals reported having gained an actionable takeaway from the experiences shared by those colleagues.

The origin of the documentary video was a meeting between two members of the project leadership team as they reflected on the valuable content provided by the participating rural school leaders in the varied settings and considered how the impact of the forums could be broadened and/or extended. A video documentary was determined to be the best option for achieving the goal of broadening and extending impact. The suggestion that led to that determination was in part informed by the awareness on the part of one of the project team members that video production was a notable strength of the college infrastructure. Awareness of and ability to activate assets/resident resources is a key tool in collaborative activity (cf. Kretzmann & McKnight, 1993).

While the videography team was a notable contribution by the university, it was not the only one. Indeed, university engagement was critical to the process by providing a source of assets and resident resources that allowed for the project leadership team to move from ideas and intentions to operational planning. Funding, technology platforms (specifically, Frame.io) that afforded the project leadership (none of whom had experience with video production) with opportunities to contribute to the creative process, and technical support all contributed directly to the work but also contributed indirectly by enhancing the contributions of the individual collaboration partners and facilitating the collaborative process itself.

The interview phase of the process, which followed the forums and was conducted in order to gain additional information about individual sites and to follow up and further probe insights shared during the forum sessions, was critical in allowing the project leadership team to capture video content of people and place. This brought a richness to what the participants shared in the forum and allowed for capitalizing on learning opportunities that emerged organically in the course of the forum discussions. For example, a participant comment about the use of paper and pencil packets for students working at home during the school closure gained greater resonance following discussion and processing among the project leadership; this led to interview questions for that participant designed to more fully explicate the comment in a way that made the takeaway more apparent to viewers.

Obtaining informed consent from participants is a standard activity for researchers. In the context of this project, that activity contributed to the overall collaborative process by providing an opportunity for being outwardly respectful of individuals, appreciating different state and national contexts, acknowledging institutional priorities, and valuing the mutual benefits of collaborating team members. As such, the essential act of securing consent to protect participants became a vehicle for enacting values and beliefs that helped frame and guide the collaborative process among university, school, and community stakeholders.

DISCUSSION AND CONCLUSIONS

This retrospective case study utilized review of extant documents, coding and analysis of archived transcripts, and participant reflection to disclose and characterize collaborative actions occurring throughout a process that emerged organically but took on structure and intentionality as it evolved. The conceptual framework for analysis was drawn from applied models of collaboration in the literature (e.g., Mattesich & Johnson, 2018), while also recognizing that collaboration theory development is in its infancy and not clearly understood (Morris & Miller-Stevens, 2016). Results for the first research question disclose and describe patterns and variations in nine collaboration elements as they occurred across the evolution of the project. All nine elements of Mayer and Kenter's (2016) typology of public-sector collaboration were present somewhere within the overall process. At least one of the nine collaboration elements was identified within each of the 21 activities, with an average of six of the nine (67%) elements identified per activity. The three elements of communication, goals, and trust appeared to be foundational to the process, and acted as affordances for the interaction and collaborative action among the principal stakeholders from the university, school, and community contexts. This is consistent with the literature, as Mayer and Kenter (2016) cited 70 authored works that address communication ($n = 22$), goals ($n = 24$), and trust ($n = 24$).

Frequent and open lines of communication are critical to promote dialogue and information sharing that lead to effective stakeholder interaction. Both quality and quality of formal and informal communications support organizational buy-in and build social capital critical for articulating and achieving shared goals and collective action in collaboration arrangements. The COVID-19 pandemic and the physical distance of Queensland Australia and the United States prevented in-person engagement of the project's four-person leadership team. Zoom conferencing and email communications became the vehicle for effective communication, thus reflecting some of the virtual team practices found by Darics and Gatti (2019) that contributed to constructing the team's shared sense of purpose, identity, and collegiality for effective collaboration. Consistent with research of Werker and Ooms (2020), the modern communications tools (i.e., virtual conferencing and e-mail technology) served as satisfactory substitutes for face-to-face contacts in the collaboration project.

Goal agreement is the second of the three collaboration elements that appeared foundational to project success. The initial, agreed upon goal of the project team was the conducting of the two principal forum sessions as an outreach exchange of service to the field in telling the stories of rural principals during early phases of the COVID-19 pandemic. This goal provided the foundation for development of the subsequent video documentary. Mayer and Kenter (2016) found, "The need for attainable, clearly articulated and agreed upon goals forms the basic foundation of the work of collaboration" (p. 52). Their review of the literature revealed the process of goal setting can enhance social capital, trust, and relationship building, and generally, the greater the social capital of the collaboration, the more collective goal congruence is possible. Their literature review led them to caution collaboration goal-setters to not overlook individual goals of stakeholders. Failure to do so may lead to many challenges and conflicts later that are exacerbated by personalities of the individuals involved. Moreover, the individual may view commitment to the collaborative goal as secondary or subservient to goals of their organization rather than for the common good of the collaborative effort. Our team success in setting the early goal (i.e., telling the story of principals in the pandemic as international virtual forum sessions) laid an important foundation for team members to evolve the goal of producing the video documentary. This is consistent with findings of Scott and Boyd (2020) in how prior successes can create a sense of joint goal commitment and also Driskell et al.'s (2018) research describing foundations of teamwork and collaboration.

Trust is the third element that appears prominently foundational to the collaborative process of the Rural School Leadership Project. Mayer and Kenter (2016) reported that trust is often cited in the literature as vital to build and sustain collaboration. It is essential in inter-organizational arrangements for working toward collective action based on mutual understanding and confidence in taking risks. Numerous authors report how building trust is time consuming, challenging, and often the most critical part of a collaboration. Trust, shared responsibility, and social capital are strongly correlated. The success of a collaboration is reduced greatly if one of these is missing, as individual and or organizational commitment fails to support the collective action necessary to attain the agreed upon goal.

Mayer and Kenter (2016) found that trust building must be an ongoing process in all phases of the collaboration. Strachwitz et al. (2021) noted that trust is the central driver of collaboration across all sectors. For example, Bond-Barnard et al. (2018) administered an online international survey to 270 self-selected respondents, with 151 usable responses, to assess the level of trust, the degree of collaboration, and the perceived likelihood of project management success they had experienced as participants in project teams. The researchers focused on three factors that influence trust: degree of knowledge exchange, dealing with uncertainty (risk), and meeting team members' expectations. Bond-Barnard et al. (2018) found that project management success becomes more likely as the degree of collaboration improves, which in turn, is influenced by an increase in the level of trust between team members. Though the degree of risk present in a project had no significant link with the level of trust experienced in a project, Bond-Barnard et al. (2018) revealed that the level of trust in a project is influenced by the expectations that members of the project team have of each other, the knowledge exchange that takes place between them, and the degree of trust that is imported from other familiar settings (imported trust). It was the early and ongoing trust fostered in the collaboration process of the Rural School Leadership Project that helped achieve successful development of the video documentary. Also noteworthy, imported trust from relationships established during the initial visit to Queensland and prior experiences with project team members enabled construction of relevant expectations, knowledge exchange and social capital required for project management success. The need to establish trust early for successful project management is well documented in the literature (Adel, 2020), including in virtual team arrangements (Mumbi & McGill, 2008).

Results for the second research question highlight and contextualize patterns and variations of involvement by the three stakeholder groups (university, school, and community) in each of the 21 activities that collectively comprise the project's collaboration process. Study findings reveal that the university stakeholder group was involved in every phase of the project's process (i.e., 21 activities) that ultimately led to the video product. The school stakeholder group was directly involved in 18 of 21 activities, and the community stakeholder group was involved in eight of the 21 activities. The university stakeholder group operated alone (or operated as the central decision maker) in the more technical activities of the process. A recurring pattern involved some form of technical activity within the university followed by outreach to school and/or community stakeholder groups for input and refining. Schools and communities commonly provided context for the technical work and facilitated the implementation. The university also commonly served the primary role of connector (Johnson et al., 2009; Morse, 2004) throughout the project.

University involvement can mean much more than institutional affiliation on the project leadership team. Nyquist and Ahonen-Jonnarth (2021) pointed out that university collaboration with surrounding society is increasingly being called *the third mission* of higher education institutions. Many of the 21 collaboration activities rely on assets and infrastructure that are not immediately available to individuals or groups outside a university setting (e.g., access to a professional videography team). In this sense, the university operates as a facilitative hub for collaboration, particularly in development of a video documentary, with university-based stakeholders leveraging available scale, scope, and resources to support non-university stakeholders and advance the collaborative process. The technical requirements of many activities led to a university stakeholder operating independently or as the lead entity in facilitating decision-making and plan-implementation for some phases of the collaboration process. Consequently, project success was heavily dependent on university group stakeholders, particularly in accessing technological resources and infrastructure for deploying such the resources. Moreover, one of the university stakeholders on the project leadership team expressed willingness to fund video development, had budget authority within the university to access the available funds, and therefore could readily direct resources to the project.

Therefore, throughout the collaborative process, the university was both a source of resources and collaborative leadership for collective action toward goal attainment (i.e., telling the story of rural principals during the COVID-19 pandemic) and video production. As importantly, however, the university served a connector role consistent with works of Johnson et al. (2009), Longo (2007), and Morse (2004) in facilitating relationships between collaboratively-determined objectives and external assets with the potential to contribute. This kind of dynamic reflects an essential component of successful collaboration as defined by Mayer and Kenter (2016): Successful collaboration partners both lead and follow within the context of their joint efforts and assume those roles in strategic alignment to their understanding of the varied assets of partners.

Results for the third research question identify seven of the 21 activities that we consider in retrospect to be the salient critical incidents (Chell, 1998; Grant & Trenor, 2010). The invitation to present at the SPERA conference and QUT laid the foundation for relationship-building that launched and sustained social capital for the collaboration process. As Mayer and Kenter (2016) found: "Social capital, the presence of existing and trusting relationships and their value, is a major component in advancing collaboration from a formative stage to a functioning outcome-oriented one" (p. 57). The early relationship-building was crucial for establishing common interests, demonstrating mutual respect, and building trust.

Visits by the U.S. university stakeholder to rural schools in Queensland (guided by the Australian school stakeholder who was one of the project team members) fostered understanding of the cultural and educational context that provided valuable insights for facilitating collective action toward planning and implementing major activities. For example, understanding similarities and differences among rural schools in the United States and Queensland Australia informed the potential for rural school leaders to learn from the successes of those in different settings that resulted in the two forum sessions, follow-up interviews of principals, and collection of information, photos, and video from community stakeholders.

The sessions of the International Rural Principals Collaborative Leadership Forums provided relevance and clarified mutual interests among rural school leaders in both countries. The forums also reinforced the value of informal learning opportunities for school principals (Ringling et al.,

2021) and dialogue among peers as a resource for professional learning by school leaders (Farag-Davis, 2013). Reflection on content and success of the international exchange forum between two U.S. members of the project leadership team stimulated ideation of the documentary video. In essence, the video documentary provided a mutually beneficial option for broadening and extending collaborative actions toward the original goal of telling the story of the rural principals during the COVID-19 pandemic. Video production embraced the awareness of and ability to activate assets and resident resources as a key tool in collaborative activity (cf. Kretzmann & McKnight, 1993).

In addition to the university stakeholder's videography team, critical university engagement also enabled project leaders to advance collective ideas and intentions for operational planning—affording opportunities for team members to participate in video production and building capacity among project leaders that may prove useful in other collaborative projects (cf. Hess et al., 2014; Kretzmann & McKnight, 1993). University expertise and technical support enhanced the contributions of university, school, and community stakeholders and the collaborative process.

The interview phase of the process, as follow-up to the forum sessions with school principals in each country, enabled project team members and videographers to gain additional information about people and places that could accurately tell the story envisioned in the video documentary. Clarifying organic experiences of schools and communities brought the rich quality of rural settings to what participants shared in the forum sessions. Among other benefits, this activity resulted in a form of thick, rich description (Holloway, 1997) that added to the credibility and trustworthiness of the experiences reported. Another more indirect outcome was that the focus and approach of the interviews (specifically, expressing appreciation for the community context and a desire to learn more from the participant about assets) offered an opportunity to further demonstrate the way the project leaders valued the individuals and their schools and communities.

In the context of this collaborative project and video production, gaining informed consent from participants, though a standard activity for researchers, took on additional meaning as a critical incident in the overall collaboration process. Much more than being a procedural compliance task or even an outward show of respect for individuals, the consent process also considered mutual values among collaborating team members, acknowledgment of institutional priorities, and appreciation of differences in state and national cultural and political contexts. The way in which this near-final activity was undertaken by the project leadership thus extended and deepened the trust established earlier in the process and strengthened/enhanced the social capital that had been built and sustained throughout (cf. Bond-Barnard et al., 2018; Mayer & Kenter, 2016).

254 ▪ J. D. JOHNSON and H. L. HARMON

RECOMMENDATIONS FOR FUTURE RESEARCH

Miller-Stevens and Morris (2016) reviewed 30 years of research on collaboration to describe trends and advance themes for future research. Among their conclusions, they suggested that much more must be understood about why collaboration projects fail, as much of the theory building has focused on investigating conditions that contribute to successful collaboration. They acknowledge, however, that given the definitional uncertainty of collaboration (and confusion with cooperation and coordination) much is unclear regarding the preconditions and/or elements in the process that are most critical for collaboration *success*—a term itself that also needs much more study.

Context and settings may play an important role in how interaction occurs among collaborating organizations or individuals, perhaps providing evidence that multiple types of collaboration are possible, even desirable. Much more needs to be understood regarding what motivates people and organizations to collaborate and the conditions under which collaboration is most appropriate for solving a policy, program, or practice issue. Skills necessary to manage collaboration remains a ripe opportunity for investigation, particularly in voluntary versus mandatory collaborative arrangements. In describing the need to better translate collaboration theory into practice, Miller-Stevens and Morris (2016) argued that a communication gap exists and noted:

> Our own research into collaboration leads us to conclude that many practitioners are drawn to the idea of collaboration, but have little idea about how to carry out a collaboration effort.... [Collaboration] success may be more a question of luck than careful deliberation and planning. (p. 284)

It is against this backdrop, the results from our retrospective reflection of the International Rural School Leadership Project and more than 50 years of combined engagement in rural education research and practice that we offer a list of general research questions as examples of topics for advancing the study of collaboration in rural contexts.

1. What knowledge, skills, and dispositions are necessary for those who seek to serve a collaborative leadership role in projects that engage school-age youth in rural community development?
2. In what ways might local and regional collaboration efforts support student access to curriculum opportunities in small rural schools for which school consolidation is often viewed as the most efficient solution?
3. What elements of collaboration are essential in university–school–community partnerships for providing high quality professional

learning opportunities to educators in high-poverty and/or remote rural settings?

4. How might collaboration offer solutions to the recruitment and retention of educators in rural school settings?
5. In what ways are collaboration strategies facilitating policymakers and practitioners in identifying and addressing gender and racial equity challenges in rural areas?
6. What innovations in telecommunications technology are necessary to facilitate collaborative research projects that maximize interdisciplinary approaches?
7. How might collaboration efforts improve the capacity of rural schools in addressing trauma and safety issues of students and educators?
8. How is collaboration succeeding or failing in supporting the sustainability movement to create rural communities that are economically viable, environmentally friendly, and socially just?
9. In what ways is collaboration contributing to informal adult education opportunities in rural areas?
10. What evaluation theories and methods are most appropriate for assessing the impact of place-based collaboration projects in rural areas?

REFERENCES

Adel, A. J. (2020). *Building trust: The step to successful project management.* PM-Panacea.

Bernard, S. C. (2007). *Documentary storytelling: Making stronger and more dramatic nonfiction films* (2nd ed.). Elsevier Inc. https://doi.org/10.4324/9780080469270

Bevan, B., & Penuel, W. R. (Eds.). (2017). *Connecting research and practice for educational improvement: Ethical and equitable approaches.* Routledge. https://doi.org/10.4324/9781315268309

Bond-Barnard, T. J., Fletcher, L., & Steyn, H. (2018). Linking trust and collaboration in project teams to project management success. *International Journal of Managing Projects in Business, 11*(2), 432–457. https://doi.org/10.1108/IJMPB-06-2017-0068

Chell, E. (1998). Critical incident technique. In G. Symon & C. Cassell (Eds.), *Qualitative methods and analysis in organizational research: A practical guide* (pp. 51–72). SAGE.

Darics, E., & Gatti, M. C. (2019). Talking a team into being in online workplace collaborations: The discourse of virtual work. *Discourse Studies, 21*(3), 237–257. https://doi.org/10.1177/1461445619829240

Driskell, J. E., Salas, E., & Driskell, T. (2018). Foundations of teamwork and collaboration. *American Psychologist, 73*(4), 334–348. https://doi.org/10.1037/amp0000241

Farag-Davis, S. A. (2013). *School leaders and networks: Understanding principal peer dialogue as a resource for professional learning* (Publication No. 3602609) [Doctoral dissertation, Lesley University]. ProQuest Dissertations Publishing. https://www.proquest.com/openview/f726c94149868bb61c1dcf586c6d167b/1?pq-origsite=gscholar&cbl=18750

Finkler, W., & León, B. (2019). The power of storytelling and video: A visual rhetoric for science communication. *Journal of Science Communication 18*(5), 1–23. https://doi.org/10.22323/2.18050202

Gibson, J. J. (1975). Affordances and behavior. In E. S. Reed & R. Jones (Eds.), *Reasons for realism: Selected essays of James J. Gibson* (pp. 401–411). Erlbaum.

Grant, D., & Trenor, J. (2010, June 20–23). *Use of the critical incident technique for qualitative research in engineering education: An example from a grounded theory study* [Paper presentation]. Annual Conference & Exposition of the American Association of Engineering Education, Louisville, Kentucky. https://doi.org/10.18260/1-2—15712

Harmon, H. L. (2017). Collaboration: A partnership solution in rural education. *The Rural Educator, 38*(1), 1–5. https://doi.org/10.35608/ruraled.v38i1.230

Harmon, H. L., Gordanier, J., Henry, L., & George, A. (2007). Changing teaching practices in rural schools. *The Rural Educator, 28*(2), 8–12. https://doi.org/10.35608/ruraled.v28i2.480

Harmon, H. L., & Schafft, K. A. (2009). Rural school leadership for collaborative community development. *The Rural Educator, 30*(3), 4–9. https://doi.org/10.35608/ruraled.v30i3.443

Hess, M., Johnson, J., & Reynolds, S. (2014). A developmental model for educational planning: Democratic rationalities and dispositions. *International Journal of Educational Leadership Preparation, 9*(1). https://eric.ed.gov/?id=EJ1024108

Holloway, I. (1997). *Basic concepts for qualitative research.* Blackwell Science.

Johnson, J., Thompson, A., & Naugle, K. (2009). Place-conscious capacity-building: A systemic model for the revitalisation and renewal of rural schools and communities through university-based regional stewardship. *Rural Society, 19*(2), 178–188. https://doi.org/10.5172/rsj.19.2.178

Kretzmann, J. P., & McKnight, J. L. (1993). *Building communities from the inside out: A path toward finding and mobilizing a community's assets.* ACTA.

Lincoln, Y. S., & Guba, E. G. (1985). *Naturalistic inquiry.* SAGE.

Longo, N. (2007). *Why community matters: Connecting education with civic life.* SUNY.

Mattesich, P. W., & Johnson, K. M. (2018). *Collaboration: What makes it work* (3rd ed.). Turner.

Mayer, M., & Kenter, R. (2016). The prevailing elements of public sector collaboration. In J. C. Morris & K. Miller-Stevens (Eds.), *Advancing collaboration theory: Models, typologies, and evidence* (pp. 43–64). Routledge.

Miller-Stevens, K., & Morris, J. C. (2016). Future trends in collaboration research. In J. C. Morris & K. Miller-Stevens (Eds.), *Advancing collaboration theory: Models, typologies, and evidence* (pp. 276–287). Routledge. https://doi.org/10.4324/9781315749242-26

Mills, A. J., Durepos, G., & Wiebe, E. (Eds.). (2010). *Encyclopedia of case study research.* SAGE.

Video Documentation of the International Rural School Leadership Project • **257**

Morris, J. C., & Miller-Stevens, K. (Eds.). (2016). *Advancing collaboration theory: Models, typologies, and evidence.* Routledge. https://doi.org/10.4324/9781315749242

Morse, S. W. (2004). *Smart communities: How citizens and local leaders can use strategic thinking to build a brighter future.* Jossey-Bass.

Mumbi, C., & McGill, T. J. (2008). An investigation of the role of trust in virtual project management success. *International Journal of Networking and Virtual Organizations, 5*(1), 64–82. https://doi.org/10.1504/IJNVO.2008.016003

Nyquist, K. J., & Ahonen-Jonnarth, U. (2021). Strategic, fundamental and means objectives of different stakeholders in collaboration between universities and surrounding society. *Perspectives: Policy and Practice in Higher Education, 26*(1), 19–27. https://doi.org/10.1080/13603108.2021.1946866

Ohlson, M., Johnson, J., Shope, S., & Rivera, J. (2018). The essential three (e3): A university partnership to meet the professional learning needs of rural schools. *The Rural Educator, 39*(2), 3–12. https://doi.org/10.35608/ruraled.v39i2.207

Penuel, W. R., & Gallagher, D. J. (2017). *Creating research–practice partnerships in education.* Harvard Education Press.

Reardon, R. M., & Leonard, J. (Eds.). (2018a). *Innovation and implementation in rural places: School–university–community collaboration in education.* Information Age Publishing.

Reardon, R. M., & Leonard, J. (Eds.). (2018b). *Making a positive impact in rural places: Change agency in the context of school–university–community collaboration in education.* Information Age Publishing.

Ringling, J. J., Sanzo, K. L., & Scribner, J. P. (2021). Elementary school principals and informal learning: Leveraging networks. *Journal of Workplace Learning, 33*(2), 109–119. https://doi.org/10.1108/JWL-03-2020-0042

Saldana, J. (2021). *The coding manual for qualitative researchers* (4th ed.). SAGE.

Scher, L., McCowan, R., & Castaldo-Walsh, C. (2018). *Regional educational laboratory researcher–practitioner partnerships: Documenting the research alliance experience* (REL 2018–291). National Center for Education Evaluation and Regional Assistance. https://eric.ed.gov/?id=ED581137

Scott, R. J., & Boyd, R. (2020). Determined to succeed: Can goal commitment sustain interagency collaboration? *Public Policy and Administration.* https://doi.org/10.1177/0952076720905002

Strachwitz, R. G., Alter, R., & Unger, T. (2021). Addressing wicked problems. Collaboration, trust and the role of shared principles at the philanthropy and government interface. *Trusts & Trustees, 27*(6), 450–459. https://doi.org/10.1093/tandt/ttab066

Werker, C., & Ooms, W. (2020). Substituting face-to-face contacts in academics' collaborations: Modern communication tools, proximity, and brokerage. *Studies in Higher Education, 45*(7), 1431–1447. https://www.tandfonline.com/doi/full/10.1080/03075079.2019.1655723

CHAPTER 12

BUILDING RECIPROCAL UNIVERSITY–SCHOOL–COMMUNITY RELATIONSHIPS TO EXPLORE THE IMPACT OF COVID-19 ON RURAL SCHOOLS IN AOTEAROA NEW ZEALAND

Jennifer Tatebe
The University of Auckland

Carol Mutch
The University of Auckland

ABSTRACT

We report on findings from research conducted by a team of university researchers in the *Te Whakatere au Pāpori*[1] research network at the University of Auckland as part of a collaborative study into rural schools in Aotearoa New

School–University–Community Research in a (Post) COVID-19 World, pages 259–286
Copyright © 2023 by Information Age Publishing
www.infoagepub.com
All rights of reproduction in any form reserved.

Zealand. The initial interest in rural schools came from Tatebe's involvement on a school board in their own rural town. As urban sprawl encroached on formerly rural towns like Tatebe's, schools and their communities faced dramatic change. Established small rural schools became overcrowded and new schools on the outskirts of housing developments were hastily constructed. As a result, communities and their schools needed to undergo rapid adjustment. This rural school study commenced in 2018 but, when the COVID-19 pandemic arrived, Tatebe initiated a pivot to take account of the unexpected conditions and challenges. That we were able to proceed at all with our research was testament to the relationships that Tatebe, the university research team, the school leadership team, and their community had forged in the early stages of data gathering. In this chapter, we share the findings from the data gathered before and during the COVID-19 pandemic to highlight how rural schools built a sense of community that helped them cope with the arrival of the COVID-19 pandemic and the subsequent interruptions and closures that they faced.

Much has been written about the impact of COVID-19 on the delivery of education both internationally (e.g., UNESCO, 2021) and nationally—in our case, in Aotearoa New Zealand (e.g., Hood, 2020). We (Tatebe & Mutch) are members of the *Te Whakatere au Pāpori* research team—which, for our project, included two research assistants as well—and we were planning the next iteration of our research to cover traumatic events and wider social issues that schools face when the government put Aotearoa New Zealand into a full national COVID-19 lockdown on March 25, 2020. When the country emerged from the first 2020 lockdown on April 27, 2020, the *Te Whakatere* team pivoted our research to focus on schools' responses to COVID-19. In this chapter, we focus on how the pandemic impacted rural schools in Aotearoa New Zealand that, due to their rural or remote locations, feel under-recognized and marginalized in mainstream educational discussions and research.

We begin this chapter by placing our research in the context of the COVID-19 pandemic before reviewing three relevant bodies of research literature regarding (a) the role of schools in disaster and crisis events, (b) the place of rural schools in Aotearoa New Zealand, and (c) university–school–community partnerships to foster educational research. The conceptual framework, arising from the three themes in the literature review will set the scene for the later discussion section. We next outline the sensitive and emergent qualitative research methodology that was important for engaging schools and their communities in our research. We will share two overarching themes drawn from the data, including how rural schools build a sense of community and how that sense of community supported them through the COVID-19 pandemic. In the discussion section, we will discuss the two themes from the findings before highlighting how the relationship

The Impact of COVID-19 on Rural Schools in Aotearoa New Zealand • **261**

between Tatebe and the members of the school communities that were built before the pandemic helped sustain research momentum despite the situation that was unfolding. We conclude the chapter with recommendations drawn from our research for building future university–school–community research collaborations.

BACKGROUND

In this section, we outline the arrival of COVID-19 in Aotearoa New Zealand and set the scene for the impact that it had on schools. Aotearoa New Zealanders first became aware of this new strain of the coronavirus in January 2020, but it was not until February that the Prime Minister, Jacinda Ardern, called a group together to plan the government's response strategy (Cameron, 2020). When people with COVID-19 began arriving in the country and several super-spreader events resulted in the transmission of the virus across the country, the government announced its four-level COVID-19 alert system (Unite Against COVID-19, 2022). The aim of "Alert Level 1—Prepare" was to introduce measures to help the country be better prepared, "Alert Level 2—Reduce" measures were intended to reduce the spread, "Alert Level 3—Restrict" measures restricted movement to stem the spread of the virus, and "Level 4—Lockdown" measures were intended to eliminate the virus altogether. On March 21, 2020, the country was put into Alert Level 2 and on March 23 into Alert Level 3. By March 25, the entire country was moved to Alert Level 4 and remained in lockdown until April 27 (Cameron, 2020; Mutch, 2021).

This sudden announcement of a nationwide lockdown meant that school leaders had little time to adjust to delivering off-site learning. The Ministry of Education decided to bring the April school holidays forward by 2 weeks so that schools and the Ministry of Education would have the opportunity to prepare resources and delivery modes (Mutch, 2021). A survey conducted by the Ministry of Education indicated that about half the schools in the country felt that their students would not be able to pivot easily to online learning (New Zealand Government, 2020). The survey finding spurred the Ministry of Education to rollout a four-channel package: first, improve access to Internet providers, modems, and devices; second, where Internet access was unaffordable or limited, send out hard-copy curriculum packs so that children could continue their education at home; third, commission two television learning channels, one in English and one in *te reo Māori* (the Indigenous language); and finally, use the Ministry of Education website to promote a range of readily available Internet resources for teachers and parents (New Zealand Government, 2020).

One of the biggest challenges for teachers and families was their lack of familiarity with the range of digital platforms that were being used to communicate, distribute materials, or deliver online learning. In one study (Hood, 2020), a teacher reported that they needed to become familiar with 15 different platforms and applications. Despite the short timeline, online, remote, or home schooling was underway for most students by April 15, 2020. Over the next 2 years, there were a series of national and regional lockdowns as the government tried to contain the spread of the COVID-19 virus, especially as new variants arrived.

Studies conducted on the impact of COVID-19 on schools in Aotearoa New Zealand (e.g., Education Review Office, 2020; Hood, 2020; Riwai-Couch et al., 2020) highlighted that the lockdowns caused disruption to students' education and increased the workloads of principals and teachers and exacerbated the social and educational disparities in Aotearoa New Zealand. Students who were able to engage successfully across the four channels typically had easy access to the Internet, appropriate learning devices, and a supportive home environment. They received suitable resources, instructions, and support from their schools and made progress with their learning. Some even thrived. On the other side of the ledger, however, there were many children and young people in Aotearoa New Zealand who had limited Internet access, unsuitable devices, lived in crowded or noisy home situations, found the instructions from their schools confusing or vague, had little contact with their teachers and were unable to gain learning support from their families. These students lost focus, were unable to engage in positive learning, and suffered from high levels of anxiety and stress (Education Review Office, 2020; Hood, 2020; Mutch, 2021; Mutch & Peung, 2021; Riwai-Couch et al., 2020).

LITERATURE REVIEW

This brief review of the literature covers three main themes: (a) the nature of disasters and crises and the role that schools play in these events, (b) rural schools in Aotearoa New Zealand, and (c) how to set up successful university–school–community partnerships to enhance educational research.

Theme 1: Schools in Disaster and Crisis Events

While a pandemic does not fit many narrow definitions of a disaster, it does meet some of the criteria. A disaster is often described as the consequences of events triggered by natural hazards or human interventions that

The Impact of COVID-19 on Rural Schools in Aotearoa New Zealand ▪ **263**

overwhelm the ability of local response services to manage or contain the impacts (Mutch, 2014; Smawfield, 2013).

Disasters do not spread themselves equally across the globe, but within the regions affected, the impact is greater on some communities than on others (Cahill et al., 2010; Ferris & Petz, 2012; Smawfield, 2013). In general, countries with higher median incomes, higher educational attainment, stronger financial systems, and less bureaucracy experience fewer losses (Ferris & Petz, 2012; Smawfield, 2013). The sectors in the affected societies with less financial, political, and social capital are the hardest hit and take the longest to recover. Women, children, the disabled, and the elderly are often the most vulnerable populations in disaster situations, especially those in lower socioeconomic communities (Cahill et al., 2010; Smawfield, 2013). Characteristically, the COVID-19 pandemic impacted countries, regions, and communities unequally.

As a large proportion of any community's population goes to, or is connected to, a school-related setting, schools are profoundly affected by local disasters and crises (Mutch, 2016). Schools might be the site of the disaster (as in a school shooting), affected to a similar degree as the rest of the community (as in an earthquake), or slightly removed but dealing with the emotional and psychological aftermath (as in a plane crash). School buildings might have been destroyed and children, parents, or staff might have lost their lives, or the school might be requisitioned as an emergency and relief center. Few systems prepare schools well for such eventualities. When disaster strikes and schools are physically unscathed, they often have the facilities and personnel to assist in response and recovery. The roles schools play through the response and recovery phases is a theme in the literature (Education Review Office, 2013; Mutch, 2014; Smawfield, 2013). They might become relief sites, communication centers, supply depots, or locations for support agencies. As places of pastoral care, they might be able to provide access to services or personnel to attend to social, emotional, and psychological needs of students and families. Getting schools up and running post-disaster is often seen as one of the first signs of normality. For students, schools can be a place of safety and calm in an uncertain and confusing time (Johnson & Ronan, 2014). Schools also play a part in the recovery of their communities by providing a stable location and social meeting space (Mutch, 2017).

While there is an emerging body of literature on schools and disasters (Johnson & Ronan, 2014; Mutch, 2014; Smawfield, 2013), there is only sporadic literature on prior epidemics or pandemics as they relate to schools. One example is the H1N1 influenza pandemic (Cauchemez et al., 2011). Most studies are conducted by medical researchers and take a mitigation approach rather than investigating the impact that epidemics have on the functioning of schools. The global impact of the COVID-19 pandemic and

Theme 2: Rural Schools

Prior to the arrival of Europeans in Aotearoa New Zealand, Māori children learned alongside their extended families in a communal apprentice-style setting. As settlers, mainly from the United Kingdom, arrived in the 1800s, they began to farm in many remote areas of the country with limited transport links. They set up small, multi-age classrooms to educate local children (Blundell, 2005; Swarbrick, 2012). As Swarbrick (2012) noted, "In remote areas some schools were in *whares* [Māori dwellings], spare rooms, and cottages" (para. 1). School supplies and finances were provided to the local education boards. In 1877, there were around 730 primary schools around the country. By 1900 there were over 1,600 state primary schools, 30% of which had fewer than 21 pupils. Blundell (2005) noted,

> These fledgling institutions, with their small clusters of wooden buildings, became the linchpin of local rural life. In many areas the school building predated the community hall, thus serving—and in many areas continuing to serve—as the social centre of the district. (para. 8)

With the arrival of bus services and reviews of rural education in the 1930s, many smaller schools were closed, and children were bussed to newly consolidated schools. Numbers of primary schools decreased from 2,600 in 1927 to 1,900 in 1947, despite population increases (Swarbrick, 2012) and reviews and consolidation of rural schools have continued. A government report in 1988 noted that rural schools "also acted as a marker of continuity, something that held together the fabric of a community, indicating the well-being of a district and the active investment made by the community in the education of its children" (as cited in Blundell, 2005, para.7). Yet, the 1990s and early 2000s saw further closing and consolidation of rural schools (Blundell, 2005; Mutch, 2017; Witten et al., 2003). The president of the teachers' union said at the time:

> With a school there comes a sense of belonging. If you look at some of these rural communities, the old Four Square store is boarded up, the village hall is in disrepair, the post office sign has faded and the Mobil petrol station is a rusting edifice. The last physical sign of that area is the local school. Take that away and you've taken the last community focal point. (Colin Tarr, as cited in Blundell, 2005, para. 52)

The Impact of COVID-19 on Rural Schools in Aotearoa New Zealand • 265

As the country's population has increased in this century, and housing developments have encroached on rural land, many rural schools have had to adjust to increased numbers of families arriving wanting to enrol their children. New classrooms have been built on some school sites and completely new schools have also been built to keep pace with increasing urban fringe growth (Tatebe, 2021). In this chapter, we highlight both established rural schools that have been forced to expand and newly built schools in once rural locations.

Theme 3: University–School–Community Partnerships

Universities engage with schools for a variety of reasons (Duncan & Conner, 2013; Martin et al., 2011; Mutch et al., 2015). Teacher preparation programs need their students to observe in classrooms and undertake periods of practical teaching. Other professional programs such as counselling or social work might also need students to have clinical placements in schools. Education faculty members need to conduct research on many aspects of school organization, educational leadership, pedagogy, or curriculum implementation. Researchers in other fields might want to trial programs, test applications, seek feedback, or otherwise engage with schools. Whatever the purpose, supportive relationships smooth access, foster communication, and reduce difficulties (Chorzempa et al., 2010; Mutch et al., 2015; Patton, 2012).

Building and sustaining these relationships is not always a smooth process. Patton (2012) claimed that a lack of mutual trust and respect between the partners, poor communication about the purpose and direction of the relationship, and reliance on one-time or infrequent interactions have sometimes marred these relationships. Hooper and Britnell (2012) observed that schools are often suspicious of university-generated research because of a history of hierarchical relationships, in which the interests of the school are rarely considered.

Mutch et al. (2015) outlined phases of relationship building and maintenance they used to keep the integrity of their research endeavor and the dignity of both parties to the fore during the (a) setting up, (b) maintaining, and (c) concluding a partnership. Setting up the partnership required clarifying the need for the relationship, the parameters of the relationship, the development of a shared understanding of the roles and activities and clarity regarding expectations and timelines. Once the activity was underway, maintaining the relationship required communicating clearly and regularly, acting ethically and sensitively, engaging in shared decision-making, respecting each other's roles and boundaries, carefully managing any issues that arose, and being prepared to be responsive and flexible. In concluding the activity, partners needed to broker agreement around ownership, presentation and dissemination of various outputs or outcomes, ensure reciprocity of benefits, acknowledge time and effort invested, and above all, keep promises.

Despite the inherent complexities, positive outcomes for both parties are feasible (Duncan & Conner, 2013; McLaughlin et al., 2006), but as Patton (2012) warned, "Despite this apparent synergy, there are relatively few published examples of successful partnerships between schools and universit[ies] aimed at mutual development and improvement" (p. 13). In this chapter, we share our experience of building and maintaining a positive university–school–community relationship that is ongoing, despite the ravages of the pandemic.

CONCEPTUAL FRAMEWORK: SCHOOLS AS COMMUNITY HUBS

Most governments aim to create a cohesive society that has common values, social order, solidarity, networks, and place attachment (Kearns & Forrest, 2000). As Gordon (2004) suggested, "Communities provide a shared life based on a common locality, culture, and routine within a communicating group in which members are united in their common identity in spite of personal differences" (p. 1). Communities consist of physical, structural, and human resources, which, along with social, cultural, and built assets, create *community capital* (Callaghan & Colton, 2008). Neighborhoods with accumulated community capital, such as strong preexisting networks and connectedness, recover equilibrium more quickly following a disaster or crisis event (Mutch, 2017; Thornley et al., 2013).

Within communities, some organizational structures hold a more significant role in maintaining the bonds in a community than others. These are sometimes termed *community hubs* or *anchors* (Community Alliance et al., 2009; Mutch, 2018). A community hub could be a place of worship, a community center, a sports club, or a local school. As schools are places of community history and identity with wide-reaching networks, they are often significant community hubs. In Aotearoa New Zealand, principals and teachers can choose the schools where they teach and the communities in which they locate themselves. Making this choice signals a commitment, not just to the school but to the community, and provides a sound footing for relationship building.

In the literature discussed in this chapter, schools as community hubs, schools in disaster contexts, and university–school–community partnerships are common elements. This literature, and our prior research, highlight a set of principles that resonate across all three fields. Schools become hubs of their communities when they foster relationships for both the educational

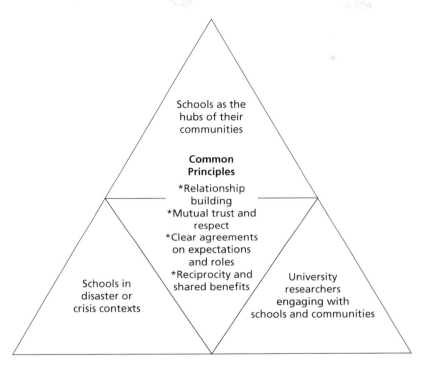

Figure 12.1 Common principles to inform school–community and university–school–community partnerships.

function they are charged with, in addition to the social cohesion function expected by society. They do this by setting out clear expectations of activities and roles but in a manner that builds on mutual trust and respect, ensuring that everyone has something useful to contribute to the success of the partnership. When this is done successfully, schools and their communities have a strong foundation for supporting each other through a disaster or crisis. If universities want to engage in activities that will benefit their organization, then we suggest that the same set of principles of reciprocal trust and relationship building need to apply—as outlined in Figure 12.1. In alignment with this conceptual framework, our methodology in this research exhibited relationship building, mutual trust, respect, and reciprocity.

METHODOLOGY

The theoretical underpinning of this study is social constructionism, in which experiences are viewed through social, historical, and cultural lenses

(Burr, 2015). Rather than seeking to establish reality, our approach focused on how the participants constructed narratives of their lived experiences and how they made sense of the events in order to absorb them into their own personal histories. Our research design was primarily qualitative and emergent (Denzin & Lincoln, 2013). We adopted a case study approach to facilitate our use of a range of data gathering methods (Stake, 1995), all focused on rural schools in changing demographic times. Our methods included gathering and analyzing documentary and digital data and conducting qualitative focus group and individual interviews to gain deeper insights. To date, we have gathered data from 84 participants across 16 school communities, including from school principals, chairs of school boards of trustees,[2] and prominent community members, such as local mayors. The school communities are part of the larger study in four different rural locations (Tatebe, 2021). For this chapter, we focused on data drawn from 16

interviews with principals and chairs of school boards of trustees about their schools during the pandemic lockdowns. The schools were in three of the fastest growing regions across Aotearoa New Zealand: Auckland and Northern Waikato, Bay of Plenty, and Canterbury with varying school demographics summarized in Table 12.1. The three regions vary demographically. Auckland and Northern Waikato are on the fringes of Auckland city, the most highly populated city in Aotearoa New Zealand. The Bay of Plenty was formerly a quieter region before becoming a housing development hot spot due to lower housing prices in comparison to major urban centers like Auckland. The third region of Canterbury is experiencing rapid growth in large part due to the earthquakes in 2011 fueling domestic migration as well as international immigration.

Ethics

We received ethical clearance from the University of Auckland and adhered to the usual ethical principles of informed consent, anonymity of the school community and personnel, confidentiality of data, and observance of cultural protocols. Given the nature of the topic (rural schools facing change) and the context (the COVID-19 pandemic), it was even more important to approach and work with the school community in a sensitive manner. There are many precedents for using sensitive and flexible approaches in difficult situations (Dickson-Swift et al., 2009; Mutch & Weir, 2016). Building relationships is a guiding principle of sensitive research. Tatebe took the time needed to build authentic relationships with the schools through a staged approach—a phone call to the principal, followed by emailing them the research brief, then one or more personal visits, until the school leaders felt they were ready to make the choice to participate in a free and informed

The Impact of COVID-19 on Rural Schools in Aotearoa New Zealand • **269**

TABLE 12.1 School, Principal, and Chair of Board of Trustees Demographics

School	Region	Enrollment	School Type	Gender Principal/ Chair of Board of Trustees
School 1	Waikato	192	Co-educational, full primary (Year 1–8)	Female/Female
School 2	Auckland	140	Co-educational, full primary (Year 1–8)	Male/Female
School 3	Waikato	494	Co-educational, full primary (Year 1–8)	Male/Male
School 4	Auckland	192	Co-educational, full primary (Year 1–8)	Female/Male
School 5	Waikato	32	Co-educational, full primary (Year 1–8)	Female/Female
School 6	Canterbury	212	Co-educational, Contributing School[a] (Year 1–6)	Male/Male
School 7	Canterbury	429	Co-educational, full primary (Year 1–8)	Male/Male
School 8	Canterbury	53	Co-educational, Contributing School (Year 1–6)	Female/Male
School 9	Canterbury	215	Co-educational, full primary (Year 1–8)	Female/Female
School 10	Canterbury	157	Co-educational, full primary (Year 1–8)	Female/Male
School 11	Canterbury	519	Co-educational, full primary (Year 1–8)	Male/Male
School 12	Bay of Plenty	340	Co-educational, full primary (Year 1–8)	Female/Female
School 13	Bay of Plenty	359	Co-educational, full primary (Year 1–8)	Male/Male
School 14	Bay of Plenty	243	Co-educational, full primary (Year 1–8)	Male/Male
School 15	Bay of Plenty	565	Co-educational, full primary (Year 1–8)	Female/Male
School 16	Bay of Plenty	250	Co-educational, full primary (Year 1–8)	Male/Female

[a] A contributing school enrolls students for primary school Years 1–6. Students then usually transition to an intermediate school for primary school Years 7–8.

manner. To build a sense of reciprocity, a *koha* (gift) was provided to the schools, usually in the form of a morning tea for the school staff. On-going reports on the research, including interview transcripts, were returned to the participants to ensure that they felt comfortable with how their words and the school situation might be portrayed later in academic presentations and articles. Once our larger research agenda is completed, articles, chapters, or presentations drawn from the data will be made available to the school communities as a way of saying "thank you" and to provide an opportunity for community members to learn from our findings. Executive summaries will also be forwarded to relevant government agencies and community councils to offer their employees insights into the needs and perspectives of those who benefit from the existence of rural schools.

ANALYSIS

Initial codes were assigned to the interview data based on the strength or quality of the idea, pattern of thought, insight, or explanation (Denzin & Lincoln, 2013). These codes were revisited many times when we added additional data to the NVivo 12 (https://www.qsrinternational.com/nvivo-qualitative-data-analysis-software/home) database. When our analysis reached saturation point—when we assigned no new codes—we grouped the codes into more abstract themes. For this article, we highlight the insights our interviewees provided into the role that rural schools played in supporting their communities before, during, and after the peak of the pandemic. In the findings section, we quote the interviewees to exemplify the themes we discerned (Denzin & Lincoln, 2013).

FINDINGS

We discerned two themes from our analysis of the interview data, each with several sub-themes. The first theme focused on the nature of rural schools and their relationships with their communities and how the schools in this study built and sustained a positive sense of community. The second theme focused on how building this sense of community supported the teachers, the students, and their wider communities served by the schools through the pandemic.

Theme 1: Rural School Communities

Discussions of community and community building pervaded the interviews, and the term community was used to describe two groups. The first group included the members of the immediate school community comprised of students and their families, teaching staff, and the board of trustees. The second group included members of the wider school community

The Impact of COVID-19 on Rural Schools in Aotearoa New Zealand • **271**

comprised of residents and members of interest groups, such as businesses and organizations, whose members may have had connections to the school. Rural identity and rural school culture were central to the understanding of community for both groups.

Principals and chairs of the school board of trustees discussed rural identity and rural school. Strong involvement of parents and *whānau* (families/extended families) was a common element of rural identity and rural school culture, exemplified by the mantra of "everyone pitching in." For principals, an emphasis on a commitment to rural identity and rural school culture was a consideration for staff recruitment and retention. Teachers who were new to rural school teaching were explicitly informed of their obligation to attend school and wider community events. The second common element of rural identity and rural school culture was the tie to agriculture and farming discussed most frequently by the chairs of the board of trustees. However, principals and chairs of the board of trustees acknowledged how urbanization was slowly shifting this agricultural base and creating more diverse school and local community demographics. We now discuss three sub-themes from the findings: the nature of rural school communities, the school as the heart of the community, and community-building strategies.

Sub-Theme 1: The Nature of Rural School Community

The importance placed on a strong school community was highlighted by each school board member and principal. Several principals identified the flexibility of teaching staff as the strength of the community. Principal School 15 stated, "I'm so fortunate to have such an adaptive, flexible group of humans that just are committed to what they do. Our [school] community are right behind us as well." Other principals described how teachers and staff of smaller rural schools were able to know their students and parents more deeply and thus be receptive to their needs. "I think that [teachers] felt they were supporting the community in the way they needed to" (Principal School 11). Approximately half the school principals participating in this research were either teaching principals with part-time classroom teaching duties or took regular classes as teaching relief when teaching staff were absent. School board members also highlighted the strength of the school community. For example, the new school board chair said:

> We've found the school community being extremely welcoming... [the] kids have settled in really quickly. You know, I've joined the board and [my partner joined] the PTA. And so, we've gotten involved. But that's because the community welcomed us with open arms as a school community that we've jumped [in] and done that. (Chair of the School Board of Trustees, school 11)

This comment demonstrates the reciprocal benefit of building a strong school community of parents, whānau, and students that fosters and maintains a community culture of belonging. Principal School 1 said their school was "like a family." Principal School 1's reference to the school being an extended family including students, parents, caregivers, and the local community residents was reinforced by their statement, "It's a bit like *Cheers* (the TV show) here, where everybody knows your name."

Although all 16 school principals and 16 chairs of the board of trustees discussed the importance of a rural school community to varying degrees, some were speaking with an authority engendered by their long-standing heritage (e.g., some schools that had been around for over 100 years), whilst others who served in newer schools found it challenging to develop a sense of school community from the ground up. As Principal School 6 of a newly established school explained, as they faced the pandemic, "I guess a disadvantage for us was that we just didn't know our [school] community well enough." Principal School 10 identified the same challenge of building a school community upon recently transitioning from an urban school. They explained how, 2 weeks into their first rural principalship, they realised that they did not know "the plan" or their new rural school's "way of doing things." They quickly had to "make relationships and build connections." Principal School 2 of another newer school explained how:

> One of the other challenges that we've had within a community is that when you first start out...from school perspective, you spend a lot of time consulting with families and, and growing a belief in what you do, and why you do it, and helping your community to understand the why around the type of environment and the kind of approaches you are providing. And you spend, you know, significant time doing that.

Sub-Theme 2: The School as the Heart of the Community

Positioning the rural school at the heart of the community was amongst the most common way our interviewees discussed the relationship between the school and the wider local community and its residents. School principals and members of boards of trustees often commented on their school communities:

> It's tiny. It serves quite a big area, but it's very much the hub of the community. Yes, and when we have events in the hall on the domain, which is just down the road, hundreds of people will turn up. People are very involved in the school. (Chair, Board of Trustees A)

This same chair drew on the example of the school's 150th anniversary to illustrate the depth and longevity of interest and commitment to the

The Impact of COVID-19 on Rural Schools in Aotearoa New Zealand ▪ **273**

school. They described how "plenty of people turned up [to the 150th celebration], people who've been at the school generations before." Other principals discussed how, in their schools, everyone was welcome, from family, whānau, and caregivers, to former students and local community groups. The sense of local community within the schools was evident in the ever-present strong contingent of parent volunteers. Principal School 9 described how local businesses had often "chipped in" with odd jobs around the school or through small donations because parents had mentioned the need for resources.

Sub-Theme 3: Community Building Strategies

Based on our interviews, school personnel—led by principals and members of boards of trustees—engaged in a range of internal and external community building strategies. The most common internal community building initiatives included open-door policies for parents, caregivers, and the community, special school events, and communication strategies such as newsletters, Facebook pages, and digital school apps. Typically, school communication came from the school principal, however, one chair of a board of trustees mentioned writing a weekly column in the community newsletter and specifically asking readers: "How's it going? We'd like to hear from you. Give us your thoughts." Special events like Calf Club Day (children rear calves at home and bring them to school to be judged), school field trips, and working bees served as methods of internal and external community building. For instance, Principal School 10 described several new community-focused initiatives:

> I'm on a big journey so I've got a long way to go, long way to go. We're having a Matariki[3] breakfast at the end of this term, bringing the whānau, bringing our whole community in to celebrate Matariki with us. That's going to be new for our school. So, you know, [we have] lots of things that we've got going on here, such as, we've invited the *iwi* (local tribe) down to join us, so it's not all us taking from them because it's a partnership. [We consider] what can we offer them as well, how could we support them.

The idea of inviting different groups into the school to participate in special events was echoed by Principal School 1. They shared their "Whānau Friday" vision in which "families would feel able to come in on a Friday and basically spend the day here if they're free to be with their families." The same principal held regular open-door schoolwide *hui* (gatherings/meetings) or assembly times where families and community members were welcome to attend. These community-focused events extended to smaller scale initiatives. For example, Principal School 14 decided to have a morning tea. They explained how it was a low key, informal event where anyone could "come and have a coffee with me, sit down...and ask questions [and] I

Theme 2: Sense of Community as Support Through COVID-19

Our second theme focused on the extent to which the sense of community forged prior to the pandemic sustained both the members of the schools and the members of the community in which the schools were located. In this section, we discuss two sub-themes: the impact of COVID-19 and how schools maintained their sense of community.

Impact of COVID-19

The COVID-19 pandemic significantly impacted rural communities in Aotearoa New Zealand. For the rural schools in this study, the implications of COVID-19 varied by context. Participants from the six schools that were in the region impacted by the 2010/2011 Canterbury earthquakes felt that they fared better than others. They cited their experience with the earthquakes for helping them put in place processes analogous to those they had initiated to that earlier disaster to respond to COVID-19. Principal School 7 explained, "Similar to the earthquakes, where we were working through procedures . . . it was easier to get that shaped up." They went on to describe how, as an outcome of the earthquakes, the school had moved all parent communication online, so the school community did not experience any communication disruptions when COVID-19 lockdowns arrived. Principal School 11, another Canterbury principal, echoed these comments about earthquake preparedness that served the school well during COVID-19. They said, "I don't know what it was like for schools that didn't experience the earthquakes . . . it helped teach us to set things up."

Despite differing levels of experience with emergency preparedness, several recurring COVID-19 themes emerged. All principals and members of boards of trustees discussed varied access to learning resources, and the additional stresses on teachers of struggling to balance working from home and supervising the education of young children—their own as well as the children in their class. Another key issue for school leadership was concern for staff, student, and family well-being and welfare.

Reliable Internet and access to Ministry of Education learning packs were the two main sources of frustration, as evidenced by Principal School 13's comment:

The Impact of COVID-19 on Rural Schools in Aotearoa New Zealand • **275**

One of the things that I underestimated, and in the COVID thing, was the pitiful Internet reception there is out in this part of the rural area. Because I know for many of our families in this part of this district, the reception and the connection to Internet was really poor. And, so they couldn't, couldn't do a lot of the online things.

Principal School 4 shared that digital technology access "was a big issue for some of our families." To mitigate the lack of connectivity and related diminished sense of community, school principals responded by quickly supplying hardware from their school budgets. Some school principals approved sending iPads and laptops to students: "We did a lot of work, actually, to support families, and we delivered. We delivered devices." Principals and teachers at some schools discussed purchasing modems and SIM card top-ups for mobile hotspots. With a school roll of just over 30 students, the smallest school participating in this study was also the most remote. Principal School 5's commentary about lack of digital access illustrates the level of frustration experienced by some schools. They described how:

None of our kids; they don't have modems and WiFi...and then we've got a third lockdown and I still don't have it. So, I'm still following up [with the Ministry of Education] saying our kids still don't have WiFi and their response is, "Oh, yeah, well, we were supposed to come and try and connect."

The lack of access to digital hardware and Internet directly influenced the students' opportunity to learn. One chair of the school board of trustees discussed at length how some "kids weren't engaged. It was hard to do that." Schools offered two common responses to this universal concern around access and connectivity. First, they offered different "versions of work" to help support families, including online and hard copy options. Secondly, schools quickly created their own learning hard packs. For example, Principal School 5 recounted how

we created our own school-based pack because we knew that the Ministry's were going to be weeks and weeks. So, we gave them all scissors, colored pencils, books, pens...and [gave families] all of our breakfast supplies. Then [a teacher] and I went, filled up my ute [pickup truck] and drove into the hills and just dropped everything off.

Principals in all the schools in our research were critical about the delays in receiving the promised Ministry of Education hard packs. Most did not receive the packs at all, or those that did received them in the tail end of lockdown which was not ideal. Principals had mixed feelings about communication from the Ministry of Education. Some schools appreciated the daily emails from the ministry offering guidance on teaching, learning, and operational matters: "I mean, none of us have navigated that sort of environment before." Others found the frequency of emails too much to process. Numerous principals described the number of daily emails as "overwhelming." Principal School 3 shared how they "so often dreaded those daily bulletins, because it was always another 'now do this' kind of thing." One board member complained that amongst the long ministry emails, they "didn't really differentiate between preschool, primary, or high school. So, you had to read the whole thing to get the pieces that you really needed." These many challenges led to a range of different techniques for schools needing to maintain relationships with their communities, as described in the next section.

Maintaining a Sense of Community

Schools focused on the specific needs of their local school communities during COVID-19 as their key response to the pandemic. Maintaining a sense of community operated at three levels (a) within the schools; (b) between the school and the school community; and (c) between the school and the wider community, including other schools. Operating within a challenging, "unknown" environment, school principals and chairs of the boards of trustees demonstrated compassionate and responsive leadership. All principals involved in our research spoke with great empathy for their teaching staff, students, and their families. Within the school, principals relied on the existing relationships with their school staff members to make lockdowns work as smoothly as possible. They recognized the varied personal and professional contexts of staff members in responding to varying COVID-19 scenarios. Principal School 1 said, "I very much had the focus of staff, parent, and student welfare, in the forefront of my mind."

After ensuring the safety and well-being of staff, principals and members of boards of trustees then moved onto organizing the shift to online learning. The same care was extended towards children and families. The message was to "do what you could," which acknowledged the varied ability of parents and whānau to support online learning. As Principal School 1 recalled,

> Teachers worked really hard to help the children set up some ability to work within the family and what the family constraints were. So, while some families were able to be beside their children quite a bit when they were working online, others had their own work to do as well. So, you know, there was a real mixture with families or children as to how much time they spent with the teacher online.

Communication with families and students was the primary method of maintaining a sense of school community. For some schools it meant "just the daily check-ins with people." These check-ins occurred via Zoom, as with teacher one-on-ones with students and families, but also extended to principal-teacher meetings. For some of the more remote rural schools, check-ins were more challenging. Principal School 8 spoke at length about numerous families who did not have a mobile phone or landline. Thus, being "out of zone, or out of service area" during lockdown meant that school personnel were unable to get in touch at all during lockdown. To maintain contact, the principal and teachers physically went to these family homes, standing in driveways to maintain social distancing, or talking to them over the fence. However, there were a few families where in-person visiting by staff members was impossible because of the cultural requirement of their needing an invitation to come onto the *marae* [Māori communal meeting place]. Principal School 2 described the benefit of the focus on health and well-being for staff, students, and their families. They indicated that, in responding to the pandemic, school personnel had "demonstrated effective leadership ... and care for our families. It put a lot of credit in the bank really for us in terms of building relationships with our families."

A benefit of wider community building came within the principals' networks. Some principals pointed to the value of the local *Kahui Ako* (Community of Learning)[4] as key sources of advice and support during the pandemic. Principal School 1 noted: "The leader of the [Kahui Ako] group organized a daily check-in with the principals in the area. And that was really valuable, as well ... it was an opportunity to, I guess, to support one another as leaders." The differing experiences of members of boards of trustees were also identified as a measure of support. Principal School 9 described how the member's voice

> was important because they came from other fields of life. So, they could say, well, in our workplace, this is how we're dealing with it or, in this group that I'm involved with, this is what the leaders are doing to manage their staff and team.

School personnel, members of boards of trustees, and members of their communities had to find alternative ways to communicate and maintain a sense of community throughout the pandemic. Whether school personnel engaged in online or in-person communication strategies, the story of navigating a messy, uncertain landscape was abundantly clear.

DISCUSSION: RECIPROCAL AND AUTHENTIC RELATIONSHIPS AND COMMUNITY BUILDING

As highlighted in the conceptual framework, building reciprocal and authentic relationships among school personnel and local community-members is the thread that holds this discussion section together. We open this section with a discussion of our rural school findings in relation to the

Rural Schools as the Hubs of Their Communities

The initiatives undertaken by the leaders who participated in our study exemplified the importance of the school in rural communities, as discussed in the literature (Autti & Hyry-Beihammer, 2014; Haynes, 2022; Witten et al., 2003). In some cases, trust had been built up over many years, as in the long-established schools, such as the one established 150 years ago. As we have previously discussed, in that case, the chair of the board of trustees noted that hundreds of wider community members would come to school–community events. Witten et al. (2003) noted, "Schools have histories and special characteristics born of place that in turn offer particular experiences to that community and facilitate the development and assertion of local knowledges and identity" (p. 206). In more recently established schools in our study, several principals described their need to be quite deliberate in their consultation and relationship-building strategies to develop a sense of community identity. Our study also highlighted that the idea of school community consisted of two layers: (a) the immediate group of school staff members, members of the board of trustees, students, parents, and families; and (b) the wider neighborhood or district and the local businesses and organizations. As Haynes (2022) noted, "A publicly funded school in a small community is often the institution with the most far-reaching impacts on citizen's daily lives as it provides a source of employment, social, cultural, and recreational opportunities" (p. 66). This was a responsibility that the principals of the newly established schools took seriously.

A school acting as a community hub was not a feature that happened by accident. As Hargreaves (2009) stated:

> The school gate may be a community "hub" for parents of school-age children (Countryside Agency, 2001, 2008), but despite recent calls for rural schools to be recognised as community hubs, parents congregating at the gate does not necessarily constitute a school-community relationship. (p. 123)

The Impact of COVID-19 on Rural Schools in Aotearoa New Zealand ▪ **279**

In our study, creating the feeling of the school as a community hub involved a set of reciprocal expectations that were built through communication, engagement, and invitations. The literature highlights that this reciprocal approach has long been part of Aotearoa New Zealand school communities: "For many New Zealand localities, schools were among the first community buildings erected, and, for generations, voluntary labor and resources, as well as tax revenues, have contributed to the maintenance of schools as a central community resource" (Witten et al., 2003, p. 220).

School leaders, mostly principals but also the chairs of their boards of trustees, took the opportunity not only to set clear communication channels in place to provide information but also to seek feedback. School principals extended open-door invitations for parents to come to the school, either to spend time in their child's class, as in Whānau Fridays, or to meet with the principal over coffee.

Building Community Capital for Coping With Disasters and Crises

All the effort that school personnel put into relationship and community building stood them in good stead when the pandemic arrived. Prior research on schools in disaster settings found that where there was a strong sense of community, local leadership, and active community networking, prior to the disaster, communities were able to thrive despite the odds (Mutch, 2016; Thornley et al., 2013). In the school community contexts in our study, building community capital (Callaghan & Colton, 2008) was a reciprocal venture. Prior to the disaster, school personnel used invitational strategies to communicate and engage their communities in educational and social activities. In response, members of the immediate and wider communities responded by supporting events, volunteering their time or providing resources. When the pandemic arrived, school personnel knew who the families were that lacked Internet connectivity and devices or would struggle to provide basic learning supplies or even food in this difficult time. Community members responded by also supporting families in need in their community, such as setting up a community pantry, where anyone with surplus food could drop it off and anyone who needed it could collect it without embarrassment.

The members of some of the school communities in our study found that prior experience of a traumatic event prepared them better for what they were to face. They already had learning and communication strategies in place for such eventualities. They also had an awareness of the disruption that such events cause and the need to be agile and adaptable. Nevertheless, as is the nature of rural and remote communities, some families were inaccessible, or their living situations meant that it was not possible for their children to engage in or be assisted with academic learning. The pandemic exacerbated the social, economic, and educational inequalities experienced by vulnerable children and young people (Education Review Office, 2020; Hood, 2020; Mutch, 2021; Riwai-Couch et al., 2020). In the most deprived rural areas, many young people did not return to school because they had lost motivation or because they had already left to find work to support their families (Mutch & Peung, 2021). Some school principals in our study expressed their frustration at the ministry's not being more proactive about engaging with rural issues or providing adequate support. Given that our research was conducted in this fraught context, in the next section we discuss how it was that our research project not only continued but was welcomed.

Building Reciprocal and Authentic University–School–Community Relationships

A primary principle in our study was building reciprocal and authentic university–school–community relationships. For many schools involved in our study, it was the first time that they had ever been involved in research. Common initial responses from members of school boards to our research invitation were "Why?" and "What would we say?" Many principals we approached were delighted to be asked to participate in our research. Several principals specifically stated how they felt overlooked by the ministry and the large-scale educational studies discussed in the media. Building authentic relationships with the personnel in these rural schools involved demonstrating a willingness to invest time and care for the school members and their communities. We employed three strategies to build these relationships—personal connection, visibility, and communication.

Building authentic relationships with each school involved our taking the time to focus on the people and places in their communities. We believed it was important to understand the nature of rurality (Haynes, 2022). School principals often held a gatekeeping role in terms of access to the members of boards of trustees. We devoted significant time to meeting with principals, some of whom were curious about the nature of the research invitation, having limited prior experience of formal educational research. The relationship building process involved explaining the impetus for the study and the role and background of Tatebe, and reiterating the goal of providing a platform for personnel in rural schools to share their experiences of rural school life. It often took several months of phone calls, in-person meetings, and even attendance at staff meetings and board meetings before we were formally welcomed into a school to begin data gathering.

The Impact of COVID-19 on Rural Schools in Aotearoa New Zealand • **281**

Our being seen in the local community furthered our identification with the school. Each visit with the school principal included asking about the local community. Learning about the geographic region and investigating some of the local landmarks and businesses demonstrated our genuine interest in building this new university–school–community relationship. Being able to talk about eating at the local cafe, describing driving around the new housing development, and even speaking with the locals was highly informative and illustrated the care and time that our research team would invest in each rural school community. In subsequent years of the study, Tatebe volunteered to participate in school events, such as Calf Club Day, school barbecues, school fairs, and local annual community events and fundraisers. Where geography and time were limitations, regular check-ins with the school principal and virtual attendance at board meetings facilitated staying connected.

Regular communication with school principals and members of boards of trustees was integral to our research. Communication included our sending back all data to the schools for their review and records, along with informing school personnel of our progress on the study through reports, emails, and phone calls. Tatebe also made efforts to forward relevant research and documents for members of boards of trustees and principals to read. Regular communication demonstrated our commitment to working with and alongside members of rural schools and communities rather than on or about them (Mutch, 2018) and reinforced Tatebe's ethic of care (Noddings, 2013) towards the study participants. Understanding more about rural schooling and rurality in Aotearoa New Zealand and abroad facilitated more informed discussions with members of school boards and principals, while also minimizing Tatebe's identity as a rural "outsider." Thus, rather than being seen as a burdensome interruption, our research was welcomed by the personnel in the participating schools as a genuine partnership in which they would have the opportunity to share their experiences with a wider audience and possibly influence policymakers.

CONCLUSION

Our chapter makes several contributions to the relevant fields. Firstly, it highlights the nature of schools as hubs of their communities and provides concrete examples of how such status is attained. Secondly, it provides insight into a rural environment that is distinctly different from that discussed in the many rural education studies based on the United States context (Haynes, 2022)—the rural schools in Aotearoa New Zealand. Thirdly, it takes up Smawfield's (2013) suggestion of conducting further research on the roles of school personnel in disaster and crisis contexts by sharing stories of their initiatives to cope with the COVID-19 pandemic. Finally, it addresses Patton's (2012) request for more examples of successful university–school partnerships. In essence, successful university–school partnerships rely on three Ps—people, project, and principles.

All relationships begin between people—while they might represent an organization, it is the bond of trust between individual people that builds and sustains relationships. In Aotearoa New Zealand, we talk of *manakitanga*[5]—mutual care and respect for and between people. This underpins our approach to building our research relationship, as exemplified by Tatebe's involvement in setting up this study. Part of *manakitanga* is that it requires time for *kanohi ki te kanohi* (literally eye-to-eye), signifying the imperative to sit down with people face-to-face and share something with them—conversation, stories, food, or, most importantly, time.

The second P is the project. What is it that brings and binds partners together? *Kotahitanga* is the Māori concept of togetherness, coming together as one. What is the *mahi*, or task, that partners have come together to complete? *Whānaungatanga* is about building authentic communal relationships for a mutual goal. It was important to us throughout our project that all parties felt informed, engaged, respected, and valued.

Finally, the third P is for principles. What are the principles that underpin the research and the values that each party brings to the endeavor? It is important that partners articulate these in words and actions. *Pūmanawatanga* invokes the power and intimacy of a beating pulse or moral purpose. If a research endeavor puts people first, builds authentic relationships, and treats the endeavor as *taonga*—a treasure—then partners have a sound footing on which to proceed. We close with the following Māori whakataukī (proverb) that speaks of coming together and sharing for the greater good.

Nāku te rourou, nāu te rourou, ka ora ai te iwi

(With your food basket and my food basket, we will sustain everyone)

ACKNOWLEDGMENT

We gratefully acknowledge the work of Drs. Lina Valdivia and Wendy Choo who contributed to the rural schools project in the data collection and analysis phases of the research. Their work advanced the project and made our sharing of study findings in this chapter possible.

The Impact of COVID-19 on Rural Schools in Aotearoa New Zealand ▪ **283**

NOTES

1. *Te Whakatere au Pāpori* was the name gifted to the research network by Hemi Dale, a Māori (Indigenous) scholar at the University of Auckland. It loosely translates as "navigating social currents."
2. In New Zealand, schools are individually governed by locally elected boards of trustees consisting of the principal, a staff representative, parents, and other community members.
3. "Twinkling in the winter sky just before dawn, Matariki (the Pleiades) signals the Māori New Year. For Māori, the appearance of Matariki heralds a time of remembrance, joy, and peace. It is a time for communities to come together and celebrate. From 2022, a public holiday marking Matariki will be held in June or July each year." https://teara.govt.nz/en/matariki-maori-new-year
4. Kahui Ako is a Ministry of Education-funded initiative where education providers (from early childhood to higher education) in a location can gather for mutual support in meeting the needs of their school communities.
5. It is challenging to maintain the multiple nuances of cultural meaning in translating Māori concepts into English. Our apologies for our shortcomings in this regard.

REFERENCES

Autti, O. M., & Hyry-Beihammer, E. K. (2014). School closures in rural Finnish communities. *Journal of Research in Rural Education, 29*(1), 1–17. https://jrre.psu.edu/sites/default/files/2019-08/29-1.pdf

Blundell, S. (2005). Yesterday's schools. *New Zealand Geographic 76* (Nov–Dec). https://www.nzgeo.com/stories/yesterdays-schools

Burr, V. (2015). *Social constructionism* (3rd ed.). Routledge.

Cahill, H., Beadle, S., Mitch, J., Coffey, J., & Crofts, J. (2010). *Adolescents in emergencies.* Youth Research Centre, University of Melbourne.

Callaghan, E. G., & Colton, J. (2008). Building sustainable & resilient communities: A balancing of community capital. *Environment, Development and Sustainability, 10*(6), 931–942. https://doi.org/10.1007/s10668-007-9093-4

Cameron, B. (2020). *Captaining a team of 5 million: New Zealand beats back COVID-19, March–June 2020.* Innovations for Successful Societies. https://successfulsocieties.princeton.edu/sites/successfulsocieties/files/NewZealand_COVID_FInal.pdf

Chorzempa, B. F., Isabelle, A. D., & de Groot, C. (2010). Our quest for mutualism in university–school partnerships. *The Educational Forum, 74*(4), 306–317. https://doi.org/10.1080/00131725.2010.507084

Cauchemez, S., Bhattarai, A., Marchbanks, T. L., Fagan, R. P., Ostroff, S., Ferguson, N. M., Swerdlow, D., & Pennsylvania H1N1 working group. (2011, January 31) Role of social networks in shaping disease transmission during a community outbreak of 2009 H1N1 pandemic influenza. *Proceedings of the National Academy of Sciences of the United States of America 108*(7), 2825–2830. https://doi.org/10.1073/pnas.1008895108

Community Alliance, British Association of Settlements and Social Action Centres, & Development Trusts Association. (2009). *Anchors of tomorrow: A vision for community organisations of the future.* Community Alliance.

Denzin, N. K., & Lincoln, Y. S. (Eds.). (2013). *The landscape of qualitative research* (4th ed.). SAGE.

Dickson-Swift, V., James, E. L., Kippen, S., & Liamputtong, P. (2009). Researching sensitive topics: Qualitative research as emotion work. *Qualitative Research, 9*(1), 61–79. https://doi.org/10.1177%2F1468794108098031

Duncan, J., & Conner, L. (2013). *Research partnerships in early childhood education: Teachers and researchers in collaboration.* Palgrave MacMillan. http://dx.doi .org/10.1057/9781137346889

Education Review Office. (2013). *Stories of resilience and innovation in schools and early childhood services. Canterbury earthquakes: 2010–2012.* Wellington, New Zealand: Education Review Office.

Education Review Office. (2020). *COVID-19: Impact on schools and early childhood services—Interim report.* https://www.ero.govt.nz/publications/COVID-19-impact -on-schools-and-early-childhood-services-interim-report/

Ferris, E., & Petz, D. (2012). *The year that shook the rich: A review of natural disasters in 2011.* The Brookings Institution. https://www.brookings.edu/wp-content/ uploads/2016/06/03_natural_disaster_review_ferris.pdf

Gordon, R. (2004). The social dimension of emergency recovery. *Emergency Management Australia. Recovery. Australian emergency management manuals series: Manual 10: Recovery* (Appendix C: pp. 111–143). Emergency Management Australia.

Hargreaves, L. (2009). Respect and responsibility: Review of research on small rural schools in England. *International Journal of Educational Research, 48*(2), 117–128. https://doi.org/10.1016/j.ijer.2009.02.004

Haynes, M. (2022). The impacts of school closure on rural communities in Canada: A review. *The Rural Educator, 43*(2), 60–74. https://scholarsjunction.msstate .edu/ruraleducator/vol43/iss2/5/

Hood, N. (2020, August 18). *Learning from lockdown: What the experience of teachers, students and parents can tell us about what happened and where to next for New Zealand's school system.* The Education Hub. https://theeducationhub.org.nz/ learning-from-lockdown/

Hooper, L. M., & Britnell, H. B. (2012). Mental health research in K–12 schools: Translating a systems approach to university–school partnerships. *Journal of Counselling and Development, 90*(1), 81–90. https://doi.org/10.1111/ j.1556-6676.2012.00011.x

Johnson, V. A., & Ronan, K. R. (2014). Classroom responses of New Zealand school teachers following the 2011 Christchurch earthquake. *Natural Hazards 72,* 1075–1092. https://doi.org/10.1007/s11069-014-1053-3

Kearns, R. A., Lewis, N., McCreanor, T., & Witten, K. (2009). "The status quo is not an option": Community impacts of school closure in South Taranaki, New Zealand. *Journal of Rural Studies, 25*(1), 131–140. https://doi.org/10.1016/j .jrurstud.2008.08.002

Martin, S. D., Snow, J. L., & Franklin Torrez, C. A. (2011). Navigating the terrain of the third space: Tensions with/in relationships in school–university

The Impact of COVID-19 on Rural Schools in Aotearoa New Zealand • **285**

partnerships. *Journal of Teacher Education, 62*(3), 299–311. https://doi.org/10.1177/0022487110396096

McLaughlin, C., Black-Hawkins, K., Brindley, S., McIntyre, D., & Taber, K. S. (2006). *Researching schools: Stories from a schools-university partnership for educational research.* Routledge.

Mutch, C. (2014). The role of schools in disaster preparation, response and recovery: What can we learn from the literature. *Pastoral Care in Education, 32*(1) 5–22. https://doi.org/10.1080/02643944.2014.880123

Mutch, C. (2015). Leadership in times of crisis: Dispositional, relational and contextual factors influencing school principals' actions. *International Journal of Disaster Risk Reduction, 14*(2), 186–194. https://doi.org/10.1016/j.ijdrr.2015.06.005

Mutch, C. (2016). Schools *as* communities and *for* communities: Learning from the 2010–2011 New Zealand earthquakes. *School Community Journal, 26*(1), 115–138.

Mutch, C. (2017). Winners and losers: School closures in post-earthquake Canterbury and the dissolution of community. *Waikato Journal of Education, 22*(1), 73–95. https://doi.org/10.15663/wje.v22i1.543

Mutch, C. (2018). The place of schools in building community cohesion and resilience: Lessons from a disaster context. In L. Shevellar & P. Westoby (Eds.), *The Routledge handbook of community development research* (pp. 239–252). Routledge.

Mutch, C. (2021). COVID-19 and the exacerbation of educational inequalities in New Zealand. *Perspectives in Education, 39*(1), 242–256. https://doi.org/10.18820/2519593X/pie.v39.i1.15

Mutch, C., & Peung, S. (2021). 'Maslow before Bloom': Implementing a caring pedagogy during COVID-19. *New Zealand Journal of Teachers' Work, 18*(2), 69–90. https://doi.org/10.24135/teacherswork.v18i2.334

Mutch, C., & Weir, A. (2016). Evaluating in traumatic contexts: Considering the contextual, ethical, emotional, and political aspects. *Evaluation Matters, 2,* 23–52. https://doi.org/10.18296/em.0010

Mutch, C., Yates, S., & Hu, C. (2015). Gently, gently: A school–university participatory research partnership in a post-disaster setting. *Gateways: International Journal of Community Research and Engagement, 8*(1), 79–99. https://doi.org/10.5130/ijcre.v8i1.4161

New Zealand Government. (2020, April 8). *COVID-19: Government moving quickly to roll out learning from home.* https://www.beehive.govt.nz/release/COVID19-government-moving-quickly-roll-out-learning-home

Noddings, N. (2013). *Caring: A relational approach to ethics and moral education* (2nd ed.). University of California Press.

Patton, K. (2012). Introduction. *Journal of Physical Education, Recreation & Dance, 83*(9), 13–14. https://doi.org/10.1080/07303084.2012.10598840

Riwai-Couch, M., Bull, A., Ellis, B., Hall, K., Nicholls, J., Taleni, T., & Watkinson, R. (2020). *School-led learning at home: Voices of parents of Māori and Pasifika students.* Evaluation Associates.

Smawfield, D. (Ed.). (2013). *Education and natural disasters.* Bloomsbury.

Stake, R. (1995). *The art of case study research.* SAGE.

Swarbrick, N. (2012). Primary and secondary education: Numbers and types of schools. *Te Ara: The Encyclopedia of New Zealand*. http://www.TeAra.govt.nz/en/primary-and-secondary-education/page-7

Tatebe, J. (2021). The "new" rural: Small and rural schools' influence on regional urban developments. *Australian and International Journal of Rural Education*, *31*(3), 15–28. https://doi.org/10.47381/aijre.v31i3.301

Thornley, L., Ball, J., Signal, L., Lawson-Te Aho, K., & Rawson, E. (2013). *Building community resilience: Learning from the Canterbury earthquakes*. Health Research Council. https://communityresearch.org.nz/wp-content/uploads/formidable/Building-Community-Resilience-report-March-2013.pdf

UNESCO. (2021). *Global Education Coalition. COVID-19 education response*. https://en.unesco.org/COVID19/educationresponse/globalcoalition

Unite Against COVID-19. (2022). *History of the COVID-19 alert system*. https://covid19.govt.nz/about-our-covid-19-response/history-of-the-covid-19-alert-system/

Witten, K., Kearns, R., Lewis, N., Coster, H., & McCreanor, T. (2003). Educational restructuring from a community viewpoint: A case study of school closure from Invercargill, New Zealand. *Environment and Planning C: Government and Policy, 21*, 203–223. https://doi.org/10.1068%2Fc05r

CHAPTER 13

EMERGENT PROGRAM EVALUATION (POST) COVID-19

Nicole Weinberg
Texas Christian University

Elissa Bryant
Texas Christian University

Kayla Bullard
Texas Christian University

Gabriel Huddleston
Texas Christian University

ABSTRACT

This chapter presents the ways in which we, at Texas Christian University's (TCU) Center of Public Education and Community Engagement (CPECE), are currently considering our work in relation to the changes we see in an emergent (post) COVID-19 context based on our recent experiences, con-

---

School–University–Community Research in a (Post) COVID-19 World, pages 287–308
Copyright © 2023 by Information Age Publishing
www.infoagepub.com
All rights of reproduction in any form reserved.

versations, and evaluative efforts with local stakeholders. Since March 2020, educators and policymakers have rapidly responded to the unexpected challenges of the COVID-19 crisis through a series of varied adaptations to institutional norms in education (da Silva Vieira & Barbosa, 2020). Continuing to navigate the aftershocks of a global pandemic will be challenging for the various community stakeholders as they plan and utilize opportunities to establish equitable outcomes. As we imagine our place in that process, we (re)consider how we, as community-based researchers, can anticipate those challenges by constructing an emergent framework grounded in core principles and practices that might facilitate collaborative responses to the evolving circumstances of schools and universities within our larger community context.

This chapter tries to emulate brown's (2017) discussion of emergent strategy by critically self-reflecting on our own processes and methodologies of conducting program evaluation. As such, we delineate the emergent elements and characteristics we aspire to embody in program evaluation through a conceptual model. Our intention for this model, and the chapter at large, is not to offer generalizable or standardized instructions of how to do program evaluation "correctly" but rather to imagine and wonder how program evaluation might exist beyond the traditionally linear paradigmatic framing(s) in which it usually resides. brown (2017) wrote:

> We have lived through a good half century of individualistic linear organizing (led by charismatic individuals or budget-building institutions), which intends to reform or revolutionize society, but falls back into modeling the oppressive tendencies against which we claim to be pushing. Some of those tendencies are seeking to assert one right way or one right strategy. Many align with the capitalistic belief that constant growth and critical mass is the only way to create change, even if they don't use that language. (p. 8)

As others have written (Hall et al., 2015; Huckaby, 2019; Huddleston, 2022), neoliberalism has heightened and calcified this type of individualistic linear organizing. It has been crystalized in the United States' response to the COVID-19 pandemic where we rely on individuals to socially distance, wear a mask, and get a vaccine to slow the spread of the disease rather than a community response that asks for synergetic cooperation and mutual sacrifice. Given this context and that we seek to be *community-based* researchers, we attempt to answer brown's (2017) question, "How do we turn our collective full-bodied intelligence towards collaboration, if that is the way we will survive?" (p. 9).

Our emerging approach to both thinking about and doing program evaluation differently is rooted in Smith and Helfenbein's (2009) framework for community-based inquiry, translational research in practice (TRIP). This chapter serves to reconsider and refine the processes and ideas presented in the TRIP model through brown's (2017) principles of emergent strategy, further exploring the interconnectedness of universities and schools within urban communities and considering how our own iterative, small-scale actions might contribute to large-scale societal impacts. We ground our thoughts in various research projects we have conducted with community partners during the pandemic, including an unpublished report entitled the *Impact of the COVID-19 Pandemic on Education in Tarrant County* (Bryant et al., 2022), which we refer to here as the ICPET study. Our purpose in referring to this and other of our unpublished reports is not to provide empirical findings but rather to consider the local context of our community-based research. Reflecting upon this work, we analyze the tensions between our ethical responsibilities and the demands made by urgent community needs, rapidly changing contexts, and stakeholder partnerships. The purpose of this chapter is twofold: First, this chapter is intended to serve as an artifact of our current mindset as we continue program evaluation work and second, we hope to spark conversation with those embarking on similar journeys.

SCHOOL–UNIVERSITY–COMMUNITY IN TRANSITION

A society in transition, according to Brazilian philosopher and educator Paulo Freire (1974), is characterized by an increased collective awareness of the "contradictions between the ways of being, understanding, behaving, and valuing" (p. 5). This description resonates with the emergent (post) COVID-19 context as institutions from global to local scales, including stakeholders in education, have rapidly responded to significant challenges posed by the pandemic, adapting educational programming in ways that were previously deemed impractical or even impossible (da Silva Vieira & Barbosa, 2020). Efforts to get industries, including education, back to normal, without challenges as the arbitrary limitations that we collectively, as a society, have imposed on ourselves in the past, become unignorable. As many individuals seek to study or work remotely to accommodate childcare, dis/ability, work/life balance, commute, or other individual circumstances, it is useful to frame institutional endeavors toward returning to "in-person" as a past which is, in the words of Freire (1974), "seeking to survive" (p. 5) rather than an inevitable reality. However, if we continue to frame the (re)consideration of these past limits and establishment of the "new normal" solely based on the needs, desires, and abilities of the individual, we run the risk of foreclosing any collective action toward our shared liberation, which, according to brown (2017), is necessary for the collective survival of life on Earth.

Systemic Failure, Holistic Effects, and Breaking Points

Our center's recent research, including the ICPET study as well as an on-going review of the evolving literature, paints a grim picture of the state of education both nationwide and in the context of our local community. Not only are the circumstances dire, but the effects of a global pandemic are complex, multifaceted, and embedded within larger institutional structures.

The existing research finds that the multifaceted shocks of the pandemic break down disproportionately along divisions of disability, race, and socio-economic status (e.g., Bacher-Hicks et al., 2020, Jaeger & Blaabaek, 2020). Historically, these inequities have long existed (Anyon, 2005), but the pandemic has exacerbated these problems due to COVID-19's impact on individuals' health and economic circumstances. Compounding the problem is that many of the services that have traditionally provided support to address these inequities have been affected negatively by the pandemic as well. Yet, measuring the consequences of the pandemic on individual health or economic outcomes alone is representative of the individualistic thinking which emergent strategies attempt to work against. An emergent approach can extend the scope of inquiry beyond individualism, instead considering the incremental and ongoing ways in which communities adapt or can adapt to ensure their collective health within and beyond classrooms.

An emergent consideration of our recent assessment of teacher and family needs indicates patterns that existed prior to the pandemic. First, teachers are suffering from a high rate of burnout which is drastically worsening an already urgent teacher shortage (García & Weiss, 2019; GBAO Strategies, 2022). Second, increasing communication between caregivers and teachers has long been seen as essential in school success (Henderson et al., 2002; Henderson et al., 2007). In the context of our local community, the center's recent qualitative findings on schools, organizations, and families suggested that increased perceptions of isolation, urgency of need, and the heightened political climate surrounding education have made effective communication more difficult and the relationships thereby more tenuous (Bryant et al., 2022; Weinburgh et al., 2021).

We witnessed an example of systemic failure when schools pivoted to online learning. Our recent findings from our local community, and the broader literature, suggest that the ability of teachers to teach, students to learn, and caregivers to provide support was directly impacted by access to the internet, availability of technology, and childcare support (Sayer & Braun, 2020; Scott, 2020; Verlenden et al., 2021; Weinburgh et al., 2021). We also observed evidence of a lack of childcare/supervision during online learning, specifically when older students had to care for their siblings, potentially at the cost of their own attendance or participation. For our community, virtual learning was a failure on many levels, but perhaps most striking was that the implementation did not consider the larger systemic issues affecting an individual's ability to engage.

Systemic failures to address the challenges of the pandemic have negatively influenced the mental and physical health of students, teachers, and caregivers, as well as made teaching and learning increasingly difficult. Yet, we cannot think our work in program evaluation to be complete once the crises have been named, analyzed, and deconstructed into their systemic failures. We must imagine alternatives and create a new future. brown (2017) wrote, "How do we move beyond our beautiful deconstruction? Who teaches us to reconstruct? How do we cultivate the muscle of radical imagination needed to dream together beyond fear?" (p. 59).

Community stakeholders in education often seek program evaluation at pivot points in their organizational planning and, at least to some extent, they are seeking innovative ideas about how to adapt their current programming; their expectation is that we, as program evaluators, will conduct and review research to generate some "answers." In these conversations, we aim to reframe our recommendations from a question of "How did we do?" to "What can we become together?"

Our stakeholders, as ourselves, are inevitably embedded within the systems of injustice that we mutually seek to change; we must resist the urge to recreate old, unsustainable patterns through "singular charismatic leaders, top down structures, money-driven programs, destructive methods of engaging conflict" and "unsustainable work cultures" (brown, 2017, p. 82). If our research is to move beyond systemic failures toward a more just future society, what would it mean to shift the practices of our research to an emergent strategy, in which complex patterns and change occur through small, iterative interactions?

brown (2017) urged us to start by considering what additional insight can be gained from paying "closer attention to this place we are from, the bodies we are in" (p. 6). For program evaluation, this requires the consideration of individuals from a holistic viewpoint, in which the connection between one's bodily health and the mind's ability to learn is essential and tied to the community that surrounds said individual (Basch, 2011; Dryfoos, 2000). Our recent findings in our local community considered how several commonly identified challenges to schools during the pandemics might be only the tip of the iceberg, or visible manifestations of embodied individual and community trauma or tension (Bryant et al., 2022). For example, we considered patterns of attendance and enrollment as interconnected with the ongoing anxieties of children and their families regarding health and safety, as well as complex social and political tensions in the school environment. Similarly, we drew connections between family or teacher-reported perceptions of youth disengagement, retrogressive developmental behaviors, increased aggression, and the adverse childhood experiences/trauma many youth experienced during lockdown (Felitti et al., 1998).

Teacher Burnout and the Virtual Aftershock

A possible cause of increased stress on schools and communities could be the continuing aftershocks of pivoting to online learning earlier in the pandemic when mitigation efforts made it necessary. This chapter does not examine whether such a move was warranted or not, but we do see that the effects of that pivot continue to resonate with both caregivers and teachers as having a negative impact on learning. In the ICPET study, the vast majority of teachers we surveyed disagreed that students continued to learn during virtual learning for various reasons. Teachers also reported an increase in work-related responsibilities, tensions, and stress during virtual learning as they struggled with tasks such as tracking online attendance and maintaining communication with students/families during virtual/hybrid learning even in the face of language barriers and unreliable access to technology.

Survey results from the National Education Association found that the number of teachers considering leaving their profession or retiring has nearly doubled since July 2020 (GBAO Strategies, 2022). The results of the ICPET confirm that many teachers are overwhelmed to the point of exhaustion with many either leaving the profession altogether or seriously considering it. As more teachers leave the profession, those remaining will be asked to do more to account for the staffing shortages.

While it would be easy to simplify the complexity of teacher burnout and attribute it to the overall stress that the pandemic is placing on everyone, what is telling is that teachers in our local community who showed signs of burnout cited reasons that have existed prior to the pandemic, such as a lack of agency and respect, often a result of perceived micromanaging (Apple, 2013; Bryant et al., 2022; Giroux, 2010; Noddings, 2007; Ravitch, 2010). Even though most districts have partly or entirely moved away from virtual learning, these prior effects are still being felt in schools. The result is learning loss, lasting emotional and mental stress on teachers, and hardship for caregivers who find it difficult to facilitate learning at home. The pandemic has increased stress for teachers along preexisting pressure points, creating daily struggles in teachers' lives which accumulate toward the larger picture of teacher burnout.

We note how the pivot to online learning is perceived by all stakeholders, ourselves as researchers included, in terms of individual repercussions such as attendance, learning loss, or mental health. Such measures represent the individualistic, linear type of pervasive thinking that brown (2017) sees as counterproductive toward a more just future. As we continue our program evaluation work within our own community, we continue to reflect upon the pivot to online learning in terms of emergence. Beyond the

Emergent Program Evaluation (Post) COVID-19 • **293**

technical success and failures of this transition and the individual ramifications, might we, and perhaps other stakeholders as well, be overlooking the ways in which formal or informal social networks were formed through this crisis? How did individuals within these organic alliances adapt and collaborate? Might such tight-knit community threads be the foundations for future collective action, resilience, and sustainable change?

Pandemic as Disaster: Philanthropic and Government Funding Landscape

Since the onset of the pandemic, we have seen an increase in private and federal funding directed toward education. Private foundations distributed $12 billion for COVID-19 response globally by June 2020, an amount far exceeding historic giving toward other recent domestic and international disaster response efforts (Sato et al., 2020). By the end of 2021, the federal government distributed $122 billion in Elementary and Secondary School Emergency Relief for public school systems (U.S. Department of Education, 2022). As stakeholders plan to utilize these resources in programmatic responses, the development and assessment of high-quality, equitable educational programming depends on educational research that portrays the complexity of school systems. Community-based research, broadly defined here as educational research in partnership with local stakeholders (i.e., program evaluation), represents fertile ground for tangibly navigating the intersections of critical theory and narrative experience. Situated amongst, but not necessarily subject to, the interests and regulations of federal and academic institutions, which might favor more positivistic approaches to educational research, community-based research is a "particularly cogent site where a policy relevant counterscience might be worked out" (Lather, 2004, p. 22).

THEORETICAL FOUNDATIONS

Translational Research in Practice

The overall framework for our center's program evaluation work is the TRIP model as implemented by the Center for Urban and Multicultural Education (CUME) at Indiana University-Indianapolis under the directorship of Smith and Helfenbein. Our goal is to not only adopt the TRIP model as guiding our practice, but also to continue to build upon and adapt the TRIP model to the specific context of our campus and the larger surrounding communities of Fort Worth and Tarrant County.

The TRIP model has its roots in professional schools such as medicine and communications, distinguishing itself from other, more traditional forms of research by valuing "the timely application of new knowledge discovered throughout the research process" (Smith & Helfenbein, 2009, p. 91). The TRIP model pushes back against what Smith and Helfenbein (2009) referred to as "traditional research," which often "looks at students/ teachers as subjects in schools as settings," constructing a false onto-epistemological separation between the school, university, and community (p. 89). As one of the possible co-mutual approaches to "further dialogue" in the school–university–community partnerships, this approach prioritizes qualitative inquiry by acknowledging the ways in which pressing problems in education are "steeped in contexts within and outside of particular schools" and are therefore "beyond what statistics can 'control' for" (Smith & Helfenbein, 2009, p. 90).

Translational research eschews traditional research models by seeking collaborative partnerships outside the university to implement evidence-based practices in a range of contexts. As Smith and Helfenbein (2009) wrote:

> Translational research differs from other forms of educational research in that the latter is predicated on the idea of the external "fly on the wall." Conversely, translational research creates a space for collaborative, co-constructed inquiry that values and utilizes the expertise of all stakeholders. (p. 91)

Emergent Strategy

While calls for adaptive programming in education existed long before the pandemic (see e.g., Valters et al., 2016), the emergent (post) COVID context continues to shatter the boundaries of how fluid and dynamic systems of education can be. In our continued commitment to working through the complex impacts of the pandemic for our schools, nation, and world, we find it useful to expand and in some ways reorient the four-step, linear TRIP model through the guiding principles of emergent strategies.

Grounding her rhetoric in Black liberatory pedagogues such as Toni Morrison, Audrey Lorde, and James Baldwin, brown's work built upon the emancipatory science fiction work of American novelist Octavia Butler. Emergent strategies have proliferated into many heterogeneous ideas and practices across sectors, all of which "let us practice, in every possible way, the world we want to see" (brown, 2017, p. 23). Efforts to change the world find a kinship with science fiction as social activists seek a deep understanding of the ways in which present actions and beliefs will shape the future and influence the next generations. For brown, envisioning a more sustainable future requires remembering the past while observing and acting in

Emergent Program Evaluation (Post) COVID-19 • **295**

the present with openness, creativity, and faith that a better future is indeed possible.

In the face of the massive scale of human-Earth suffering, emergent strategies are practices in which we heal ourselves, each other, and the world through means such as dialogue, curiosity, and wonder (brown, 2017, p. 17). Emergent strategies often look to the natural world and complex sciences in efforts toward biomimetics, or biomimicry, or attempts to imitate "the models, systems, and elements of nature for the purpose of solving complex human problems" (p. 23). Such examples include the cooperative work and collective sustainability of ant colonies, the interconnectedness and detoxifying function of mycelium, and the decentralized resilience of dandelions (p. 45). brown identified the following principles of emergent strategy:

> Small is good, small is all (The large is a reflection of the small).
> Change is constant (Be like water).
> There is always enough time for the right work.
> There is a conversation in the room that only these people at this moment can have. Find it.
> Never a failure, always a lesson.
> Trust the People (If you trust the people, they become trustworthy).
> Move at the speed of trust. Focus on critical connections more than critical mass—build the resilience by building the relationships.
> Less prep, more presence.
> What you pay attention to grows. (p. 41)

In considering the ways in which we might shift inequitable systems, we must consider the relationship between our team's practices and the future worlds we envision as fractals. brown (2017) described fractals as "infinitely complex patterns that are self-similar across different scales" (p. 51). As small, iterative actions in our lives constitute the larger world in which we live, we hope to become "the seashell representation of a galactic vision for justice" (p. 23). Fractals invite us to recognize that, in the words of brown, "What we practice at the small scale sets the patterns for the whole system" (p. 53), meaning that transforming the world begins—but does not end—with the active healing and transformation of our own lives, practices, and relationships. By acknowledging the complex ways in which we are embedded within the patterns of relations which we seek to change, we respond to Lather's (1991) call to "take responsibility for transforming our own practices" that might create space for agency and justice (p. 164). What would it mean for us to conduct program evaluation through practices of love and care rather than the destructive competitive practices and resulting burnout typical to academia and the larger cultural context of education in America?

PROGRAM EVALUATION IN THE SCHOOL–UNIVERSITY–COMMUNITY BEEHIVE

Incorporated to the broader scope of school–university–community collaboration, program evaluation constitutes fertile grounds for collaborative re-imaginings of the school in the (be)coming aftermath of COVID-19 (Dryfoos, 2000; Dryfoos & Maguire, 2019; Noddings, 2001; Pattison, 2022). We believe in a future world in which program evaluation promotes community dialogue and engagement in service of equity. Our work draws from—and seeks to adapt—resources such as the Community Science (2022) guides for using theory of change models and logframes to diagnose biases within institutional and social structures.

In hopes that we might also practice collective efficacy, we offer Program Evaluation in the School–University–Community Beehive (Figure 13.1) as an expansion of the four-step, linear TRIP model proposed by CUME (Smith & Helfeinbein, 2009, p. 93) and an artifact of our team's conversations and shared envisioning forward. The model also represents our strategic intentions, which brown (2017) described as a "north star" or

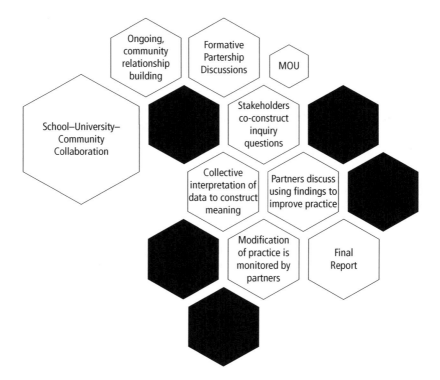

Figure 13.1   Program evaluation in the school–university–community beehive.

Emergent Program Evaluation (Post) COVID-19 • **297**

imperfect, fluid map that might serve as a "way to adapt in real time while still holding direction" (p. 237). Looking toward nature to inspire a model of sustainability, we look toward the collective efficacy of a beehive.

In Figure 13.1, the interconnected, ordered chaos of the beehive represents our collective and connective approach to our work.[1] While honeycombs do not typically qualify as fractals, each of the individual cells builds into the honeycomb and larger beehive, in which the former may retain a similar shape. Each of the hexagonal cells represents a stage or thing in the program evaluation process; the process consists of concrete steps that often flow non-linearly downward like honey. The black hexagonal cells represent an acknowledgement of the incompleteness of this model, alluding to the aspects of program evaluation which exist beyond these identified elements.

Ongoing Community Relationship Building

The influx of grant applications available from federal and private actors to address the challenges of COVID-19 to the education system can result in organizations competing for increased, but still limited funds (brown, 2017). Instead of reproducing the competitive and individualistic practices which often feed into the very problems we seek to address, we envision program evaluation as work that listens for and creates opportunities for purposeful collaboration and recognizes a diversity of resources as potential community assets. This requires our team to focus on critical connections, prioritizing the relationships we are building over winning larger grants or having greater visibility, more money, or more projects/partnerships.

The mission of our work at CPECE is to advocate for public education by informing others on issues that impact students, educators, schools, and communities. We study, support, and strive to strengthen public education by building partnerships, engaging in a variety of initiatives, and promoting research. We acknowledge education as a civil and human right as well as a public good and put resources into the community to help high school students find their path to college. CPECE builds collaborative partnerships, engages in a variety of initiatives, and disseminates research on current topics relevant to education and schooling.

The TRIP model centers ethics in program evaluation by positioning the role of the urban university as a part of the surrounding community, conferring upon the institution a duty to leverage its resources as an "engine of knowledge" for the benefit of the greater community (Smith & Helfenbein, 2009, p. 100). The TRIP model requires that researchers gather essential knowledge of community stakeholders as collaborators as well as an understanding of the inner workings of their organizations. Through this reciprocal evaluative process, researchers thereby seek long-lasting relationships with community organizations that extend beyond a one-and-done/extractive approach to evaluation research.

Promoting an ethical foundation in this type of community-based work, as well as transparency in our values and intentions, our work is currently grounded in the four core commitments of the TRIP model: commitment to learning, commitment to people, commitment to teaching, and commitment to work (Smith & Helfenbein, 2009). The first of these, a commitment to learning, relates to our team's capacity for listening to foster reflection, reflexivity, and communicative understanding in key conversations with community partners. Our commitment(s) to people, as individuals and as members of the community as a whole, drives our purposes toward social advocacy in determining both the projects we undertake and with whom we collaborate. Our commitment to teaching refers to our internal, ongoing process of professional development and communication with graduate assistants and staff on the nature and processes of our work. Finally, our commitment to work is a commitment to work *through* the ongoing challenges to doing this type of work, including both practical elements and complex ethical dimensions of community collaboration by utilizing emergent and responsive research methodologies that seek to retain the rich complexities expressed in our qualitative findings.

Patti Lather (1993) described Deridian rigor/rhizomatic validity as research which can "act via relay, circuit, multiple openings, as 'crabgrass in the lawn of academic preconceptions'" (p. 680). This approach resonates with the emergent strategy of biomimicry as it constructs truth as non-linear and understands relationships within intersecting networks with key nodes, which are hard to pin down. In our program evaluation work with/in school–university–community collaborations, we aim to build a rhizomatic network of partnerships, characterized by "interdependence" and mutually beneficial strategies, as well as "decentralized innovation and leadership" (brown, 2017, p. 98).

Formative Discussions of Partnership

Community stakeholders seeking to facilitate community recovery through strategic interventions have the responsibility to acknowledge the complex and emergent nature of the pandemic; they should design flexible and adaptive programmatic structures that incorporate ongoing evaluation elements and respond to new information relevant to the program design (see Valters et al., 2016). This strategic adaptability has potential for what Lather (2016) refers to as a "cockroach theory of social change" in which

Emergent Program Evaluation (Post) COVID-19 • **299**

a "blueprint for change is gradually produced" by incremental subversive iterations (p. 127).

Promising institutional partners, whether nonprofits, foundations, coalitions, or schools, tend to operate within a general sense of urgency. They are passionate about their mission and impatient for a better future world, as are we. However, many individuals and organizations that seek social change tend to burn themselves out through unregulated impatience that rushes to solutions, especially those who are early in their work. We are not immune from this tendency and must remind ourselves, each other, and our partners that if solutions to complex social problems were simple, they would have already been solved. We aim to cultivate a strategic type of impatience in our work which acknowledges urgency without sacrificing intentionality.

We are seeking partners who are open to such strategic impatience and are open to a more emergent and adaptive evaluative process, capable of fostering deeper understandings, authenticity, and community/connective dialogue. Taking the time to build relationships with each other and together allow the work to be an evaluative process rather than an "evaluation" or the final product/report.

The integration of emergent strategies into program evaluation work requires a more relational and reflexive approach to partnerships and teams, methods that center adaptability and contextualized ethics rather than global generalizability and project timelines that make space for ethical methodologies and the emergence of rich and complex findings. As CUME learned in the early years of the center, the funding context of doing program evaluation and the exciting nature of the work can easily slip into "responding, more often than internationally planning, the direction of the work" (Smith & Helfenbein, 2009, p. 96). brown (2017) invites us to practice mindfulness and intentionality in our work; when our partnerships and practices no longer align with our core values and mission, we must be willing to reinvest our attention elsewhere and question our overall research processes, from research design, to data collection, to analysis and report writing.

Importantly, formative conversations of partnership, whether formal or informal, should be regularly communicated throughout the evaluative team. To facilitate meaningful, collective reflection and shared visioning within our own team, we intend to make space at least once a semester for loosely structured self-assessment sessions. Using tools from brown's (2017) "emergent strategy journal" as a point of departure, we intend for these internal, dialogic spaces to assess our "embodiment of emergent strategy at this moment" (pp. 184–190), relating focal topics such as adaptability, interdependence, and resilience to our work as it relates to internal process, network-building practices, methodological choices, and ongoing partnerships. Our hope is for these self-assessment sessions to facilitate an ongoing practice of reflexive accountability to our commitments and expand the

300 • N. WEINBERG et al.

possibilities of our work and vision for moving forward by dedicating time and space for "holding up the mirror to the work" as we seek a deeper understanding of the essential elements of emergent strategy (Smith & Helfenbein, 2009, p. 97).

In addition to these internal, self-assessment sessions, we plan to make time and space for formative and ongoing conversations with current and/or potential partners, drawing inspiration from the topics and activities identified in brown's (2017) emergent strategy facilitation guide (pp. 217–270). The extent to which partnerships are in service of our commitments, as well as those of the partner, will be considered on an ongoing basis. Rather than a stagnant representation of the plan forward, we frame the memorandum of understanding (MOU) as an artifact of the shared understandings developed through our early conversations with partners and initial vision for the project. Co-creation of the MOU fosters liberated partnerships through radical honesty that acknowledges the desires, boundaries, and responsibilities of both organizations and opens possibilities for co-evolution in working through the work on a shared foundation.

Stakeholders Invited to Co-Construct Inquiry Questions via Connective Dialogue

As we seek deep understanding of the nature of processes of oppression, the emergent approach to ethics proposed by Barad (2006) suggests that the oppressor, as well as the oppressed, are inherently co-constituted. Understanding the co-constitution of matter, education becomes, what Barros (2020) described as a humanization that "rests on a view of pedagogy that is anthropologically and ethically grounded in people as part of Creation's autopoiesis," adopting an interpretation of critical consciousness in which teaching is an act of searching for new social orders which "are able to reproduce and sustain themselves adaptively" (p. 163).

Freire (1974) posed dialogue as a "relationship between two subjects" (p. 45); if the subjects are not two separate elements but inherently co-constituted in each other, then dialogue is not an exchange between them. Rather, it is a creative act in which knowledge is produced, intra-acting with matter far beyond the subjects themselves and extending the intentions of love and understanding into the world. This connective dialogue is central to not only partner relationships but must first be present in our own team's daily practices.

Honesty and Trust

For translational research to emerge, collaboration must start within our own team and be predicated on a level of honesty and trust which is uncommon in school–university–community collaborations, utilizing shared decision-making strategies and co-constructing the objects and methods of inquiry at every step of the process. Smith and Helfenbein (2009) noted that building trust is no small feat, and they urged researchers to carefully consider the culture of distrust that often exists between schools and university researchers. We recognize the necessity for and the legitimacy of distrust in the communities with violent histories of settler colonialism. Our own present positionality cannot be separated from the contexts in which academic institutions, including our own, have historically marginalized populations, utilized violent and extractive research methods, and which continue to cause great systemic harm to Black and indigenous people of color in our community today. Not only does our positionality within a high-resource, private, predominately White institution mean that this trust must be earned, but we understand that our center does not have an inherent right to attain this trust. Radical honesty acknowledges the dynamics at play between organizations and lets "the relationship build inside all that reality" (brown, 2017, p. 143).

Listening and Humility

In doing this work as it relates to our positionality, we approach the task of emancipatory work "hesitantly and with humility" (Mohanty, 2003, p. 499), understanding that we do not "live simply under the gaze of Western eyes" but "also live inside it and negotiate it every day" (p. 530). Radical honesty is a willingness to be vulnerable through the uncertainty and shifting dynamics of power. Our approach of utilizing the TRIP model as one of the possible approaches to further dialogue in school–university–community collaborations is an acknowledgement that there are other ways of conducting program evaluation. As a practice in humility, this requires all stakeholders, especially our own team, to be willing to remain reflexive and responsive to critique at every stage in the process, holding ourselves accountable to recommitting over and over to the community-centered purpose of the work (brown, 2017).

Collective Interpretation of Data to Construct Meaning

Looking towards that which is not yet, we imagine our work as "making an impact" and overcoming "ignorance that perpetuates suffering." We imagine being "the one who knows" (Sedgwick, 2008), revealing inequity towards accomplishing some degree of social change. This begins with an effort of subversion and humility in which we are considering our program evaluation efforts, which are necessarily rooted in qualitative methodologies, as ruins. As the funding landscape for education programming becomes somewhat of a mega-audit culture, the "recharged positivism" of neoliberal-technocratic hegemony results in the disciplining or instrumentalism of qualitative research (Lather, 2013, p. 636). As a result, ethical concerns are often neglected after approval by the institutional review board, leading to aporias of representation and interpretation. Considering program evaluation as ruins draws upon Lather's logic of aporia, "reframing the victor narratives of empirical impact as a sort of self-wounding laboratory for discovering the rules by which truth is produced" or transparently non-innocent space (Lather, 2018, p. 246).

Through clashing/mirroring American discourses of qualitative inquiry with those "trained in the ruins of the empire" of program evaluation, we hope to make possible what Lather (2012) referred to as an "engaged social science" working "towards the something to come that is already at work, incalculable" (p. 1024). Through intentionally transgressing certain norms in evaluative practice, such as the premeditated nature of traditional research designs, new ways to engage in dialogue about educational programming might provide fertile ground for emerging meta-methods and systems of social relations to imagine forward towards a becoming (re)constructions of qualitative research and program evaluation.

In our qualitative research, data analysis is often an emergent process which is customized, revised, and choreographed (Miles et al., 2013). We rely on data collection principles that promote diversity, strive for equity, and practice inclusivity while recognizing the instability and limiting nature of identities. If we are to, as Lather (2008) suggested, embrace the complexity and uncertainty of identities as qualitative researchers, we must commit to "tracing the assemblages," or the situated contexts, "in which these categories gain a momentary hold" (Tsing, 2015, p. 29). In negotiating the ethical dilemmas and methodological nuances of qualitative research, we continue to seek out and learn from unique qualitative methodologies that approach rupture through attempts to explore rather than reconcile differences (Adair & Pastori, 2011; Fothergill & Peck, 2015; Lather, 1993; Lather, 2018).

Partners Discuss Ways to Use Findings to Improve Practice

In the context of a society in transition, program evaluation plays an important role in "distinguishing clearly which elements truly belonged to the transition and which were simply present in it" (Freire, 1974, p. 7). The impacts of the pandemic are situated, embedded, and voluptuous where you can't see where one issue ends and the other begins, a tapestry of interwoven issues. The challenges currently facing practitioners in education represent what Pietrocola et al. (2020) described as "wicked problems"

Emergent Program Evaluation (Post) COVID-19 • **303**

since they "not only lack solutions *a priori*" but potential interventions that have seen some perceived success in other contexts "may no longer be acceptable in further moments" (p. 18). As such, translating or comparing program evaluations across contexts can be problematic.

While we might see some similarities in our educational response to the COVID-19 pandemic to previous disasters such as Hurricane Katrina, the evaluations of previous interventions must be considered as having broad, national implications rather than certain solutions to challenges facing our current, local context. Instead, emergency relief efforts such as Hurricane Katrina might draw our attention to overarching, historic patterns where influxes of federal funding have not responded to the needs of communities of color (Buras, 2020). Researchers should cautiously consider evaluations of policy or interventions and not assume that reforms implemented to address other disasters or contexts would naturally be successful in the current context (Phillips & Schweisfurth, 2014). Program evaluation might begin to organize a few problem areas in schools during the pandemic in terms of complexity to help inform the actions and priorities of our partners going forward.

Modification of Practice Is Monitored by Partners

In Figure 13.1, the cell representing the final report shares a border with the ongoing modification and monitoring of practice because this work does not "end at the conclusion of studies or funding cycles, indeed they are often merely the beginning" (Smith & Helfenbein, 2009, p. 101). The honeycomb thus becomes situated within the beehive as one process of program evaluation flows into the next.

The beehive is not an example of individualistic, linear organizing, but rather a seemingly chaotic network of collective action toward shared survival. While the fractal nature of the beehive metaphor represents how small, iterative actions contribute to larger societal change, it is not an affirmation of neoliberal scalability in which what works in one context can be uprooted and replanted into a foreign soil. On the contrary, the beehive might represent what Tsing (2015) termed a "theory of nonscalability" that is rhizomatic in nature, adapting to interruptions in the underlying assumptions, situating itself within, and allowing for interruptions to the framework, a method in which the "research object is contaminated diversity" and the "unit of analysis is the indeterminate encounter" (p. 37). The beehive is a reminder that it is not what we are doing in our work, but rather how we go about doing the work that will either work toward or against a more just future. Thus, we plan to proceed through continually re-committing to our mission and envisioning forward by working through contradictions, contamination, and complexity.

CONCLUSION

The emergent (post) COVID-19 context of education has contributed to our collective imagination of our shared future, both in terms of apocalyptic inequality and disconnection as well as a renewal of hope in the "extraordinary human resources and potential" in our schools (da Silva Vieira & Barbosa, 2020, p. 27). Addressing the impact of the COVID-19 pandemic is an enormous task and responsibility, but we cannot continue to use the same compensatory strategies born of the individualistic, linear thinking which created the conditions for the current crisis. We cannot leave schools—their leaders, teachers, families, and students—alone in the recovery from a global crisis and burdened with unsustainable expectations and practices; rather, envisioning the emergent (post) COVID-19 context should be—and is always already—a collaborative effort in which all stakeholders come together. Rather than the top–down organizing of the past which has continuously proved unproductive, we view program evaluation as a critical node in the rhizomatic network of community listening, imagining, and creating compelling futures together. As we embrace adaptivity and complexity, we hope that our community can continue to co-evolve toward an "interdependence of lots of kinds of people with lots of belief systems," a purposeful, "continued evolution" (brown, 2017, p. 57).

For those who are skeptical such relations can exist in the context of our work with/in school–university–community collaborations, we too consider such an aim as other-worldly in the contexts of our lived realities; and yet, we reject the notion that generative relationships between education researchers and the broader community exist only within science fiction. Envisioning a world that we have yet to experience requires a strategic and intentional approach, as well as a regenerative supply of imagination and, most importantly, hope.

NOTE

1. Much has been retained in this visual model from the TRIP model proposed by CUME, in which the original four stages were (a) "faculty are invited to co-construct inquiry questions," (b) "data are shared with school partners; collective interpretation for meaning," (c) "partners discuss ways to use findings to improve practice," and (d) "modification of practice is monitored by partners" (Smith & Helfenbein, 2009, p. 93). Our expansion of this work includes a few small changes in language; for example, we replace the term

"faculty" with "stakeholders" in anticipation of the diverse partnerships we may encounter. In addition, we have added some elements mentioned in the text but not present in their visuals such as "ongoing, community relationship building," the memorandum of understanding (MOU), and the final report.

REFERENCES

Adair, J. K., & Pastori, G. (2011). Developing qualitative coding frameworks for educational research: Immigration, education and the Children Crossing Borders project. *International Journal of Research & Method in Education, 34*(1), 31–47. https://doi.org/10.1080/1743727X.2011.552310

Anyon, J. (2005). *Radical possibilities: Public policy, urban education, and a new social movement.* Routledge.

Apple, M. W. (2013). Controlling the work of teachers. In D. J. Flinders & S. J. Thornton (Eds.), *The curriculum studies reader* (4th ed., pp. 167–181). Routledge.

Bacher-Hicks, A., Goodman, J., & Mulhern, C. (2020). *Inequality in household adaptation to schooling shocks: Covid-induced online learning engagement in real time* (Working Paper 27555). National Bureau of Economic Research. http://www.nber.org/papers/w27555

Barad, K. M. (2006). *Meeting the universe halfway: Quantum physics and the entanglement of matter and meaning.* Duke University Press.

Barros, S. (2020). Paulo Freire in a hall of mirrors. *Educational Theory, 70*(2), 151–169. https://doi.org/10.1111/edth.12413

Basch, C. E. (2011). Healthier students are better learners: A missing link in school reforms to close the achievement gap. *Journal of School Health, 81*(10), 593–598. https://doi.org/doi:10.1111/j.1746-1561.2011.00632.x

brown, a. m. (2017). *Emergent strategy: Shaping change, changing worlds.* AK Press.

Bryant, E., Weinberg, N., Huddleston, G., & Weinburgh, M. (2022). *Impact of the COVID-19 pandemic on education in Tarrant County: Preliminary analysis and recommendations* [Unpublished manuscript]. The Center for Public Education and Community Engagement (CPECE) at Texas Christian University.

Buras, K. L. (2020). *From Katrina to COVID-19: How disaster, federal neglect, and the market compound racial inequities.* National Education Policy Center. https://nepc.colorado.edu/sites/default/files/publications/PM%20Buras.pdf

Community Science. (2022). *Doing evaluation in service of racial equity: Diagnose biases and systems.* W. K. Kellogg Foundation. https://communityscience.com/?wpdmdl=7443

da Silva Vieira, M., & Barbosa, S. M. (2020). School culture and innovation: Does the post-pandemic world COVID-19 invite to transition or to rupture? *European Journal of Social Science Education and Research, 7*(2), 23–34. https://doi.org/10.26417/922sju94c

Dryfoos, J. (2000, March). The mind-body building equation. *Educational Leadership, 57*(6). https://cccoi.org/i/u/2043019/i/JoyDryfoos_Healthy_Minds_and_Buildings.doc

Dryfoos, J., & Maguire, S. (2019). *Inside full-service community schools.* Simon & Schuster.

Felitti, V. J., Anda, R. F., Nordenberg, D., Williamson, D. F., Spitz, A. M., Edwards, V., & Marks, J. S. (1998). Relationship of childhood abuse and household dysfunction to many of the leading causes of death in adults: The adverse childhood experiences (ACE) study. *American Journal of Preventive Medicine, 14*(4), 245–258. https://doi.org/10.1016/s0749-3797(98)00017-8

Fothergill, A., & Peek, L. (2015). *Children of Katrina* (1st ed.). University of Texas Press.

Freire, P. (1974). *Education for critical consciousness.* Continuum.

García, E., & Weiss, E. (2019, March 26). *The teacher shortage is real, large and growing, and worse than we thought: The first report in 'The Perfect Storm in the Teacher Labor Market' series.* Economic Policy Institute. https://www.epi.org/publication/the-teacher-shortage-is-real-large-and-growing-and-worse-than-we-thought-the-first-report-in-the-perfect-storm-in-the-teacher-labor-market-series/

GBAO Strategies. (2022). *Poll results: Stress and burnout pose threat of educator shortages.* National Education Association. https://www.nea.org/sites/default/files/2022-02/NEA%20Member%20COVID-19%20Survey%20Summary.pdf

Giroux, H. A. (2010). Dumbing down teachers: Rethinking the crisis of public education and the demise of the social state. *The Review of Education, Pedagogy, and Cultural Studies, 32*(4–5), 339–381. https://doi.org/10.1080/10714413.2010.510346

Hall, S., Massey, D., & Rustin, M. (2015). *After neoliberalism? The Kilburn Manifesto.* Lawrence Wishart.

Henderson, A. T., Averett, A., Donnelly, D., Jordan, C., Orozco, E., Buttram, J., & Wood, L. (2002). *A new wave of evidence: The impact of school, family, and community connections on student achievement. Annual synthesis, 2002.* National Center for Family & Community Connections With Schools. https://eric.ed.gov/?id=ED474521

Henderson, A. T., Mapp, K. L., Johnson, V. R., & Davies, D. (2007). *Beyond the bake sale: The essential guide to family–school partnerships.* The New Press.

Huckaby, M. F. (2019). *Researching resistance: Public education after neoliberalism* (Vol. 5). Myers Education Press.

Huddleston, G. (2022). Cultivating whiteness: How White supremacy continues to matter in qualitative research. *International Review of Qualitative Research, 14*(4), 649–668. https://doi.org/10.1177/19408447211049515

Jaeger, M. M., & Blaabaek, E. H. (2020). Inequality in learning opportunities during Covid-19: Evidence from library takeout. *Research in Social Stratification and Mobility, 68,* 100524. https://doi.org/10.1016/j.rssm.2020.100524

Lather, P. (1991). *Getting smart: Feminist research and pedagogy with/in the postmodern.* Routledge. https://doi.org/10.4324/9780203451311

Lather, P. (1993). Fertile obsession: Validity after poststructuralism. *Sociological Quarterly, 34*(4), 673–693. https://doi.org/10.1111/j.1533-8525.1993.tb00112.x

Lather, P. (2004). This is your Father's Paradigm: Government intrusion and the case of qualitative research in education. *Qualitative Inquiry, 10*(1), 15–34. https://doi.org/10.1177/1077800403256154

Lather, P. (2008). (Post)Feminist methodology: Getting lost OR a scientificity we can bear to learn from. *International Review of Qualitative Research, 1*(1), 55–64. https://doi.org/10.1525/irqr.2008.1.1.55

Lather, P. (2012). The ruins of neo-liberalism and the construction of a new (scientific) subjectivity. *Cultural Studies of Science Education, 7*(4), 1021–1025. https://doi.org/10.1007/s11422-012-9465-4

Lather, P. (2013). Methodology-21: What do we do in the afterward? *International Journal of Qualitative Studies in Education, 26*(6), 634–645. https://doi.org/10.1080/09518398.2013.788753

Lather, P. (2016). Top ten+ list: (Re)thinking ontology in (post)qualitative research. *Cultural Studies & Critical Methodologies, 16*(2), 125–131. https://doi.org/10.1177/1532708616634734

Lather, P. (2018). Postmodernism, post-structuralism and post(critical) ethnography: Of ruins, aporias and angels (2001). In *(Post)critical methodologies: The science possible after the critiques: The selected works of Patti Lather* (pp. 239–260). Routledge.

Miles, M. B., Huberman, A. M., & Saldaña, J. (2013). *Qualitative data analysis: A methods sourcebook* (3rd ed.). SAGE.

Mohanty, C. T. (2003). "Under Western eyes" revisited: Feminist solidarity through anticapitalist struggles. *Signs: Journal of Women in Culture and Society, 28*(2), 499–535. https://doi.org/10.1086/342914

Noddings, N. (2001). Care and coercion in school reform. *Journal of Educational Change, 2*(1), 35–43. https://doi.org/10.1023/A:1011514928048

Noddings, N. (2007). *When school reform goes wrong.* Teachers College Press.

Pattison, H. D. (2022). Lessons from lockdown: Could pandemic schooling help change education? *Pedagogy, Culture & Society,* 1–22. https://doi.org/10.1080/14681366.2022.2026455

Phillips, D., & Schweisfurth, M. (2014). *Comparative and international education: An introduction to theory, method and practice.* Bloomsbury.

Pietrocola, M., Rodrigues, E., Bercot, F., & Schnorr, S. (2020). Risk society and science education: Lessons from the Covid-19 pandemic. *Science & Education, 30*(2), 209–233. https://doi.org/10.1007/s11191-020-00176-w

Ravitch, D. (2010). *The death and life of the great American school system: How testing and choice are undermining education.* Basic Books.

Sato, G., Kumar, S., Coffman, S., Saronson, B., Webster, R., Gulliver-Garcia, T., Moore, K., & Entcheva, R. (2020). *Philanthropy and COVID-19 in the first half of 2020.* Candid & Center for Disaster Philanthropy. http://doi.org/10/gg72df

Sayer, P., & Braun, D. (2020). The disparate impact of COVID-19 remote learning on English learners in the United States. *TESOL Journal, 11*(3), e00546. https://doi.org/10.1002/tesj.546

Scott, I. (2020). Education during COVID-19: Pivots and consequences. *The Clinical Teacher, 17*(4), 443–444. https://doi.org/10.1111/tct.13225

Sedgwick, E. K. (2008). *Epistemology of the closet.* University of California Press.

Smith, J. S., & Helfenbein, R. J., Jr. (2009). Translational research in education: Collaboration & commitment in urban contexts. In W. Gershon (Ed.), *The collaborative turn; Working together in qualitative research* (pp. 89–102). Brill Sense.

Tsing, A. L. (2015). *The mushroom at the end of the world: On the possibility of life in capitalist ruins.* Princeton University Press.

U.S. Department of Education. (2022, January 18). *U.S. Department of Education announces distribution of all American Rescue Plan ESSER funds and approval of all 52 state education agency plans* [Press release]. https://www.ed.gov/news/press-releases/us-department-education-announces-distribution-all-american-rescue-plan-esser-funds-and-approval-all-52-state-education-agency-plans

Valters, C., Cummings, C., & Nixon, H. (2016, March). *Putting learning at the centre: Adaptive development programming in practice.* Overseas Development Institute. https://cdn.odi.org/media/documents/10401.pdf

Verlenden, J. V., Pampati, S., Rasberry, C. N., Liddon, N., Hertz, M., Kilmer, G., & Barrios, L. C. (2021). Association of children's mode of school instruction with child and parent experiences and well-being during the COVID-19 pandemic. *Morbidity and Mortality Weekly Report, 70*(11), 369–376. https://doi.org/10.15585/mmwr.mm7011a1

Weinburgh, M., Anderson, S., Bryant, E., Ezzani, M., Hernandez, F., Huddleston, G., Lacina, J., & Roach, W. (2021). *Non-profit organization serving families and youth during the Covid-19 pandemic: Impacts and recommendations* [Unpublished manuscript]. The Center for Public Education and Community Engagement (CPECE) at Texas Christian University.

ABOUT THE EDITORS

R. Martin Reardon (PhD, Educational Policy Planning and Leadership, The College of William and Mary in Virginia, 2000) is associate professor in the Educational Leadership Department of the College of Education at East Carolina University (ECU), Greenville, NC. His instructional contributions to the Educational Leadership Department focus on teaching academic writing and mixed methods approaches to research in the context of the problem-of-practice-oriented education doctorate program.

Reardon oversaw the 2017 implementation of a recently completed $1,000,000, 5-year National Science Foundation grant to integrate computational thinking with the teaching of music and visual arts in middle schools in three rural counties in North Carolina. Since 2018, he has also served as an affiliate faculty member of the Rural Education Institute within the College of Education.

Stemming from his then 6 years as chair of the School–University–Community Collaborative Research (SUCCR) Special Interest Group (SIG) of the American Educational Research Association (AERA), Reardon co-edited a book in 2016 with two former leaders of the SUCCR SIG that extended an earlier model of school–university collaboration to incorporate the vital role of the community. Subsequently, beginning in 2017, he embarked on an in-depth exploration of the SUCCR theme as the lead editor in an ongoing series—Current Perspectives on School–University–Community Research. The most recent of the prior eight volumes in the series was titled *School–University–Community Collaboration for Civic Education and Engagement in the Democratic Project* (Information Age Publishing, 2022).

School–University–Community Research in a (Post) COVID-19 World, pages 309–310
Copyright © 2023 by Information Age Publishing
www.infoagepub.com
All rights of reproduction in any form reserved.

310 ▪ About the Editors

Reardon is one of four co-editors of a 60-chapter, two-volume current undertaking under the auspices of the British Educational Research Association (BERA) to publish the *BERA-SAGE International Handbook of Research-Informed Education Policy and Practice* with an anticipated publication date of 2024 (https://www.bera.ac.uk/news/the-bera-sage-international-handbook-of-research-informed-education-policy-and-practice-call-for-authors)

Jack Leonard, EdD, served the Boston Public Schools as a teacher, administrator, and then principal of an award-winning turnaround high school. After earning his EdD from Boston University in 2002, he joined the faculty at the University of Massachusetts Boston. As an associate professor in the leadership in urban schools program at UMass Boston, he directed the graduate programs and educational administration. Leonard retired from the university in 2017. His research focuses on school leadership, school partnerships, and educational history. In addition to his ongoing work with the Current Perspectives in School–University–Community Research series, he recently published two articles on a new performance assessment for principal licensure.

ABOUT THE CONTRIBUTORS

Eleanor R. Anderson (she/her) is an assistant professor of research–practice partnerships in the Department of Educational Foundations, Organizations, and Policy at the University of Pittsburgh. She joined the Pitt faculty in Fall of 2020 after earning her PhD at Northwestern University and serving as a postdoc with the National Center for Research in Policy and Practice. Prior to graduate school, she was inspired to pursue her current path by her experiences working at youth-serving nonprofits in her hometown of New York City. Her frustration with the lack of accessible, trustworthy, relevant information available to practitioners sparked an interest in the complex relationship between research and practice. Eleanor's research is motivated by a perennial problem of practice: how to make promising equity-oriented educational practices "stick." She addresses this question from multiple perspectives, drawing on conceptual tools from the learning sciences, policy implementation, and organizational science—especially institutional theory. She also uses design-based implementation research methods to collaborate with educational stakeholders seeking to implement equity-focused initiatives more sustainably. Her work has spanned both formal and informal learning environments and addressed content ranging from math and science teacher learning, to restorative justice practices, to museum education.

Elissa Bryant, MEd, is a doctoral candidate in curriculum studies at Texas Christian University. In her current work, she engages with qualitative research methodologies, critical theories, and liberatory pedagogies to fos-

---

School–University–Community Research in a (Post) COVID-19 World, pages 311–326
Copyright © 2023 by Information Age Publishing
www.infoagepub.com
All rights of reproduction in any form reserved.

312 ▪ About the Contributors

ter practices of self-care and collective conscious action through radical love and inter-religious femme spirituality. She has attained certifications in both women and gender studies (WGST) and comparative race and ethnic studies (CRES) and is passionate about cultivating spaces for diverse communities to come together, challenge their assumptions, transcend their limitations, and co-create a better world for us all.

Kayla Bullard, PhD, is an independent scholar in educational leadership who led community-based research and engagement projects at the Center for Public Education and Community Engagement (CPECE) at Texas Christian University (TCU) for several years as a graduate student. Dr. Bullard received her bachelor's in business education along with her teaching certification from the University of Nebraska at Kearney before completing her master's in instructional technology from University of Southern Mississippi. In her hometown of Freeport in the Bahamas, Dr. Bullard taught courses in business education and information technology for a number of years and assisted in the development of the IT curriculum for local schools as well as supervised new business education teachers. In both her scholarship and current work in the classroom, Dr. Bullard is a passionate advocate for culturally responsive school leadership and student agency in the classroom, especially for international and emergent bilingual and multilingual students.

Wendy Cukier, MA, MBA, PhD, LLD (hon), DU (hon), M. S. C., is a professor of entrepreneurship and strategy in the Ted Rogers School of Management at Toronto Metropolitan University (formerly known as Ryerson). As the founder of the Diversity Institute, she leads a team of 100 research staff and collaborates with scholars around the world as well as with more than 200 industry, government, and community partners. She is also the academic research director of the Future Skills Centre, the Women Entrepreneurship Knowledge Hub, and the Inclusive Innovation and Entrepreneurship Network in addition to leading other large collaborative projects. She is the author of more than 200 papers on entrepreneurship, innovation, and inclusion and has co-authored the Canadian best seller *Innovation Nation: Canadian Leadership From Java to Jurassic Park* (Wiley, 2002). In addition to several scholarly prizes, she has received numerous awards for her efforts as a changemaker including one of Canada's highest civilian honors—the Meritorious Service Cross. In 2000, the University of Toronto named her one of "100 alumni who shaped the century."

Alonzo M. Flowers III, PhD, is an associate professor in the School of Education at Drexel University. He specializes in educational issues, including academic identity development of African American and Latino males in STEM education. He also focuses on issues including diversity, teaching

About the Contributors • **313**

and learning, and college student development. Specifically, Flowers's research focuses on the academic experiences of academically gifted African American male students in the STEM disciplines and impacts the needs of underrepresented students in education. He was selected to join The Massachusetts Institute for College and Career Readiness (MICCR) at Boston University as a Senior Research Fellows program. To date, he has completed 40 peer-reviewed national conference presentations, including several presentations at the Association for the Study of Higher Education (ASHE) and American Educational Research Association (AERA). In 2014, Flowers served as one of the keynote speakers at the first annual Texas African American Males in College Achievement & Success Symposium. Flowers is also a member of the editorial board of *The Journal of Race and Policy*. Additionally, he is a reviewer for several educational journals, including *Journal of African American Males in Education* (JAAME). He authored or coauthored several book chapters and articles that focus on students of color and their academic experiences; this includes his recently published textbook *The African American Students Guide to STEM Careers* (Greenwood, 2016). Ultimately, Dr. Flowers' professional aim is to advocate for equity for all students across the educational pipeline.

Chris Fornaro, BS, MEd, is a third-year PhD candidate studying STEM education in the School of Education at Drexel University. Chris started his career as a process engineer and then transitioned to teaching as a Noyce Scholar. During his time as a teacher, he was a math, science, and STEAM teacher. His last position was at The Shipley School where he was tasked with starting the STEAM department; creating STEAM courses; and designing and managing the school's MakerSpace. Before becoming a teacher, he worked as a process engineer for approximately 3 years. He holds a BS in chemical engineering from Rutgers University and a MEd in secondary math education from Temple University. His research focuses on out-of-school time STEM programming, integrated STEM teaching, and self-efficacy of STEM instructors.

Patrice Forrester, PhD, is a licensed independent clinical social worker. She received her PhD in social work from the University of Maryland, Baltimore in 2021. She also has a master's in social work. Prior to obtaining her PhD degree, she served as a youth director at a church-based youth program. She also provided mental health services to children, teenagers, and adults affected by psychological trauma, HIV/AIDS, and chronic mental illness in community-based mental health programs. During her time in the PhD program, she worked on quantitative and qualitative research projects exploring social service provisions and child and adolescent well-being. Her dissertation study explored how youth development workers build and maintain relationships with older adolescents (14–17 years) and emerging

314 · About the Contributors

adults (18–29 years). Patrice's research interests are in positive youth development, including youth development workers and community-based youth programs that promote the healthy development of older adolescents and emerging adults.

Donna Fradley, BES, BEd, is an accomplished educator and administrator. She has extensive experience working to strengthen and advance reconciliation initiatives and decolonizing practices within educational institutions. Her areas of expertise are First Nations education and gender studies. She currently works as a research assistant with the Toronto Metropolitan University's Diversity Institute. Donna holds a BES and a BEd and is currently pursuing an MEd at the Ontario Institute for Studies in Education at the University of Toronto.

Hobart L. Harmon, PhD, is a leading expert on public education in rural America and leader of Strategic Advancement at Intermediate Unit 8 in Altoona, PA. He holds a courtesy appointment as a senior research associate in the Department of Educational Leadership at Kansas State University. A former director of two investing in innovation (i3) projects ($6 million) funded by the U.S. Department of Education and deputy director of a NSF Rural Systemic Initiative ($10 million), previous positions held by Dr. Harmon include executive assistant to the state superintendent of schools, high school agriculture teacher, university visiting professor, Regional Educational Laboratory R&D specialist, ERIC Clearinghouse on Rural Education and Small Schools' interim director, and state Rural Development Council vice-chair. Additional appointments include adjunct associate professor of educational leadership at Penn State University, with affiliation in the Center on Rural Education and Communities, and as a graduate faculty scholar in the College of Graduate Studies at the University of Central Florida. Harmon is a two-time recipient of the National Rural Education Association's Stanley A. Brzezinski Memorial Rural Education Research Award. Author of numerous rural education articles, Harmon serves on the editorial board of *The Rural Educator* and as a reviewer for the *Journal of Research in Rural Education.* Dr. Harmon holds PhD and master's degrees (The Pennsylvania State University), a Master of Science degree (The Ohio State University), a Bachelor of Science degree (West Virginia University [magna cum laude], and an associate degree from Potomac State College of West Virginia University.

Theresa Harrison, MS, MPA, is the project manager for the Carolina Family Engagement Center (CFEC). The work of CFEC is focused primarily on underserved families and their students (low income, English learners, those with disabilities, those in foster care, migrants, homeless, and marginalized communities). In this role, she has had the opportunity to serve as a co-PI on a research project "Examining Black–White Disparities

About the Contributors • **315**

and Identifying Empowerment Solutions Among Custodial Grandparent-Headed Families During COVID-19 in South Carolina: A Mixed-Methods Community-Based Study." Theresa has worked at the University of South Carolina (UofSC) since 2011 in various administrative roles within community service and service-learning programs, residence life, and integrative and experiential learning. She is also a doctoral student in the Educational Foundations and Inquiry program at UofSC and a scholar in the Grace Jordan McFadden Professors program. Her research interests include community–university relationships and partnerships, critical race and decolonizing pedagogies, and abolition studies. She is an active member of professional organizations such as the National Society for Experiential Education and the International Association for Research on Service-Learning and Community Engagement.

Gabriel Huddleston, PhD, Huddleston is an associate professor of curriculum studies, director of the Center for Public Education and Community Engagement and chair of the Counseling, Social, and Inquiry Department at Texas Christian University. He is also core faculty with both the Women and Gender Studies and Comparative Race and Ethnic Studies departments. He teaches classes in curriculum studies and qualitative inquiry. His work in curriculum studies utilizes a cultural studies theoretical framework within qualitative research to examine intersections between schools and society broadly and, more specifically, relationship between neoliberal education reform and teachers. His other research interests include popular culture, spatial theory, new materialism, and postcolonial studies. He has publications in several journals, including *Taboo: The Journal of Culture and Education*; the *Journal of Curriculum and Pedagogy*; the *Review of Education, Pedagogy, and Cultural Studies*; *Critical Literacy: Theories and Practices*; and the *Currere Exchange Journal*. He served as managing editor of the *Journal of Curriculum Theorizing* (JCT) from 2013–2018. During this time, he was also the program chair and co-organizer for JCT's annual conference: the Bergamo Conference on Curriculum Theory and Classroom Practice. Gabriel has also served as the chair for the Critical Issues in Curriculum Studies and Cultural Studies Special Interest Group of the American Educational Research Association.

Detra D. Johnson, PhD, is an assistant professor in the Department of Educational Leadership and Policy Studies at the University of Houston (Texas). With over 15 years of experience as a K–12 practitioner, her experience includes being a classroom teacher, a campus administrator, a district administrator, and an educational consultant for Region 4 Educational Service Center (a statewide educational support center for school staff, teachers, and administrators). She also served in rural, suburban, and urban school districts in multiple educational capacities. Her higher education experi-

316 ▪ About the Contributors

ences include the development and training of teachers as an alternative teacher certification coordinator, adjunct math professor, and tenure track faculty member in educational leadership and policy studies. Detra's teaching earned her a national award—Social Justice Teaching Excellence Award in Education Administration—from the Leadership for Social Justice (SIG) with AERA. Her research agenda focuses on educational leadership, policies, politics, programs, and practices based on systemic and structural issues of equity, race, and social justice that intersect with disparities among marginalized, underrepresented, and diverse groups of people in K–12 educational systems. Dr. Johnson's service records include both national and international levels as well as university, college, department, and program commitments. More so, Detra has served as the AERA Division A secretary, the AERA Research on Women in Education (RWE) SIG chair and Diversity Task Force co-chair, and as her university's UCEA plenum representative. Dr. Johnson has also served on both AERA Division A Planning Convention Planning and UCEA Conference Planning Committees.

Jerry D. Johnson, EdD, is the Phoebe Moore Dail distinguished professor in Rural Education at East Carolina University. He holds a BA in political science from Eastern Kentucky University, an MA in English literature from Eastern Kentucky University, and an EdD in educational administration from Ohio University. A former English teacher and high school principal, Johnson has taught in educational leadership programs for 16 years and served from 2003–2008 as policy research director for the Rural School and Community Trust, a national nonprofit organization addressing the crucial relationship between good schools and thriving communities. The 2017 recipient of the Stanley A. Brzezinski Memorial Rural Education Research Award from the National Rural Education Association, he is the author of more than 60 publications on rural education policy, school-based leadership, and place-based learning. Johnson's research has been supported by external funding from the U.S. Department of Education's Institute for Education Sciences and Office of English Language Acquisition, state departments of education, private foundations, and local school districts. Current leadership roles in professional organizations include serving as associate editor of the *Journal of Research in Rural Education*, advisory board member for the Center for Community Schools, and editorial advisor to the journal *Education Leadership Review*–doctoral research.

Stefan Karajovic, MIRHR, BComm, is a researcher and educator in the areas of organizational behavior and workplace diversity. Stefan has a decade of experience working as a teaching assistant, lecturer, researcher, and business partner in both the public and private sectors. Stefan is currently a PhD candidate at York University. He also holds a Master of Industrial Rela-

About the Contributors • **317**

tions and Human Resources degree from the University of Toronto and a Bachelor of Commerce degree from Toronto Metropolitan University.

Gina M. Kunz, PhD, is an independent consultant and a licensed psychologist. She received her PhD in psychology at Louisiana State University with school psychology as her program of study. She conducts large-scale research to identify evidence-based practices for children, families, and teachers. She has secured more than $25 million as PI/co-PI in federal funding. She was co-PI for the National Center for Research on Rural Education. She is project co-director for two current grant-funded projects housed in the University of South Carolina: "Carolina Family Engagement Center (CFEC)," a 5-year, $5 million grant funded by the U.S. Department of Education, and "The South Carolina Teacher Education Advancement Consortium through Higher Education Research (SC-TEACHER)," funded through the South Carolina Commission on Higher Education. She has held faculty positions at the University of Nebraska Medical Center, Louisiana State University Health Sciences Center, University of Nebraska-Lincoln, and University of South Carolina. Her areas of expertise include behavior management for children and adolescents with behavioral and social-emotional challenges and attention deficits, academic assessment and intervention for children and adolescents with academic challenges, professional development and instructional coaching for adults who teach and support children and strengthen home–school partnerships. She also has provided behavioral health services as a licensed psychologist through private practice. As an independent consultant, she provides consultation for faculty development in grantsmanship. She also provides academic intervention and enrichment supports through private services for students with a wide range of needs from challenged to gifted and from early grade levels through college.

Kimberly Lee is a parent of two youth with disabilities and a parent advocate in private practice who provides advocacy to Chinese families of students with disabilities. She helps families understand the U.S. special education process and their parental rights and provides them with information and resources about how to seek available support and services that are appropriate for their children with disabilities.

Sue Levkoff, ScD, is a professor in the College of Social Work and endowed chair in SeniorSMART, a SmartState Center of Economic Excellence. Prior to joining the University of South Carolina in 2010, Levkoff was associate professor in the Harvard Medical School Department of Psychiatry at Brigham and Women's Hospital. She continues to hold an appointment as part-time lecturer in the Harvard Medical School Department of Global Health and Social Medicine. She currently serves as associate editor for

318 • About the Contributors

both the *International Journal of Gerontechnology* and *Frontiers in Public Health and Health Promotion*. Currently, Dr. Levkoff is serving as a topic editor for a special journal issue of *Frontiers in Public Health* entitled, "Technological Innovations to Address Social Isolation and Loneliness in Older Adults." She was a 2019 inductee as a fellow into the American Academy of Social Work and Social Welfare's Society for Social Work and Research.

Ashlee Lewis, PhD, is a research associate professor in the REM Center at UofSC. Dr. Lewis holds a PhD in foundations of education and an MEd in educational research—both from the University of South Carolina. Dr. Lewis is the lead evaluator of UofSC's teacher induction program, and she also has served as lead evaluator for the U.S. Department of Education and National Science Foundation grants. Dr. Lewis's work regularly places her in contact with the daily routines and inner workings of schools in South Carolina. Her work has provided her with many opportunities to interact extensively with teachers, instructional specialists, principals, and district administrators, and she highly values the opportunity to partner with school personnel and other stakeholders on research and evaluation efforts.

Lusa Lo, EdD, is faculty member at the University of Massachusetts Boston. Her research focuses on family–school–community partnerships and educational planning and practice for English learners with and without disabilities at PreK–12 levels. Dr. Lo trains pre- and in-service teachers and paraprofessionals who seek special education teacher licenses. She also partners with schools, communities, organizations, and government agencies to develop parent training programs and make policy changes nationally and internationally, so students with disabilities and their families—specifically ones from diverse backgrounds—can be well supported.

José Rogelio Manriquez-Hernandez, BA, is a 2022 graduate from the University of Colorado Boulder who majored in leadership/community engagement and history and has a minor in education. He comes from a family of immigrants who came from Michoacan all the way to Colorado so that their family could have an education. Growing up in Aurora and Denver, Colorado, he realized how impactful the community members and teachers were in his life; they smoothed his path, and he has a duty to work for and give back to that same community. Some of his past experiences include working in research, teaching, and community environments such as working with the Museum of Boulder and organizations such as Young Aspiring Americans for Social and Political Activism (YAASPA) that work for the Aurora community by supporting youth education. While Manriquez-Hernandez aspires to become a teacher, he has had the opportunity to work in various environments such as museums and he has taught at summer camps including Aquetza—a youth leadership, education, and empower-

About the Contributors • **319**

ment program—and through the CU Pre-Health Scholars program. Manriquez-Hernandez has also earned a micro-credential for his employment at the museum at the University of Colorado Boulder for the CHANGE Collective which conducts bi-weekly team meetings focused on personal/ professional development and an in-depth series of activities to cultivate awareness of self and others. Featured activities included self-assessments, peer shadowing, regular journaling, interviewing professionals, collecting and reviewing inspirational media, and presenting on the CHANGE Collective at a public showcase.

As an educator, **Jay Matthew**, BA, MA, has served as a hands-on teacher and administrator at the secondary level in a suburban district. As a servant educational leader, Mr. Matthew's daily objective is centered on being overtly immersed in doing whatever it takes to help both students and teachers succeed in the classroom. Jay is now focused on completing his doctoral program at the University of Houston and becoming a contributor to educational research and the discovery of educating under privileged students in our communities across the country. While growing up, Jay has been an avid writer and has produced several stage plays.

Elizabeth Holliday Morgan, PhD, is an assistant professor in the doctorate in educational leadership program at California State University Sacramento (CSUS). A developmental scientist and educator by training, she earned her PhD in human development from the University of California Davis and a master's in education from the Harvard Graduate School of Education. Elizabeth has supported early childhood practitioners in utilizing developmentally appropriate practice and inclusion strategies since 2004. Her area of research focus includes early childhood and early intervention services with a specific interest in under-represented populations. Before arriving at CSUS, Elizabeth worked as a researcher at the UC Davis MIND Institute and recently completed an NIH T36 Training grant with the Global Alliance for Training in Health Equity Research (GATHER) program where she spent a month interning for the African Population Health Research Center in Nairobi, Kenya. When she is not thinking about autism service equity, Elizabeth enjoys the theater and spending time with her family and their dog, Billie Jean.

Carol Mutch, PhD, is a professor of critical studies in education in the faculty of education and social work. She is also the education commissioner for UNESCO New Zealand. Dr. Mutch came to The University of Auckland following many years as a primary teacher, teacher educator, and policy advisor. During her career, Dr. Mutch has lived and worked overseas as a teacher in Canada and the United Kingdom, a visiting professor in Japan (Nagoya & Waseda) and the United Kingdom (LSE), and taught at the

320 ▪ About the Contributors

National University of Samoa. Her teaching and research interests are in research methods, education policy, curriculum development, and social education. She has published in scholarly books and journals on research methods, social studies and citizenship education, education history and policy, curriculum theory, and, most recently, the role of schools in disaster response and recovery—including schools' responses to COVID-19. Her disaster-related research has taken her to Australia, Japan, Samoa, Vanuatu, Nepal, and China. Dr. Mutch sits on numerous international editorial boards, as well as international and national association executive boards, advisory committees, and reference groups.

Christina Payne-Tsoupros, MEd, JD (she/her/hers), is an attorney and law professor. Previously a visiting assistant professor of law at the University of the District of Columbia David A. Clarke School of Law (UDC Law), Chris recently joined the National Association of the Deaf as its Education Policy Counsel. She continues to teach courses at UDC Law and also at Monterey College of Law. She is pursuing her doctorate in deaf education at Gallaudet University. She received her JD from William & Mary School of Law, MEd from the University of Houston, and BA from Cornell University. Chris is licensed to practice law in the District of Columbia and Virginia (inactive).

Holly Plank, MEd (she/her), is a graduate student researcher and PhD student in the learning sciences and policy program in the Department of Teaching, Learning, and Leading at the University of Pittsburgh. She fell in love with outdoor and environmental education serving in various roles at Camp Kirchenwald in Lebanon, Pennsylvania. After graduating with a degree in earth and space science and secondary education from Shippensburg University of Pennsylvania, she went on to teach middle school and physical science while continuing to pursue opportunities for informal, outdoor education. Holly also served as a science department chair, school leader, and instructional coach. As an instructional coach, she supported preservice and novice K–12 teachers in various core subjects and STEM electives with curriculum development, culturally sustaining pedagogy, learning environment planning, family engagement, real-time coaching, and more. She earned her master's in educational administration, curriculum, and supervision from the University of Oklahoma and has served as a manager of teacher leadership development and science content facilitator with Teach for America-Greater Tulsa, as well as a school director with Teach for America's National Institute. Holly's research focuses on science teacher education, environmental justice, computational thinking, and research–practice partnerships. She has worked on several grant-funded projects using RPP models as a graduate student at Pitt. Holly also teaches in the Master of Art in teaching program for secondary STEM.

About the Contributors · **321**

Joseph L. Polman, PhD, is a professor of learning sciences and human development, as well as associate dean for research, in the School of Education at University of Colorado Boulder. He received his PhD in learning sciences from Northwestern University. Dr. Polman designs and studies project-based learning environments for youth and adults in schools and community-based programs. He seeks to design learning environments that involve people with powerful tools for democratic participation, in pursuing personal and civic action, and in creating a more just and flourishing world. He focuses on learning and identity development connected to practices of communities of people pursuing science, literacy, history, and journalism. In collaborative work with other educators and scholars in universities, research and development organizations, community-based organizations, museums, and schools, he seeks to identify and make accessible practices from the disciplines and professions that learners can find meaningful and transformative in their lives. He is a past president and fellow of the International Society of the Learning Sciences and has served on the editorial boards of the *Journal of the Learning Sciences, Cognition, & Instruction; American Educational Research Journal;* and the *Journal of Research in Science Teaching.* He was program co-chair of the International Conferences of the Learning Sciences in 2014 and 2016. He has authored and co-authored numerous scholarly works, including the books *Designing Project-based Science: Connecting Learners through Guided Inquiry* (Teachers College Press, 2000), *Compose Our World: Project-based Learning in Secondary English Language Arts* (Teachers College Press, 2021), and *Situating Data Science: Exploring How Relationships to Data Shape Learning* (Routledge, 2022, edited volume).

Cassie Quigley, PhD (she/her), is an associate professor of science education and department chair in the Department of Teaching, Learning, and Leading at the University of Pittsburgh's School of Education. She received her doctorate in Curriculum & Instruction at Indiana University in 2010. As a former biology and physics teacher, she wondered how science was distancing students by eliminating certain knowledges and voices. She has always been concerned with the question of voice (whose voice has power and whose perspective is privileged) and how does this influence and privilege inform understandings of science, knowledge, and methods? While her scholarship on voice and power began many years ago, studying discourse practices in science classrooms, the same underlying questions form the arc of her current research, which asks, "How can STEM be transformed to embrace multiple knowledges, a critical stance towards content and schooling?" She centers those individuals and communities, most often on the margins, as the focus of her work by asking critical questions about their participation in science. Cassie teaches in various teacher education pro-

322 ▪ About the Contributors

grams, including the MEd in curriculum and instruction, Master of Arts in secondary science, and STEAM education certificate program.

Marc T. Sager, MS, is an education PhD student in the Department of Teaching and Learning at Southern Methodist University, with a concentration in STEM education. Marc's research interests integrate three topics: (a) inquiry, (b) food systems and food justice, and (c) data modeling. Most of his research involves working with urban farms to study how novices construct knowledge in these spaces, as well as how their lived experiences mediate their learning. He is also currently conducting research on research practice partnerships between a large public university and a large urban school district, considering their use of inquiry-based computer science curriculum and using augmented reality to support informal math learning. Prior to pursuing his graduate degree, Marc worked in food production, agricultural sales, and taught secondary agricultural sciences in both formal and informal contexts. His research continues to span both in-school and out-of-school learning environments. Marc teaches courses on topics within the learning sciences and is active in the education research community through service on committees.

Margaret L. Sebastian, PhD, is the TRIO student support services program director at Salisbury University in Salisbury, Maryland and the owner of MLS & Associates: Peaceful Processes—a dissertation editing and coaching business. She has more than 10 years of higher education experience, including work in TRIO grant programs, housing and residence life, and Title IX compliance and equity. Additionally, Dr. Sebastian has teaching experience in the Department of Leadership, Policy, & Development at the University of Northern Colorado and in the School of Health Sciences & Wellness Department and University Seminar Department at Northwest Missouri State University. Dr. Sebastian has a bachelor's degree in history and leadership studies, a master's degree in guidance & counseling, a certificate in organizational leadership, and a PhD in higher education and student affairs leadership with an emphasis in applied statistics and research methods from the University of Northern Colorado. Her research interests include student affairs administrators, qualitative research methods, campus climate, and organizational change. In her spare time, she coaches doctoral students as they complete their degree programs all over the country. She has successfully graduated 20+ such students.

Kanwardeep Kaur Singh, MEd, is currently a second year EdD student at California State University Sacramento. She earned her bachelor's and master's from the University of California Davis (UCD). At UCD, she worked under Dr. Nicole Sparaponi in the Care Lab conducting research on inclusion and access strategies for students on the autism spectrum in K–12 schools. She currently teaches high school computer programming and advanced robotics. After completing her degree, she hopes to continue her work in educational equity.

Aaron Smajda, MSc, BEd, OCT, is an Ontario certified teacher with 15 years of experience who specializes in the integration of information and computer technology into classroom instruction. He holds a Master of Science degree in education with a focus on disrupting gender stereotypes in physics education. He currently oversees Toronto Metropolitan University's Study Buddy program—a free tutoring initiative that pairs K–12 students with teacher candidates from multiple Ontario universities.

Kristina M. Stamatis, PhD, is an assistant professor of literacy in the College of Education, Health, and Human Sciences at the University of Nebraska Omaha. She received her PhD in learning sciences and human development from the University of Colorado Boulder. Dr. Stamatis began her career as a secondary reading specialist and English language arts teacher working with young people in Aurora, Colorado. Her research focuses on narrative and storytelling as a means of re-storying dominant narratives and engaging in anti-racist pedagogies. She is currently examining playful learning in community with the Omaha Urban Thinkscapes project, as well as collaborations focused on identity development through narrative, jazz as a model for understanding anti-racist education, and community-based research as a nexus for relational learning. She leads "The Throughlines Project," a youth narrative project aimed at reimagining the world through story. She is also collaborating with the "Denver Writing Project" to research the ways that youth develop identities as civic participants in society. Previous collaborations have included project-based learning initiatives in English language arts classrooms, explorations of STEM identities and creative learning with families, and multimodal literacies with youth in makerspaces. Her work can be found in the *Journal of Literacy Research*; *Urban Education*; and *Teaching and Teacher Education*; and in the book *Compose Our World: Project-Based Learning in Secondary English Language Arts* (Teachers College Press, 2021).

Kimberly Sterin, MEd, is a third-year PhD candidate studying education policy and leadership in the School of Education at Drexel University. She has 7 years of experience as a public school English teacher in both middle and high school settings. Sterin earned a master's in secondary education from Johns Hopkins University through their School Immersion Master of Arts in Teaching (SIMAT) program. She holds bachelor's in English language & literature and Spanish language & literature, as well as a minor in creative writing with a concentration in poetry, from the University of Maryland, College Park. Informed by her teaching experience, Sterin aims

324 ▪ About the Contributors

to bridge gaps between education research, policy, and practice. Her research focuses on how school, district, and federal level finance policies can be leveraged to enhance resource equity and close educational disparities.

Katrina Struloeff, MAM, is an experienced K–12 urban educator with a background in nonprofit operations, educational development, and communications. Prior to joining Drexel, Katrina spent 7 years in the New Orleans public charter school landscape as a middle school and high school administrator focusing on operations, facilities, transportation, and student community relations. She has facilitated national training for organizations that serve youth and families in vulnerable positions; taught arts, STEM, and entrepreneurship to youth; engaged with community activism and social enterprise incubation; and led partnerships with numerous national and regional organizations for information-sharing and innovative evidence-based programming. She earned a master's from Carnegie Mellon University Heinz College in public policy, with a focus on nonprofit management. Her research interests focus on leadership and education policy including equity gaps and representation for women and minoritized populations, civic education, policy design, and the connection of schools and communities.

Jennifer Tatebe, PhD, Tatebe is a senior lecturer in the sociology of education specializing in equity and social justice. Originally from Vancouver, Canada, she graduated from the University of British Columbia (UBC) with a master's in higher education, Bachelor of Education (Secondary), and Bachelor of Arts in English literature and history. Her work is informed by her teaching experience in primary, secondary, and alternative education settings in the United Kingdom and Canada, and professional tertiary roles in student development and cooperative education. Her research and teaching examine the transformative potential of education in disadvantaged contexts by exploring the socioeconomic and political contexts of these educational spaces and their influence on teaching and learning.

Karen M. Utter, JD, is the associate director of the South Carolina School Improvement Council (SC-SIC) and the project director of the Carolina Family Engagement Center (CFEC), which are housed in the College of Education at the University of South Carolina. Utter has over a decade of experience providing training and technical assistance to support the growth of effective school–family–community partnerships across South Carolina. Her approach to family engagement draws from several well-recognized models including the National Network for Partnership Schools' Action Team for Partnerships (Epstein et al.), the Dual Capacity-Building Framework for Family–School Partnerships version 2.0 (Mapp et al.), and the SC Framework for K–12 Family Engagement (SC Department of Education). Her work in family

About the Contributors • **325**

engagement is an extension of her commitment to ensuring that all children in South Carolina graduate from high school college or career ready as envisioned by the Profile of the South Carolina Graduate.

Nicole Weinberg, MA, is from North Richland Hills, Texas. After earning her undergraduate degree from the University of Texas, Nicole completed her MA in education, health promotion, and international development from the University College London Institute of Education. Her professional background includes early childhood education and nonprofit initiatives in London, Tanzania, Austin, and Fort Worth. She is currently a second-year doctoral student in curriculum studies as well as a graduate assistant in the Center for Public Education and Community Engagement (CPECE) at Texas Christian University. Her research interests include early childhood/elementary teacher education and well-being, critical perspectives on educational technology and youth digital literacies, and (post) qualitative methodologies.

Jeanna R. Wieselmann, PhD, is an assistant professor of STEM education in the Department of Teaching and Learning at Southern Methodist University. She holds a PhD in curriculum and instruction from the University of Minnesota and was a recipient of the National Science Foundation's Graduate Research Fellowship program. Dr. Wieselmann's research focuses on integrated STEM education at the PreK–12 levels, including curriculum development, instructional strategies, the development of STEM-focused schools, and support for teachers implementing integrated STEM curricula. She has received a National Science Foundation grant to explore elementary teachers' self-efficacy and effectiveness in teaching integrated STEM. Dr. Wieselmann is also currently conducting research on students' small group interactions during integrated STEM activities, exploring patterns of participation and how these patterns may vary based on students' gender, race, ethnicity, first language, and special education needs. Prior to pursuing her graduate degrees, Dr. Wieselmann taught elementary STEM in both formal and informal contexts, and her research continues to maintain a focus on both in-school and out-of-school STEM learning opportunities. She is particularly interested in equity in relation to STEM and maintaining diverse students' STEM interest and engagement as they progress through elementary and middle school. Dr. Wieselmann teaches courses for preservice and in-service science and STEM teachers and is active in the science education research community through service on committees of international organizations and on numerous editorial review boards for scholarly journals.

Bincy Wilson, PhD, is a social science researcher with over a decade of experience managing research projects and monitoring and evaluating develop-

326 ▪ About the Contributors

ment programs in both South Asia and North America. She has extensive field-based research experience in both academia and nonprofit settings. Her areas of expertise include gender-based violence, rights-based approaches, gender equality and empowerment, monitoring and evaluation, mixed research methodologies, and grant writing. She has both published articles in international peer-reviewed journals and written manuals and technical reports for various international nonprofits (e.g., UNICEF, The Freedom Fund, Terre des Hommes Netherlands, World Vision, etc.). Dr. Wilson holds a PhD in social welfare from the University at Buffalo and a master's in social work from India.

Yanfeng Xu, PhD, is an assistant professor in the College of Social Work and an affiliate faculty associate for the Research Consortium on Children and Families and Walker Institute of International and Area Studies at the University of South Carolina. She earned her PhD in social work from the University of Maryland School of Social Work. Xu's research is focused on the well-being of children and their caregivers in kinship care and nonkinship foster care. She has led several projects that examined multiple challenges in kinship care and their associations with kinship caregivers' parenting practices and kinship children's educational and behavioral health outcomes. Xu has authored more than 30 peer-reviewed articles, book chapters, and book reviews and made more than 45 presentations at national and international conferences. Her work has been featured in top-tier journals, such as *Child Abuse and Neglect* and *Children and Youth Services Review.*